£2.35

BLACK'S NEW TESTAMENT COMMENTARIES

GENERAL EDITOR: HENRY CHADWICK, D.D.

THE EPISTLES
OF PETER AND OF JUDE

A COMMENTARY ON
THE EPISTLES
OF PETER AND OF JUDE

J. N. D. KELLY, D.D., F.B.A.
PRINCIPAL OF ST EDMUND HALL, OXFORD

ADAM & CHARLES BLACK
LONDON

PRINTED IN GREAT BRITAIN BY R. & R. CLARK, LTD., EDINBURGH

CONTENTS

PREFACE

THERE should be no need to apologize for bringing out a new commentary on the three epistles included in this volume. English-speaking students of 1 Peter have been fortunate in having access to the splendid editions of E. G. Selwyn and F. W. Beare, but in their original form these were published in 1946 and 1947 respectively, and since then the debate about the epistle has been vigorously continued and extended. Excellent short editions (one would mention with particular respect that by A. M. Stibbs) have occasionally appeared, but their scope has of necessity been limited. 2 Peter and Jude have been much less well served, and indeed (apart again from short editions with restricted aims) have been virtually neglected by English editors since J. Moffatt (1928) and J. W. C. Wand (1934). This is a great pity, for while neither has the magnificent qualities of 1 Peter, they both provide fascinating glimpses of Christianity as it developed in the epoch immediately succeeding that of the apostles.

All three epistles contain passages of exceptional difficulty, but I have striven (it has not always been easy) to sort out the often complicated issues as simply and clearly as possible. Even so, there is probably rather more technical discussion of knotty points of syntax, the background of obscure words, and the like, than some Greek-less readers may find to their taste. This could not, however, be avoided if the meaning was to be brought out; and having derived a great deal myself from struggling with these passages, I would urge the student to persist and profit likewise. My chief personal regrets are that I have not found it possible, within the compass of a single volume, to give these three works as thorough and detailed a treatment as I could have wished, and that the need to keep my translation reasonably literal has prevented me from even attempting to convey the interesting stylistic qualities of the original texts.

Like all who venture to comment on the New Testament, I am deeply conscious of the long line of masterly predecessors on whose work I have drawn. On 1 Peter I am especially indebted to the remarkable editions of Windisch-Preisker, R. Knopf, E. G. Selwyn, F. W. Beare, K. H. Schelkle, and, more recently, C. Spicq. The single study which has helped me most is W. J. Dalton's brilliant monograph on 1 Pet. iii. 18-iv. 6. Although this came into my hands only after the completion of my first draft, I was delighted to find that its general line coincided with the one I had myself adopted and that I was able to weave a number of its insights into my final text. On 2 Peter and Jude the expositions which have proved of greatest assistance have been those of R. Knopf and J. Chaine.

I am grateful to my friend the Revd J. L. Houlden, Fellow of Trinity College, for taking the trouble to read through the Introduction to 1 Peter and for making many perceptive comments of which I have taken advantage. I owe a different kind of debt to the General Editor, Professor Henry Chadwick, who by persuading me to undertake a second volume in this series and thus divert a share of my attention from the patristic field, has stimulated me to further exploration of the New Testament. I am particularly grateful to my brother, Nevill Davidson Kelly, and my elder sister, Marjory McCracken, as to their families, for their long-suffering indulgence in allowing me, when staying with them in Edinburgh and Kelso last summer, to remain closeted in a room with my typewriter while I hammered out the final version of the book.

J. N. D. K.

Oxford
St Valentine's Day, 1969

ABBREVIATIONS

1. General

AV	Authorized, or King James, Version of the Bible.
CIG	Corpus Inscriptionum Graecarum.
CIL	Corpus Inscriptionum Latinarum.
Corp. Herm.	Corpus Hermeticum.
LXX	Septuagint (Greek version of the Old Testament).
m (e.g. AVm)	Alternative reading in margin or footnote.
Moffatt	J. Moffatt's translation of the Bible.
MS(S)	Manuscript(s).
NEB	New English Bible (New Testament).
NT	New Testament.
Old Latin	Pre-Vulgate Latin versions of the Bible.
OT	Old Testament.
Pap. Hib.	Collection of papyri found at El-Hibeh.
Pap. Oxy.	Collection of papyri found at Oxyrhynchus.
PG	*Patrologia Graeca*, edited by J. P. Migne.
RSV	Revised Standard Version of the Bible.
RV	Revised Version of the Bible.
SB	Strack-Billerbeck: *Kommentar zum Neuen Testament aus Talmud und Midrasch*.
TWNT	Kittel-Friedrich: *Theologisches Wörterbuch zum Neuen Testament*.
Var. lect.	Variant reading.
Vulgate	The Vulgate (Jerome's Latin version of the Bible).
ZNTW	*Zeitschrift für die neutestamentliche Wissenschaft*.

2. Non-Biblical Works Cited without Author's Name

Apoc. Bar.	The Syriac Apocalypse of Baruch (2 Baruch).
Apoc. Pet.	The Apocalypse of Peter.
Asc. Is.	The Ascension of Isaiah.
Ass. Mos.	The Assumption of Moses.
Barn.	The Epistle of Barnabas.
1 Clem.	The First Epistle of Clement.
2 Clem.	The Second Epistle of Clement.
Cod. Theod.	The Theodosian Code.
Const. apost.	The Apostolic Constitutions.
Did.	The Didache, or Doctrine, of the Twelve Apostles.
Didasc.	Didascalia Apostolorum.
1 En.	1 Enoch (the 'Ethiopic Enoch').

2 En.	2 Enoch (the 'Slavonic Enoch').
Ep. ad Diogn.	The Epistle to Diognetus.
Ep. apost.	The Epistle of the Apostles.
Ep. Arist.	The Letter of Aristeas.
Jub.	The Book of Jubilees.
3 and 4 Macc.	The Third and Fourth Books of Maccabees.
Mart. Polyc.	The Martyrdom of Polycarp.
Orac. Sibyll.	The Sibylline Oracles.
Pass. Perp. et Fel.	The Passion of Perpetua and Felicitas.
Ps. Clem. *Hom.*	The Pseudo-Clementine Homilies.
Ps. Clem. *Recog.*	The Pseudo-Clementine Recognitions.
Ps. Sol.	The Psalms of Solomon.
1QGnApoc	Qumran: Genesis Apocryphon.
1QH	Qumran: Hymns.
1QM	Qumran: War Rule.
1QpHab	Qumran: Commentary on Habakkuk.
1QS	Qumran: Community Rule.
1QSa	Qumran: Rule Annexe.
1QSb	Qumran: Book of Blessings.
4QpHos	Qumran: Commentaries on Hosea.
4QpNah	Qumran: Commentary on Nahum.
4QpPs37	Qumran: Commentary on Psalm xxxvii.
6QD	Qumran: Damascus Document.
Targ. Onk.	Targum of Onkelos.
Test. Reub. etc.	The Testaments of the XII Patriarchs.
Vit. Ad. et Ev.	The Life of Adam and Eve.
Vit. Cypr.	The Life of Cyprian.

3. MANUSCRIPTS

References to MSS have been kept to the minimum; the following are the symbols employed:

Pap. 72	Papyrus Bodmer vii-ix (3rd cent.).
Codex Sin.	Codex Sinaiticus (4th cent.).
A	Codex Alexandrinus (5th cent.).
B	Codex Vaticanus (4th cent.).
C	Codex Ephraemi rescriptus (5th cent.).
K	Codex Mosquensis (9th cent.).
L	Codex Angelicus (9th cent.).
P	Codex Porphyrianus (9th cent.).
69	Codex Leicestrensis (cursive: 15th cent.).

INTRODUCTION TO 1 PETER

1. Preliminary

THIS letter, one of the most pastorally attractive and vigorously confident documents in the NT, presents itself as a message of encouragement from the Apostle Peter to Christian communities in Asia Minor which are bewildered by the cruel treatment and persecution to which they are being subjected. As Christians, it reminds them, they are God's chosen people and their sufferings are a purely temporary testing of their faith; the End is at hand, which will bring destruction to their enemies and, if they stand firm, everlasting glory to themselves. So far from being disheartened by malice and misunderstanding, they should seek to disarm them by making their conduct in every department of life a reflection of their holy calling. Christ Himself, innocent though He was, accepted death patiently, and indeed by undergoing it has conquered the powers of evil and been raised to glory. They should take Him as their example, for participation in His sufferings will lead to participation also in His triumph. So they should reckon their present tribulations not only a challenge to steadfastness, but a positive ground for rejoicing.

Not surprisingly, in the light of this summary, the epistle has acquired a heightened actuality in the present age. Christians have always found it inspiring, but it must be particularly so at a time when they are actively persecuted in several countries and in many more are, or have been reduced to, a minority with beliefs and standards which their neighbours view with puzzlement, even resentment. For the student, however, it has a special interest because of the many fascinating problems it raises; even if they are not all susceptible of final solution, their discussion cannot fail to deepen our understanding of primitive Christianity. Who, for example, really wrote 1 Peter, and how is it related to other NT texts? To what date should its composition be assigned? What is its theology, and how far does it represent the writer's personal standpoint? If he incorporated

1

traditional material, what was its nature? Again, is 1 Peter, as the casual reader might suppose, a literary unity, or does its façade disguise the piecing together of originally separate documents? Then there are the Christians to whom the letter claims to be addressed: who were they, and (a vitally important issue) what was the exact character of the persecutions to which they were exposed?

All these questions are closely connected; the answers we give to any one will have repercussions on our answers to the others. They will be examined, though inevitably less thoroughly than they deserve, in the following sections; and particular points will receive a more detailed treatment in the Commentary. Here it is appropriate to recall that the church historian Eusebius (c. 260–c. 340), whose testimony on these matters merits attention, takes (*Hist. eccl.* iii. 3. 1) 1 Peter's canonicity for granted, including it among the writings which have been accepted from ancient times. As a matter of fact the earliest evidence we have of the respect accorded to it, and of its attribution to the Apostle, comes in the Bible itself, in 2 Pet. iii. 1 (see note), i.e. early in the 2nd cent. at latest. Polycarp of Smyrna quotes from it several times in his *Letter to the Philippians* (c. 135), and Eusebius reports (*Hist. eccl.* iii. 39. 17) that Papias of Hierapolis (in Phrygia: c. 60–c. 130) used it. The first father to speak of it as by Peter is Irenaeus (*Haer.* iv. 9. 2; 16. 5; v. 7. 2: c. 185). Clement of Alexandria (c. 150–c. 212) commented on it in his *Hypotyposes*, and elsewhere quotes from every chapter of it. Curiously enough, definite traces of knowledge of it in the west are lacking until Tertullian, who cites it in works written around the first decade of the 3rd cent. (*De or.* xx; *Scorp.* xii. 2 f.). There is no mention of it in the Muratorian Canon, which lists the NT books accepted at Rome in the latter part of the 2nd cent. On the other hand, there are possible echoes of it in Hermas's *Shepherd* (c. 140) and the Gnostic *Gospel of Truth* (before 145), which both originated in Rome.

2. DESTINATION

Although not everyone is agreed, there can be little doubt that, at any rate in its final form, 1 Peter is a piece of genuine correspondence. This holds good whatever the elements out of which one believes it to be constructed and whatever one's theory of date and authorship. Its character as a letter is borne out not only by superficial traits like the address, with its conventional greeting (i. 1 f.) followed by an expression of thanks (i. 3-12), and the closing salutation, with its references to Silvanus and Mark (v. 12-14), but also by the warm pastoral tone which pervades it, its direct hortatory language, and such touches as the repeated 'Dear friends' (ii. 11; iv. 12) and the special word of advice to church leaders (v. 1 ff.). Nothing goes to show that the writer and his correspondents are personally acquainted, and in any case one would not expect him to include messages to individuals in a circular letter (cf. the analogy of Galatians). Nevertheless he does not confine himself to generalities; there are plenty of hints that he has an accurate picture both of the background of the people he is addressing and of the acutely painful situation in which they are placed.

The communities to which they belong are scattered over an enormous area. Pontus and Bithynia, Galatia, Cappadocia, and Asia are the titles of the four provinces of the Roman empire which in the 1st and 2nd cents. covered the whole of Anatolia between the Taurus range and the Black Sea, i.e. the bulk of Asian Turkey. The area would be considerably reduced if, as some scholars have proposed, the names are used in a popular or ethnic rather than a political sense, Galatia denoting the old northern kingdom without the districts (parts of Phrygia, Lycaonia, etc.) incorporated in the Roman province after 25 B.C., and Asia only the north-east portion of the province. The fact that Pontus and Bithynia, officially departments of a single province, are mentioned separately has been held to favour this interpretation, as has the absence of any mention of Paul, which some think would have been natural had the destination included centres (e.g. Iconium and Ephesus) first evangelized by him. This latter point is open to question; but, leaving aside the doubtful propriety of thus restricting Asia, this address at the head of a letter probably coming from Rome would most naturally suggest to contemporaries the four provinces, especially as the territory they comprised formed a recognized geographical entity (Strabo, *Geog.* ii. 5. 31; Cassius Dio, *Hist.* lxxi. 23).

Although we can only speculate how and by whom, there is no valid reason why Christianity should not have been brought to the shores of the Black Sea and the pastoral uplands and rugged mountain recesses of Cappadocia by, say, the sixties of the 1st cent. The possibility cannot be excluded of Peter's having reached these regions himself; but apart from this it is likely that, with the first-class communications available, the gospel spread very rapidly (Colossae and Laodicea are examples which spring to mind) northwards and eastwards from the missions planted by Paul.

As a result of successsive migrations, Anatolia could boast a motley, unevenly distributed mixture of races, cultures and religions. Much of it (especially Asia and Bithynia-Pontus) had long been thoroughly Hellenized; and even where the indigenous or Celtic stock retained vitality (Cappadocia and Galatia) it was overlaid, at any rate in towns, with a firm Hellenistic veneer. Almost everywhere the Jews (e.g. Philo, *Leg. ad Gai.* 245; 281; Josephus, *Ant.* xiv. 110-18), with their synagogues and the special privileges granted them by the government, formed a numerous and commercially important element. On a hasty reading one might be tempted (with the Greek fathers, Erasmus, Calvin and others) to conclude that the intended recipients of 1 Peter are converts from Judaism. After all, they are saluted (i. 1) as 'exiles of the Dispersion', and the writer makes lavish use of OT quotations and seems to assume a first-hand knowledge of Jewish ideas and traditions. But such an inference would be mistaken; it is reasonably certain that the addressees, or the majority of them, have a pagan background. This is the clear implication of the statements that they have been rescued from a futile way of life inherited from their fathers (i. 18), that having formerly been 'no people' they have now become 'God's people' (ii. 10), and that previously they had been idolaters indulging in typically Gentile excesses (iv. 3: cf. i. 14; ii. 9; iii. 5f.). The description of them as the Dispersion is a simple instance of the early Church's habit of transferring to itself, as the new Israel, the language appropriate to the experience of the old. The author, himself undoubtedly a Jew, was entitled to expect them to have some familiarity with the OT because it had provided the scriptural basis of their catechetical training—

4

perhaps also because many of them, prior to their conversion, had been attached to synagogues as 'God-fearers', like the centurion Cornelius (Acts x. 2).

The letter leaves the impression that these Christians form small, closely knit fellowships (cf. 'brotherhood' concretely used in ii. 17; v. 9) in their respective localities. If the author's choice of topics supplies reliable hints, their social level is for the most part humble (slaves, but not masters, are singled out for advice), and a good proportion of them are young. They include, however, at any rate some well-to-do women who can afford fashionable clothes and hair-styles, and whose husbands are still pagans (iii. 1-6). The frequent references to their former paganism and to baptism seem to imply that many are fairly recent converts, as does the mention (i. 12) of 'those who preached the good news to you'. The organization of the communities is in the hands of 'elders', a term which can denote equivocally either rank (v. 1) or age (v. 5), but ordinary members who possess some spiritual or practical 'gift' are encouraged to exercise it (iv. 10 f.). Their organization is therefore comparatively rudimentary, and this (as we shall see in §7) may have some significance for the date of writing.

3. THE PERSECUTIONS

Running through the whole letter, sometimes overtly expressed but never far below the surface and giving point to the writer's reiterated appeal to Christ's sufferings as a precedent and a ground for confidence, is the assumption that the recipients are being, or at any moment are liable to be, subjected to trials and persecutions. It is clearly vital to form as accurate an assessment of their situation as possible, and as scholars have given very different verdicts we must now scrutinize the relevant passages more closely. By and large there are two related questions which call for an answer. The first is whether the ill-treatment alluded to in i. 3-iv. 11 is actual or merely potential, for while everyone agrees that in iv. 12 ff. the author is dealing with harsh realities, many hold that in the earlier chapters he is speaking more generally of possible eventualities. The second concerns the character of the ill-treatment, viz.

whether it is official persecution initiated by the imperial government, or private and local harassment, capable of course of attracting the attention of municipal authorities, but basically the product of the ill-will of the Christians' fellow-citizens.

(1) In his very first paragraph (i. 6) the writer dwells eloquently on the joy his readers feel, in spite of being 'distressed by various trials', because they know that God is keeping them safe for an imperishable inheritance. He gives no clue to the form these trials take, but highlights their severity by likening their effect to the refining action of fire on gold. According to many, his language is general: the trials have not yet taken place, but are viewed as a distinct possibility. This, however, is an erroneous interpretation resulting from a misreading of the clause, and in particular of the seemingly hypothetical 'if need be', where 'if' (see note) has almost the force of 'since'. The participle 'distressed' is aorist in tense and can only mean 'although you *have been* distressed'. Moreover, the urgency of the encouraging message developed in i. 3-12 is lost, and the paradox of exultation in suffering integral to the writer's theology is blurred, if the distress is something which may or may not be realized instead of a painful fact of present experience.

(2) In ii. 11 ff. the writer urges his readers to cultivate the highest standards of conduct so that their pagan neighbours may have no excuse for 'vilifying them as evil-doers'. He elaborates this in a series of paragraphs sketching the demeanour appropriate in their relations both to one another and to the emperor, governors, masters and pagan husbands: its keynotes should be submissiveness, charity towards all men, and complete abstention from resentfulness. He then asks (iii. 13) who is going to hurt them if they show this passion for goodness. The question is plainly rhetorical, and becoming more realistic he points out (iii. 14-17) that, even if they should suffer because of their upright behaviour, they need have no fear but should count themselves privileged. Whenever requested to give an account of their Christian hope, they should be prepared to make their defence courteously and reverently. So long as their conscience is clear, their transparent rectitude will put slanderers to shame. It is no doubt disgraceful to have to suffer for doing

6

wrong, but (as Christ's example proves) to suffer for doing right, if God should will it so, brings glory.

The argument is awkwardly arranged, but the points which interest us can be easily disentangled. First, does the maltreatment envisaged in iii. 13-17 take the form of judicial prosecution and condemnation? Some of the language used at first sight supports this: both 'make a defence' and 'call to account' seem to imply legal proceedings (though before what kind of court is not clear). But they do not necessarily do so; the two expressions (see notes) could equally well refer to giving a reasoned explanation of the faith to inquirers, and indeed this agrees better with 'your hope', since the surviving records of trials before Roman magistrates do not indicate that the latter were concerned with such questions. The context, moreover, is more consistent with widespread popular prejudice and obloquy, liable to erupt in violence. Not only are abuse and slander the only specific injuries mentioned in the passage, but it cannot be separated from the lengthy preceding section insisting on great circumspection and avoidance of all provocation. In itself the remark about suffering for doing right does no more than reproduce the advice given to slaves when bullied by their masters (ii. 20).

Secondly, is the ill-treatment regarded only as a future possibility? This is the inference commonly drawn from the optatives 'if you should suffer' (iii. 14) and 'if such should be God's will' (iii. 17). It is admittedly a tenable one in strict syntax, but one wonders whether this approach does not spring from too narrow a view of the situation. Quite apart from i. 6, the writer has made it abundantly plain, both in ii. 12 and in his counsel to different classes of people, that misunderstanding, malice and defamation are ever-present realities with which his correspondents have to live. What he is doing is urging them to take every possible precaution to prevent these exploding in more violent forms. Even with the best will in the world, they are not likely to be completely successful, and so he paints a glowing picture of their blessedness if the worst should happen. What makes life miserable for a hated and despised minority, as recent history confirms, is not that cold-shouldering, insults and beatings-up are everyday occurrences (the individuals directly affected may be comparatively few), but that in the prevailing atmosphere of suspicion no one knows whom, or when, the blow will strike next. We are given a shocking little picture of the Asian Christians' actual plight a couple of paragraphs later, when the writer recalls (iv. 4) that their pagan neighbours are infuriated by their refusal to join them in boisterous debauches.

(3) In iv. 12-19 he bids his readers not to be surprised by the 'fiery ordeal' through which they are passing, 'as though something strange were happening' to them; it is a testing of their faith, and they should welcome the opportunity of sharing Christ's sufferings as a foretaste of the glory to come. None of them, he insists, must suffer as a criminal; but no disgrace attaches to suffering 'as a Christian'. Judgment-time has come (the End, he has already pointed out in iv. 7, is at hand), and the scripture teaching that the judgment is to begin with 'the house of God', i.e. the Church, should help them to understand why they are singled out. Things will be much worse for those who reject the gospel; so in the meantime they ought to entrust their souls confidently to God and continue in well-doing.

The problem of this passage is whether it envisages the same situation as the earlier chapters, or a fresh and altogether fiercer, more definite crisis which has broken on the churches. Many claim that the latter is the case, some adding that this is the first reference to actual persecution in the letter. They argue that 'fiery trial' must connote an exceptionally drastic experience, that suffering 'for the name of Christ' and 'as a Christian' points to criminal proceedings of a capital nature, and that this is confirmed by the remarkable parallel with the correspondence between Pliny and Trajan in 110 (see pp. 28 f. below), from which it emerges that merely being a Christian counted then as a crime. In part this thesis depends on the premiss that the earlier allusions to suffering are quite general, unrelated to anything that has actually occurred; and reasons have been given for doubting this. Much of its plausibility also comes from giving 'fiery trial' a much more fearsome content than the Greek warrants, and even exaggerating this in translation (cf. F. W. Beare's 'fiery ordeal that is raging among you'). In fact, as the gloss which follows shows, the word simply connotes testing by fire, thus exactly repeating the image used in i. 7; as such it aptly describes the smouldering animosity by which, as we have seen, the Christians are daily surrounded.

Similarly the warning against suffering as a criminal does no more than reiterate, with slightly altered phrasing but essentially the same ideas, the caution given to servants in ii. 19 f. and more generally in iii. 17. The comparison with the punishment meted out to murderers and thieves may conceivably be a hint that Christianity is now a capital offence, but is much more probably thrown in to set the same plea in high relief. As for suffering 'for the name of Christ', no special significance should be read into the formula, for in the 1st cent. Church this was a stock way of describing the kind of ill-treatment assumed in every part of the letter. These points are more fully discussed in the Commentary as are the difficulties of identifying the situation with that delineated by Pliny (see also pp. 28 f. below). The proposal that the language is best explained by a sudden, entirely fresh outburst is also hard to substantiate. 'Do not be surprised' does not denote a paralysing shock, but simply the bewilderment which decent people are bound to feel when all their efforts to fulfil God's will are met with uncomprehending brutality. The fact that the imperative is not aorist, as we should expect if the surprise were a reaction to a new crisis, but present suggests that the writer knows that his readers are living in just such a state of bewilderment. In the same way the use of the present participle 'happening to you', instead of 'has happened to you', emphasizes that the painful experience is not new, but one of some standing which they have to get used to. The encouragement to positive good works in iv. 19 bears this out, for it presupposes that martyrdom is not envisaged.

(4) In v. 6-10 the writer invites his readers to accept God's chastisement humbly, confident that He cares for them and, after they have 'suffered for a little while', will exalt them. They need to be watchful, for the Devil is prowling around seeking victims to devour; they should resist him, fortified by the knowledge that afflictions of the same kind are the lot of their fellow-Christians in the world. Again the reference to the Devil suggests that persecution, with the temptation to apostasy, is the atmosphere in which Christians permanently live; and the

9

assurance that their sufferings will be of short duration picks up the similar assurance in i. 6, like it being based on the conviction that the End is near. The final statement may be of crucial significance, for on the most obvious interpretation it confirms that the troubles referred to in iv. 12 ff. are in no way exceptional but have their counterpart in a great many places. Attempts have been made (see note) to evade this conclusion, but they are based on imaginary difficulties and result in strained translations. If it is accepted, it creates great embarrassment for any theory that the tribulations mentioned in this section, or in the rest of the letter, are the effect of direct state intervention, for (even allowing for exaggeration in phrasing) there is no evidence for any very extensive persecution initiated by the government in the 1st or early 2nd cents.

We are now in a position to summarize the results of this analysis. First, it is clear that throughout the entire letter the writer is dealing with a persecution-situation which actually exists. The suspicions, vexations and general abuse the Christian communities have to put up with in i. 3-iv. 11 are just as concrete as those referred to in iv. 12 ff., and are in fact identical with them. If there is a heightening of tone, a greater compactness and a more urgent note in iv. 12 ff., this is because the writer is recapitulating his message and, like a good teacher, using his climax to ram it home. Secondly, taken *en ensemble* the references leave the firm impression that the persecution is private and local, originating in the hostility of the surrounding population. The technical terms for official persecution (*diōgmos*, etc.) are noticeably absent, nor is there any unambiguous mention of formal accusation (*katēgoria*), much less of imprisonment or execution. The picture we obtain is of minority groups living in an environment charged with dislike, misrepresentation and positive hostility, probably with sporadic explosions of violence. Action by local magistrates cannot be excluded, for any disorders resulting from communal squabbles were bound to attract their attention, and Christians, popularly regarded as haters of mankind and guilty of every conceivable enormity (e.g. Tacitus, *Ann.* xv. 44; Suetonius, *Nero* xvi. 2), could not look for much sympathy if involved. But the writer's attitude to the imperial government is positive: it exists to administer justice

10

and promote good citizenship, and he clearly (ii. 13-17) does not fear it as necessarily hostile to Christianity.

4. LITERARY AND THEOLOGICAL AFFINITIES

The relation of 1 Peter to other NT writings is the next question we ought to examine. In particular, much stress has been laid on its affinities to the Pauline epistles; some have even declared that, if it did not appear under the name of Peter, we should have inferred that it was the work of one of Paul's disciples and admirers. The opening salutation seems modelled on the Pauline ones, and Paul's characteristic 'in Christ' occurs thrice (iii. 16; v. 10; 14). Several passages, it is suggested, are reminiscent, in thought and language, of Romans, the following being the chief: i. 14 (Rom. xii. 2); i. 22 (Rom. xii. 9 f.); ii. 5 (Rom. xii. 1); ii. 6-8 (Rom. ix. 32 f.); ii. 10 (Rom. ix. 25); ii. 13-17 (Rom. xiii. 1, 3, 4, 7); iii. 8 f., 11 (Rom. xii. 16-18); iv. 7-11 (Rom. xii. 3, 6). Equally close correspondences, again of ideas as well as wording, have been detected with Ephesians: e.g. i. 3 (Eph. i. 3); i. 10-12 (Eph. iii. 2-6); i. 20 (Eph. i. 4); ii. 1 (Eph. iv. 25, 31); ii. 2-6 (Eph. ii. 18-22); iii. 1 (Eph. v. 22); iii. 22 (Eph. i. 20 f.). Resemblances with other acknowledged Paulines and the Pastorals are rather more remote, but the following may be singled out from the latter: i. 3-5 (Tit. iii. 4-7); ii. 1 (Tit. iii. 3); ii. 9 (Tit. ii. 14); iii. 1-6 (1 Tim. ii. 9-11). Finally, the theology of 1 Peter has been described as Pauline to a degree unexampled in the rest of the NT, its teaching on the redemptive effects of the passion (ii. 24; iii. 18; iv. 13), on the Church (ii. 4 ff.), on suffering with Christ leading to participation in His glory (iv. 13; v. 1), and on His resurrection as effecting salvation (i. 3; iii. 21) being among the instances adduced.

Parallels with 1 Peter have also been discovered in both James and Hebrews. The following are the most striking of the former: i. 1 (Jas. i. 1); i. 6 f. (Jas. i. 2 f.); i. 23 (Jas. i. 18); i. 24 (Jas. i. 10 f.); ii. 1 (Jas. i. 21); iv. 8 (Jas. v. 20); v. 5 f. (Jas. iv. 6 f.); v. 9 f. (Jas. iv. 7-10). For Hebrews the following are sometimes cited: i. 1 and ii. 11 (Heb. xi. 13); i. 2 (Heb. xii. 24); ii. 24 (Heb. x. 10); ii. 25 and v. 4 (Heb. xiii. 20); iii. 9 (Heb. xii. 17). In addition numerous texts have been noticed which seem to betray knowledge of the synoptic tradition: e.g. i. 10 f. (Mt. xi. 13; xiii. 17); i. 17 (Mt. vi. 9); ii. 7 (Mt. xxi. 42); ii. 12 (Mt. v. 16); iii. 9 (Mt. v. 44); iv. 13 f. (Mt. v. 10); v.8 (Mt. v. 25; Lk. xviii. 3). Outside the NT but still within the 1st cent., 1 Peter stands in a close relation with *1 Clement* (*c*. 95). Both use a vocabulary containing a large number of striking words which are rarely or never found elsewhere in early Christian literature, both open with the same salutation and characterize Christians as 'sojourners', and both cite OT texts in the same distinctive form (iv. 8: *1 Clem.* xlix. 5; v. 5: *1 Clem.* xxx. 2). Other passages showing kinship of thought or wording are i. 11 (*1 Clem.* viii. 1); ii. 9 (*1 Clem.* lix. 2); ii. 21 (*1 Clem.* xvi. 17); iii. 6 (*1 Clem.* iv. 8; xxxi. 2); v. 1-5 (*1 Clem.* lvii. 1).

What are we to make of this necessarily meagre and selective summary? We may leave aside *1 Clement*, for any theory that 1 Peter is indebted to it would demand a much later date for the latter than seems at all likely. The correspondences are best explained by the hypothesis either of *1 Clement's* familiarity with 1 Peter or (more plausibly) of the emergence of both in the same milieu. The more urgent question is whether the NT data suggest literary dependence. To earlier scholars this seemed the obvious and natural way of accounting for most, if not all, of the overlaps; it has even been argued that our author must have been acquainted with virtually the whole of the NT. Nowadays such solutions tend to be greeted more sceptically, if only because they fail to reckon with the character of 1st cent. Christianity and thus artificially limit the range of possibilities. The primitive Church was essentially a traditional Church, witnessing to saving truths which had been committed to it and giving expression to these in its distinctive mode of life and forms of worship. Long before stereotyped creeds, codes and liturgies were formed, it had its characteristic exegesis of select OT testimonies and its record of the Lord's passion, mighty acts and sayings, its outlines of essential doctrines and its 'type of instruction' (Rom. vi. 17). Preachers were embroidering the message along recognized lines, and the structure of the baptismal and eucharistic actions had been plotted out. This shared tradition of faith, worship and conduct, fluid in wording and continually developing but set in relatively fixed patterns, must have pervaded and left a deep impress on the thinking of 1st cent. Christians, and not surprisingly underlies the NT as a whole. Indeed all the NT documents, however diverse their aims and the degree to which they reflect their authors' individual genius, can properly be viewed as variations, more or less elaborate, on its fundamental themes.

If this is the true position, we should hesitate to explain resemblances between NT passages in terms of literary dependence except where there is transparent evidence of this. Occasionally the evidence is all but incontrovertible, as when we consider the relation of Matthew to Mark or of 2 Peter to Jude (see pp. 225-227). Very often, however, what at first sight strikes us as straightforward borrowing will, on closer inspection, look more like an instance of two writers independently availing themselves, consciously or unconsciously, of the traditional material (catechetical, hortatory, credal, liturgical, etc.) by which the life and thought of the primitive Church were nourished. No one today, for example, would insist that 1 Peter shows knowledge of the gospels as such, for we are certain that collections of the Lord's sayings were in circulation long prior to, as well as after, their composition. Similarly there would be wide agreement today that the parallels in 1 Peter with most of the acknowledged Paulines, the Pastorals and Hebrews are proof, not of direct acquaintance, but of the influence of accepted patterns of teaching and preaching, traditional ideas and ways of looking at things, and a common vocabulary.

Because the coincidences they show are more numerous and closer, some scholars are inclined to treat James on the one hand, and Romans and Ephesians on the other, as exceptions; but it is doubtful if the evidence warrants this. Several of the correspondences between 1 Peter and James listed above appear striking, but a meticulous comparison will reveal that many of the verbal similarities are superficial (e.g. the same word used in different senses), that sometimes the same OT texts or identical Christian ideas are applied in very different ways and with different intentions, or that the parallels in question patently reflect conventional Christian motifs or turns of phrase. For an exhaustive treatment the reader should consult M. Dibelius's *Der Brief des Jakobus* (11th ed., 1964). As the Commentary will also attempt to show, a close scrutiny in their contexts of the parallels with Romans and Ephesians yields equally negative results. C. L. Mitton, it is true, has put in a special plea for certain passages of Ephesians (most of them figure in the list above) which are plainly based, he thinks, on Colossians but also seem related to 1 Peter. Whatever may be said of the other correspondences (and he freely grants that they might be equally well accounted for by the hypothesis of the independent use of traditional material), these at any rate demonstrate, he claims, that the author of 1 Peter had read Ephesians. His argument might conceivably hold water (granted, of course, that the priority of Ephesians were on other grounds acceptable) if the coincidences of thought and wording were very close indeed; but in fact they are not. All too often the common words he carefully counts are everyday NT words or are used in contrasting senses (e.g. 'prophets' in i. 10 and Eph. iii. 5), the common phrases are standardized forms or involve stock OT testimonies, the alleged similarities of thought belong in fact to different contexts of ideas (e.g. the growth of a baby in ii. 2; the erection of a building in Eph. ii. 21), and the themes treated as well as the setting and style of their treatment are divergent. Even in these passages, therefore, it seems easier and more natural to conclude that the agreements of Ephesians and 1 Peter are evidence of a shared tradition working independently on the two writers.

If the case for 1 Peter's familiarity with other NT documents seems weaker than used to be supposed, we may turn briefly to its alleged Paulinism. Most students would agree that it has, superficially at any rate, a Pauline colouring, but the precise significance of this needs to be defined. The Apostle's teaching was widely influential in the primitive Church; he was its great creative genius, working of course with traditional material, but remoulding it in forms which had a powerful and immediate impact far beyond his personal circle. A Pauline note has been overheard not only in 1 Peter, but in James, Hebrews and several other NT books. Two considerations should warn us against exaggerating the Paulinism of our epistle. First, many of the so-called Pauline traits are found in passages where the author is drawing on sources which Paul himself exploited.

Secondly, his theology is in important respects different from, and markedly less advanced than, the Apostle's. He has no inkling, for example, of justification by faith, of the tension between faith and works, of the problem of the Law, or of the Church as the body of Christ; indeed, the terms 'church' (62 times in Paul), and 'cross' and 'crucify' (18 times), are totally lacking. His own cast of mind is Hebraic, and this comes out, e.g., in his definitely OT doctrine of God, to Whom he restricts the title 'Lord', and in his conception of the relation of Christians to Israel. Again, 'sin' is usually for him the concrete act, while for Paul (who rarely uses the word in the plural) it tends (esp. in Romans) to be a menacing, almost personal power. His anthropological language, too, has a different cast, 'soul' (*psuchē*) bearing the Semitic sense of 'self' or 'life' in contrast to Paul's equation of it with the lower, natural man, and 'flesh' standing neutrally for man's bodily nature without any suggestion of its being the seat of sin. Finally, his view of Christ's sufferings as exemplary is not a Pauline theme.

5. LITURGICAL HYPOTHESES

The argument of the preceding section prompts us to probe beneath the surface of 1 Peter for clues to its composition. At first sight it looks like a mosaic of pieces, of various sizes and colours, without much connection or plan. Many, for example, have sensed a sharp break at the doxology in iv. 11, finding confirmation in the more urgent note perceptible in iv. 12-v. 11. Other apparent breaks have been noticed between the extended opening thanksgiving (i. 3-12) and the compact exhortation i. 13-ii. 10, with its eloquent contrast between the readers' former paganism and the holiness of their new Christian calling; and again between this and the diffuse admonitory section stretching from ii. 11 to iv. 11. This latter, too, seems to subdivide into a detailed catalogue of advice to particular groups in the communities (ii. 11-iii. 12), a part specifically concerned with persecutions (iii. 13-iv. 6), and a paragraph of more general advice set in an eschatological framework (iv. 7-11). The style of some of the pericopae, as H. Preisker has pointed out, seems to differ from that of others. Finally, it has been observed that the theme of baptism is prominent in certain passages (cf. esp. the mention of rebirth in i. 3; 23; ii. 2, and the short explanation of the sacrament in iii. 21), whereas it is entirely absent from others. Certain other passages seem to contain fragments of primitive creeds or hymns.

To account for these peculiarities various theories of composite structure have been advanced, although there is general agreement that a single redactor was responsible for the final form of the document. An important group of these concentrates on the baptismal allusions, reaching the conclusion that the epistle, or the major portion of it, reproduces features of the ancient service of baptism. Thus, according to R. Perdelwitz, i. 3-iv. 11 consists largely of a baptismal homily addressed to recent converts with the object of demonstrating the superiority of the Christian sacrament to the initiation rites of pagan mystery cults. As it stands it has been filled out with scraps of instructional and hortatory matter, and prefixed to a letter intended for persecuted Christians living in areas where these cults flourished. A number of scholars have been attracted by his thesis, although few have accepted his view of the large-scale influence of the ideas and terminology of the mysteries. One obvious weakness of this approach (others perhaps more fundamental will be adduced later) is that, by visualizing this long section almost exclusively as a sermon, it scarcely does justice to all the heterogeneous elements composing it. Another is that, while later practice makes it likely that addresses were given to the newly baptized, it is doubtful whether any single such address would have ranged over such a wide variety of topics, if indeed it touched on some of them at all.

Others who have worked on these lines have sought a purely liturgical solution to the problem. H. Preisker has been the pioneer here, making the bold claim that 1 Peter is in fact the transcript of a Roman baptismal liturgy. The bulk of the epistle (i. 3-iv. 11) represents the service for candidates receiving baptism, and according to his minute analysis eight successive stages can be distinguished. Thus it opens (i) with a 'prayer-psalm' (i. 3-12), eschatological in flavour and highlighting the future safety (cf. 'guarded' in i. 5) the baptized will enjoy, and passes (ii) into a 'teaching-discourse' (i. 13-21), including credal phrases which point to their imminent baptism. The baptismal act (iii) takes place immediately after i. 21; the convention (*disciplina arcani*) of drawing a veil over the Church's mysteries prevents any description of it, but its occurrence is clearly implied (Preisker argues) by the abrupt change to perfect tenses in i. 22 f. Then comes (iv) a short 'baptismal dedication' (i. 22-25) couched in soberly practical terms so as to dampen excessive enthusiasm; and this is followed (v) by a 'festal song' in three strophes (ii. 1-10), contributed by an inspired member of the congregation. After this we have (vi) an 'exhortation' (ii. 11-iii. 12), which is delivered by a 'new preacher' and which the congregation interrupts by bursting into a hymn about Christ (ii. 21-24); and then (vii) a 'revelation' (iii. 13-iv. 7a), imparted apparently by another charismatic bystander. Finally, redrafted now in epistolary style, comes what would originally have been (viii) the 'closing prayer' (iv. 7b-11). But this is not all. The candidates having been thus initiated, the section iv. 12-v. 11 is an open service for the whole body of the faithful; this explains why persecution is now spoken of as a stern reality and no longer, as it was for the candidates, as a future possibility (although it remains obscure why the persecutors should make this subtle distinction between baptized Christians and would-be Christians undergoing instruction).

Preisker suggests that the several parts of this liturgy were subsequently put together by Silvanus, a 2nd or 3rd generation Christian, and despatched as a letter in the name and spirit of the martyred Apostle to churches in Anatolia which had known him. More recently F. L. Cross has put forward what is essentially a simplified version of the same thesis, shorn of the somewhat arbitrary extempore outbursts and more realistically related to such information as we have about 2nd cent. baptismal imagery and procedure. Agreeing with Preisker that i. 3-iv. 11 constitutes the early Roman service of baptism, with the immersions taking place immediately after i. 21, he offers the following analysis: (i) opening prayer by the presiding minister (i. 3-12); (ii) his formal charge to the candidates before baptizing them (i. 13-21); (iii) his welcome to the newly baptized on entering the redeemed community (i. 22-25); (iv) his address on the fundamentals of the Christian life, concluding with the eucharist and first communion of the baptized (ii. 1-10); (v) his address on the duties of Christian discipleship (ii. 11-iv. 6); (vi) his closing admonitions, with doxology (iv. 7-11). Cross's special contribution is to associate the service with the Easter rites of baptism, confirmation and eucharist described in detail in Hippolytus's *Apostolic Tradition*, written in Rome *c.* 115 but probably preserving the usage of a much earlier epoch; in fact it is 'the Celebrant's part for the Paschal Vigil, for which, as the most solemn occasion in the Church's year, the Baptismal-Eucharistic text must have been very carefully prepared'. Easter in the early Church was the season *par excellence* for baptism, and the connection with it, he claims, is clearly indicated by the repeated occurrence of *paschein* ('suffer') and its correlates in 1 Peter, since there are plenty of parallels in early paschal homilies to the word-play *pascha* (Easter)-*paschein*. Further, in the early Church the Exodus was interpreted as prefiguring both the Christian Pasch and baptism, and Cross thinks he can trace this typology throughout 1 Peter. He backs his case for an Easter baptismal-eucharistic setting by his exegesis of numerous individual texts (e.g. i. 13: girding up the loins as in Ex. xii. 11; i. 18: paschal lamb; ii. 3: baptismal eucharist; iii. 3: removal of clothes before immersions).

Both Preisker's and Cross's theses are impressive in their breath-taking ingenuity, and (like Perdelwitz's) they oblige us to take seriously the baptismal echoes which can be heard in parts of the letter—echoes which should not surprise us when we recall the extent to which (as the NT abundantly shows) the great sacrament of initiation dominated the thoughts of 1st cent. Christians. It is impossible, however, to feel much confidence either in the detail of their analyses or in their schemes as wholes. In some cases their exegesis of texts is forced and un-natural; in others where it is correct it scarcely warrants their far-reaching deductions. The assumption on which their whole argument hinges, that the immersions take place after i. 21, depends on ignoring the palpable fact that the persons addressed in i. 3 ff. have already been baptized, and on pressing unduly the change of tenses in i. 22 f. (cf. the aorist in i. 3). As regards the schemes themselves, Preisker's reconstruction can only be described as a *tour de force* of subjective improvisation; we know little enough of baptismal procedures in the 1st cent., but what little we know gives no support to his conjectural picture. Cross's simpler scheme is superficially more plausible, but when closely examined presents none of the appearance of 'a very carefully prepared liturgy'. For one critical stage of the proposed scheme (the baptismal eucharist) he has to resort largely to guesswork; of the other stages the best that can be said is that, while the subject-matter roughly conforms with the titles given them, much of it would be more satisfyingly located in other, non-liturgical settings. The paronomasia *pasch-paschein* which he postulates is particularly unconvincing. Not only is it hard to see how anyone could be expected to recognize it since the key-term *pasch* is nowhere used, but the references to suffering are naturally and adequately accounted for by the situation of the addressees; six out of the eighteen instances of *paschein* or *pathēma* are in any case found in iv. 12-v. 11, which lies outside the supposed liturgy. A further daunting question is what sense the recipients of the letter as finally redrafted would be likely to make of a liturgy without any accompanying word of explanation.

Two more general considerations may now be advanced. First, it is intrinsically improbable that, in the period within the limits of which 1 Peter must have originated, the baptismal liturgy had acquired the elaboration, much less the relative fixity of its several parts, that the liturgical hypotheses presuppose. In short, they owe what plausibility they possess to assigning the term 'liturgy' a fluid, indeterminate sense which robs it of all practical relevance. In so doing they make the mistake of proposing a perilously over-simplified solution of the problem. In principle there is much to be said for the suggestion that, in composing his letter, the writer exploited traditional material; if we also recognize, as it is easy to do, that his organization of it is sometimes cumbersome, we have a straightforward and reasonable explanation of the resultant patchwork effect. But the traditional material at his disposal cannot have been exclusively liturgical. It must have been more variegated than these hypotheses allow, and in seeking to identify it we should be well advised to cast our net more widely.

Secondly, the theories of Perdelwitz and Cross (Preisker's too, but from a different angle) assume that iv. 12 ff. is a separate entity, and that the epistolary form has been subsequently imposed. Others who accept a break at iv. 11 take a more moderate line: iv. 12 ff. is an appendix added either because news of an intensive outbreak of persecution has suddenly reached the author, or as an alternative version for the benefit of certain communities which are in the thick of actual persecution. Behind these conjectures lies the conviction shared by most editors that it has 'no definite plan or logical evolution of a train of thought' (C. Bigg). We should like to maintain that it is, and always has been, a genuine unity, with a single consistent message, and was written as a real letter to the churches named in the address. In the previous section an attempt was made to show that we are not entitled to separate iv. 12 ff. from i. 1-iv. 11 on the ground that it envisages present, as opposed to hypothetical, persecution; the notes will indicate that arguments based on the doxology at iv. 11 are equally unconvincing. The clue to the letter's unity is the plight of the addressees, which is hinted at as early as i. 5 ('kept safe by God's power'), is explicitly mentioned in such passages as i. 6; ii. 12; ii. 20 f.; iii. 14-17; iv. 4, as well as iv. 12-19; v. 6-10, and throughout is the motive prompting all the writer's exhortations, appeals for exemplary conduct, and glowing delineations of Christ's victory over evil powers and the baptized Christian's share in it. Moreover, the themes in the several parts are exactly the same (it is better to suffer for doing right than the reverse: iii. 17; iv. 15 f.; brief tribulation to be succeeded by glory: i. 6 f.; v. 10; rejoicing in suffering: i. 6, 8; iv. 13 f.); and the same strongly eschatological note is present everywhere (i. 20; iv. 5; 7; 17; etc.), the same threatening talk about those 'who disobey the gospel'. Whatever material the writer may have taken over, he has evidently moulded it so as to conform to his overriding purpose of comforting and encouraging his correspondents in their painful testing.

6. STRUCTURE AND AIMS

If we are persuaded of the inadequacy of any theory that 1 Peter is simply a sermon or liturgy dressed up as a letter, we may now make a fresh attempt to sort out its component elements and expose to view the plan which seems to underlie them. The most practicable procedure will be to go through the successive pericopae, seeking to identify the author's sources of inspiration and to show how he has integrated them in his argument. In so doing we shall be treading in the footsteps of E. G. Selwyn, who in his exhaustive analysis of types of material current in the mid-1st cent. Church distinguished (i) hymns and embryonic credal forms, (ii) a homiletic or hortatory document compiled to assist evangelists and teachers, (iii) catechetical paradigms, and (iv) sayings of Christ. There can be little doubt that his approach was in principle correct, for (as C. Spicq has aptly remarked) 1 Peter is pre-eminently 'the epistle of tradition'; his chief mistakes were to think too much in terms of written documents and to propose an artificial degree of schematization for the ancient catechism. The form-critical technique has also been successfully applied by, among others, E. Lohse and M. E. Boismard (who has cautiously re-emphasized the influence of liturgies); and W. J. Dalton has brilliantly vindicated the unity of the epistle. The reader should be warned, however, not to look for clear-cut, confident conclusions. If it is certain that the author drew on conventional outlines (catechetical, liturgical, etc.), it is also certain that they were not verbally fixed, and that he felt completely at liberty to expand or recast them as suited his purposes.

(1) The form of the prescript (i. 1 f.), often alleged to be copied from Paul's, is in fact independent (note esp. the absence of Paul's characteristic 'from God our Father etc.'), reflecting the two-membered salutation customary in Jewish official correspondence which Paul himself adopted, although here we have the conventional Jewish 'be multiplied' (which he omits). In filling it out the writer incorporates traditional elements, such as the idea of Christians as the new Israel and a primitive Trinitarian formula. The former of these, and the mention of 'sanctification' and 'obedience', announce ideas which will be taken up later.

(2) The paragraph i. 3-12 opens with an ecstatic doxology glorifying God for regenerating us and making us eligible for an imperishable inheritance which will be finally ours at the last day; it then passes over in 6 ff. into a long parenthesis extolling

the jubilation which, despite their temporary trials (cf. v. 10), the recipients should feel at this assurance. The baptismal setting of i. 3-5 is made evident by 'born again', and after his parenthesis the writer harks back to it in i. 13-ii. 10 (e.g. i. 23; ii. 1 f.). As many have noted, there are remarkable correspondences between i. 3-5 and the similarly baptismal Tit. iii. 5-7, highlighted by the mention of *rebirth, inheritance, hope*, eternal *life*, and of God's *saving us by His mercy*; similar ideas are echoed in Rom. viii. 14-24; Col. iii. 1-4; 1 Jn. ii. 29-iii. 2. The structure, too, is strophe-like, and the inference seems inescapable that underlying these texts is a common baptismal thanksgiving, possibly a hymn, which the several authors have paraphrased more or less freely in accordance with their immediate needs. For example, the sudden switch from 'us' to 'you' in 4, and the interpolation of the reassuring 'who are kept safe etc.', confirm that the writer is modifying the original before him in the light of his correspondents' situation. He concentrates directly on this in i. 6-12, mingling personal references (6; 8; 12b) with Christian commonplaces about rejoicing in suffering and the opposition between present tribulation and eschatological glorification. There is nothing baptismal about these themes, which recur elsewhere in the letter and the NT and seem largely worked up in his own language; but it seems clear that one of his sources is a type of exhortation which the primitive Church took over from later Judaism and transmuted by its conviction that the day of salvation had dawned.

(3) The long section i. 13-ii. 10 makes a somewhat more homogeneous whole, dominated by the thought that as baptized Christians the readers are now God's chosen people, called to holiness but also the beneficiaries of His mercy in the new era which is opening. The raw materials which have gone to its composition are extremely varied in character. It is packed, for example, with paraenetic clichés; in particular, we note the conventional contrast between the converts' pre-Christian immoralities and the demands of the new life (cf. Eph. iv. 22-24; Tit. iii. 3-7), the insistence on unrightness, purity and brotherly affection as its tokens, and the rudimentary catalogue of vices (ii. 1) introduced by the tell-tale 'put off'. At i. 20 and 21 we find incorporated what are probably excerpts from a hymn and a creed;

and the paragraph throughout, particularly in the second half, is a veritable mosaic of stock OT testimonies. Its atmosphere, again most obviously in the second half, is sacramental, pervaded by what seem to be reminiscences of baptism (e.g. i. 23; ii. 1 f.) and the eucharist (ii. 3; 5). With such a motley texture it is difficult to believe that the pericope reproduces a baptismal homily, or even the paraphrase of one; much more probably the writer has been freely plundering catechetical, liturgical and other commonplaces in the interests of his message. The references in i. 14; 18; ii. 10 to his readers' having previously been pagans make it plain that they are in the forefront of his mind. So too (though this has been generally overlooked) are the persecutions they have to put up with, as the repeated echoes of Ps. xxxiv (see note on ii. 3) and the prophecy of doom for those 'who disobey the word' (ii. 7 f.) confirm. Indeed what knits together all these disparate scraps, so diverse in their provenance, is his confident promise that, however harassing his experiences, the Christian who sets his hope on Christ will never be put to shame, since God has raised Him from the dead and given Him glory (e.g. i. 13; 21; ii. 6).

(4) The abrupt 'Dear friends' at ii. 11 marks the opening of a fresh pericope, which continues to iii. 12 and forms a relatively compact unity. Style, subject-matter and arrangement, as well as the numerous parallels in other NT epistles, indicate the writer's dependence here on a type of ethical code which was apparently in circulation in the primitive Church and which it took over, with suitable Christian modifications, from models supplied by Jewish and Judaeo-Hellenistic propaganda and popular pagan philosophy. Prescribing the right attitude to the civil authorities and the conduct appropriate to different categories of people, its setting was not necessarily, and certainly not exclusively, baptismal. Like Paul and James, the author of 1 Peter handles his material (the wording of which was in any case far from fixed) very freely, adapting it in the light of his readers' special situation. It is his concern for this which prompts him, in recalling Christ's patience in suffering, to insert what look like fragments of a creed and a Christological hymn at ii. 21-25, to hold up the picture of God as the just judge (ii. 23) and of Christ as his correspondents' sure guardian (ii. 25), and

3

to wind up the section with a warning against retaliation (iii. 9) based on a saying of the Lord and flowing over into a citation from Ps. xxxiv, both items belonging to community tradition.

(5) Taking up the closing word of his psalm citation ('harm'), he comes to grips in the rest of the letter (iii. 13-end) with the Asian Christians' painful predicament. Thus we get vivid glimpses of the interrogations and abuse to which they are subjected (iii. 15 f.), of the indignation excited by their abstention from loose revelries (iv. 4), and of a 'fiery ordeal' capable perhaps of landing them in court cases (iv. 12-16), as well as a statement that such anti-Christian action is world-wide (v. 9). Throughout his motive is to brace their spirits by pointing to the precedent of Christ's passion and the privilege of sharing it, but more particularly by holding up the glory in prospect for them, by reminding them that they have an unshakable ground for confidence in Christ's triumph over the powers of evil (iii. 18-22), and by announcing the certain doom which the approaching judgment spells for their opponents (iv. 5; 17 f.). The whole section is to a large extent his own composition, but the influence of traditional forms is everywhere discernible. For example, his emphasis on rejoicing in suffering and on ill-treatment as a blessed testing, while expressed in his own words, reflects a theme which, as we remarked on i. 6 ff., was a commonplace of primitive Christianity. Again, he reinforces his affirmation of Christ's victory through suffering with excerpts (iii. 18 f.; 21c-22) from a Christological hymn or creed, interweaving with them current baptismal teaching in such a way as to insinuate that the baptized share in that victory and escape the destruction it brings to the wicked. In v. 1-5 he inserts some advice to 'elders' and young people which properly belongs to the ethical code of ii. 11-iii. 12, but which he has transferred here, not by oversight, but because this is the appropriate place to dwell on the responsibilities of leaders and the cohesion necessary to the community. Elsewhere, too, interspersed with what is obviously his own writing, traditional scraps, turns of phrase and ideas keep reappearing, as in the mention of spiritual armour in iv. 1, the contrast between past and present in iv. 3, the credal tag 'to judge living and dead' in iv. 5, the brief admonitory section iv. 8-11a, and the call to humility, submission to God's will and

resistance to the Devil in v. 5-9a (cf. the close parallel in Jas. iv. 6-10).

This rapid survey, conjectural though much of its detail must be, should at least help to illustrate the wide variety of traditional elements which the author has pressed into service. Some of them are patently catechetical; others seem to have a liturgical or homiletic ring; here and there snatches from hymns or creeds stand out. In citing scripture he handles a recognized corpus of OT texts, applying them in the light of already established exegetical principles; and in dealing with suffering he speaks from a tradition which has its roots far back in Judaism. At the same time his letter is far from being an unoriginal pastiche. Complex though his material is, he succeeds in shaping it to subserve his purpose of sustaining and encouraging the Asian Christians, and to be the vehicle of his own characteristic and supremely confident convictions about Christ's victory and the vindication of His faithful adherents. His correspondents' troubles are the ever-felt background of every paragraph, sometimes emerging into the open, but always determining his selection and manipulation of catechetical, liturgical and hortatory matter; and it is they, illuminated by the passion of Christ Himself, which inspire and give point to his paradoxical summons to exultation.

The tone of the epistle being thus mainly practical, we should not look to it for theology in the strict sense. It is, of course, packed with theology, but theology which is for the most part taken for granted rather than consciously expounded. The most interesting features of this (e.g. in regard to baptism, or Christ's proclamation to the spirits) will be more usefully treated in the Commentary, and here we need only observe its generally simple, traditional character. The writer's conception of God, as remarked above, is very close to the OT conception, and he thinks of Jesus as the Messiah of whom the prophets had spoken, seeing Him prefigured in Isaiah's Suffering Servant. He identifies 'the Spirit of Christ' with the Spirit which was in the prophets, and while he includes an archaic Trinitarian formula in i. 2, his references to the Holy Spirit are noticeably sparse. Christ is sinless, and His death is not only exemplary but has an atoning effect; as crowned by the resurrection, it represents

God's final triumph over evil. For much of this teaching, however, he relies on stereotyped formulae. So far as the Church is concerned, Christians are the new Israel, the people of God who were once no people, strangers and sojourners in the world awaiting their heavenly inheritance.

Two aspects of his theology are peculiarly significant for understanding his exhortations. The first is the strongly eschatological perspective in which he places the experiences of his readers. The Messiah has been revealed and the End has already begun (i. 20); redeemed and regenerated, Christians have the promised salvation already within their grasp. Although the full glory is yet to come (i. 4 f.; iv. 13), their temporary sufferings are themselves proof that it is just round the corner (iv. 7; 17: cf. v. 10); the final conflict of God and His saints with the Devil has been effectively won, so that they can face every sort of ill-treatment with confidence, even exultation. Linked with this is the remarkable emphasis on exemplary behaviour which characterizes the epistle. Not only should Christians be tenderly affectionate to each other, but they are asked to observe the highest standards in their relations with pagan neighbours and the civil authorities. There is no thought in the writer's mind that good works will procure them salvation, for he believes they have obtained that through Christ. One reason for recommending such conduct is that it will help to silence calumniators (ii. 15) and even win sceptics over to the faith (iii. 1 f.), but the real motive lies deeper. The commonly accepted norms of behaviour are things of the past for them (iv. 1 ff.), for they are denizens of the heavenly order which is breaking in; holiness is the vocation of God's people (i. 15), and in this time of judgment His favour is on the righteous (iii. 12).

7. Date, Author and Place

1 Peter represents itself as a message from the Apostle, and the writer's description of himself as a witness of Christ's sufferings (v. 1: but see note) and of Mark as his spiritual son (v. 13) lends colour to this claim. Scholars who accept it generally conclude, on the assumption that Peter perished in Nero's pogrom, i.e. in 64 or shortly thereafter (although Eusebius puts his death

in 68), that the epistle was written from Rome in the early sixties of the 1st cent. On the other hand, many find the theory of Petrine authorship and the early date it necessitates incredible. Their scepticism is grounded partly on the refined Greek style and literary vocabulary of the letter, its habit of citing the OT exclusively from the Greek LXX, and the sparseness of its personal allusions to Jesus (all surprising features, as they think, if it comes from the Galilean fisherman who was His constant associate), partly on its apparent dependence on the Pauline correspondence, the indications it seems to contain that Christianity is now a criminal offence in the eyes of the law, the numerous traces some have detected of the ideas and practices of the mystery-cults, and the comparative lateness of its attestation. They are also troubled by the absence of any reference to Paul if the addressees included communities he had evangelized, and (on the alternative hypothesis) by the lack of any evidence that Peter worked in northern Anatolia. Critics who are impressed by considerations like these, while agreed that 1 Peter must be pseudonymous, are divided about its probable date. Some place it in the reign of Domitian (81–96), traditionally reckoned a persecutor of Christianity. Others assign it to the first decades of the 2nd cent., being convinced that it reflects the very situation sketched by Pliny the Younger when, as governor of Bithynia-Pontus, he wrote to Trajan in 110 for advice about how to deal with Christians.

(1) DATE. The arguments favouring a late date differ greatly in value. Few, for example, would attach as much importance to the impact of mystery-cults as R. Perdelwitz did in 1911. The background of the traits on which he and his followers fastened (e.g. the conception of baptism as rebirth in i. 3; 23, and of 'pure, spiritual milk' in ii. 2; the notion of being called from darkness into God's light in ii. 9) is, as the Commentary will try to show, in all probability totally alien from Hellenistic religion. Indeed, the cast of the writer's mind has been more affected by Palestinian influences than Hellenistic. As regards recognition, the Muratorian Canon's failure to mention 1 Peter (especially if it is a Roman document) is distinctly puzzling, and the attempts made to explain it by the mutilated state of the text are not really satisfactory. There is, however, an element of

chance in these matters, and on any estimate the reference to
1 Peter in 2 Pet. iii. 1, its repeated citation by Polycarp and
its reported use by Papias (see p. 2) are obstacles to placing it
outside the 1st cent. If admitted, the allegation that it draws on
Paul's letters is bound to carry great weight, even allowing for
the fact that the Apostle's influence, especially in places (e.g.
Rome) where he had personally worked and preached, was
powerful and immediate. Yet its force, once considered overwhelming, diminishes to vanishing-point if we accept the view
(see §4) that most, if not all, the correspondences result from
the independent use of community tradition by the two writers.

The persecutions might be expected to furnish a definite
clue. If the letter indicates that they spring from government
intervention and that the very profession of Christianity has
become an indictable offence, we must conclude that it was
written after the great fire of Rome of 64, since prior to that we
have no evidence of action by the imperial authorities against
Christianity as such. At some time after 64, certainly well before
109–111 when Pliny was imperial legate in Bithynia-Pontus,
Christianity came to be regarded as an abomination deserving
the severest penalties. The theory that there was a general edict
outlawing it, enacted by Nero or Domitian, has been widely
abandoned; it seems much more likely that in repressing it
provincial governors were exercising *coercitio*, i.e. their ordinary
responsibility for enforcing public order at their own discretion,
without reliance on specific legislation. The actual grounds for
singling out Christianity as such for prosecution remain obscure,
and are still debated among Roman historians; the most probable explanation is that the government accepted at its face
value the popular view, engendered by its exclusiveness and
total rejection of the Roman religion, that it was an anti-social
phenomenon fraught with danger to the state and possibly shel-
tering all sorts of detestable practices. This was certainly the
position in 110, when Pliny (*Ep*. x. 96), reporting that he had
executed some Bithynians who had been 'denounced to me as
Christians', disclosed to Trajan his uncertainty whether it was
'the name itself, even in the absence of crimes, or crimes associated with the name', which constituted the offence; and the
emperor in his rescript, while stipulating that Christians must

not be hunted out nor anonymous accusations accepted, confirmed that Pliny had acted correctly (i.e. in punishing confessed Christians for the name only). The coercitial procedure, it should be noted, was not inquisitorial but accusatorial, i.e. the guilty parties had to be delated to the magistrate, and he had to determine whether to take action or not; this explains why the early persecutions were relatively few, sporadic and short-lived.

At first sight there might seem a remarkable resemblance between the situation hinted at in iv. 14-16 (cf. the stress on 'the name of Christ' and on suffering 'as a Christian') and that more circumstantially described by Pliny, especially as Bithynia is involved in both cases; and, as already remarked, several scholars have inferred that they are in fact the same. Even if such a very late date is on other grounds (see below) improbable, it is reasonable enough to appeal to the Pliny–Trajan exchange as evidence that the persecutions belong at any rate to, say, the last third of the 1st cent., when we may presume the mere profession of Christianity to have become a crime. Nevertheless caution is necessary; if iv. 14-16 is studied in the context of the other allusions to trials and sufferings, it becomes plain that this is not the only interpretation that is possible, nor the most plausible. As we saw in §3, the impression which the letter as a whole conveys is not of juridical prosecutions by the government (these seem ruled out by the references themselves, by the statement that the ill-treatment is world-wide, and by the respect shown to the emperor), but of an atmosphere of suspicion, hostility and brutality on the part of the local population which may easily land Christians in trouble with the police. It is relevant to observe that the threat mentioned in iv. 14 is 'being insulted for Christ's name', which conjures up precisely such an atmosphere; and that while iv. 15 f. might conceivably have trials before provincial governors in view, its language is at least equally compatible with petty prosecutions before civic magistrates. Acts, the Pauline letters and the rest of the NT provide ample proof that such harassment was a routine experience of Christians from the apostolic age onwards, and numerous texts (e.g. Mt. v. 11 f.; Mk. xiii. 13; Lk. xxi. 12; Acts v. 41) confirm that this was conventionally spoken of as suffering 'for the name'.

If we are satisfied that the persecutions are of this kind, we still have not settled our problem. As far as we can judge, Christians were liable to become the objects of local maltreatment at almost any time in the first two centuries. There are, however, certain phenomena which incline one to favour a relatively early date, just conceivably even a date before 64, rather than one towards the end of the 1st cent. First, the persons addressed, or at any rate a large proportion of them, seem to be recent converts; there is no hint of second-generation Christianity. This kind of situation, prevailing in a fair number of communities in Anatolia simultaneously, is more likely to have obtained earlier rather than later in our period. Secondly, the type of church order they possessed, with pastoral oversight in the hands of 'elders' who are also seniors in age, seems comparatively undeveloped, especially when we remember (cf. Ignatius's letters) how rapidly an elaborate ministerial hierarchy evolved in Asia Minor. In this connection the later one places the epistle, the more remarkable becomes the modest self-description 'fellow-elder' put into Peter's mouth (v. 1). Thirdly, its theology has a distinctly primitive flavour; among the points listed on pp. 25 f. we may stress the archaic Trinitarian formula in i. 2 and the identification of Jesus in ii. 21 ff. with Deutero-Isaiah's Servant of the Lord. Though extremely ancient, the Servant-Christology soon receded in the Church, being already in retreat in Paul and hardly traceable in the 1st cent. after him. Lastly, 'the eschatological structure of the thought, with its close inter-penetration of future hope and present realization' (F. L. Cross), the eschatological setting of the ethics, and the exultant anticipation of the glory which will shortly be revealed, are all tokens of an early epoch.

(2) AUTHOR. The question of authorship is even more difficult than that of dating, and critical scholarship is not equipped to produce a finally convincing settlement. A reasonable case can of course be made out for the traditional view that the epistle comes from Peter. His name stands in its superscription, and (unlike, e.g., 2 Peter) it exhibits none of the telltale pointers to pseudonymity, such as a self-conscious straining after verisimilitude or the barely concealed assumption that the apostolic age lies in the past. Rome has strong claims (see below) to be its place of origin, and few today would question that the

Apostle spent a period there before his martyrdom. His close relationship with Mark (v. 13) is well attested, and Mark's residence in Rome is also vouched for (Phm. 24; 2 Tim. iv. 11; Papias in Eusebius, *Hist. eccl.* iii. 39. 15). If the argument of the preceding paragraphs is accepted, both contents and tone are fully consistent with apostolic times. The objection based on the lack of personal reminiscences of Jesus is easily countered; not only does it overlook the sayings of the Lord recalled in the letter, but it reflects anachronistically a modern biographical preoccupation. As for the absence of references to Paul, such references would be out of place since some at any rate of the churches addressed cannot have been founded by him; and the movements of Peter himself after the activities described in Acts and Galatians are too obscure to form the basis of speculations. Some indeed profess to discover, scattered throughout the letter, traces of the Apostle's teaching as transmitted to us in Acts (e.g. the Servant Christology), and even of his Master's charges to him (e.g. v. 2: cf. Jn. xxi. 17).

Of course, if he is the author of 1 Peter, he can hardly have composed it himself; the character of the Greek weighs heavily against this. The argument on this score is often misconceived, and we need to be clear about the real issue. It is not the case, as is commonly assumed, that an 'uneducated' (Acts iv. 13) fisherman like Peter could not have expressed himself in Greek, or would not have used the LXX. His family, engaged in business in bilingual Galilee, must have been at home with Greek, and his brother Andrew in fact bore a Greek name; in any case Greek rather than Aramaic must have been the tongue in which he had conversed during the past thirty years with Hellenist Jews in Jerusalem and Antioch, and the LXX the Bible for his missionary work abroad. What is decisive is rather the literary quality of the epistle, the Greek of which has a certain scholarly correctness. Its style certainly does not deserve the extravagant eulogies it has received, being unimaginative, monotonous and at times clumsy (cf. L. Radermacher: ZNTW xxv, 1926, 287 ff.), but the writer does deploy a limited range of rhetorical conventions, and has evidently had a technical training which we could not plausibly attribute to Peter. Thus almost all who believe him to be responsible for the letter are convinced that he committed the drafting to a trusted colleague, probably but not necessarily Silvanus (see on v. 12). It is naïve to caricature such a hypothesis as a resort to a 'ghost-writer'. In the ancient world, as today, not only statesmen like Trajan but private persons dealt on occasion with correspondence in this way; and it was entirely natural that a man like Peter, fluent in conversational Greek but without a formal education, should do so when writing officially to Greek-speaking communities.

The case for Petrine authorship, at any rate in this sense, is a strong one, but even so doubts are bound to obtrude themselves. At least three reasons why its most ardent adherents should abstain from dogmatism can be suggested. First, however firm our conviction that 1 Peter is relatively early, we must concede that this description, like most of the facts on which it is based, is just as compatible with a date shortly after 64, or even in the seventies, as with one shortly before it. Secondly, the argument has largely consisted of weighing probabilities, and if our assessment of the crucial issues had been slightly different the balance would have tilted in the other direction. For example, we have argued that it is much more likely that 1 Peter and the Pauline letters drew independently on common material than that the former borrowed from the latter; but 'much more likely' is not equivalent to 'certain'. The alternative view remains a possibility; and if we decide that it is even in some degree correct, and further agree with many scholars that Ephesians is post-Pauline, the Petrine case is proportionately weakened. Thirdly, there is a great unknown which casts its shadow over the whole debate, the personality of Peter himself. The parallel discussion about, say, the Pastorals is vastly different, for we know a great deal about Paul, his theology, his style, his relationship with his colleagues, etc. We have no such direct, trustworthy insight into the mind and method of Peter, for the speeches reported in Acts are at best second-hand summaries reconstructed long after the event, while the attempts to recapture his traits and accents in this or that passage of the letter are largely romantic guesses.

This being the position, the possibility that 1 Peter is after all pseudonymous certainly cannot be excluded, and in the Commentary we have preferred to speak of 'the writer' rather than name him. A moderate version of the theory of pseudonymity is that Silvanus wrote the letter after the Apostle's death, perhaps at the request of the Roman church, but at any rate sincerely believing that he was carrying out his intention. This would resolve the difficulty, if difficulty it is, why Peter is depicted as corresponding with churches which, as far as we know, were strange to him, but many of which Silvanus had visited (Acts xv. 40; xviii. 5; I Thess. i. 1); since Silvanus had been Paul's constant companion and had shared in writing 1 Thessalonians, it would also explain any Pauline traits in construction, manner and theology. An awkward problem, of course, is posed by the self-eulogy which, on this theory, he inserted at v. 12. A more radical version would postulate an unknown writer and would treat all the personal references as deliberately contrived so as to suggest a convincingly lifelike setting. The reader must make his own decision, but it seems proper to repeat that, taken as a whole, the evidence inclines towards an early date, and the earlier we place it the more difficult it becomes to deny some connection, indirect if not direct, with the Apostle.

(3) PLACE. Since the 2nd cent. (Eusebius, *Hist. eccl.* ii. 15.2) 'Babylon' in v. 13 has been generally accepted as a figurative description for Rome, but even if this should prove to be a mistaken exegesis (see note), there are other pointers to Rome as the probable place of origin. One thinks particularly of the mention of Mark (v. 13), whose residence in Rome is attested (Col. iv. 10; Phm. 24: cf. 2 Tim. iv. 11) and who is generally supposed to have written his gospel there, and of the likelihood (see above, p. 12) that 1 Peter derives from the same milieu as the unquestionably Roman *1 Clement*. The silence of the Muratorian Canon, also a Roman document, is admittedly embarrassing, but there may be some explanation of this which eludes us. On the assumption that the Apostle himself or one of his immediate circle is the author, the claim that the letter was despatched from Rome is entirely acceptable, for it accords with reliable tradition about the closing phase of his life. Even on a theory of pseudonymity in the strict sense, there is nothing intrinsically objectionable in a Roman origin; in the Neronian persecution, and possibly later, the church of the capital had a specially poignant experience of suffering, and might well have

felt moved to send a message of encouragement, in the name of its martyred hero, to other communities faced with similar testing. A theory of pseudonymity, however, clearly leaves the field much more open. Some of its adherents argue that, wherever the epistle was actually written, it was natural to give it a Roman address in view of the accepted facts about Peter's movements. Others (e.g. M. E. Boismard), pointing out that 'Babylon' does not necessarily stand for Rome, have pressed the view that, in its final form, it may have been put together at Antioch. Points in favour of this are the detailed knowledge it shows of Christian communities in Asia Minor, its early use by Papias of Hierapolis and Polycarp of Smyrna, and the fact that where the name 'Christian' occurs elsewhere in the NT the environment is Syrian. With so many different factors competing for consideration a firm decision is not easy, but the tradition connecting it with Rome still seems much more solidly based than any rival hypothesis.

SELECT BIBLIOGRAPHY TO 1 PETER

COMMENTARIES

F. W. Beare, *The First Epistle of Peter* (Oxford, 2nd ed. 1958).

C. Bigg, *The Epistles of St. Peter and St. Jude* (International Critical Commentary. Edinburgh, 1901).

A. Charue, *Les Épîtres catholiques* (Paris, 3rd ed. 1951).

C. E. B. Cranfield, *1 and 2 Peter and Jude* (Torch Commentary. London, 1960).

J. Felten, *Die zwei Briefe des hl. Petrus und der Judasbrief* (Regensburg, 1929).

R. Franco, *Cartas de san Pedro* (Madrid, 1962).

Fr. Hauck, *Die Briefe des Jakobus, Petrus, Judas und Johannes* (Göttingen, 8th ed. 1957).

F. J. A. Hort, *The First Epistle of St. Peter i. 1-ii. 17* (London, 1898).

R. Knopf, *Die Briefe Petri und Judä* (Göttingen, 7th ed. 1911).

A. R. C. Leaney, *The Letters of Peter and Jude* (Cambridge Bible Commentary. Cambridge, 1967).

R. Leconte, *Les Épîtres catholiques* (La sainte bible de Jérusalem. Paris, 1953).

J. Moffatt, *The General Epistles* (Moffatt NT Commentary. London, 1928).

B. Reicke, *The Epistles of James, Peter and Jude* (The Anchor Bible. New York, 1964).

K. H. Schelkle, *Die Petrusbriefe, Der Judasbrief* (Herders Theologischer Kommentar zum NT. Freiburg im Breisgau, 2nd ed. 1964).

J. Schneider, *Die Kirchenbriefe* (Das NT Deutsch. Göttingen, 1961).

E. Schweizer, *Der erste Petrusbrief* (Zürich, 2nd ed. 1949).

E. G. Selwyn, *The First Epistle of St. Peter* (London, 2nd ed. 1955).

C. Spicq, *Les Épîtres de saint Pierre* (Sources Bibliques. Paris, 1966).

A. M. Stibbs, *The First Epistle General of Peter* (Tyndale NT Commentaries. London, 1959).

J. W. C. Wand, *The General Epistles of St. Peter and St. Jude* (Westminster Commentaries. London, 1934).

H. Windisch (rev. by H. Preisker), *Die Katholischen Briefe* (Handbuch zum NT. Tübingen, 3rd ed. 1951).

G. Wohlenberg, *Der erste und zweite Petrusbrief und der Judasbrief* (Kommentar zum NT. Leipzig-Erlangen, 3rd ed. 1923).

STUDIES AND ARTICLES

F. W. Beare, 'The Teaching of First Peter' (*Anglican Theological Review* xxvi, 1944-45).

35

THE EPISTLES OF PETER AND OF JUDE

E. Best, 'Spiritual Sacrifice—General Priesthood in the NT' (*Interpretation* xiv, 1960).

M. E. Boismard, 'Une Liturgie baptismale dans la Prima Petri' (*Revue Biblique* lxiii, 1956).

'La Typologie baptismale dans la première épître de s. Pierre' (*La Vie spirituelle* xciv, 1956).

Quatres Hymnes baptismales dans la première épître de Pierre (Paris, 1961).

'Pierre (Première épître de)' (*Dictionnaire de la Bible*, Supplément vii. Paris, 1966).

W. Bornemann, 'Der erste Petrusbrief, eine Taufrede des Silvanus?' (ZNTW xix, 1919–20).

W. Brandt, 'Wandel als Zeugnis nach dem 1. Petrusbrief' (*Verbum Dei Manet in Aeternum*: Festschrift O. Schmitz. Witten, 1953).

R. Bultmann, 'Bekenntnis- und Liedfragmente im ersten Petrusbrief' (*Coniectanea Neotestamentica* xi. Lund, 1947).

C. E. B. Cranfield, 'The Interpretation of 1 Peter iii. 19 and iv. 6' (*Expository Times* lxii, 1958).

F. L. Cross, *1 Peter, A Paschal Liturgy* (London, 1954).

W. J. Dalton, *Christ's Proclamation to the Spirits* (Rome, 1965).

J. Daniélou, *Sacramentum Futuri* (Paris, 1950).

J. H. Elliott, 'The Elect and the Holy' (*Novum Testamentum*, Supp. xii. Leiden, 1966).

F. V. Filson, 'Partakers with Christ: Suffering in First Peter' (*Interpretation* ix, 1959).

K. Gschwind, 'Die Niederfahrt Christi in die Unterwelt' (*Neutestamentliche Abhandlungen* ii, 1911).

J. Jeremias, 'Zwischen Karfreitag und Ostern' (ZNTW xlii, 1949).

E. Kamlah, *Die Form der katalogischen Paränese im NT* (Tübingen, 1964).

J. Knox, 'Pliny and 1 Peter: a Note on 1 Pet. iv. 14-16 and iii. 15' (*Journal of Biblical Literature* lxxii, 1953).

A. R. C. Leaney, '1 Peter and the Passover: an Interpretation' (*New Testament Studies* x, 1964).

E. Lohse, 'Paränese und Kerygma im 1. Petrusbrief' (ZNTW xlv, 1954).

Märtyrer und Gottesknecht (Göttingen, 1955).

P. Lundberg, *La Typologie baptismale dans l'ancienne Église* (Uppsala, 1942).

E. Massaux, 'Le Texte de la 1a Petri du Papyrus Bodmer VIII' (*Mélanges G. Ryckmans*. Louvain, 1963).

C. L. Mitton, 'The Relationship between 1 Peter and Ephesians' (*Journal of Theological Studies*, NS i, 1950).

C. F. D. Moule, 'Sanctuary and Sacrifice in the Church of the NT' (*Journal of Theological Studies*, NS i, 1950).

'The Nature and Purpose of 1 Peter' (*New Testament Studies* iii, 1956).

SELECT BIBLIOGRAPHY TO 1 PETER

W. Nauck, 'Freude im Leiden' (ZNTW xlvi, 1955).
'Probleme des frühchristlichen Amstverständnisses' (ZNTW xlviii, 1957).

R. Perdelwitz, *Die Mysterienreligion und das Problem des 1. Petrusbriefes* (Giessen, 1911).

C. A. Pierce, *Conscience in the New Testament* (London, 1955).

L. Radermacher, 'Der erste Petrusbrief und Silvanus' (ZNTW xxv, 1926).

B. Reicke, *The Disobedient Spirits and Christian Baptism: A Study of 1 Pet. iii. 19 and its Context* (Copenhagen, 1946).
'Die Gnosis der Männer nach 1 Petr. iii. 7' (ZNTW, Beiheft xxi, 1954).

E. G. Selwyn, 'Eschatology in 1 Peter' (*The Background of the NT and its Eschatology*, ed. W. D. Davies and D. Daube: Cambridge, 1956).

G. E. M. de Sainte-Croix, 'Why were the Early Christians Persecuted?' (*Past and Present* xxvi, 1963; xxvii, 1964).

A. N. Sherwin-White, 'The Early Persecutions and Roman Law Again' (*Journal of Theological Studies*, NS iii, 1952).

T. C. G. Thornton, '1 Peter, A Paschal Liturgy?' (*Journal of Theological Studies*, NS xii, 1961).

W. C. van Unnik, 'The Teaching of Good Works in 1 Peter' (*New Testament Studies* i, 1954).
'Christianity according to 1 Peter' (*Expository Times* lxviii, 1956).

J. W. C. Wand, 'The Lessons of First Peter: A Survey of Recent Interpretation' (*Interpretation* ix, 1959).

S. Wibbing, 'Die Tugend- und Lasterkataloge im NT' (ZNTW, Beiheft xxv, 1959).

THE FIRST EPISTLE OF PETER

1. ADDRESS AND GREETING

i. 1-2

(1) Peter, apostle of Jesus Christ, to God's scattered people settled temporarily in Pontus, Galatia, Cappadocia, Asia and Bithynia who have been chosen (2) as a result of God the Father's foreknowledge, by the sanctifying action of the Spirit, with a view to obedience and sprinkling with the blood of Jesus Christ. May grace and peace be multiplied to you.

The conventional opening of Greek letters in the 1st and early 2nd cents. followed the formula, 'A to B, greeting'. NT examples are the decree of the Council of Jerusalem and the letter of Claudius Lysias to Felix (Acts xv. 23; xxiii. 26). By contrast the address of Jewish letters was divided into two sentences, the first containing the names of sender and recipient, and the second a prayer for peace and other blessings, usually in the second person. For examples, cf. Dan. iv. 1; vi. 25 (in both 'Peace by multiplied to you'); Apoc. Bar. lxxviii. 2; Bab. Talmud, San. 11b. In addition, while the Greek prescript was barely and tautly constructed, the names in the Jewish were often embellished with elaborate descriptive attributes.

As the NT shows, it was the Jewish rather than the Greek pattern that primitive Christian writers took over and christianized (E. Lohmeyer, ZNTW xxvi. 158-64), and a comparison between the present address and those of Paul's letters illustrates different ways in which this might be done. There is no sound reason (see Introduction, p. 21) for detecting Pauline influence on it. The writer's concern is to emphasize, in the most solemn manner, the supernatural vocation of his correspondents, which should be their sheet-anchor in their trials; but first he

4

1 quietly reminds them of his authority. He is **Peter, apostle of Jesus Christ.** For the question of authorship, see Introduction, pp. 30-3. The bare name (the Greek equivalent of the Aramaic *Kēphas*, or 'rock', applied by Jesus to Simon, son of John: Mt. xvi. 17 f. Jn. i. 42) is enough, for Peter's leading position was widely acknowledged in the primitive Church. There is nothing defensive in **apostle**, i.e. representative or delegate, **of J.C.,** as there usually is in Paul's parallel claims. No one is likely to question Peter's right to the title; he is simply making it plain from the start that his message is not so much his own as the Lord's, whose authorized agent he is.

He then describes his correspondents as **God's scattered people settled temporarily** in various parts of Asia Minor **who have been chosen . . .** On a hasty reading one might be tempted to infer that they are Jewish Christians: so most of the Greek fathers, but not Jerome or Augustine. The Greek noun translated **scattered people** is *diaspora* (i.e. 'Dispersion'), a technical term among Greek-speaking Jews (there is no exact equivalent in the Hebrew Bible) for members of their race dwelling outside Palestine in heathen countries. Similarly **chosen** was the epithet regularly used by the Jews to express their conviction that God had singled them out from all nations to be His special people (e.g. Dt. iv. 37; vii. 6; xiv. 2; Ps. cv. 6; Is. xlv. 4). In Maccabean times and later the growing consciousness of living in a hostile environment strengthened this conviction (e.g. Jub. ii. 20); at Qumran, too, the sectaries regarded themselves as God's elect (e.g. 1QS viii. 6; xi. 16; 1QpHab. x. 13). Actually, however, we have good reasons for believing (see Introduction, pp. 4 f.) that the addressees, or the majority of them, are Gentile Christians. Thus in transferring to them the hallowed language appropriate to God's own people the writer is tacitly implying that the Christian Church has succeeded to that privileged role.

This assumption that the Church is the new Israel, the appointed heir of both the revelation and the promises made to the old, is a NT commonplace (e.g. Gal. vi. 16; Phil. iii. 3; Jas. i. 1) which goes back to our Lord's interpretation of His person and mission in the light of key-ideas of the OT. The writer embroiders the theme in ii. 9 f. In the present passage the point he wishes to emphasize, in view of his readers' difficult situation, is that as Christians they have no abiding home on earth. In earlier times the Jews read their successive deportations as divine punishments (e.g. Dt. xxix. 25-28; Jer. xxxiv. 17; Jdt. v. 18), but later, as their foreign settlements prospered and increased in number, they began to view them less gloomily (e.g. Orac. Sib. iii. 271; 1 Macc. xv. 16-24: cf. TWNT II, 98-101). Even so, *diaspora*, adopted as a euphemism for the harsher expressions formerly used, conveyed a wistful hope of returning to their homeland (e.g. Neh. i. 9; Ps. cxlvii. 2; 2 Macc. i. 27). This hope is more frankly stated in **settled temporarily** (*parepidēmoi*: cf. i. 17; ii. 11), a term which connotes one who is merely passing through a territory, with no intention of permanent residence. So what the writer is suggesting is that, just as the Jews of the Dispersion were a **scattered people** cut off from their country but with the prospect of ultimately going back, so Christians are bound, wherever they are, to be transitory sojourners yearning for home. The difference is that for them 'home' cannot be identified with any place on earth, but only with the new order which God is bringing in. For closely related ideas, cf. Eph. ii. 19; Phil. iii. 20; Heb. xi. 13-16; *Ep. ad Diognetum* v (esp. 9: 'they [i.e. Christians] pass their time on earth, but belong as citizens to heaven').

The writer next defines the destination of his letter as **Pontus, Galatia, Cappadocia, Asia and Bithynia.** These names (see Introduction, pp. 3f.) denote the four Roman provinces which covered all Asia Minor north of the Taurus range, but it is not clear whether he has the whole or only parts of this vast area in mind. Paul had brought Christianity to sections of it (Galatia, Ephesus and the neighbouring region in Asia), but we have no information about missionary work by Peter in Anatolia. Since the writer seems to have some knowledge of the communities, this has been used as an argument against Petrine authorship, but not much can be built upon it since the knowledge is not circumstantial, and in any case we are almost wholly in the dark about Peter's movements. The order in which the names are listed has puzzled commentators, especially as Bithynia and Pontus had been departments of a single province since Pompey's time (64 B.C.) and lay adjacent to each other on the

Black Sea coast. If explanation is required, the most natural remains F. J. A. Hort's, viz. that, the letter being a circular one, the order reflects the courier's expected itinerary. There were excellent highways from Amastris and Sinope, the Black Sea ports of Pontus, southwards through Galatia to Cappadocia, and then westwards from the latter's capital, Caesarea, to Ephesus in Asia, whence several roads ran to Bithynia and its ports in the north-west; indeed Herod the Great made precisely such a journey, from Sinope via Paphlagonia and Cappadocia to Ephesus, in the spring of 14 B.C. with Marcus Agrippa, Augustus's son-in-law (Josephus, *Ant.* xvi. 21-23).

Having thus located his correspondents geographically, the writer explains the nature and purpose of the special calling in virtue of which they have become (ii. 9) 'God's own people'. His elaborate statement is built around a Trinitarian formula of archaic pattern: cf. the order Father-Spirit-Jesus Christ. Though correct, this interpretation has been queried on the ground that in the original **chosen** comes near the beginning of 1, being separated from 2 by eight words ('settled temporarily . . . Bithynia'). Many of the ancient commentators (e.g. Cyril Alex., Ps. Oecumenius, Theophylact), therefore, preferred to take the three prepositional clauses comprising 2 as qualifying **apostle,** while some moderns connect them with both **apostle** and **chosen.** But, in addition to the latter's entailing a needlessly complicated construction, both these exegeses have to face the objections that (a) **apostle** is even further from 2 than **chosen**; (b) they suggest that Peter's authority as an apostle needed bolstering, which is a hardly tenable proposition whether we regard the Apostle himself or a pseudonymous disciple as the author; and (c) they fail to notice that the writer is deliberately impressing on his readers the dignity of *their* vocation.

If these clauses are linked, as in the translation, with **chosen,** he first affirms that the Asian Christians' election has come

2 about as **a result of,** i.e. is grounded in, **God the Father's foreknowledge.** For him God's **foreknowledge** (*prognōsis*: cf. i. 20) is much more than knowing what will happen in the future; it includes, as it does in the language of the LXX (e.g. Num. xvi. 5; Jdt. ix. 6; Am. iii. 2) and in the thought of the Qumran

sect, His effective choice. He shares Paul's belief (Rom. viii.
29 f.: cf. ix. 11; Eph. i. 11 f.) that 'those whom he foreknew he
also predestined . . . And those whom he predestined he also
called'. (For God's predestination to disaster, see on ii. 8.) In so
doing God reveals Himself in His true character as **Father,** a
title which here stresses not only His role as Creator but also the
love by which He calls His own. Thus the Christians addressed
in the letter, and Christians in every age, owe their membership
of the redeemed community, not to any act of choice they
have made themselves, but wholly to God's gracious providence.

This predestinating choice, the writer continues, has been
made operative **by the sanctifying** (i.e. 'making holy') **action
of the Spirit.** Paul enunciates almost the same thought in
identical language (the formula was evidently a cliché) in 2
Thess. ii. 13. In the context the phrase cannot, as some propose, mean 'spiritual sanctity of character'; God's people, it is
implied, are 'holy', i.e. cleansed from sin and consecrated to His
service, and the agent of this is **the Spirit.** His **sanctifying
action,** we infer, became real for the Asian Christians in the
movement of faith which led them to Christ and, supremely, in
their baptism (cf. 1 Cor. vi. 11: 'you were washed, you were
sanctified'); these events are probably in mind here. But the
Spirit is continually present in the daily life of believers, developing their faith and deepening their sanctification (cf. i.
15 f.; iii. 15). Indeed, if their election originates in God's eternal
decree and is made effective by the Spirit's presence, its end
and object are **obedience and sprinkling with the blood of
Jesus Christ.**

The noun **obedience** (*hupakoē*) is an important one in
1 Peter (cf. i. 14; 22); it is also a favourite with Paul (11 times).
Its use has been taken as evidence of Pauline influence, or
simply of the common Christian vocabulary both writers employed. Many couple **Jesus Christ** with it, translating 'obedience to J.C. and sprinkling with His blood'. But (a) this entails
treating the genitive *Iēsou Christou* as simultaneously objective
(with **obedience**) and subjective (with **the blood**), which is
difficult; and (b) we have examples of *hupakoē* standing on its
own (i. 14: cf. also Rom. xvi. 19; 2 Cor. vii. 15). Taken absolutely, it implies that, viewed from the human side, a man's

calling as a Christian finds expression in **obedience.** This no doubt in part connotes conformity to the Christian moral ideal; but in view of i. 22 (cf. also ii. 8; iv. 17), and also of the Pauline usage (cf. esp. Rom. i. 5: 'obedience to the faith'), its chief emphasis is on the believer's submissive acceptance of the gospel, with its proclamation of Christ's saving act.

So much for the human side of the Christian's calling; but it is only the obverse of the divine side, which is brought out in **sprinkling with the blood of J.C.** By **the blood of J.C.** the writer means the Lord's sacrificial death, as a result of which the new covenant between God and His people has been ratified; being sprinkled with Christ's blood, stripped of metaphor, connotes accepting His saving death by faith and entering the new community inaugurated by it. R. Perdelwitz believed that a contrast is being drawn with the rites of Mithras, in which the votaries descended into a pit where the blood of a bull dripped on them from a grid. But this is absurdly far-fetched; it is plain that the imagery is derived from the vivid narrative of Ex. xxiv. 3-8 describing the sealing of the covenant between Yahweh and His people (cf. its use in Heb. ix. 19-21 also). There we have the same stress on obedience (7: 'and they said, All that the Lord has spoken we will do, and we will be obedient') followed by sprinkling; and just as there the Israelites were initiated with blood into the old covenant, so here those who have been chosen are introduced into the new by blood. In the Exodus story Moses poured the blood first on the altar, to signify the dedication of the people to Yahweh, and then on the Israelites to show that they now shared in His blessing and protective power. The new covenant is made possible by the forgiveness of sins accomplished by Christ's sacrificial death, which He Himself seems to have interpreted (Mk. xiv. 24: 'my blood of the covenant') in the light of Ex. xxiv. 8 in conjunction with Jer. xxxi. 31 ff. and Is. liii.

In this highly compressed statement we can sense the confidence and hope, grounded in their assurance of God's call, which in spite of their apparent weakness and very real perils must have inspired the little Christian communities in the 1st cent. The greeting which follows contains the formula **grace and peace** which Paul employs in all his letters. It is commonly held to be a Christian adaptation of the pagan epistolary 'Greeting' (*charis* being substituted for *chairein*), but in fact reproduces the pious wishes conventional in Jewish letters. By **grace** is meant the loving favour which God shows to sinners, and which He has made supremely manifest in Christ; while **peace** was the regular Hebrew salutation on meeting and parting as well as in letters (see on i. 1). In the OT 'peace' (Heb. *shālōm*) was much richer in content than its Greek (*eirēnē*) or Latin (*pax*) equivalents, including all blessings, material and spiritual, bestowed on man by God, more particularly in the eschatology of the prophets (e.g. Is. ix. 6 f.; lii. 7; Zech. ix. 10) the salvation which He will bring about in the Messianic age. So in the NT, especially in greetings like this (cf. Jud. 2; 2 Pet. i. 2), it does not simply denote inner tranquillity or repose in the psychological sense. Rather it is the objective condition of being right with God, with all the blessedness which flows from that. It is therefore a gift which God bestows in Christ, for He is 'the God of peace' (e.g. Rom. xv. 33; xvi. 20; 1 Cor. xiv. 33; 1 Thess. v. 23; Heb. xiii. 20), who has established peace 'through the blood of Christ's cross' (Col. i. 20). See further TWNT II, 398-416.

While Paul regularly omits the verb, the writer adds the distinctively Jewish prayer that these blessings may **be multiplied.** For OT examples, cf. Dan. iv. 1; vi. 25: for NT and other early Christian ones, cf. 2 Pet. i. 2 (influenced by this verse); Jud. 2; *1 Clem.* praescr.; *Ep. Polyc.* praescr.

2. THANKSGIVING AND ASSURANCE OF SALVATION

i. 3-12

(3) Blessed be the God and Father of our Lord Jesus Christ, who in his great mercy has caused us to be born again to a living hope through the resurrection of Jesus Christ from the dead, (4) to an inheritance which cannot be destroyed, polluted or made to decay, and which is preserved in heaven for you (5) who through God's power, as a result of your faith, are being kept safe for a salvation

which is all ready to be revealed in the last time. (6) In this you exult, even though now you have been distressed for a short while (since it has to be) by various trials, (7) so that the sterling quality of your faith may be found to be more precious than gold (which is perishable even though it is tested by fire) and so redound to your praise and glory and honour at the revelation of Jesus Christ. (8) Without having set eyes on him, you love him; though you do not at present see him, you believe in him and exult with joy inexpressible and full of glory, (9) receiving as the consummation of your faith the salvation of your souls. (10) It was this salvation that the prophets who prophesied about the grace which was to be yours searched for and inquired after, (11) inquiring what time or circumstances the Spirit of Christ within them was pointing to when foretelling the sufferings in store for Christ and the glories that would follow them; (12) and it was revealed to them that it was not for themselves but for you that they were ministering these things—things which have now been proclaimed to you through those who preached the good news to you in the Holy Spirit sent from heaven, and into which the angels desire to look.

After the address, the letter proper starts by offering praise and thanks to God for the wonderful inheritance upon which the recipients have entered through their baptism. The consciousness that the promised salvation is already within their grasp gives them ground for rejoicing in their troubles. Like Paul, the writer is following the pattern of ancient letters, Jewish and pagan, which commonly opened with thanksgiving for the welfare of the persons addressed and a prayer for its continuance. The present passage, in length and elaboration, recalls 2 Cor. i. 3-11; Eph. i. 3-14; 2 Thess. i. 3-12, but the baptismal note of i. 3-5 (cf. the reference to rebirth) is unmistakable. The same complex of ideas is found in a baptismal setting in Tit. iii. 5-7 (cf. also Rom. viii. 14-24; Col. iii. 1-4; 1 Jn. ii. 29-iii. 2), and both writers may well be reproducing, with a good deal of rephrasing, the lineaments of a common liturgical text or hymn (see Introduction, p. 22).

The opening formula, **Blessed be** . . . (*eulogētos*) followed by 3 the name of God, was a time-honoured Jewish one. It occurs again and again in scripture, often with a clause expatiating on the particular act of mercy which evokes gratitude: e.g. Gen. ix. 26; Ps. lxvi. 20 ('Blessed be God, because he has not rejected my prayer'); lxxii. 18 ('Blessed be the Lord, the God of Israel, who alone does wondrous things'); cvi. 48; 2 Macc. xv. 34; Lk. i. 68 ff. (the Benedictus). It was a constant element in Jewish prayers, most strikingly in the Eighteen Benedictions (*Shemoneh 'Esreh*), which were recited thrice daily in the synagogue and each of which ended with the refrain, 'Blessed be thou, O Lord'.

Primitive Christianity naturally took over the idiom with suitable adaptations. Thus the writer gives glory not just to God or the Lord, but to **the God and Father of our Lord Jesus Christ** (this rendering is preferable to 'God, the Father of . . .'). The expression (Rom. xv. 6; 2 Cor. i. 3; xi. 31; Eph. i. 3) early became stereotyped, so that there is no need to suspect dependence on Eph. i. 3; and indeed it crystallizes the essence of the gospel. Christian worship is not directed to Deity as such, but to the God Whom Christ has revealed and Whose Son in a unique sense He is. For **our Lord**, cf. the invocation *Marana tha* ('Our Lord, come') in 1 Cor. xvi. 22, which indicates that the phrase must have established itself among groups which still used Aramaic. 'Jesus is Lord' was probably the earliest Christian confession (cf. Acts viii. 16; xix. 5; Rom. x. 9; 1 Cor. xii. 3; 2 Cor. iv. 5; Phil. ii. 11). It is unlikely that the title was used in Jesus's lifetime; it came to be ascribed to Him as risen and ascended, being possibly suggested by His own appeal to Ps. cx. 1 (Mk. xii. 36 f.). *Kurios* ('Lord') was the customary LXX rendering of the divine name; the naturalness with which NT writers apply OT texts containing it to the exalted Jesus is thus proof of their recognition of His status. The addition of **our** underlies the special, personal bond between Christians and their Lord.

The reason for this hymnlike outburst is that God **in his great mercy has caused us to be born again.** The statement, though using a different image, recalls Paul's claim (Eph. ii. 4 f.) that 'God, who is rich in mercy . . . made us alive, together with Christ'. The salvation He bestows is not something human beings procure by their own efforts, any more than

children are responsible for their natural birth; it derives from
His loving initiative and compassion (Rom. iii. 24; Tit. iii. 5).
What He has done (note that the participle is aorist; the addressees have already been **born again**) is described here under the
figure of rebirth, the reference being clearly to baptism; and the
use of **us** instead of the 'your' we might expect (cf. 4) confirms
that the writer is freely citing a current baptismal thanksgiving.
The new life to which Christians are introduced by their sacramental rebirth is then defined as **a living hope.** Like the hints
in 1 that the Christian's true home is heaven, this word is
intended to give encouragement to the addressees, but it also
brings out a significant feature of Christianity itself. Although he
has a very real foretaste of it, the baptized believer does not yet
enjoy the full possession of what has been promised to him; he
lives in **hope** of sharing in the glory of God and the blessings of
eternal life. But his **hope** is not 'dead', i.e. insubstantial and
unfruitful, but **living,** i.e. certain and therefore effective even
now (cf. Rom. v. 5: 'hope does not disappoint us').

This transformation of our existence, made real in baptism,
is brought about **through the resurrection of Jesus Christ
from the dead.** Grammatically these words attach in the first
instance to **living hope,** suggesting that Christ's resurrection
is the ground and guarantee of our resurrection hope (i. 21: cf.
Rom. viii. 10 f.; 1 Cor. xv. 12-22; 1 Thess. iv. 14); but since the
verb **has caused us** governs the whole pericope, we must infer
that all the mysteries of salvation, the rebirth of which baptism
is the effective sign included, are attributed to His victory over
death. By that event the whole situation of mankind has been
altered in a revolutionary way (cf. Rev. xxi. 5: 'Behold, I make
all things new'); men and women who embrace the risen Lord
by faith are transported into a wholly new order, in which
they can 'walk in newness of life' (Rom. vi. 3-14). For the
link between baptism and Christ's resurrection, cf. iii. 21 (see
note).

The writer uses the same metaphor of supernatural begetting in i. 23; in ii. 2 he addresses his readers as 'newly born
children'. Elsewhere in the NT this imagery recurs relatively
rarely. According to Jn. iii. 3-8, he who would see the kingdom
of God must be 'born again' (or 'from above'), while in 1 Jn. ii.

29; iii. 9; iv. 7; v. 1; 4; 18 the Christian is 'born of God'. Jas.i.18 states that God 'brought us to birth by the word of truth', and Tit. iii. 5 speaks specifically of 'the bath of regeneration'. Behind all these passages, more or less overtly, lies the great sacrament in which the believer is made, in an ultimate sense, a new man. Paul, it should be observed, prefers different figures, likening the change to dying and rising again (Rom. vi. 4-9), or else to being created afresh (2 Cor. v. 17; Gal. vi. 15), although he describes the result, in terms very similar to those used here, as 'walking in newness of life' (Rom. vi. 4). But after the middle of the 2nd cent. (Justin, *1 Apol.* lxi. 3; lxvi. 1; *Dial.* cxxxviii. 2) baptism is regularly portrayed by the fathers as a 'regeneration'.

The question whence the early Church derived this imagery has been much debated. Some have argued that its background is Jewish, pointing to the rabbinical maxim (which probably applied in NT times) that the convert to Judaism who has received proselyte baptism 'is like a new-born child' (for the evidence, see SB II, 422 f.). But by itself this is hardly convincing. The maxim does not say that the proselyte is actually reborn (there was no such word in Hebrew or Aramaic), and compares him to a baby only in the sense that he is, as it were, starting life afresh with a new legal status. The pagan mystery cults offer much more promising material, for we know that the votaries of Isis (Apuleius, *Met.* xi. 21), Mithras (cf. A. Dietrich, *Mithrasliturgie*, 1923, 12), and Cybele (CIL VI, 510: date 376), to mention no others, were held to be 'reborn' (Lat. *renati*) as a result of their sacramental initiation. Early fathers like Hippolytus (*Ref.* v. 8. 10; 23) and Tertullian (*De bapt.* v. 1) confirm this testimony. Admittedly these authorities belong to a much later epoch; but the mysteries were centuries old by the NT period and there can be no serious doubt that their characteristic ideas were operative then. The concept of 'birth in the Spirit' or 'rebirth' is also found in the earlier Hermetic texts (*Corp. Herm.* xiii. 1; 3; 7) and Gnostic writings (cf. Hippolytus, *Ref.* v. 8. 21; 23; Clement Alex., *Exc. ex Theod.* lxxvi. 4; lxxx. 1).

Hellenistic influences can hardly be denied, but we should be clear about the way they worked and on our guard against concentrating exclusively on them. First, they concerned terminology rather than substance (see below); the early Christians found themselves inevitably slipping into forms of speech which were current in their milieu. Secondly, they were probably indirect, for by the 1st cent. Hellenistic Judaism had become receptive to pagan philosophical and religious idioms. Josephus, e.g., speaks (*Ant.* iv. 319) of God 'begetting' the Law, while Philo is familiar with the idea of a divine sowing and begetting, using the latter term of God's creation (*Leg. alleg.* iii. 219: cf. *De ebr.* 30); for men as God's sons, cf. *Spec. leg.* i. 317 f.; *De confus.* 63; 145-8. Such assimilations of language may have helped to form a bridge. But, thirdly, the ultimate source must have been the primitive tradition itself. On the one hand, there was the Lord's teaching (Mt. xviii. 3; Mk. x. 15; Lk. xviii. 17) that those who would enter the kingdom of heaven must become as little children, and the word underlying His reported statement (Jn. iii. 3 ff.) to Nicodemus. On the other hand, there was the conviction that the Messianic age, which in Jewish thought (e.g. Is. lxv. 17; lxvi. 22; Dt. xxxii. 12-Targum of Onkelos; Apoc. Bar. xxxii. 6; xliv. 12: cf. Mt. xix. 28) was expected to involve a new creation, had already been inaugurated in the person and work of Christ. Later Judaism actually envisaged God's elect in that age as His children (Mal. iii. 17 f.; Wis. ii. 18; v. 5; Ps. Sol. xvii. 30; Jub. i. 24 f.; 1 En. lxii. 11; Ass. Mos. x. 3: also Mt. v. 9). Within the framework of these ideas it was easy and natural for Christianity to take up a Hellenistic term like regeneration and reinterpret it in its own sense. That this differed radically from the Hellenistic one is clear from the fact that its perspective was eschatological. Further, Christian rebirth in baptism contained no element of ecstasy, as did the mystery cults, nor was it the privilege of an élite, as was that of Gnosticism; it was effected by God's word (i. 22), and was the response of His grace to the catechumen's pledge (iii. 21).

The thanksgiving now enlarges on the content of the bap-
4 tismal hope, describing it as **an inheritance.** The figure is inspired by the previous one of rebirth, since children have the status of heirs. The term used (*klēronomia*) had rich associations for readers of the OT, according to which the Jews as physical descendants of Abraham inherited the promises made to him. In its older strata this inheritance was equated with Canaan (e.g. Dt. xv. 4; xix. 10: 'the land which the Lord your God gives

you for an inheritance'), but after the exile it came to be understood less and less of material possessions. Sometimes it was
identified with God Himself (Ps. xvi. 5; lxxiii. 25 f.), sometimes
with eternal life (Dan. xii. 13: cf. Ps. Sol. xiv. 10; xv. 15; 1QS
xi. 7). In the NT Paul makes the point (Rom. viii. 17; Gal. iv. 7)
that as God's adopted sons Christians are His 'heirs', and their
inheritance is variously interpreted as eternal life (Mk. x. 17;
Tit. iii. 7), glory with Christ (Rom. viii. 17), immortality (1 Cor.
xv. 50), the kingdom of Christ (Eph. v. 5), salvation (Heb. i. 14),
the heavenly city (Rev. xxi. 2-7), etc. In 1 Peter it is elsewhere
defined as 'the grace of life' (iii. 7) and 'a blessing' (iii. 9).

An inheritance comes to the heir freely, not as the result of his
own efforts; and this shade of meaning is present here. Moreover, the inheritance which God has in store for His children is
one **which cannot be destroyed, polluted or made to decay.**
This clause translates three ornate, solemn-sounding adjectives,
each beginning with a-privative, which corroborate the liturgical character of the passage; all three are used in Wisdom (xii. 1
and xviii. 4; iv. 2; vi. 12) to describe heavenly realities. Their
purpose is not, as some think, to contrast the Christians'
promised land with the earthly territory occupied by Israel and
for centuries subjected to devastation, moral and religious impurity, and decay. Rather it is to emphasize that the blessedness
the baptized inherit is totally unlike ordinary human possessions; neither catastrophes, nor human sin, nor the transitoriness
to which the whole natural order is prey (*amarantos* applies
particularly to never-fading flowers: cf. v. 4) can affect it.

This inheritance is also (like the Christians' hope in 3)
absolutely certain; whatever harm overwhelms the readers,
they can rely upon it, for it is kept safe in God's custody. This is
the assurance conveyed by **which is preserved in heaven for
you.** In the Bible 'heaven' is God's dwelling place, the sphere
of salvation and blessedness; what is **preserved** there must be
immune from disaster. So Paul speaks (Col. i. 5) of 'the hope
laid up for you in heaven'. The Christian's citizenship is also
'in heaven' (Phil. iii. 20), and so is the true Jerusalem (Gal.
iv. 26; Heb. xii. 22; Rev. iii. 12). The notion of blessings kept
in reserve in heaven (Mt. xxv. 34), to be brought out at the decisive moment, was thoroughly Jewish, being familiar both to

apocalyptic (1 En. xlviii. 7; lviii. 5; Asc. Is. viii. 25 f.) and to the rabbis (SB III, 762; IV, 1146 f; 1156 f.).

This last point is developed in the next clause, in which the writer, breaking away (as **for you** shows) from his liturgical source to take note of the Asian Christians' cruel plight, assures
5 them that **through God's power, as a result of** their **faith they are being kept safe for a salvation which is all ready to be revealed in the last time.** If the inheritance is being vigilantly guarded, so are those who are predestined to receive it; there is a conscious correspondence between the two participles (*tetērēmenēn* and *phrouroumenous*) in the Greek, and the second is a military term evoking the picture of a fortress defended by a garrison. The time of the End, the writer is convinced (cf. 6; 20; iv. 5; 7; 17; v. 10), is very close, and it was notoriously to be preceded by severe trials and afflictions (cf. v. 8: also Mk. xiii; 2 Thess. ii. 3-12; 2 Tim. iii. 1; etc.). God's chosen stand in need of protection; they are guaranteed this **through** (the Greek reads 'in', but the preposition has lost its local force) **God's power,** which **as a result of** their **faith** makes victory certain. As is 7; 9; 21; v. 9 (cf. also Heb. xi), **faith** connotes steadfast trust based on confident belief (TWNT VI, 208).

Though grammatically dependent on **are being kept safe, salvation** denotes the object of **living hope** and the content of **inheritance,** and in 1 Peter (see also 9) is equivalent to the full enjoyment of eternal glory (iv. 13 f.; v. 1; 4). The term (*sōtēria*: lit. 'safety', 'preservation', 'deliverance') was not borrowed by Christianity from paganism, which had gods and even rulers hailed as 'saviours' and was quite familiar with 'salvation' from sin and death, demonic powers, etc. Its immediate source, like that of its cognates 'save' (*sōizein*) and 'saviour' (*sōtēr*), was the LXX and later Judaism, for which it meant, in the religious sense, deliverance or preservation bestowed by God, more specifically deliverance from His wrath at the final judgment. In the NT, while having a variety of nuances, it is linked with Christ's person and work, and the eschatological note is strongly to the fore (e.g. Rom. i. 16; v. 9; xiii. 11). Hence the writer's eager assurance that it is **all ready to be revealed in the last time.** This latter expression (cf. i. 20) brings out afresh

his certainty that the last act of history has begun and that
the yearnings of himself and his readers are about to be fulfilled.

In this, he continues, i.e. in the experience of rebirth and the 6
anticipation of salvation, **you exult with joy,** in spite of the
afflictions you have to put up with temporarily. This is the
likeliest interpretation of a verse which contains both syntactical and textual difficulties. The opening words *en hōi* ('in
which' or 'in whom') could refer either (a) right back to 'the
God and Father . . .' in 3, or (b), more immediately, to **in the
last time.** Objections to (a) are that (i) it separates the relative
clause too far from its antecedent; (ii) it seems natural that the
ground of the Asian Christians' rejoicing should be, not God
Himself, but the wonderful experience and promise just
delineated. The fatal flaw in (b) is that **the last time,** though
imminent, is still to come. It would be a plausible exegesis if we
could accept the alternative reading 'you will exult' (future
agalliasesthe instead of present *agalliasthe*: so Origen, *Exhort.
ad mart.* xxxix; also several ancient versions); but this has no
support in Greek MSS, and is a patent correction (the present
is *prima facie* more difficult) made by readers who felt that 'in
which' must be connected with the preceding **last time.**

The verb **exult** (*agalliasthai*) belongs to the vocabulary of the
LXX and NT, in both often having a strongly eschatological
flavour; it connotes the joy of the created order, and especially
of God's chosen people, when He is revealed as Judge and
Saviour (e.g. Ps. xcv. 11 f.; xcvi. 1; Is. xii. 6; Mt. v. 12; 1 Pet.
iv. 13; Jud. 24; Rev. xix. 7). So far as its form goes, it might be
an imperative here, but a confident statement of fact accords
better with the mood than a command. And his readers' jubilation, the writer implies, is not diminished but is actually
enhanced by the fact that they **have been distressed for a
short while (since it has to be) by various trials.** The
rendering **since it has to be** is intended to bring out the force of
ei deon (lit. 'if it is necessary'), which though conditional in
form states what he regards as in fact the case (for the usage,
see Blass-Debrunner, *A Greek Grammar of the N.T.* §372).
The common assumption that the clause is strictly hypothetical
is ruled out by the aorist participle **have been distressed**

(*lupēthentes*), which indicates in the clearest possible fashion the actuality of the **trials.**

This is the first explicit mention (there is a veiled allusion in **kept safe** above) of the Asian Christians' sufferings; for a discussion of their nature, see Introduction, pp. 5-11. As his language implies, the writer is not thinking of future possibilities, but of concrete ill-treatment which his readers have been, and still are, facing, and which he tries to set in the perspective of Christian faith. First, it will only last **for a short while** (*oligon*: of duration, as its association with **now** shows, rather than of degree), for the Lord's Coming is at hand: again the note of eschatological urgency, reminding one of 'a little while' in Jn. xvi. 16-19. Secondly, **it has to be,** having been ordered by God's providence. In the Bible He is viewed as Lord of history, and what 'must' happen (for *dei* in this deeply significant sense, cf., e.g., Dan. ii. 28; Mt. xvi. 21; Mk. ix. 11; Lk. iv. 43; Rev. i. 1) can be traced to His sovereign will. Thirdly, these **trials,** the result no doubt of the machinations of Satan (v. 8), have the

7 effect of putting **the sterling quality of** the readers' **faith** (here again the word has the sense of steadfast loyalty) to the test and showing up its intrinsic purity and strength. In the Greek **the sterling quality** represents a neuter adjective (*dokimion*, i.e. 'approved', 'assayed') used with the article as a noun; 'the genuineness of your love' in 2 Cor. viii. 8 is an exact parallel.

The translation given, **may be found to be more precious than . . . and so redound to . . .,** gives the best construction and sense. Most versions (AV; RV; RSV; etc.) take **more precious than gold** as standing in loose apposition to **sterling quality** and continue: 'may be found to result in' or the like. But (a) the writer's point is that the quality of his correspondents' faith is actually brought to light by their testing experience; and (b) it is awkward to have the adjective **more precious** hanging in the air on its own, and no less awkward to have **may be found** followed simply by **to your praise** etc. In spite of the interposition of **which is perishable . . . fire, more precious** is much more naturally understood as the predicate of the verb, and **to your praise** etc. as an additional predicate setting out the further consequences.

For the idea that fire, so far from destroying, purifies and brings out the best in something, cf. 1 Cor. iii. 13. The same comparison of the way God disciplines men with the refining of precious metals is frequent in the OT (e.g. Ps. lxvi. 10; Prov. xvii. 3; xxvii. 21; Zech. xiii. 9; Mal. iii. 3; Wis. iii. 6): see further TWNT VI, 929-48. The writer selects gold as being proverbially the most valuable of commodities (e.g. Philo, *De ebr.* 86: 'reason, more precious than all the gold in the world'), but points out that the Asian Christians' **faith** is even **more precious** since gold, however much **tested by fire,** is ultimately doomed to perish. Though they may feel sorry for themsslves now, this special quality will be abundantly recognized **at the revelation of Jesus Christ** (i. 13; iv. 13: cf. 1 Cor. i. 7; 2 Thess. i. 7), i.e. on the day of the Lord, when Jesus Christ will be manifested in power and glory as judge of living and dead. Then it will **redound to** their **praise and glory and honour.** These have of course nothing to do with human commendation or reward. The first denotes the **praise** which the righteous Judge will bestow (cf. the great eschatological picture of Mt. xxv. 31-46) and which alone counts (Rom. ii. 29; 1 Cor. iv. 3-5) on the last day. Both **glory** and **honour** are essentially divine attributes, denoting the radiance and majesty which belong to God's being and which He has imparted to Christ (i. 21). The supreme blessedness of faithful Christians is to be given a share in them when the consummation comes (for **glory,** cf. v. 4; Rom. viii. 17; Col. iii. 4: for **honour,** cf. ii. 6 f.; Rom. ii. 7).

There is a remarkable verbal resemblance between 6 f. and Jas. i. 2 f., so that mutual borrowing has been widely suspected. That there is some connection seems undeniable, but we should notice (a) that while 1 Peter speaks of **the sterling quality of your faith,** James uses the same words to mean 'the testing of your faith'; and (b) that while both are concerned with the significance of 'trials', 1 Peter sees them as purifying a man's faith, James as making him 'complete and perfect'. More to the point, perhaps, is the fact that the theme of 6 f., the paradox of exulting in persecutions, which runs through the whole letter (cf. esp. iv. 13), recurs not only in Jas. i. 2 f. but in a host of NT passages (e.g. Mt. v. 11 f.; Lk. vi. 22 f.; Acts v. 41; Rom. v. 3 f.; viii. 18; 2 Cor. iv. 17; vi. 10; vii. 4; viii. 2; 1 Thess. i. 6; Heb.

5

x. 32-36), frequently in an eschatological setting contrasting the short duration of the present afflictions with the eternal glory to come. It was therefore a Christian commonplace, a very primitive one too since it is woven so naturally into, e.g., Paul's argument, and must have been a routine topic of catechetical instruction which many writers reproduced independently. It may be based directly on the Lord's sayings (E. G. Selwyn), but we must reckon with the possibility that, as reported, these themselves may reflect its influence. There is in fact evidence (see W. Nauck, ZNTW xlvi. 68-80) that the heroic attitude of rejoicing at being made to suffer in God's cause was well established in later Judaism, being inspired by the cruel but glorious experiences of Maccabean times: cf. e.g. 2 Macc. vi. 28-30; 4 Macc. vii. 22; ix. 29; xi. 12; Jdt. viii. 25-27; Wis. iii. 4-6 (the ref. here is to the Maccabean struggles; the parallel to 6 f. is especially close). In assimilating it the Church reinterpreted it in the light of its conviction of the imminence of the End and of Christ, who Himself had suffered, as the ground of its jubilation.

The writer now develops this aspect of the paradox, dwelling on the personal relation of his correspondents to their glorified 8 Lord: **Without having set eyes** (*idontes*) **on him, you love him; though you do not at present see him, you believe in him.** Instead of the first clause several MSS and fathers read 'Without having known (*eidotes*) him'; but this is a corruption which has probably arisen (a) from the common confusion, due to identity of pronunciation in late Greek, of 'i' with 'ei'; and (b) from a sense of the clumsiness of juxtaposing so closely two different participles of the verb 'see'. As the sentence stands, it has been read as hinting at a contrast between the writer's own position as an eye-witness (cf. v. 1: also Lk. i. 2; Jn. i. 14; 1 Cor. ix. 1; xv. 5; 1 Jn. i. 1-3) and that of the Asian Christians, whose knowledge of Jesus comes through reports of others. If correct, this might be a pointer to Petrine authorship; but equally (if we are obliged to look for a subtle nuance) it might be a lifelike touch inserted by someone claiming to write in the Apostle's name.

While many in the original community had been directly acquainted with the Lord, the majority of Christians of the first and all of later generations were of course differently placed, and in the NT we notice attempts made to show that they were at no disadvantage. So Paul insists (2 Cor. v. 7) that 'we walk by faith, not sight'; and the Fourth Gospel extols (xx. 29) the blessedness of 'those who have not seen but have believed' (cf. Rom. viii. 24 f.; x. 14; Heb. xi. 27). Naturally these attempts become particularly obvious in the sub-apostolic age (see on 2 Pet. i. 1). The present verse also witnesses to the increasing emphasis in the apostolic (or sub-apostolic) Church on personal love for Jesus. In the synoptic gospels, as in the OT, the first command-ment is to love God (Mk. xii. 30). The idea that we should love Jesus is completely absent from them, but becomes prominent in John (viii. 42; xiv. 15; 21; 24; xxi. 15-17). Paul expects us to love God (Rom. viii. 28), but can pronounce a curse (1 Cor. xvi. 22: a primitive liturgical formula?) on anyone who 'has no love for the Lord'; he can also wish grace (Eph. vi. 24) to 'all who love our Lord J.C. with undying love'.

With love is linked faith: they **believe in him.** Here faith stands for unswerving trust, the confidence that, although they cannot **at present see him,** they will, for He is the Christ whose Coming is at hand. Though definitely Christocentric, the conception of faith is akin to that of Heb. xi. 1. As a result they **exult with joy inexpressible and full of glory.** For the present **exult** (*agalliasthe*) the Old Latin, Vulgate, Irenaeus, Augustine and some MSS substitute the future 'will exult' (*agalliasesthe*: Lat. *exultabitis*), but this is clearly a prosaic cor-rection springing from a failure to grasp the paradox. By any ordinary assessment their exultation should belong to the future, when the Lord will appear to reward His saints; but for the writer the **joy** of the End overflows into the present, irradiating the wretched plight of those to whom he writes (cf. 2 Cor. iv. 8-10; vi. 8-10). This is a mystery of faith, contradicting everyday experience, and so the **joy** is **inexpressible.** It is also **full of glory,** i.e. shot through with the radiance which belongs to God's very essence (see on i. 7) and which He imparts to His chosen. Cf. Paul's claim in Rom. viii. 30 that God 'has glorified' (the tense is aorist) those whom He has predestined, called and justified.

The following clause, **receiving as the consummation of** 9

your faith the salvation of your souls, brings out the underlying cause of the readers' paradoxical joy. The verb used
(*komizesthai*) literally means 'carry off for oneself', often with
reference to a prize or a punishment one has earned (cf. v. 4;
2 Cor. v. 10; Eph. vi. 8; Col. iii. 25; Heb. xi. 13). The present
participle is significant, highlighting the tension between present
and future; the hoped for **salvation** is already in process of
being realized. For **salvation,** see on i. 5; it is the **consummation** (*telos*: for this sense of the word, cf. 1 Tim. i. 5) of their
devoted trust and loyalty (cf. i. 5). For salvation as the outcome
of faith, cf. Acts xv. 11; xvi. 31; Eph. ii. 8; 2 Tim. iii. 15; also the
Roman baptismal liturgy: 'What does faith give you?—Eternal
life'. The expression **salvation of your souls** deserves note, not
least because it points to a radical difference between the writer's
anthropology and Paul's. On a hasty reading it sounds as if he
distinguished between soul and body, restricting salvation to
the former and thus implicitly accepting the characteristically
Greek dichotomy of the human make-up; and so his words have
often been understood. Actually 'soul' (*psuchē*) is a term of
which he is fond, using it in i. 22; ii. 11; 25; iii. 20; iv. 19, and
in all these passages it most naturally bears the distinctively
Semitic sense (e.g. Gen. ii. 7) of man as a living being, as a self
or person (so Mt. xvi. 25 f.; Heb. x. 39). Here **salvation of your
souls** (there is in fact no **your** in the Greek, but it is implied) is
virtually equivalent to 'your salvation', just as in, e.g., iv. 19
'your souls' simply means 'yourselves'. By contrast in Pauline
usage *psuchē* and its related adjective *psuchikos* tend to have a
disparaging flavour, connoting man's weak and sin-inclined
nature.

10   The fact that they already enjoy a foretaste of **this salvation,**
of which the inspired writers of the OT had only an obscure
presentiment and even the angels long to catch sight, is a
measure of the Asian Christians' privileged position. **It was**
precisely **this salvation that the prophets . . . searched for
and inquired after.** It has been argued (E. G. Selwyn) that
these are Christian prophets (for their presence and activity in
the apostolic age, cf. esp. Acts xi. 27 f.; xiii. 1; xxi. 10 f.; 1 Cor.
xiv. 3-5; 24-32; 1 Tim. i. 18; iv. 14) on the grounds that (a) this
'seeking' and 'inquiring' seem to imply a searching of the

scriptures which was not characteristic of the OT prophets; (b) the mention of **the Spirit of Christ** working in them is more readily understood of Christian prophets; and (c) the lack of the definite article before **prophets** in the original points to their being individuals familiar to the communities rather than the classical prophets.

Among the serious difficulties facing this exegesis is the fact that **the prophets** are manifestly contrasted with, and seem to belong to an earlier epoch than, the readers and those who evangelized them. No significance need be attached to (c), for the omission of the article is in keeping with the writer's style; while (a) attempts to wrest too precise a meaning out of the rhetorically vague **searched for and inquired after** (perhaps a reminiscence of 1 Macc. ix. 26, where there is nothing about scrutinizing texts). For the answer to (b), see on 11 below. We are therefore justified in taking **the prophets** in its obvious and natural sense, i.e. as referring to the OT prophets, indeed to the OT in general, since the Law and the Writings (cf. esp. the Psalms) were regarded by early Christians as prophetic. Like Christ Himself as portrayed by the evangelists (e.g. Lk. iv. 17-21; xxviv. 25-27) and the NT as a whole, our author takes it for granted that the men of the OT had their gaze focussed on the Messiah, i.e. Jesus the Christ, and His coming. This point of view does not, of course, evince a complete appreciation of Hebrew prophecy. In their historical setting the prophets were not so much concerned to peer into the future as to announce God's verdict on the world in which they lived. Inevitably, however, with their eschatological approach to history, their attention was directed to the Day of the Lord, when the condemnation of the wicked and the **salvation** of God's chosen would be finally accomplished, and they scanned the horizon for signs of its advent.

As things worked out, for all their earnest searching, the OT saints were doomed to disappointment themselves. **The grace** (*charis*: 'favour', 'free gift', i.e. the whole gracious action of God of which **salvation** is the consummation) which was their constant theme was not for them, but **was to be yours** (the original reads 'the grace to you': for the compressed construction, cf. 'the sufferings to Christ' below and 'his grace towards

me' in 1 Cor. xv. 10; also Polybius, *Hist.* i. 7. 12; 69. 7 for this
use of 'to'), i.e. was destined to be enjoyed by believers who
lived, like the writer and his correspondents, in the last times
and so had the blessedness, as Jesus had stated (Lk. x. 23 f.;
Mt. xiii. 16 f.), of seeing 'what many prophets and kings desired
to see . . . and did not see it'. They themselves, he suggests, had
been groping in the dark, assured by divine inspiration of the
deliverance to come, but with only a blurred vision of its details
11 and timing. So he represents them as **inquiring** (he repeats the
second of the verbs previously used) **what time or circumstances the Spirit of Christ within them was pointing to
when foretelling the sufferings in store for Christ and the
glories that would follow them.** (*N.B.* Literally rendered,
the Greek reads 'what or what manner of time . . .', and the
'what' could be a separate object, thus justifying the RSV
rendering 'what person or time . . .'.)

Four points deserve notice in this important passage. First,
the writer's picture of eager, not to say anguished, speculation
about when the Messianic age will dawn applies accurately
enough to the atmosphere of later Judaism. Illustrations are
provided by Dan. ix-end (where the prophet struggles to make
sense of the 70 years which, according to Jeremiah, must pass
before the desolations of Jerusalem end) and 2 Esd. iv. 33-v. 13,
as well as by the preoccupation of apocalyptic with 'the signs
of the End' (cf. the material in the synoptic gospels, 1 and
2 Thess., etc.). Similar anxieties exercised the Qumran sectaries:
e.g. they held that Habakkuk had had no inkling of the bearing of
his prophecies, but God had disclosed to the Teacher of Righteousness that they would be fulfilled now, in the time of eschatological salvation (1QpHab vii. 1-8). Secondly, by **the Spirit
of Christ** (*pneuma Christou*: B omits *Christou* through failure to
appreciate the doctrine of inspiration implied) the writer evidently means, not the Spirit which the NT describes as descending on, belonging to or sent by Jesus, but Christ Himself
conceived of as divine spirit (2 Cor. iii. 17 f.). Christ is for him
pre-existent (see also i. 20), and he presupposes a Spirit-
Christology of which traces appear elsewhere in the NT (e.g.
Rom. i. 4; 1 Tim. iii. 16; Heb. ix. 14).

Thirdly, consistently with this view, it was Christ in His pre-existent Spirit-being **(the Spirit of Christ within them)** who inspired, or rather spoke through, the OT prophets. The idea that He appeared to and inspired them was popular among the early fathers: e.g. Ignatius, *Magn.* viii. 2; *Barn.* v. 6; Hermas, *Sim.* ix. 12. 1 f.; Justin, *1 Apol.* xxxi-xxxiii; lxii. 3 f.; *Dial.* lvi f.; Irenaeus, *Haer.* iv. 20. 4. It is not evidenced in the NT generally, the usual theory being that the Holy Spirit was the inspiring agent (e.g. Acts i. 16; 2 Pet. i. 21), and this latter established itself in the orthodox teaching of the Church (cf. 'the Holy Spirit . . . who spoke by the prophets' so frequent in creeds). We should not expect, however, the precisions of the later theology of the Holy Spirit in the 1st cent. On the other hand, the pre-existence of Christ was very early accepted, and we find Paul, e.g., dilating on His activity in creation (Col. i. 15-17) and in the wilderness (1 Cor. x. 4).

Lastly, the writer teaches that the prophetic witness of the OT was to **the sufferings in store for Christ** (lit. 'the sufferings to Christ') **and the glories that would follow them.** The Lord's passion, understood as in Hebrews primarily as His death, is central in his thinking (cf. ii. 21; iii. 18; iv. 1; 13; v. 1), and he holds it up, with its triumphant sequel, as a model and inspiration to his readers. His language, deliberately made parallel to 'the grace to you' above, suggests that both were ordained by God. It is evident from passages like Lk. xxiv. 25-27; Acts ii. 23; xvii. 3; 1 Cor. xv. 3 f., as well as from a critical analysis of the synoptic passion-narratives, that the primitive Church strained every effort to demonstrate from scripture that, as a result of 'God's definite plan and foreknowledge', it had been 'necessary for Christ (i.e. the Messiah) to suffer and enter into His glory'. So by **the glories that . . .** the writer means His resurrection, ascension, enthronement on high (cf. the list in iii. 21 f.; also 'glory' in i. 21) and, not least, His final 'revelation' (i. 7; 13; iv. 13) as judge of living and dead (iv. 5). He is in agreement with Jn. xii. 41, according to which Isaiah in his vision (vi. 1 ff.) foresaw Christ's glorification. E. G. Selwyn's interpretation of 'the sufferings to Christ' as 'the sufferings of the Christward road', i.e. which Christians will have to bear in following Christ, and of **the glories . . .** as the vindication assured to them, while required by his equation of 'prophets' in

10 with Christian prophets, is linguistically difficult, not to say impossible. It also misses the point that what reconciled Christians of the apostolic age to the initially shocking enigma of a crucified Messiah was their persuasion, confirmed by the resurrection etc., that it was an essential element in God's saving plan as attested by prophecy.

The prophets must have longed themselves to witness the realization of the salvation they dimly descried (Lk. x. 24). 12 Nevertheless **it was revealed to them that it was not for themselves but for you that they were ministering these things,** i.e. the substance of their vision, in effect Christ's passion and glorification. The view that the OT is a forward-looking book is not far from the mark; its writers had a presentiment, based as they believed on God's authority, that the divine intervention they expected was not intended for their own day (e.g. Num. xxiv. 17; Dt. xviii. 15; Hab. ii. 1-3; 2 Esd. iv. 51 f.; cf. 1 En. i. 2: 'I understood what I saw; and it is not for this generation, but for a remote one in the future'). Thus they **were ministering** (the imperfect tense betokens the length and continuity of their witness) these hopeful tidings for a privileged age to come—in fact, for the Asian Christians and others like them. The choice of 'minister' is significant, for in the primitive Church the verb and its cognates were used to denote types of service in the community (e.g. Acts vi. 1 f.; Rom. xv. 25; 1 Cor. xvi. 15; 1 Tim. iii. 10; Heb. vi. 10). So the insinuation here is that prophecy, in fact the OT revelation as a whole, has a function of service in relation to the Christian revelation. Thus we have implied the conviction that OT and NT form a unity, the hope of Israel being once for all fulfilled in the gospel.

The writer now spells out his point in terms calculated to heighten his readers' confidence: the glorious denouement which the prophets had obscurely but accurately discerned has **now been proclaimed to you through those who preached the good news to you.** In other words, they should recognize in Christ's passion and subsequent glorification the accomplishment of the prophets' dream, the saving intervention of God which makes sense of their present sufferings. And this, he adds, is guaranteed to them by the fact that the missionaries who brought the gospel to them acted under the influence of **the**

Holy Spirit sent from heaven. While there is probably here
a reference to their recent conversion, there is also a hint that
the writer himself was not one of these missionaries. It was fully
accepted in the apostolic Church that the Spirit assisted and
confirmed the preaching of the gospel (e.g. Acts i. 8; v. 32; 1 Cor.
ii. 4; 1 Thess. i. 5; Heb. ii. 4). There is no allusion to the Spirit's
descent at Pentecost in **sent from heaven**; the phrase simply
underlines His divine origin.

Finally, to highlight his correspondents' privilege, the writer
asserts that the saving events they have had declared to them,
the blessed fruits of which they are beginning to experience,
were not only the object of the prophets' vain yearning; they are
things into which **the angels desire to look.** It is not clear
whether his point is that their position is equal or superior to
that of the angels. The verb used (*parakuptein*) suggests in Lk.
xxiv. 12; Jn. xx. 5 stooping down and peering into the Empty
Tomb, but not necessarily that the glance was momentary. It
often occurs in the LXX with the sense of looking out, or in,
through a window, while in 1 En. ix. 1 it describes the four archangels looking down from heaven at events on earth. In Jas. i. 25
it perhaps denotes continuous regard. According to many **desire**
(*epithumousin*) does not suggest unfulfilled longing, but rather
the angels' intense interest in the work of redemption; and the
idea that they had inside knowledge of this was not unfamiliar
to Jewish and Christian thinking (e.g. Dan. vii. 16; Zech. i. 9;
Philo, *De fug. et inv.* 203; Lk. xv. 7; Eph. iii. 10; Heb. i. 14). On
the other hand while the basic meaning of *parakuptein* is 'bend
down to look', in some of the passages cited it suggests a fleeting
glance ('peep', 'catch a glimpse of'), and **desire** is a fairly
strong verb consistent with a longing not yet fulfilled. So the
writer's argument may be that even the angels, for all their eagerness, are denied a vision of the final denouement; and this interpretation makes his climax more effective. The thought that
the knowledge of the heavenly powers is restricted has parallels
elsewhere: e.g. Mk. xiii. 32; Rom. xvi. 25; 1 Cor. ii. 8; 1 En. xvi.
3; 2 En. xxiv. 3; Ignatius, *Eph.* xix. 1.

The contention has been advanced that there are correspondences of thought and wording between 10-12 and Eph. iii. 2-6
which oblige us to infer literary dependence, but on close

inspection of the texts it is seen to be unfounded. Both contain
the idea of a divine plan concealed from earlier generations which
has now been made manifest, but in 10-12 it is 'the time and
circumstances of the End', in Eph. iii. 2-6 the admission of the
Gentiles. The idea is in any case integral to the Christian understanding of revelation, and its statement in 1 Peter, with its
stress on the unfulfilled longing of the OT saints, is much more
akin to such passages as Mt. xiii. 17; Lk. x. 24; Jn. viii. 56;
xii. 41; Heb. xi. 13-16 than to Eph. iii. 2-6, which speaks of 'the
sons of men in other generations'. Several of the alleged verbal
coincidences should also be discounted, for 'prophets', 'grace'
and 'Spirit' are all used in different senses in the two passages.

3. CALL TO HOLINESS AND BROTHERLY LOVE

i. 13-25

**(13) Gird up therefore the loins of your mind, be sober and
set your hope unreservedly on the grace which is being
conveyed to you at the revelation of Jesus Christ. (14) As
children of obedience, do not be conformed to the passions which in your ignorance formerly dominated you,
(15) but as he who has called you is holy be yourselves
holy too in all your conduct, (16) since it is written, 'You
are to be holy, for I am holy'. (17) And since you invoke as
Father One who judges impartially in the light of what
each has done, conduct yourselves with fear for the duration of your temporary stay. (18) You know that it was
not with perishable goods, like silver or gold, that you
were ransomed from the futile mode of conduct you inherited from your ancestors, (19) but with the precious
blood of Christ, as of a lamb without blemish or stain (20)
—predestined before the foundation of the world, but
made manifest at the end of the times for your sake, (21)
who through him have faith in God, who raised him from
the dead and gave him glory, so that your faith and hope
are fixed on God. (22) Now that through obedience to the
truth you have purified your souls for sincere love of your**

brothers, love one another strenuously from the heart, (23) having been born afresh, not from perishable seed but from imperishable, through God's living and abiding word. (24) For 'all flesh is like grass, and all its glory like the flower of grass. The grass has withered and its flower has fallen; (25) but the Lord's utterance abides for ever.' This 'utterance' is the good news which has been preached to you.

In his exordium the writer has sketched in glowing colours the splendid inheritance to which his readers have been admitted as baptized Christians. Their salvation is so close at hand and so assured that they can afford to rejoice in their afflictions. From i. 13 to iii. 12 he draws out, in various ways, the practical consequences of their regenerate status, stressing in particular that the hope they look forward to with such certainty demands a distinctive pattern of behaviour. Some of the principles underlying this are expounded in i. 13-ii. 10, which forms a close-knit whole and into the texture of which traditional paraenetic themes, probably baptismal in provenance, have been woven (see Introduction, pp. 22ff.). This first part concentrates on holiness, fear and brotherly affection, reminding the readers of the costliness of their redemption.

It opens with a summons to alert expectancy: **Gird up there-** 13 **fore** (i.e. in view of your having been born again, etc.: the position of the particle is emphatic in the Greek) the **loins of your mind, be sober.** The first picture is of a man gathering up his long main garment and tucking it into his belt so as to leave his limbs free for action. For the practice, cf. e.g. 1 Kgs. xviii. 46 (preparing to run); Jer. i. 17 (getting up to prophesy); Lk. xvii. 8 (for waiting at table). Here the girding up is metaphorical, signifying the Asian Christians' preparedness for the Lord's coming. Nevertheless, since the section seems built up of echoes of baptismal homilies and the Exodus was for the early Church the type of baptism, the imagery is probably inspired by the story (Ex. xii. 11) of the Israelites eating the Passover with their loins girded. By **mind** (*dianoia*) the writer does not primarily mean the intellect. The noun has a wider connotation, and he wants his readers to be alert and ready in their

whole spiritual and mental attitude For 'girding up the loins'
applied to mental alertness, cf. Job xxxviii. 3; xl. 7; Eph. vi. 14:
the Greeks could speak of 'the sinews of the soul' (Plato, *Resp.*
411b; Philodemus, *De ira*, col. xxxi. 35).

With **be sober** he introduces a second picture. Primarily
sobriety means abstention from alcohol (Tit. ii. 2), but in the
NT generally it denotes self-control and the clarity of mind
which goes with it (iv. 7; v. 8; 1 Thess. v. 6; 8; 2 Tim. iv. 5).
This is the sense it bears here; Christians need these qualities as
they enter upon the fulfilment of their hope. When it occurs in
the NT, the context usually has an eschatological colouring. In
much the same fashion the way of death is characterized in the
Hermetic literature (Gnostic: 1st–3rd cent.) as drunkenness,
aberration and darkness, the way of life as sobriety, lucid
apprehension and light (e.g. *Corp. Herm.* i. 27 f.).

We then come to the point of this preparedness: **set your hope
unreservedly on the grace which is being conveyed to
you at the revelation of Jesus Christ.** The imperative is
aorist (*elpisate*), the tense striking a more urgent, insistent note
than the present would: not just 'hope', but 'fix your hope
purposefully'. The adverb **unreservedly** (*teleiōs*: lit. 'perfectly', 'absolutely') reinforces it; their hope should not be
half-hearted or indecisive. In the Greek it is not clear whether
teleiōs goes with **be sober** or **set your hope,** and many editors
prefer the former. A decision is difficult, for the writer frequently places the adverb (contrary to the commoner practice)
after the word it qualifies; but the idea of degrees of hope is perhaps more natural in the context than degrees of mental clarity.
The main emphasis of the challenge, moreover, falls on **set your
hope** (in the Greek the other two verbs are participles); it is
here that any hesitation or faltering would be most detrimental.

The object on which their hopeful gaze is to be focussed is the
salvation which, as so eloquently stated in the preceding paragraph, is already assured for baptized Christians and is about to
be finally accomplished on the last day, when Christ will come
again in glory (for this meaning of **at the revelation of J.C.,**
see on i. 7). The writer defines this briefly as **grace** (*charis*), a
term which therefore does not stand for some influence, power
or favour emanating from God which can be viewed in separation

from Christ's person, but (as in i. 10) is virtually equivalent to 'the salvation which is all ready to be revealed at the last time' (i. 5). Much the same identification of 'grace' with God's redemptive action in the Parousia is found in the well-known prayer in the Didache (x. 6): 'May grace come, and the present world pass away'. We should notice that the participle rendered **which is being conveyed** (*pheromenēn*) is present. Although a present participle can have a future force (Lk. ii. 34; Jn. xvii. 20; etc.), its use here is in keeping with the writer's conviction that the object of their hope is already virtually within his readers' grasp.

He then rapidly summarizes some of the practical demands which their baptismal status imposes—obedience to God (14), holiness (15 f.), godly fear (17), mutual charity (22)—at the same time underlining the motives which should animate Christians. Thus he reminds them that they are **children of obedience. 14** Some detect an echo of Eph. ii. 1-3, where a contrast is similarly drawn between the transformed life of the baptized and their earlier sensuality, and Paul speaks of 'sons of disobedience' and 'children of wrath'. The contrast, however, was a baptismal commonplace, and the odd-sounding expression is a characteristic Semitic circumlocution (e.g. Dt. xiii. 13: 'sons of worthlessness'; 2 Sam. vii. 10: 'children of wickedness'; Mt. viii. 12: 'sons of the kingdom'; Mk. ii. 19: 'sons of the bride-chamber'). The genitive is not simply one of quality ('obedient children' would be inadequate), but fastens on an essential property or role of the persons described. The prominence of **obedience** in the letter has already been mentioned (see on i. 2). Here it has a special nuance: Christians should frame their lives according to their baptismal promises.

These have both negative and positive implications. First, there must be a complete break with the past: **do not be conformed to the passions which in your ignorance formerly dominated you.** In the Greek the verb (*suschēmatizomenoi*) is the present participle, and some render it so (RV: 'not fashioning yourselves'). It is clear, however, that the participle is in effect an imperative, as frequently in this and other NT letters (ii. 18; iii. 1; 7-9; iv. 8-10; Rom. xii. 9-19; Eph. iv. 2 f.; v. 19-21; Col. iii. 16; Heb. xiii. 5). This is not, as was once supposed, a

Hellenistic grammatical development, but reproduces, as is now recognized, the rabbinic Hebrew practice of using participles to express, not direct commands, but rules of conduct and even religious precepts. As all the NT passages concerned consist of codes or scraps of community admonition, they probably represent translations of Hebrew or Aramaic originals, extremely primitive material which the authors have taken over and remodelled to suit their purposes. The verb used here (derived from *schēma*, i.e. 'form' or 'shape', conveying the idea of copying a pattern) is found elsewhere in the Bible only in Rom. xii. 2 ('Do not be conformed to this world'), which many therefore think may have influenced our writer. But since Paul employs the Hellenistically more correct imperative, this seems excluded; both were independently appropriating a Christianized version of a Jewish apophthegm.

As baptized Christians, the writer reminds his readers, their new life must be the antithesis of the sensuality of their previous existence; in iv. 3 he will give a thumb-nail sketch of this. The Greek noun (*epithumia*: lit. 'desire') translated as **passions** could be morally neutral, but in 1 Peter (ii. 11; iv. 2 f.) and most NT passages has a strongly pejorative colouring; it denotes the baser appetites which, unless strictly controlled, keep a man from God (e.g. Mk. iv. 19; Gal. v. 16; 1 Jn. ii. 16 f.) and drive him to sin. The writer attributes their earlier absorption in these to their **ignorance.** His choice of word is significant, for to the Jew or Jewish-bred Christian **ignorance** conveyed much more than unawareness of the moral law. In the vocabulary of OT (e.g. Ps. lxxix. 6; Jer. x. 25; Wis. xiv. 22) and NT (e.g. Acts xvii. 30; Gal. iv. 8 f.; Eph. iv. 18; 1 Thess. iv. 5) alike it is a routine characterization of the Gentiles 'who know not God'. Its use here only makes sense if, as other texts suggest (i. 18; ii. 9 f; 25; iii. 6; iv. 3 f.), the majority at any rate of the addressees are converts from paganism. It is not far-fetched to detect a further allusion to the Exodus-baptism typology in this warning. Egypt was to Jews the symbol of the pagan world; and just as the Hebrews, after the Exodus, were bidden abandon their former Egyptian habits of life (Lev. xviii. 2-4: just before the call to holiness in xix), so must baptized Christians cut free from their pagan past.

So much for the negative side of the baptismal challenge. Its positive aspect comes out in the invitation, **as he who has** 15 **called you is holy be yourselves holy too.** God Himself, and not any system of abstract ideals, much less rules, is to be their standard, for as a result of His calling (the stock NT image for the divine initiative in saving men: ii. 9; 21; iii. 9; v. 10) He has made them His own. So Paul expects (1 Thess. ii. 12) his correspondents 'to lead a life worthy of God, who is calling you into his kingdom and glory'; while John (1 Jn. iii. 3) argues that 'everyone who thus hopes in him purifies himself as he is pure'. Like the Psalmist (e.g. xv; xxiv. 3-6) and Isaiah in his moment of vision, the writer knows that the holy God expects holiness of His worshippers (for the same demand, cf. Rom. vi. 19; Eph. i. 4). Holiness thus understood does not stand for mere ritual purity, as certain strata of the OT (e.g. Ex. xxviii. 2; xl. 9; Lev. xxii. 3 ff.; Ezr. ix. 2) might at first sight seem to indicate; rather it connotes the freedom from sin and absolute moral integrity which fellowship with God makes imperative.

As such it should extend to **all your conduct.** So Clement of Rome, after stating (xxx. 1), 'Since we are a holy portion, let all our actions accord with holiness' (a sentence probably deriving from the same catechetical source), spells out the all-embracing implications of Christian holiness with down-to-earth, practical examples—avoidance of slander, impure associations, drunkenness and violence, abominable pride, etc.; and in later sections our author will be giving some idea of what he has in mind. He will also be making the pastoral point, specially relevant in view of the hostile environment, that a Christian's manner of comporting himself (*anastrophē*: cf. esp. ii. 12; iii. 1; 16, where he employs the identical noun) is an effective form of witness to pagan neighbours.

In the meantime he rams home his insistence on holiness with the authority of the Bible: **it is written, 'You are to be holy,** 16 **for I am holy.'** These words run like a refrain through Leviticus (xi. 44; xix. 2; xx. 7; 26); indeed, because of its preoccupation with holiness the legal section Lev. xvii-xxvi has been designated the Holiness Code. The conception is of crucial importance in the whole Bible and looms large in this letter. Basically, 'holy' (Heb. *qādōsh*) means 'separate', 'marked off', the opposite of what is common or profane; the idea comes to birth in the awareness of the numinous, which is the primal religious experience. In the Near Eastern religions generally holiness was understood as a dangerous, quasi-naturalistic power or explosive force inhering in cult objects, places, activities or persons. In the OT, however, it is God Himself, in His awful majesty and perfection, who is in the authentic sense the Holy One. This shift of emphasis derives, of course, from the unique encounter of the Hebrew people with the living, personal God. But the result is that, according to OT thinking, holiness normally has an ethical element present in it; it expresses the nature and will of One who reveals Himself as righteous, merciful and loving. The Holiness Code itself provides an illustration, for mixed up with ritual injunctions it contains a mass of commands of profoundly moral import. It was the work of the prophets, with their enhanced insight into God's will, to enrich and deepen this ethical element, stressing, e.g., His desire for obedience (Jer. xi. 6 ff.), justice (Is. i. 10-17), and mercy (Hos. vi. 6); while the Psalmists (e.g. xv; li) exposed the hollowness of worship without moral purity and penitence.

In harmony with the original meaning of the term, but with this altogether different perspective, the OT takes it for granted that God imparts holiness to whatever objects or people He appropriates to Himself. Thus Jerusalem is holy (Is. xlviii. 2); so is mount Sion and the Temple on it (Is. lxiv. 10). Above all Israel is holy because God has chosen it as His people and dwells in its midst (e.g. Num. xv. 40; Dt. vii. 6; xxvi. 19; Lev. xvii-xxvi). This language passed to Qumran; the sectaries called themselves holy (e.g. 1QM iii. 5; xvi. 1), and the community as a whole was 'the congregation of saints' (1QM xii. 7; 1QSb i. 5). The NT writers, as we have seen and as 1 Peter preeminently shows (esp. ii. 4-10), took over and developed these conceptions. For them the Church is God's holy people, and its members are 'saints', i.e. holy in virtue of being called by God; and, like their Jewish predecessors, they are conscious of the moral challenge this holiness presents. The main differences are that God's chosen are no longer limited to a particular race but comprise all who accept Christ by faith, and that their under-

standing of God's will for them has been given a fresh dimension
by the recognition of Jesus as the Messiah.

The writer at once advances a further motive (this is the force
of **And**) for exalted standards of behaviour: the consideration of **17**
God's role as judge. As he puts it, **since** (*ei*: lit. 'if') **you invoke
as Father One who judges impartially in the light of what
each has done, conduct yourselves with fear for the rest
of your temporary stay.** The precise movement of his thought
is not absolutely certain. Some place the emphasis on **Father,**
translating 'if you invoke the impartial judge as *Father*', i.e.
have the privilege of approaching Him in that specially intimate
relationship, and in harmony with this interpret **fear** as the
reverence which children owe their parents. Coming so soon,
however, after the mention of the divine judgment, **fear** is much
more naturally understood of the awe ('godly fear') which it
should inspire. The accent is rather on the definition; the
writer's point is that, since the God whom his readers address
as Father is to be their judge, they would be wise to have a
healthy dread of His judgment and shape their behaviour
accordingly. In particular, they should not rely on their privileged status as His children (cf. John the Baptist's similar
rebuttal of the Jews' claim, 'We have Abraham as our father' in
Mt. iii. 9), for His decisions will be determined solely by the
quality of each man's actions.

As in the previous verse, the writer is working with basically
Jewish conceptions, although he and his correspondents read
them with Christian eyes. To **invoke** God **as Father** recalls
passages like Ps. lxxxix. 26; Jer. iii. 19; Mal. i. 6; but Christ has
taught His followers to apprehend God's fatherhood in a closer,
more personal way (there is conceivably a reminiscence of the
Lord's Prayer here). This consciousness of their sonship might
tempt them to expect favourable treatment. God's impartiality
as judge was a cliché of Judaism (e.g. Dt. x. 17; 2 Chron. xix. 7;
Ecclus. xxxv. 12; Jub. v. 16; Ps. Sol. ii. 18); the NT writers take
it for granted and hold it up as a model (e.g. Rom. ii. 11; Eph.
vi. 9; Col. iii. 25; Jas. ii. 1). The 'fear of the Lord' is also a
familiar OT idea, suggesting man's appropriate response to the
holiness of God; indeed 15-17 are probably inspired by Ps.
xxxiv. 9 ('Fear the Lord, you his holy ones'), which is never far

from the writer's thoughts (see on ii. 3). It is central in 1 Peter (ii. 17; 18; iii. 2; 15), and here, as elsewhere in the NT (e.g. Mt. x. 28; 1 Tim. v. 20; Heb. iv. 1; x. 31), it includes the awe which even those who are convinced of God's love must feel as they face His judgment. The imperative **conduct** . . . is aorist, conveying a sense of urgency ('set about . . .'). In **for the rest of your temporary stay** the writer takes up his earlier (i. 1: see note) picture of Christians as transitory dwellers on earth. The Greek word so translated (*paroikia*: cf. *paroikos* at ii. 11) denotes residence in a place without taking out or being granted citizen rights. With its cognates it is frequently used in the LXX (e.g. Lev. xxv. 23; 1 Chron. xxix. 15; Ps. xxxiii. 5; xxxviii. 13; cxviii. 19) both in the literal sense and with a metaphorical nuance analogous to the present one; in Acts xiii. 17 it is applied to the Israelites' sojourn in Egypt. See also TWNT V, 840-52.

From the thought of God as holy and as judge the writer passes to a third, even more compelling motive for moral earnestness—the awed thankfulness his readers must feel when they recall what their rescue from their previous pointless existence has cost. He appeals to elementary articles of Christian belief:

18 **You know that** . . . (in the Greek the verb is a participle; we might paraphrase—'knowing as you do'). Exactly the same participial expression (*eidotes hoti*) is found frequently in Paul's letters (e.g. Rom. v. 3; vi. 9; 1 Cor. xv. 58; 2 Cor. i. 7; iv. 14; v. 6), and in the majority of cases the pithy, even epigrammatic character of the sentence so introduced suggests that it embodies an excerpt from standardized teaching. One is therefore led to suspect that i. 18-21 has been filled out with catechetical, credal or liturgical material. This is borne out (a) by the traditional themes and baptismal echoes it contains; (b) by the balanced structure of 20 and the awkward join between it and 21; and (c) by the fact that much of the detail is extraneous to the argument, which simply required a reference to Christ's saving death.

The writer continues: **You know that it was not with perishable goods, like silver or gold, that you were ransomed.** His words contain a reminiscence of Is. lii. 3 ('you were sold for nothing, and not with silver shall you be ransomed'). The same verb *lutrousthai* is used in Tit. ii. 14 to describe the effect of Christ's passion; related words involving the same metaphor occur elsewhere in the NT—*antilutron* ('ransom') in 1 Tim. ii. 6; *lutrōsis* ('redemption') in Heb. ix. 12; and, most frequent of all, *apolutrōsis* ('redemption') in Rom. iii. 24; 1 Cor. i. 30; Eph. i. 7; Col. i. 14; Heb. ix. 15. According to the synoptic tradition (Mk. x. 45: cf. Mt. xx. 28), the imagery goes back to Jesus Himself, who declared that the purpose of His mission was to 'give His life as a ransom (*lutron*) for many'. The writer is thus working with long established Christian ideas, but it is the parallel with Tit. ii. 12-14 that is most illuminating. There too, as in 1 Pet. i. 13-15; 18; 22; ii. 9, Christ's ransom is linked with the Christian's eschatological hope and made the motive of moral purification and the formation of a new people of God. The pattern of thought is identical; and the baptismal hint in Tit. ii. 14 ('purify'), as well as the pointed reference to baptism in Tit. iii. 5, confirms that both writers are handling stock baptismal material, liturgical or homiletic.

What follows is, as we shall see, in harmony with this. In the Hellenistic world of the 1st cent. *lutron*, or 'ransom', was a technical term for the money paid over to buy a prisoner-of-war or slave his freedom; in the latter's case it could be temporarily deposited in the shrine of a god, whose property he thus by a legal fiction became. Gentile readers may conceivably have understood the phrase in this sense (F. W. Beare), but we must posit an OT background for the thought of the writer himself and his source. Both the noun and the related verb were extensively used in the LXX, their original meanings including the redemption of a property held in mortgage (e.g. Lev. xxv. 25-28) and the payment of a sum to God either for the first-born (e.g. Num. xviii. 15) or as a ransom by a man whose life was forfeit (e.g. Ex. xxi. 30; xxx. 12). Later the verb came to be used metaphorically of deliverance from enemies (e.g. Ps. cvi. 2), from sin (e.g. Ps. cxxix. 8), from death (e.g. Ps. xxxiii. 23; Hos. xiii. 14), or from exile (e.g. Is. xli. 14; xliii. 1; 14), but particularly of God's mighty deliverance of Israel from Egypt (e.g. Ex. vi. 6; xv. 13; Dt. vii. 8)—the event which Christians regarded as foreshadowing baptism and which probably prompted the choice of word here. At this stage the image of a price paid has completely faded, but here (cf. **silver or gold**), as in Mk. x. 45

and Tit. ii. 14, it retains its vigour. For later theology this was
to raise far-reaching questions, such as why a 'ransom' should
be necessary; but these were as remote from our writer's mind
as from that of Mark, with whose teaching on Christ's work
his own has close affinity. Yet without actually stating it he
clearly implies that God is the recipient of the ransom, accepting Christ's obedient surrender of His life as an offering which
once for all abolishes the disobedience of sinful mankind.

He is more explicit about the Egypt-like bondage from which
his readers have been **ransomed.** It is not the power of Satan
(the theory of a price paid to him was to fascinate later theologians, but is not found in the NT), but rather **the futile mode
of conduct** (again *anastrophē*, consciously echoing the same
noun in 15 and the related verb in 17) **you inherited from your
ancestors.** The adjective **futile** (*mataios:* 'vain', 'powerless',
almost 'non-existent') gives a further unmistakable hint that
they had been pagans. It is scornfully applied in the LXX to the
gods of the heathen, in contrast to the one living and true God
(e.g. Lev. xvii. 7; 2 Chron. xi. 15; Jer. viii. 19; x. 15), or else to
those who have never known Him (e.g. Wis. xiii. 1) or have
apostatized from Him (e.g. Jer. ii. 5). NT usage is in line with
this: cf. Acts xiv. 15; Rom. i. 21; viii. 20; 1 Cor. iii. 20; Eph. iv.
17 (the Gentiles walk 'in the futility [*mataiotēs*] of their minds').
An early Christian would never have described the ancestral
upbringing of converts from Judaism in such terms (see further
TWNT IV, 525-30; SB III, 763).

The price of their ransom or rescue, the writer has explained,
does not consist, as was normal in such transactions, of **silver or
gold.** These are **perishable goods,** i.e. material and therefore
transitory, incapable of effecting a lasting spiritual deliverance.
For the high value he sets on incorruptibility and his consequent
disparagement of its opposite, cf. i. 4; 7; 23 f.; iii. 4. In fact it is
19 **the precious blood of Christ** (where the adjective sharply
underscores the contrast with the 'perishableness' of money).
At this point the imagery he employs, or finds in his source,
changes and becomes frankly sacrificial; Christ is likened to **a
lamb without blemish or stain,** i.e. a sacrificial victim. The
first adjective (*amōmos:* cf. Ex. xxix. 1; Lev. xxii. 17-25; Ezek.
xliii. 22 f.) recalls the Jewish requirement that such an offering

74

must be faultless; the second (*aspilos*) does not occur in the LXX, but is added so as to emphasize that in Christ's case the fault-lessness which makes the victim acceptable must be understood in terms of sinlessness and holy consecration (Heb. ix. 14). Eph. v. 27 has *amōmos* and *spilos* (the root noun of *aspilos*) in a single sentence, but both wording and subject-matter are so different that to speak of the present verse as a reminiscence is fanciful. For **blood** connoting blood shed or life laid down in sacrificial death, see on i. 2.

Different conceptions intermingle in the key-word **lamb**. In Is. liii. 7 the Suffering Servant is depicted as 'a lamb led to the slaughter'; in view of his interest in this passage as a clue to Christ's passion (ii. 22-24), the writer must have had it in mind here. But it is also likely that he is thinking of Christ as the pass-over victim (Ex. xii; etc.), which though not necessarily a lamb was usually one. Its original purpose, of course, was not to remove sin, but apotropaic, as a sign to the Destroyer (Ex. xii. 13); but in later Jewish thought and practice this was submerged in its general role in the deliverance from Egypt, and deliverance from captivity, not removal of sin, is the primary theme here. Our writer was not alone in using this image, for when Paul wrote 1 Cor. v. 7 he took it for granted (cf. Jn. xix. 36, with its citation of Ex. xii. 46) that Christ was the true paschal offering. The fact that, in contrast to Jn. i. 29; 36; 1 Cor. v. 7; Rev. *passim*, he does not speak of Christ as actually the lamb, but only com-pares Him to it, may be a pointer to the early date of his material. In any case the implied reference to the Exodus is additional evidence of its pervasively baptismal character.

The next verse at any rate—**predestined before the founda-** 20 **tion of the world, but made manifest at the end of the times**—bears all the marks (balanced antithesis, solemn tone, etc.) of being an excerpt from either a credal text or, more plausibly, a Christological hymn: for a liturgical scrap of kindred pattern and ideas, cf. 2 Tim. i. 9 f. It is tempting, in view of the similar structure and theme, to connect this with the hymn of which fragments seem to be reproduced at iii. 18-22 (see note). In citing it the writer desires to impress on his readers that the redemption in which they now share through baptism is part of a plan which God has been preparing from all

75

eternity with them in view. A more literal rendering of **pre-destined** (*proegnōsmenou*) would be 'foreknown', but we have already noticed (see on i. 2) that for him God's foreknowledge includes His creative will and determination. This whole conception of history, especially salvation-history, as the working out of God's age-old purpose had been familiar to later Judaism (e.g. Is. xxxvii. 26; 2 Esd. vi. 1-6; 1 En. xlviii. 6; lxii. 7), and was an accepted article of the apostolic Church (Rom. xvi. 25 f.; 1 Cor. ii. 6-10; Eph. iii. 3-6; 9-11; Col. i. 26; Tit. i. 2 f.). In the light of God's loving predestination the Christian can begin to make sense of events which might otherwise seem inexplicable; and the synoptic tradition (Mk. viii. 31 and parr.) suggests that in interpreting Christ's passion in this way we have the authority of the Lord Himself.

Two other points call for remark. First, a corollary of this view of history is that crucial importance attaches to **the end of the times,** i.e. its climax, for the divine purpose, hitherto veiled, is then fully and decisively disclosed. Like Acts ii. 16 ff.; 1 Cor. x. 11; Heb. i. 2; ix. 26; etc., the present passage witnesses to the conviction of primitive Christianity that with the incarnation, passion and resurrection of Christ the last age has dawned. Secondly, the conclusion can hardly be avoided that Christ's pre-existence, in some sense at any rate, is assumed. This is implied, not by **predestined,** since God's foreknowledge extends to every being destined at any time to come into existence, but by **made manifest** (for the verb, cf. 1 Tim. iii. 16; Heb. ix. 26), which hints that He existed with God, outside the process of history, prior to the incarnation. For this Christology, cf. i. 11 with note.

Moreover, Christ has been manifested **for your sake.** The writer adds this, breaking away from his citation, in order to inspire his readers with the confidence they need. The goal of the gospel is intensely personal; God's plan is focussed on the Church, or rather on the individual members of it, just as according to Paul (1 Cor. x. 11) all the experiences of Israel were really designed as lessons 'for us, upon whom the end of the ages has come'. Its fulfilment is realized when men and women, by faith, embrace the blessedness which He has been preparing
21 from all eternity. This is brought out in what follows: **who**

through him (i.e. Christ) **have faith in God.** Their **faith** has been mediated through Christ (a) because He has revealed the Father (Mt. xi. 27; Jn. i. 18; xvii. 6), but (b), more importantly, because as God's instrument for reconciling the world to Himself (2 Cor. v. 19) Christ by His redemptive work has once for all opened up man's approach to God (iii. 18; Rom. v. 1). Peter's words in Acts iii. 16 ('the faith which is through Jesus') provide a striking parallel.

In the MSS the Greek word translated **have faith** varies between the adjective *pistous* and the present participle *pisteuontas*. Besides having somewhat superior MS support, the former is to be preferred as the more difficult reading; the adjective *pistos* with two prepositional phrases is definitely awkward, and the participle is a correction which would naturally occur to scribes. There is a slight difference of sense: as well as 'believing' (the predominant idea here), the adjective can mean 'loyal', 'faithful', while the participle simply means 'who believe'.

The writer characterizes the God in whom his readers believe as Him **who raised him** (i.e. Jesus) **from the dead and gave him glory.** Again the clauses have the ring of a stereotyped formula, and we have evidence (e.g. Rom. viii. 11; 2 Cor. iv. 14; Gal. i. 1; Eph. i. 20; Col. ii. 12; 1 Thess. i. 10) that the former at any rate very early became one. But it is not attached here as mere ornamental padding. The fact that God has raised Christ from the dead, indeed has exalted and glorified Him (cf. esp. Phil. ii. 9-11, where Paul dwells on the name above every other name, i.e. 'Lord', which God has bestowed on Him), eloquently confirms that He is the living God Who can impart life to what seems stricken down and dead. As such it awakens **faith,** in the sense of assurance and trust, and **hope** too, since the believing reader can be confident that the resurrection life and glory which God has given to Christ belong to him too. So the writer can add, enlarging on his mention of **faith** only, that as a result **your faith and hope are fixed on God.**

The rendering adopted assumes that *hōste* **(so that)** expresses, as it commonly does, consequence. But it can also express intention (e.g. Mt. xxvii. 1; Lk. xx. 20), and the alternative translation 'so that . . . may be fixed on God' (cf. AV; RV) is possible. A decision is difficult, the more so as the Semitic mind did not distinguish sharply between purpose and result; but an affirmation of what is actually the case agrees better both with **have faith** above and with the writer's confident tone. Some (e.g. J. Moffatt; R. Bultmann in TWNT VI, 208 and 211) construe **hope** as a predicate, translating 'so that your faith is (or 'may be') also hope in God'. This is syntactically possible, gains superficial support from the absence of the definite article before **hope,** and avoids tautology with 21a. But against this (a) there is no real tautology, for 'faith and hope in God' has a different nuance than 'faith in God who raised . . .' in 21a; (b) **faith** and **hope** in 1 Peter both connote confidence and are virtually two aspects of one thing (cf. 'who hoped in God' in iii. 5); (c) after **faith in God** in 21a it is natural to take **in God** with **faith** here; (d) the weight of the clause falls on its climax **in God,** which is thus in effect the predicate. Pap. 72, it should be noted, inserts an article before **hope**, showing that some 3rd cent. readers treated **faith** and **hope** as coordinate.

In the preceding four verses, packed as they are with evocative liturgical tags, the writer might seem to have been diverted from his task of expounding the Christian, as opposed to the pagan, way of life (i. 15; 17; 18). Now he returns to it, adding brotherly charity to holiness and godly fear as a mark of the baptized Christian. This is laid upon the Asian Christians, he explains,

22 because **through obedience to the truth** they **have purified** their **souls,** an experience which issues, or should issue, in **sincere love of** their **brothers.** Here **obedience** and **purified** (perfect participle of *hagnizein*, i.e. 'sanctify' or 'make holy') carry us back to i. 2; 14 and i. 2; 15 respectively, just as **having been born afresh** in 23 recalls i. 3. This strongly suggests that i. 22-25 forms a literary unity with i. 1 f. and i. 3-21 and is not, as the liturgical hypothesis proposes, a separate address on its own. The participial clause (for **your souls** as in effect equivalent to 'yourselves', see on i. 9) is 'an archaic description of baptism' (C. Spicq), underlining the cleansing from sin and the restoration of a right relationship with God which it brings about (cf. esp. 1 Cor. vi. 11; Eph. v. 26; Tit. iii. 3-7; Heb. x. 22). In the LXX *hagnizein* denotes a purely ceremonial cleansing by means of washings or sacrifices, and as the sacramental reference

shows the cultic element is not lacking here; but in the NT it is the moral and spiritual transformation which is stressed (e.g. Jas. iv. 8; 1 Jn. iii. 3). So too **obedience to the truth** points to baptism. As often in the NT (e.g. Gal. v. 7; Eph. i. 13; 2 Thess. ii. 12; 1 Tim. iv. 3), **the truth** means, not truth in general, but God's revelation of Himself in the gospel. It is therefore His word, the writer implies, when the believer obediently responds to it, which is the effective agent in the sacrament. The Qumran sect, it is interesting to observe, held a similar doctrine of the cleansing power of God's truth (1QS iii. 4-8; iv. 20 f.).

The words **for sincere love of your brothers** are closely attached to what precedes; they define what is involved in the baptismal engagement. The writer's point is that, through submitting to the gospel and being baptized, his correspondents have entered a community in which **love** is the rule of conduct (for the 'new commandment', cf. Jn. xiii. 34 f.; xv. 12; 17: also 1 Jn. iii. 11-18). The noun he uses (*philadelphia*: cf. Rom. xii. 10; 1 Thess. iv. 9; Heb. xiii. 1; 2 Pet. i. 7), literally translated, is 'brotherly love'; it does not connote love of mankind in general, but love between members of the Christian brotherhood (for the collective noun *adelphotēs*, cf. ii. 17). In this relationship love becomes a caricature of itself if any tincture of hypocrisy is present; hence it should be **sincere** (*anupokritos*: always used in the NT of or in relation to love—Rom. xii. 9; 2 Cor. vi. 6; 1 Tim. i. 5; Jas. iii. 17). The expression brings out the warm sense of being brothers which, as the NT shows (e.g. Acts xiv. 2), bound Christians together in the apostolic age and excited the admiration or incredulity of pagans (cf. Lucian's sneer in *De mor. Pereg.* xiii: 'Their first lawgiver persuaded them that they are all brothers of one another'). Stemming from our Lord's description of His disciples, this attitude was a development of Jewish practice, for in the OT and later Judaism those who belonged to the Jewish people and religion were spoken of as brothers; the same idiom prevailed in the Qumran sect (1QM xiii. 1; xv. 4; 7; etc.). What is distinctive about the new Christian family is that admission to it no longer depends on physical or racial kinship but on acceptance of God's will and total commitment to Christ (Mk. iii. 31-35; x. 30).

So the writer, using what had become a catechetical cliché,

bids his correspondents **love one another strenuously from the heart** (again the imperative, as at i. 13; 17, is the ingressive aorist: 'set about . . .'). Is his evident anxiety on this score (ii. 17; iii. 8; iv. 8) perhaps prompted not only by the need for unity in the face of danger, but also by the knowledge that frictions are manifesting themselves in the little communities (K. H. Schelkle)? The Byzantine text, with a formidable array of supporting MSS, gives 'with a pure (*katharas*) heart' (so AV), but the adjective is redundant after the preceding clause and must be an interpolation suggested by 1 Tim. i. 5. The adverb (*ektenōs*: cf. Jdt. iv. 12; Joel i. 14; Jon. iii. 8; Lk. xxii. 44; Acts xii. 5) implies energetic activity rather than fervour (AV; RV). But how is this strenuous fraternal love possible in the world in which men have to live? The writer meets this unspoken objection by recalling

23 that their existence now has a new dimension: they have **been born afresh, not from perishable seed but from imperishable, through God's living and abiding word.** This takes up the image of baptismal rebirth already used in i. 3 (where see note) and contrasts natural generation, which is brought about by human and therefore **perishable seed,** with the new birth in Christ which men undergo in baptism, and which results from the impact of divine and therefore **imperishable** seed, here identified with **God's living and abiding word.** God's word is always **living** in the sense of life-giving or creative (Gen. i. 3 ff.; Ps. xxxiii. 9; Phil. ii. 16; Heb. iv. 12); it is **abiding** since it 'abides forever' (Is. xl. 6-8 below). Many editors, with the Vulgate, prefer to construe 'through the word of the living, abiding God', quoting Dan. vi. 26 where precisely the same epithets qualify 'God'. But (a) the position of **God,** after **living** and before **abiding,** is against this; (b) stress on the creative, lasting quality of the word is appropriate to the argument; (c) the appeal to Is. xl. 6-8 in the next verse confirms the usual exegesis.

The same contrast between human and divine generation, and the different orders of existence which result, is drawn in Jn. i. 12 f. Jas. i. 18, too, speaks of God as 'bringing us forth by the word of truth'. There, as here, 'the word' is not the divine Logos, as in Jn. i. 1, but (cf. 1 Cor. xiv. 36; 2 Cor. ii. 17; Col. i. 25 f.; 1 Thess. i. 6; 2 Thess. iii. 1) the gospel message. When 1 Jn. iii. 9 f. describes a man who has been regenerated by God as unable to sin 'because His seed abides in him', it is very likely that 'seed' stands for the word of God, i.e. the gospel. Other points of contact between I Peter, James and I John (e.g. ii. I f.: Jas. i. 21; i. 3-5: I Jn. ii. 29-iii. 2; i. 13-16: I Jn. iii. 3; i. 18-20: I Jn. iii. 5) have been noticed (M. E. Boismard), and it is tempting to infer that, notwithstanding their very different settings, all three texts bear the imprint, more or less blurred, of a common baptismal schema (see on i. 3). Here the writer's thought is that, as a result of accepting the gospel and being baptized, the Asian Christians have been supernaturally born into a new order of being of which the characteristic note is divine charity.

In support of what he has just said about God's word he appeals to Is. xl. 6-8, which compares **all flesh,** i.e. all human **24** existence, with **grass,** which **has withered,** and **the flower of grass,** which **has fallen** (the LXX aorists vividly express the rapid blooming and fading of herbage), and sets in contrast **the 25 Lord's utterance** (as the Greek gives *rēma*, not *logos* as in 23b, this translation has been adopted rather than 'word'), **which abides for ever.** Jas. i. 10 f. also appeals indirectly to this text, but to illustrate the ephemeralness of riches. The prophet's object had been to console the despondent Jews exiled in Babylon with the assurance that, while their oppressors' might was already on the wane, God's promise to restore them to their homeland could be trusted implicitly. Our writer's interest is focussed, not of course on the historical situation recalled by the passage, but on the way it highlights the enduring reliability of **the Lord's utterance.** By altering the LXX 'God's utterance' to **the Lord's utterance** he gives it a specifically Christian slant, and is able to equate **utterance** with **the good news which has been preached to you,** i.e. the gospel.

4. THE ELECT PEOPLE OF GOD
ii. 1-10

(1) Having therefore put off all wickedness, all deceit, pretences and jealousies, and all recriminations, (2) new-born babes as you are, crave for the milk of the word that

is free from deceit so that by it you may grow up to salvation, (3) seeing 'you have tasted that the Lord is good': (4) to whom coming, the living stone, rejected indeed by men but chosen and honoured in God's sight, (5) you are yourselves, like living stones, built up as a spiritual house, so as to form a holy priesthood to offer spiritual sacrifices acceptable to God through Jesus Christ. (6) For it is set down in scripture, 'See, I appoint in Sion a choice and honoured corner-stone, and he who has faith in it will not be put to shame'. (7) The honour, therefore, belongs to you who have faith; but for those who lack faith, 'the stone which the builders rejected, this has been made the head of the corner', (8) indeed 'a stone to trip men up, a rock to stumble over'; for they stumble when they disobey the word—the lot for which they were appointed. (9) You, however, are a chosen race, a royal house, a priesthood, a holy nation, a people for God's possession, that you may proclaim the mighty deeds of him who has called you out of darkness into his marvellous light, (10) you who were once no people but are now God's people, who had not received mercy but now have received mercy.

This involved section flows logically and naturally out of i. 13-25, gathering up the exhortation set down there and eloquently unfolding some of the implications of being a baptized Christian. The imagery changes with disconcerting suddenness: first the Christians addressed are children, then blocks of stone in a temple, then a body of priests, finally a specially chosen nation, but throughout the connecting theme is their election. The bulk consists of a recondite exposition (*midrāsh*), typically rabbinic in method but Christian in application, first of Ps. xxxiv. 8, and then of two centos of OT texts grouped around the ideas of Christ as the Stone and of the new Israel. The writer has already exhibited his flair for such exegesis in i. 24 f., and Paul's letters and Hebrews are full of it. Though the detail of his argumentation seems obscure, his broad message is clear enough: as Christians his readers, in contrast to their unbelieving persecutors, have a surpassingly glorious vocation, and hence (this is the underlying motive) should not be shattered by their present afflictions. With its links with what precedes and its direct allusion to the Asian Christians in 10, the passage does not read in the least like a hymn (H. Windisch), still less like a song contributed by a 'pneumatic' bystander at a service of baptism. In spite of its exalted tone, its style smacks more of learned exegesis than of poetry; and in its subject-matter it carries to its climax the summons to holiness in i. 13 ff. As before, we can detect several sacramental reminiscences, but nothing to indicate that as a whole it is an excerpt from a liturgy.

The particle **therefore** (*oun*) is resumptive, referring back to i. 22 f. and reminding the readers that in their baptismal rebirth they have already taken the first, negative step towards fulfilling the command to love one another. They have formally **put off**, or renounced, **all wickedness, all deceit, pretences and jealousies, and all recriminations.** Here we have one of those roughly standardized lists of unbecoming kinds of conduct which crop up frequently in the NT (Rom. i. 29 f.; 2 Cor. xii. 20; Eph. iv. 31; Col. iii. 8; 1 Tim. i. 9 f.), and which were in common use in Hellenistic popular diatribe and in the ethical propaganda of later Judaism (also in the Qumran sect: e.g. 1QS iv. 9-11; x. 21-24). From the start the Church seems to have taken over such codes and adapted them to its catechetical instruction. The faults selected here broadly represent types of behaviour incompatible with brotherly love (i. 22), but since the material is conventional it does not allow us to form a precise picture of the Asian Christians' situation. If distinctions are to be drawn, **wickedness** (*kakia*: an all-inclusive term) and **deceit** stand for general attitudes disruptive of community life, while the remaining three words are plurals denoting the practical expressions of hypocrisy, envy and slanderous backbiting.

The verb **put off** (*apotithesthai*) deserves special note. It is used in exactly the same way in Rom. xiii. 12; Eph. iv. 22; 25; Col. iii. 8; Jas. i. 21—all passages summarizing forms of conduct characteristic of the readers' pre-Christian past—and therefore seems to have been a technical term. The Pauline texts clearly show that the image behind it is that of stripping off one garment in order to don another. The early Christian practice of baptism

by immersion entailed undressing completely; and we know
that in the later liturgies the candidate's removal of his clothes
before descending naked to the pool and his putting on a new
set on coming up formed an impressive ceremony and were
interpreted as symbols of his abandonment of his past unworthy
life and his adoption of a new life of innocence (Hippolytus,
Trad. apost. xxi; Cyril of Jerusalem, *Cat. myst.* ii. 2; *Procat.* 4).
As all our NT texts have the Christian's break with his past in
view, and as this was sacramentally enacted in baptism, there is
a strong presumption that this symbolism, at any rate so far as
the undressing was concerned, had established itself in the
apostolic age, and the 'putting off' has a definite baptismal
reference. This interpretation enables us to restore what is
probably the proper force of the aorist participle (*apothemenoi*)
here. Most translations veil it by giving either a present participle ('laying aside': AV; RV) or even an imperative ('So put
away': RSV; NEB), as if the writer were requesting his readers
to begin repudiating uncharitable behaviour now. His plea,
however, is that they have already done this formally at their
baptism, and should therefore now be prepared for growth in
positive Christian living.

2   So he encourages them, **new-born babes as** they **are, to
crave for the milk of the word that is free from deceit so
that by it** they **may grow up to salvation.** His graphic description of them as **babes** carries one stage further the picture
of rebirth he has already used in i. 3; 23. Advocates of the
liturgical hypothesis (see Introduction, pp. 15-18) claim that
new-born (*artigennēta*: lit. 'recently born') implies that their
baptism has taken place immediately before, the passage thus
reproducing a service actually in progress; but this entails
squeezing more out of the prefix than it contains, and is in any
case quite unnecessary. The adjective need mean no more than
that the Asian communities included a substantial proportion
of fairly recent converts (as is likely if the letter is early).

The writer elaborates his imagery realistically. Milk is the
natural diet of infants, and they do not simply desire it but are
drawn with a powerful instinctive urge to the breast. The strong
verb **crave for** (*epipothein*) brings this out well: cf. its use in
Ps. xlii. 1 (of the thirsty stag's yearning for water); cxix. 174 (of

the soul's longing for salvation). He has chosen it deliberately because he wants his readers to have a passion for what he calls **the milk of the word that is free from deceit.** In the Greek **milk** is qualified by two adjectives which pick up and play on expressions he has employed a moment previously. The second (*adolos*: lit. 'guileless', 'without deceit') obviously echoes 'deceit' (*dolos*) in ii. 1; having renounced deceit, it is fitting that their drink should be **free from deceit.** Later Greek papyri and inscriptions (e.g. Pap. Hib. 85, 16 f.; 98, 19 f.; Pap. Oxy. 729, 19; Dittenberger, *Syll. inscr. Graec.* 736, 100) prove that *adolos*, as applied to corn, wine and other foodstuffs, had the technical sense of 'unadulterated', 'pure'. The first adjective (*logikos*) is generally translated 'spiritual' (RV; RSV; NEB), as in Rom. xii. 1 ('spiritual worship': its sole other occurrence in the NT), on the assumption that the writer is simply contrasting non-material, or heavenly, with literal milk. It seems hardly credible, however, that he is not also consciously referring back to God's 'word' (*logos*), about which he was so concerned in i. 22–25. It should be noted that in most of the passages cited in support of 'spiritual' (Epictetus, i. 16. 20; iii. 1. 26; Philo, *Migr. Abr.* 185; *Corp. Herm.* i. 31; xiii. 18; 20), while 'spiritual' or 'intelligible' gives the correct sense, the idea of 'word' (*logos*) is never far from the surface. Hence AV's **milk of the word** seems to express the intention of the phrase more accurately.

There has been much speculation about the background which suggested the image. On the one hand, milk figured prominently both in pagan mythology and in the mysteries. The Egyptian devotees of Isis, e.g., regarded it as imparting immortality, and in the initiation rites of Cybele the 'reborn' initiates were fed on milk (Sallust, *De deis* iv: for other texts see TWNT I, 645). Our writer's thought-world, however, seems much too remote for these ideas to have had any direct influence. On the other hand, we know that in the late 2nd and early 3rd cents. newly baptized persons were presented with milk mixed with honey, a symbol of the promised land which they had now entered (Hippolytus, *Trad. apost.* xxiii. 2; Tertullian, *Adv. Marc.* i. 14; *De cor.* iii. 3). As the writer has built so much baptismal material into this section, there may be a fleeting reference to this practice here, although the absence of any mention of honey (always linked with milk in our main texts, as in Ex. iii. 8) discourages confidence. Actually, the comparison of religious teaching with milk is found in 1 Cor. iii. 2; Heb. v. 12, and is used by Philo (*Agric.* 9; *Migr. Abr.* 29), and a very striking parallel is provided by the Qumran hymns (vii. 21, where 'the children of grace' are pictured as drinking in true doctrine as infants drink milk at the breast). So, too, in the Christian but markedly Semitic Odes of Solomon (viii. 16: cf. xix. 1-5) the enlightenment which the Lord bestows is likened to milk from His breasts. All this evidence tends to suggest that the writer did not need to look beyond his Jewish environment for his imagery.

When children feed on good milk, they **grow up** to physical maturity; the Christian who drinks in the gospel is nourished **by it** for **salvation,** i.e. the glory and blessedness which God has prepared for His elect at the End (see on i. 5). The Greek original for **by it** (*en autōi*) literally means 'in it' or even 'in him'. It would have been more natural to write 'through it' (*di' autou*), but he prefers the ambiguous *en autōi* because he does not distinguish between the word which is the Christian's **milk** and Christ. His thought has already shifted to Him, and as a spur 3 he evokes his readers' experience: **seeing 'you have tasted that the Lord is good'.** For **seeing** the Greek has *ei* (lit. 'if'), where the particle is not conditional but, as frequently in the NT (cf. i. 17; Mt. vi. 30; Lk. xii. 28; Rom. vi. 8; etc.), states as a supposition what is actually the case. The sentence is a loose quotation from Ps. xxxiv. 8, where the LXX gives, 'Taste and see that the Lord is good'. In the original 'the Lord' of course denotes Yahweh, but the Christian understanding of the Psalter naturally transferred the title to Christ. The verse brings out the full significance of the spiritual nourishment by which Christians are sustained. If in a sense it is God's word, in a deeper sense it is Christ Himself, whom they receive in word and sacrament. For a fine parallel, cf. Od. Sol. xix. 1: 'A cup of milk was presented to me, and I drank it in the sweet graciousness of the Lord'. The adjective (*chrēstos*) should not be translated 'kind' or 'gracious', a meaning which would be appropriate in other contexts; as applied to foods it had the special sense 'delicious to the taste' (e.g. Jer. xxiv. 2-5; Lk. v. 39), which is the one required here.

Our writer's citation of Ps. xxxiv. 8 is not haphazard; the whole psalm was present in his mind as he wrote the letter, and must have been familiar to his readers. He will have recourse to it again in the next verse; in iii. 10-12 he will quote verses 12-16, and there are close vebal correspondences between i. 15-18 and the LXX of verses 4, 9 and 22. Its theme is broadly the same as that of the letter: if in distress you seek the Lord, He will deliver you from all your troubles (4), for 'though the afflictions of the righteous are many, the Lord will rescue them out of them all' (19). In appealing to 8, however, is he thinking in general terms of the satisfaction his readers have derived from the gospel, or of something more specific? Because of its obvious aptness Ps. xxxiv came to be closely associated with the euchar- ist, being sung during the communion (*Apost. const.* viii. 13. 16; Cyril of Jerusalem, *Cat. myst.* v. 20; Jerome, *Ep.* lxxi. 6; Liturgy of St. James; Mozarabic Liturgy), and 8 in particular was applied by the fathers to partaking of it. In what follows the writer will be dwelling on the priestly aspect of the Christian community and on its 'spiritual sacrifices'. In this context (note also the suppression of 'and see' in the LXX) it is hard to evade the conclusion that the psalm was already being understood in a eucharistic sense and that he is reminding the Asian Christians of the blessings they have received through sacramental fellow- ship. If accepted, this interpretation runs counter to the theory that the bulk of 1 Peter is a baptismal liturgy; if it were, the imperative in Ps. xxxiv. 8 ('Taste . . .') would surely have been preserved as a fitting invitation to the communion which fol- lowed baptism, whereas the alteration to **you have tasted** insinuates that the readers are already communicants.

The writer now comes to his main thought, that as Christians they form an élite community assured of God's protection. His opening words, **to whom coming,** are a further echo of Ps. 4 xxxiv, verse 5 of which reads in the LXX, 'Come to him (*proselthate pros*: the same verb and preposition) and be en- lightened'. The idea he is working up to is that of triumph in the midst of apparent disaster. So, suddenly switching from his picture of Christ as the Christian's spiritual sustenance, he represents Him as **the living stone, rejected indeed by men but chosen and honoured in God's sight.** This description combines two OT texts which were much pondered in the primitive Church and were charged with Christological significance for himself and his readers. The first is Ps. cxviii. 22 ('the stone which the builders rejected has been made the head of the corner': cited in full in 7), where the stone stands in the original for Israel, harried by the world-powers and thrown away as useless, but in spite of all given marvellous honour by God. There is some slight evidence (SB I, 876) for the messianic interpretation of this text in later Judaism, and Christians very early (Acts iv. 11) began reading verse 22 as a prophecy at once of Christ's passion and death at the hands of men and of His vindication by God as shown by His resurrection and glorification; indeed they traced this application to Jesus Himself (Mk. xii. 10). So here, as in 7 below, the contemptuous discarding of **the stone** directly alludes to the Lord's rejection and execution and, by implication, to the sufferings of the Asian readers. To explain **living** many refer to 'the spiritual rock' which in 1 Cor. x. 4 is identified as Christ, but the context of ideas is quite different. The adjective is added to emphasize that Christ is the Risen One, alive again after being dead and able to impart life to those who suffer in His cause.

Because he is planning (as we shall see below) a more detailed exegesis for 'head of the corner', the writer breaks away for the moment from Ps. cxviii and, to balance Christ's rejection by a reminder (again pregnant with encouragement to his readers, also rejected by their fellow citizens) that God has set His seal of approval on Him, seizes on an excerpt from Is. xxviii. 16, which he will cite in full in 6 and which runs in the LXX: 'See, I shall lay for the foundations of Sion a precious, chosen stone, an honoured corner-stone for her foundations; and he who has faith in it [him] shall not be put to shame'. There is nothing corresponding to 'in it [him]' in the Hebrew, but the addition is probably older than the NT; and the Hebrew original of 'will not be put to shame' is 'will not be in haste', i.e. will not have to flee. The prophet is addressing the rulers of Jerusalem who, threatened with invasion by Assyria, have spurned his advice and made an alliance with Egypt. Using metaphors drawn from the solid fabric of the Temple, he insists that Israel's true refuge lies, not in political pacts or military power, but in confidence in God,

Whose sovereignty is their sure foundation. In rabbinical exegesis (TWNT IV, 276) the stone was paraphrased as 'the mighty king, heroic and terrible', i.e. the Messiah, whom Yahweh would establish in Sion and in whom the righteous might confidently place their trust; at Qumran the image of the stone was applied to the community as the eschatological congregation of the last day (1QS v. 5; vii. 17 f.; viii. 7 f.; etc.). Not unnaturally, therefore, Christians read the passage as a prediction of Christ, and found especial encouragement in the promise made explicit in the LXX that faith in Him would not be disappointed.

While **chosen** and **honoured** stress in the first instance God's vindication of Christ, both epithets are intended to impress on the readers that, humiliated and distressed though they are, they will enjoy a no less signal victory, and prepare the way for the fuller account the writer is going to give in 6-10 of the honour and privileges of God's people. In the meantime, in a bold phrase, he assimilates them to the risen Lord; like Him they are, as it were, **living stones,** sharing through baptism in an 5 existence which is triumphant over disaster and death. As such they **are** being **built up as a spiritual house.** So far as its form goes, the verb (*oikodomeisthe*) might be an imperative, and many prefer a translation such as (RSV) 'be yourselves built up'. The builder, however, is surely God; thus the imperative would have to mean 'allow yourselves to be built up', which is not easy to extract from the Greek. Further, the previous relative clause **to whom coming** indicates that the writer is now drawing out the doctrinal corollary of his exhortation; as a result of faith in Christ his readers are in fact being formed into a close-knit unity which may be pictured as **a spiritual house** (cf. 'house of God' in iv. 17). The noun used (*oikos*) can convey the sense of 'household' (cf. Acts x. 2; xi. 14; 1 Cor. i. 16; etc.), but his mention of stones and building reveals that this is not his only or main thought. His conception of the Christian life is through and through corporate, not individualistic; but here, as frequently in the LXX (e.g. Ps. lxix. 9; Is. lvi. 7), **house** also specifically denotes 'temple'. He is making the twofold point (a) that, as baptized and united with Christ, his readers form the true temple of God which is Christ Himself; and (b) that this new temple, in contrast to the localized and material Temple of the old Law, is a **spiritual** one (impregnable, by implication, to earthly vicissitudes).

Both these ideas are deeply embedded in primitive Christian propaganda and apologetic. For the former, cf. 1 Cor. iii. 9-17 (Christians are God's temple, with Christ as the foundation and the Spirit dwelling in them); 2 Cor. vi. 16 f. ('we are the temple of the living God'); Eph. ii. 20-22 (where the building metaphor is elaborated in detail); 1 Tim. iii. 15; Heb. iii. 2-6 ('we are his house if . . .'); x. 21. For the conviction that God does not inhabit material temples, cf. esp. Acts vii. 48; xvii. 24. There is synoptic evidence (Mk. xiv. 58; xv. 29: cf. Jn. ii. 19) that Christ Himself spoke of raising a temple not made with hands to replace the one on Sion; and Mt. xvi. 18 represents Him as referring to His new community as a building. So widespread was this imagery, and so varied the forms in which it clothed itself, that we must infer that it was traditional, so that there is no need to posit a direct connection between this passage and, say, Eph. ii. 20-22 (where the word for 'temple' is *nāos*). There was in fact nothing novel in thinking of the Church as a spiritual temple; at Qumran the Teacher of Righteousness was conceived of as 'building . . . the congregation' (4QpPs37 ii. 16), the community itself as a house of God built on a rock (e.g. 1QH vi. 25-28), and its council as 'an everlasting plantation, a house of holiness for Israel . . . a house of perfection and truth in Israel' (1QS viii. 5-10).

Thus the Church is **a spiritual house,** where the adjective primarily denotes that the Spirit both brings it into existence and pervades its life, but also by implication points the contrast with material, man-made temples. At this point, however, the kaleidoscope makes yet another turn, and the writer envisages his correspondents, not so much as a temple, but as the **holy priesthood** who inhabit it and offer the pure worship which is appropriate to the new order established by Christ. Literally rendered, the Greek is 'for a holy priesthood', and some prefer the translation 'to exercise holy priestly functions'; but the use of the same noun (*hierateuma*) in 9 makes it likely that it has the collective sense 'body of priests' here too. In contrast to other religious communities, where the priests are a caste demarcated off from the people, and in particular to Judaism, where they were in theory descendants of Aaron, the Christian community as a whole is a priestly body (cf. Ambrose, *Expos. in Luc.* v. 33: 'All the sons of the Church are priests; for we are all anointed ... offering ourselves to God as spiritual sacrifices'). Moreover, as such it is **holy,** the adjective being intended not so much to contrast their priesthood with that of pagan religions as to highlight once again the Church's status as a holy people consecrated to God (Ex. xix. 6).

Further, it is the function of priests to offer sacrifice, and just as the temple of the new covenant which they in effect constitute is **spiritual,** so the Christian community in its priestly capacity is called upon **to offer spiritual sacrifices.** Again a distinction is drawn (probably with an apologetic intent, for critics habitually fastened upon the Christians' apparent lack of any cultus) between the worship appropriate to the new order and the material offerings whether of Judaism or of the paganism in which the Asian Christians had been reared. Many OT writers had already glimpsed the truth that what pleases God is not external sacrifice in itself, but rather such things as prayer and praise, thankfulness, a broken and contrite heart, and a life of justice and compassion (e.g. Ps. l. 14; li. 16-19; lxix. 30 f.; cxli. 2; Hos. vi. 6; Mic. vi. 6-8). The Qumran sectaries, cut off from the Temple at Jerusalem, worked out a spiritual reinterpretation of sacrifices on similar lines, arguing (1QS ix. 3-5) that 'prayer rightly offered shall be as an acceptable fragrance of righteousness, and perfection of way as a delectable free-will offering'. The apostolic Church was quick to perceive that with Christ's supreme sacrifice all material sacrifices, even the divinely ordained ones of the Law, had been finally abrogated. The true worship of Christians, according of Paul (Rom. xii. 1; Eph. v. 2; Phil. iv. 18), is the surrender of themselves, individually and corporately, to God in loving service to one another and faith; according to Heb. xiii. 15 f., the sacrifice they continually offer consists of praise and thanksgiving, charity and mutual sharing. This worship is **spiritual** both in the sense of non-material, as indicated above, but also more positively as inspired by the Spirit. The writer's doctrine is thus richer than that of Rom. xii. 1, where Paul's *logikē latreia*, also commonly rendered 'spiritual worship', lacks the positive reference to the Spirit's activity contained in **spiritual** (*pneumatikas*) here.

There has been much discussion whether the writer's thought embraces the eucharist. Most commentators have decided against this, mainly on such grounds as that 'the thought of any Christian rite as a sacrifice is foreign to the NT' (F. W. Beare). This overlooks the fact that 2nd cent. writers, who were as stoutly opposed to sacrifice as conventionally understood as any NT author, did not hesitate to describe the eucharist as a sacrifice in their own, highly analogical sense, believing it to be 'the pure offering' foretold in Mal. i. 11 (e.g. *Did.* xiv; Justin, *Dial.* cxvii. 1). All the elements mentioned in Rom. xii. 1; Heb. xiii. 15 f.; etc. were gathered up in the eucharist, the culmination of which was the offering over the bread and wine of praise and thanks to God by the redeemed community, all in a setting expressive of the mutual charity which is the fruit of our redemption (e.g. Justin, *1 Apol.* lxv; Hippolytus, *Trad. apost.* iv. 2-12). In the light of this and of the liturgical overtones of the passage, the technical sense of **offer** (*anapherein*: the correct cultic term, from which 'anaphora' is derived), and the mention of 'proclaiming God's mighty deeds' in 9 (where see note), we should probably infer that, while by no means limited to it, these **spiritual sacrifices** include the eucharistic action.

In any case they are **acceptable to God through Jesus Christ.** The whole object of sacrifice, whether conceived of as a material offering to God or, at the Christian level, as thanksgiving and a humble striving to fulfil His will, is that it should please Him and win His approval. But the NT teaches that Christ is the mediator through whom our approach to God is made possible. Here it is not clear whether the last three words are to be taken with the verb **offer** or the adjective **acceptable.** If the former, the thought is akin to that of Heb. xiii. 15 f.: Christ is the high priest of the new order who, having entered the heavens, presents our sacrifices to God. If the latter, there is the tacit admission that the best we can offer, in loving service and thankfulness, falls short of what God requires until united with Christ's sacrifice and offered in His name. The latter is on balance preferable as suiting the order of the words in Greek better; but the expression has become almost stereotyped, and it may be doubted whether the author was conscious of the fine distinction.

He now proceeds to substantiate his plea by writing out in full the scripture texts which have been in his mind and adding others which develop his argument. First come the two passages (Is. xxviii. 16 and Ps. cxviii. 22) which we have already discussed in part, along with a third (Is. viii. 14): **'a stone to trip 8 men up, a rock to stumble over'.** They are introduced by the formula **For it is set down in scripture,** where the verb 6 (*periechei*) is absolute and impersonal (lit. 'it includes': cf. Josephus, *Ant.* xi. 104; Pap. Oxy. 249, 24; etc.) and the article customary in the NT when an individual text is being cited is noticeably absent before **scripture.** In all three Christ is likened, according to an exegesis which he evidently expects to be familiar to his readers, to a stone; their common theme, as he expounds it, is that the destiny of men, and of the readers and their persecutors in particular, is determined by their attitude to Him. Those who esteem Him as God does, i.e. as **a choice and honoured corner-stone,** and who recognizing His vindication by God have **faith in** Him, **will not be put to shame.** To drive his message home, the writer interpolates a midrashic gloss at 7a, picking up the prophet's word **honoured** and applying it directly to the Asian Christians: because they **have faith,** i.e. 7 believe and hold fast, **the honour belongs to** them. This **honour** includes (a) their privileged status here and now, on which he will dwell more fully in 9 f., but also (b) their triumph over their mocking assailants and their salvation on the last day.

On the other hand, a different fate is in store **for those who lack faith:** a threat of general import, but here pointedly directed at the Asian Christians' tormentors. Like the trustless builders, they will have the mortification of seeing **the stone which** they **rejected . . . made the head of the corner.** The crucified Christ who seemed abandoned has been promoted by God to glory, and so (such is the writer's message) will be His faithful servants in Asia Minor whom they seek to humiliate. Thus He has proved, as it were, an awkward stone over which they have stumbled, and so will go headlong to disaster. In Is. viii. 13-15 the prophet's point had been that the Lord would be a sanctuary for those who held Him in proper awe and reverence, but would bring destruction (hence the image of 'the stone of stumbling') to all who underrated His power and goodness (as did Ephraim by its aggression and Judah by its want of faith). In the rabbinic literature the text was sometimes given a messianic interpretation (TWNT IV, 277). In the case of unbelievers like the Asian pagans the cause of their stumbling

8 is precisely the fact that **they disobey the word** (cf. iii. 1; iv. 17). The gospel message is conceived of as a challenge demanding men's obedience (the negative *apeithein* has the same root as *pisteuein*, i.e. 'believe' or 'have faith', but carries the stronger sense of 'refuse belief', 'disobey'), and where this is withheld a terrible retribution follows. And this retribution, the writer sharply interjects, is **the lot for which they were appointed.** The verb he uses (*tithenai*: employed also in 6 above) is the one specifically applied to God's predestination (e.g. Is. xlix. 6; 1 Thess. v. 9). Just as in i. 2 he represents his readers as marked out by God for salvation, so here he envisages their adversaries as predestined to destruction; but in both cases his mention of obedience or its opposite implies that the personal decision of the individual is involved. No more than other NT writers does he provide a clue to the solution of the baffling problems which this tension raises.

Two further points call for note. First, it is by no means obvious what particular architectural feature is denoted by 'head of the corner' and 'corner-stone'. J. Jeremias has contended (e.g. TWNT I, 792 f.; IV, 275-83) that, at any rate in the LXX version of the texts, the terms used stand, not for the foundation-stone, but for the keystone or coping-stone of a building. This may well be correct of LXX Ps. cxviii. 22 and Is. xxviii. 16, as well as of Mk. xii. 10; Acts iv. 11, but it is doubtful if this usage is consistently adhered to in the NT. In Eph. ii. 20, e.g., where 'corner-stone' (*akrogōniaios*) is also found, it must signify a distinctive, structurally important stone at the corner of the foundations (which in fact is the sense of 'corner-stone' in the Hebrew of Is. xxviii. 16). In the present passage the writer's thought seems to fluctuate. In 4 and 7, where the exaltation of the rejected is to the fore, the keystone motif fits best, but in 6 the idea of a foundation-stone is more in place; while 'the stone of stumbling' in 8 is clearly on the ground in reach of a man's foot. Probably his concern is not so much with the stone's function in a building as with its character as **chosen and honoured.**

Secondly, the writer was not alone in reading these three texts, with the stone image they contain, in a Christological sense. Ps. cxviii. 22 was widely interpreted as foreshadowing Christ's rejection and vindication (Mt. xxi. 42 f.; Mk. xii. 10 f.; Lk. xx. 17; Acts iv. 11), and Eph. ii. 20 echoes Is. xxviii. 16. The latter and Is. viii. 14 are conflated, in an abbreviated form but in a translation which differs from the LXX almost exactly as 1 Peter does, in Rom. ix. 33. This striking fact has been seized on by many as proof positive that our writer must have copied Romans. Had this been the case, however, we should have to suppose that he not only went to the trouble of disentangling the passages, which Paul weaves closely together, but then supplied the bits of Is. xxviii. 16 which Paul omitted in a version somewhat divergent from the LXX. The procedure is possible, but unlikely. Much the most plausible explanation is that all three texts, so different in their original bearing but linked together by the common image of the stone, formed a group, or part of a group, of Christ-testimonies current in the primitive Church on which the NT writers drew independently. As we have seen, both the rabbis and Qumran sectaries gave them a messianic/eschatological exegesis, and so in interpreting them Christologically the Church was simply adapting a ready-made tradition. Whatever may be said of the hypothesis of 'testimony-books', there is little doubt that Christians in the apostolic age had recognized catenae of OT texts which they regarded as significant, and the discoveries of Cave IV at Qumran suggest that the practice of compiling such collections had a precedent in sectarian Judaism.

So much for the fate of the unbelieving persecutors of the Asian Christians. In contrast to this (**You, however** is emphatically adversative) the writer dwells in heightened tones on the status of these latter as God's elect people, enlarging on his remark in 7 that **honour . . . belongs to** them. In the opening sentence of his letter (see on i. 1) he had hinted that the Church is the true Israel, the rightful heir of all the privileges pertaining to the old Israel and all the promises made to it. So here, calling in aid yet another cento of OT texts, he tranfers to the Christian community a string of honorific titles which in the original applied to Israel. They are all, it should be noted, corporate in character, denoting the Church as a body rather than individual Christians. He begins with a conflation of LXX Ex. xix. 6 and Is. xliii. 20 f. (loosely quoted from the LXX). In the former Yahweh announces to the children of Israel, 'And you shall be to me a kingdom of priests and a holy nation', where the motivating idea is not polemic against the Levitical priesthood but simply that, provided they remain loyal to the covenant, they will have the holy God for their king and, like priests, will have a specially intimate relationship with Him. In the latter the Lord, promising Israel liberation from captivity in Babylon, describes her as ' . . . my chosen race, the people which I have made my possession to declare my mighty deeds'.

Thus it is the Church, the believing community which stands fast under persecution, which is in the true sense God's **chosen race.** While starting off with Ex. xix. 6 (*humeis de,* i.e. **You, however,** reproduces its opening words exactly, although *de* has the adversative sense **however,** which it lacks in the LXX but which the present context requires), the writer immediately brings forward **chosen race** from Is. xliii. 20 and inserts it here. He does this partly because the expression picks up **choice** (*eklekton*: the same word) in 6 and so accentuates the parallelism between Christ and His followers, and partly because it strikes the keynote, election, of his theme. Israel after the flesh, on which God's choice originally fell, has been supplanted because it was found wanting in faith. He then reverts to Ex. xix. 6, saluting the Church in the persons of his correspondents as **a royal house, a body of priests.** In the light of the promise made to the children of Israel, these predicates now belong to it, and to the Asian Christians in particular, because it has obeyed God's word and is loyal to His new covenant. The former gives a fresh turn to the image of 'spiritual house' in 5; the community is **a royal house** because the King dwells in its midst. In the same way the second echoes 'a holy priesthood' in 5; again the noun is a collective one, designating Christians in their corporate capacity rather than as individuals.

Traditionally the two Greek words thus translated (*basileion hierateuma*) have been taken together, being identified as an adjective and a noun respectively, and the ordinary rendering (AV; RV; RSV; etc.) is 'a royal priesthood'. At first sight this seems the natural translation as well as the one supported by LXX Ex. xix. 6; further, since each of the other three collective nouns in the sentence is qualified either by an adjective or by a phrase equivalent to one, an adjective seems appropriate before 'priesthood'. Against it, however, the following points have been made (see J. H. Elliott, *The Elect and the Holy*). (a) The Hebrew lying behind the first of the two words is, as we have explained, a noun, viz. 'kingdom'. (b) While *basileios* can mean 'royal', its use as an adjective is exceedingly rare in Biblical Greek (twice only in the LXX, if we exclude Ex. xix. 6; xxiii. 22 as being subject to discussion). (c) Much the most common use of the word in the LXX is as a neuter noun *basileion*, and this is found frequently in secular Greek too. In the latter it generally has the sense of 'royal residence' (Xenophon, *Cyrop.* ii. 4. 3; Herodotus, *Hist.* i. 30. 178—in plural), or else 'royal capital' (Polybius, *Hist.* iii. 15. 3); while in the LXX the meanings 'sovereignty', 'crown', 'monarchy' (2 Sam. i. 10; 1 Chron. xxviii. 4; Wis. i. 14; 2 Macc. ii. 17), or (mostly in plural) 'palace' (Esth. i. 9; ii. 13; Prov. xviii. 19; Nah. ii. 7; Dan. vi. 19), predominate. (d) In the exegesis of Hellenistic Judaism *basileion* in LXX Ex. xix. 6 was interpreted as a substantive: cf. 2 Macc. ii. 17 ('kingdom'); Philo, *De sobr.* 66 and *De Abr.* 56 ('royal house'). (e) The author of Rev. i. 6; v. 10 also seems to have read the relevant words of Ex. xix. 6 as two independent nouns (cf. 'a royal house, priests to God . . .'; 'a royal house and priests'). (f) Stylistic considerations in fact favour our taking *basileion* as a substantive, for had it been an adjective we should have expected it to be placed, like the other adjectives in the sentence, after its noun.

The case is an impressive one and, in spite of the awkwardness (more visible in the Greek than in the English) of having the two nouns juxtaposed without adjectives, hard to resist. If *basileion* is a substantive, its probable meaning is 'royal residence'. The word rarely, if ever, denotes 'kingdom', and a correspondence with **spiritual house . . . holy priesthood** in 5 seems intended. This rendering has an important bearing on our understanding of the passage. According to a very widely accepted exegesis the usual translation 'a royal priesthood' indicates that there is no priestly caste in the new Israel; every believer has both a royal function derived from Christ's kingship and a priestly one derived from His priesthood. On any interpretation this is probably a misreading of the text, for throughout (as has been already explained) it is the Church as a whole that is being addressed; the emphasis is not on the role of Christians as individuals but as a corporate body. The recognition, however, that *basileion* is itself a collective noun, picturing the community as the house in which the King chooses to dwell, sets **body of priests** in perspective as merely one in a series of corporate descriptions, without any title to be specially singled out. The common factor which unites these predicates, each containing a different image, is simply the idea of election. Through faith in Jesus, 'the choice and honoured corner-stone' which the world has rejected, Christians baptized with the Spirit become God's choice and honoured people, with all the privileges of Israel of old.

Some (so J. H. Elliott) would go further, arguing that **body of priests** carries no specifically priestly implications but is merely another image illustrating the electedness and holiness of God's new community. More precisely, it denotes a people peculiarly close to God and as such called to the exercise of a holy life of obedience and well-doing. But it would surely have been paradoxical for the writer to fasten on this particular image if he had intended to evacuate it of all priestly connotation; and his language in 5 makes it unlikely that he wished to do so. Admittedly it can be shown that neither in the OT nor in subsequent exegesis was Ex. xix. 6 given a priestly interpretation, still less understood as arguing in favour of a priesthood of all Israelites as against a Levitical system. Admittedly, too, the writer's dominant motive was to highlight the exalted status of the Christian community as God's chosen people. Even so, **a body of priests** seems to convey something more than the idea of a community enjoying unique closeness to God; the idea of performing holy service in His honour (cf. 'spiritual sacrifices' in 5) must also be included as a subordinate but none the less consciously intended motive.

Further, the Church is **a holy nation,** again a title originally appropriated to Israel and an element in the covenant formula in Ex. xix. 6. It is **holy,** not in the sense that either it or its members are in actual fact paragons of virtue, but because it has been set apart for God's service (see on i. 15 f.) and is inspired and sustained by His Spirit. The former idea is repeated and elaborated in the final title, **a people for God's possession,** i.e. a community which God has singled out and made peculiarly His own and which finds the end of its existence in this fact. Here we are brought back to Is. xliii. 21. The curious expression used (*eis peripoiēsin*) represents a modification of the prophet's words as they appear in the LXX (*hon periepoiēsamēn*: 'whom I have made my private possession'), but is itself found with exactly the same meaning in Mal. iii. 17. The term used for **people** is *lāos*, the word which in the LXX is the designation *par excellence* of the people of God. And the whole object of their election to this role, the writer reminds the Asian Christians, is **that you may proclaim the mighty deeds of him who has called you out of darkness into his marvellous light.**

The first of these clauses carries on the quotation from Is. xliii. 21, with the verb changed from an infinitive to a second-person plural subjunctive so as to address the readers directly, and the more graphic **proclaim** (*exaggellein*) substituted for the LXX 'recount' (*diēgeisthai*). The second clause, in **called, darkness,** and **light,** seems to contain reminiscences of the preceding context in Is. xlii. 6 f. Instead of **mighty deeds** the older translations give 'praises' (AV), 'excellences' (RV), or the like; but the Greek *aretai*, when applied to a god, does not denote his virtues or intrinsic qualities but the manifestations of his power (TWNT I, 457-61). In a Jewish-Christian setting these must be God's saving acts, the signal disclosures of His mercy towards His chosen: cf. 'mighty acts of God' in Acts ii. 11. For Israel the divine redemptive act which had above all others sealed its election, and which Jews regularly commemorated with gratitude (e.g. at the Passover), was the Exodus; this was in the prophet's mind in Is. xliii. 1 ff. For the new Israel it is God's raising up Christ from the dead, in spite of rejection and humiliation, and giving Him glory, as a result of which believers too triumph over earthly assaults and are brought to salvation.

The verb 'call' (*kalein*) is the technical term in both LXX and NT for God's saving initiative: for its use in 1 Peter, cf. i. 15; ii. 21; iii. 9; v. 10. The dualism of light and darkness is deeply rooted in the Bible; cf. also the antithesis drawn at Qumran between 'the sons of light' and 'the sons of darkness'. In Judaism light was associated with the Messiah and the messianic age (SB I, 161 f.: e.g. rabbinical comment on 'in thy light we see light' of Ps. xxxvi. 9); and so for primitive Christianity Jesus was the light (Jn. i. 4 f.; 8 f.; viii. 12; etc.), while those who accepted Him as Lord were thought of as entering into and walking in the eschatological light (e.g. Jn. xii. 35; Acts xxvi. 18; Eph. v. 8; Col. i. 12; 1 Thess. v. 5; 1 Jn. i. 5-ii. 11). Their pre-Christian past was regarded as 'darkness', and their baptism as 'enlightenment' (Rom. xiii. 12; Eph. v. 14; Heb. vi. 4; x. 32; Justin, *1 Apol.* lxi. 12 f.; lxv. 1; *Dial.* cxxii. 1). So routine an element in catechetical instruction was this imagery that the glowing mention of God's having called the readers from darkness **into his marvellous light** must contain a reminder of their baptism; there is possibly also a further echo of Ps. xxxiv (cf. 5: 'Look to him and be enlightened'). This being the setting, the attempts of R. Perdelwitz and others to trace the language to the pagan mysteries, in which the initiate advanced through a darkened chamber into a blaze of light, are unnecessary and indeed far-fetched.

The Church, then, as God's elect people, has the function of proclaiming His saving acts. This it does, we may presume, both by rehearsing them in its daily life with exultant thankfulness and, as Israel of old was expected to do (e.g. Is. xliii. 10; 12; xliv. 8), by bearing witness to them before mankind. In testing circumstances, such as the readers were faced with, this rehearsal was calculated to stiffen the resolution of Christians and fill their opponents with dismay. Again, however, as at 5, it is hard not to overhear a eucharistic note in the words. In the early 2nd cent. we know that the eucharist was understood primarily as a sacrifice of praise and reached its climax in a prayer (Justin, *1 Apol.* lxv. 3; lxvii. 5; *Dial.* xli. 1; Hippolytus, *Trad. apost.* iv.) giving glory and thanks to God for His goodness in creating us, in sending His Son, in redeeming us, etc.—in short, proclaiming His **mighty deeds.** It is entirely likely that in the 1st cent. too, when Christians met together for the breaking of bread, such a recital featured prominently in the memorial they made of Christ; and the regular use of **proclaim** (*exaggellein*) in the LXX with the sense of cultic proclamation, or the rehearsal in adoring language of God's righteousness and praises, suggests that this is at any rate part of what is covered by the verb here.

The writer then concludes his eloquent description of his readers' elect status by recalling, with a backward glance at his veiled reference to their conversion and baptism, that they **were 10 once no people but are now God's people,** and that whereas previously they **had not received mercy,** they **now have received mercy.** Once again he is conflating LXX texts, this time from Hosea, and his words evoke Hos. i. 9 ('And he said, "Call his name Lo-ammi [i.e. Not-my-people], because you are not my people and I am not your God"'); i. 10 ('And in that place where it was said to them, "You are not my people", it shall be said to them, "Sons of the living God"'); i. 6 ('... and he said to him, "Call her name Lo-ruhamah [i.e. Who-has-not-received-mercy], because I shall no longer have mercy on the house of Israel"'); and ii. 23 ('... and I shall have mercy on Who-has-not-received-mercy, and I shall say to Not-my-people, "You are my people"'). The prophet had seen in these strange, divinely appointed names of the children Gomer bore him a parable of God's rejection of Israel and subsequent readiness to receive it back, but the present writer interprets the story as prefiguring the drastic and wonderful change the Asian Christians have experienced as a result of their conversion. Previously as pagans they had been **no people,** for the noun used (*lāos:* see on 9) was reserved in the OT and later Judaism for Israel alone, the correct term for Greeks and barbarians alike being *ethnē* (i.e. 'nations'). Now, through accepting the gospel and being regenerated in baptism, they have become in the full Christian sense **God's people.** The corollary of this is that, whereas formerly they had no claim on God's **mercy,** as shown in His rescuing them from the attacks of their enemies and assuring them of salvation in the messianic age, they have **now** become actual beneficiaries of it.

It is interesting to observe that Paul also, in Rom. ix. 25 f., conflates Hos. ii. 23 and i. 10, mentioning the prophet by name and treating his words as evidence of God's intention to adopt the Gentiles as His people. This has led many to infer that our writer must have taken Rom. ix. 25 f. as his model; but such dependence seems excluded by the facts (a) that, whereas he speaks of **who had not received mercy,** Rom. ix. 25 has 'who was not beloved', thus apparently reflecting an alternative version of the Hebrew; (b) the two passages make a rather different selection from the Hosea texts, so that it is hard to understand why, if our writer had Rom. ix. 26 before him, he did not reproduce its striking sentence, 'they will be called sons of the living God'; (c) there is a perceptible divergence between the lessons which the two writers deduce from the texts, the one stressing the universalistic motif, and the other (while not over-looking this) the eschatological blessedness which his readers now enjoy as a result of accepting the gospel. The true explanation, as in ii. 6-8, is that both were making independent use of a pre-canonical tradition which already recognized this group of sayings as prefigurative of the new Israel.

5. PRACTICAL ADVICE: (i) RELATIONS WITH PAGANS

ii. 11-12

(11) I appeal to you, dear friends, as aliens and temporary sojourners, to abstain from the passions of the flesh which wage war against the soul. (12) See that your conduct among the pagans is good, so that in cases where they vilify you as wrongdoers, they may, through taking note of your good actions, glorify God on the day of visitation.

At this point a fresh section which extends to iii. 12 commences. So far the writer has expatiated on the election and separation of baptized Christians as the new Israel; now he draws out some of the practical implications of this changed status for his readers in the testing situation in which they are placed. He makes the transition by 'appealing' (the verb *para-kalein* is regular in such exhortation: e.g. Rom. xii. 1; 1 Cor. i. 10; 1 Thess. iv. 1) to them as **dear friends** (*agapētoi*: lit. 'beloved'), a form of address which is rarely used in non-Christian Greek to mark an affectionate relationship, but which is frequent both in the Pauline letters (Rom. xii. 19; 1 Cor. x. 14; 2 Cor. vii. 1; 1 Thess. ii. 8; etc.) and in the Catholic Epistles (Jas. i. 16; 19; ii. 5; 1 Pet. iv. 12; 2 Pet. iii. 1; 1 Jn. ii. 7; etc.). Derived from the distinctively Christian noun *agapē*, it harks back to the advice given in i. 22, and while primarily denoting the writer's love for his correspondents, also evokes the thought of the love which God has for them and the mutual charity which should characterize the Christian community.

To highlight the special quality of the life to which they are called, the writer reminds the Asian Christians that they are **aliens and temporary sojourners.** The expression recalls Abraham's words to the children of Heth (Gen. xxiii. 4), 'I am a stranger and a sojourner with you', and the Psalmist's cry (Ps. xxxix. 12), 'I am a stranger with thee, and a sojourner, as all my fathers were'. It also looks back to i. 1 and i. 17 (see notes), where the same images are used to drive home the Christian's transitory allegiance in the world. Taken strictly, the terms are mutually exclusive, for while 'alien' (*paroikos*) connotes a man who is domiciled in a foreign country, 'temporary sojourner' (*parepidēmos*) suggests a visitor making a brief stay in one. The writer, however, is less concerned with such niceties than with the doctrine, shared by the saints of Israel, Paul and others, that 'here we have no lasting city' (Heb. xiii. 14), for 'our commonwealth is in heaven' (Phil. iii. 20). Neither he nor the NT writers generally interpret this in an escapist sense. On the contrary, the corollary which he, like them, draws from it is that the ideals and motives of the heavenly city should inspire the Christian's daily life.

Thus he exhorts his readers, since their true home is elsewhere, **to abstain** (*apechesthai*: for the infinitive some MSS give the imperative *apechesthe*) **from the passions of the flesh, which wage war against the soul.** The NT more than once resorts to the imagery of warfare to describe the interior moral

8   103

struggle in a man (e.g. Rom. vii. 23; 2 Cor. x. 3; Jas. iv. 1: all using the same verb *strateuesthai* or a compound), while the tension between his spiritual or rational nature and his appetites is a commonplace of Greek, Hellenistic and late Jewish literature (for the last, cf. Philo, *Leg. alleg.* ii. 106; 4 Macc. i. 20 ff.; iii. 1 ff.; vii. 16-18). The verb 'abstain from' is a catchword which the Church's ethical catechesis, of which this verse is a sample, took over from a long tradition, Greek as well as Jewish, going back at least to Plato (e.g. *Phaed.* 82c) and Aristotle (e.g. *Eth. Nic.* ii. 2. 7; 9). As in i. 14 (where see note), **passions** (lit. 'desires') has the pejorative meaning 'wrongful appetites'; and most commentators attribute a pejorative sense to **of the flesh** (the Greek has the adjective 'fleshly') too, citing Paul's 'desires of the flesh' (Gal. v. 16 f.; 24; Eph. ii. 3) and finding here his doctrine of 'the flesh' (*sarx*) as the whole nature of man in its unredeemed condition, the seat and vehicle of sin (cf. esp. Rom. viii. 4-13). They may be correct, but we should hesitate to admit such a distinctively Pauline interpretation unless there is positive evidence in its favour. Against it we should note that (a) in i. 24; iii. 18; iv. 1; 6 'flesh' (*sarx*) is a morally neutral term, connoting simply man's physical nature or sphere of existence as such; (b) the present expression is matched by 'passions of men' in iv. 2; and (c) the distinction between bodily desires and desires springing from the soul was familiar to Hellenistic-Jewish diatribe (e.g. 4 Macc. i-iii). It seems wiser, therefore, to gloss **passions of the flesh** by 'disorderly appetites connected with the body', without reading out of the words any innuendo that physical appetites are intrinsically sinful.

Thus the writer is not warning his readers against a multiplicity of sins of various kinds like 'the works of the flesh' listed by Paul in Gal. v. 19 ff.; he is thinking specifically of types of immorality which will (see next verse) ruin their reputation with their non-Christian neighbours. In the meantime he introduces a more fundamental reason for avoiding such excesses (the Greek for **which** is *haitines*, which here is more than a simple relative, virtually meaning 'because they'), viz. that they **wage war against the soul.** The noun he uses for **soul** is *psuchē*, which makes it tempting to see here the conventional distinction between soul and body as 'parts' of human nature. His employment of the word elsewhere (see note on i. 9), however, should put us on our guard against such a conclusion. Here, as in the other passages where he uses it, **soul** denotes the man himself, considered as a living being or person, and unbridled appetites are condemned as being destructive of the true, divine life he has been given by Christ.

He follows up this negative warning with a positive exhortation: **See that** (the Greek gives the present participle 'having') 12 **your conduct among the pagans is good.** For **conduct,** see on i. 15; the same phrase (*kalē anastrophē*) recurs in Jas. iii. 13 and may have been a catechetical cliché. This concern for the Church's fair name among non-Christians is frequent in the NT (1 Cor. x. 32; Col. iv. 5; 1 Thess. iv. 12; 1 Tim. iii. 7; v. 14; vi. 1; Tit. ii. 5-10: also ii. 15; iii. 1; 16). Here, however, an additional, evangelistic motive is advanced, viz. **so that in cases where they vilify you as wrongdoers they may, through taking note of your good actions, glorify God on the day of visitation.** The admonition seems inspired by our Lord's command (Mt. v. 16), 'Let your light so shine before men that they may see your good works and glorify your heavenly Father'. The language (cf. esp. **vilify you as wrongdoers**) is strong, and shows up in an arresting way the perilous situation in which 1st cent. Christians were liable to find themselves. While their faith as such may not have been legally a crime (see Introduction, pp. 10; 28 f.), they were the object of blind suspicion and detestation, and so exposed to all sorts of victimization, possibly even police charges arising out of public disorders. The grim backcloth is supplied by Tacitus's remark (*Ann.* xv. 44) that Christians were 'loathed because of their abominations', as well as by Suetonius's unconcealed approval (*Nero* xvi. 2) of Nero's violent measures against 'a class of people animated by a novel and mischievous superstition'.

The cumbrous phrase **in cases where** is an attempt to do justice to the elusive Greek *en hōi* ('in which' or 'in what'—a favourite expression of the writer's: cf. i. 6; iii. 16; iv. 4). Some render it simply 'whenever', but this indeterminate temporal sense is excluded by the specific future reference in **glorify** (*doxasōsin*). The meaning is brought out by such a paraphrase as 'in the very matter in which . . .'. The Greek represented by

through taking note . . . is also awkwardly expressed, and a literal translation would be 'as a result of your good works, as they observe them'. The verb used (*epopteuein*) is in the present participle, and thus suggests observing for a continuous period, perhaps also reflecting about what they see. In the mystery religions it acquired a technical meaning, standing for the privileged glimpse of the cult objects to which the higher initiates (hence called *epoptai*) were admitted. Some argue that it hints at esoteric spiritual vision here, but such ideas are quite foreign to the context; the straightforward, natural meaning is entirely adequate, as also at iii. 2, where the same verb is similarly used.

In the Bible **visitation** (*episkope*) is generally a divine prerogative, an inquest which God conducts into men's doings, and while it can result in punishment (Is. x. 3; Jer. vi. 15; x. 15; xi. 23), it can also bring acquittal and blessing (Gen. l. 24; Job x. 12; Is. xxiii. 17; Wis. iii. 7; iv. 15). In Lk. xix. 44 (cf. i. 68) 'the day of visitation' refers to the Messiah's offer of salvation. Commentators tend to equate **the day of visitation** here either with the day of judgment or with some intermediate intervention which brings the truth of the gospel home to unbelievers, but the antithesis fails to take account of the eschatological tension presupposed in the letter. For the writer God's final **visitation** is close at hand, is indeed already breaking in and taking effect. So it is his hope that, persuaded by the attractiveness of the Asian Christians' lives, their hitherto slanderous neighbours will not only form a favourable opinion of the Church (this idea is not expressed, but is present), but will themselves be converted to the same faith. Thus God's **visitation** will be merciful, for He will find them 'glorifying' Him for the grace inspiring and revealed in the **good actions** which have changed their hearts.

This last point needs underlining if his preoccupation with practical Christianity, which comes to the fore whatever topic he is treating and is exemplified by his constant references to 'conduct' (i. 15; 18; ii. 12; iii. 1; 2; 16) and 'doing good' (*agathopoiein*, etc.: ii. 14; 15; 20; iii. 6; 17; iv. 19: cf. also iii. 13), is to be seen in true perspective. Good actions, as he understands them, are not 'good works' of the Jewish type, i.e. works done for the benefit of widows, the poor, the dead, etc. They cover, as paragraph after paragraph shows, the whole range of upright behaviour, and are to be practised to one's neighbour as such, regardless of his status, condition, religion or race. Their mainspring is not human goodness, but God's call (cf. i. 15); and their object is not to merit glory for oneself, but to fulfil one's Christian vocation and commend the gospel to unbelievers. Thus his concern does not betoken (as is sometimes alleged) a bourgeois, second-generation Christianity, but has its source in our Lord's teaching; it finds an apt parallel in Paul's insistence (Gal. vi. 9: cf. Rom. ii. 7; 2 Cor. ix. 8; 2 Thess. ii. 17) that we should not 'grow weary in well-doing'.

6. PRACTICAL ADVICE: (ii) THE CHRISTIAN CITIZEN
ii. 13-17

(13) Be subject for the Lord's sake to every human creature—whether to the emperor as sovereign, (14) or to governors as sent under his commission for the punishment of wrongdoers and the commendation of those who do right. (15) For such is God's will, that by doing right you should put the ignorance of foolish men to silence. (16) Live as free men, but without using your freedom as a covering for wickedness—in fact, as servants of God. (17) Do honour to all, love the brotherhood, fear God, honour the emperor.

To give practical illustrations of the 'good actions' (ii. 12) required by the gospel, the writer inserts a lengthy passage (ii. 13-iii. 12) which consists in the main of a series of short codes of duties, each adapted to a particular class or grouping of persons (citizens, wives, slaves, etc.). Numerous examples of such codes are found elsewhere in the NT (e.g. Eph. v. 21-vi. 9; Col. iii. 18-iv. 1; 1 Tim. ii. 8-15; Tit. ii. 1-10) and other early Christian documents (e.g. *Did.* iv. 9-11; *1 Clem.* i. 3; xxi. 6-9; *Barn.* xix. 5-7; Polycarp, *Phil.* iv. 2-vi. 2). We have plenty of evidence that the arrangement of ethical instruction in classified lists of this kind (e.g. duties to one's gods, country, parents, brothers, wife, children, etc.) had become conventional practice in popular Stoic morality (cf. esp. Epictetus, *Diss.* ii. 14. 8; 17. 31; Seneca, *Ep.* xciv. 1; Hierocles, in Stobaeus, *Anth.* i. 3. 53), and that a closely similar pattern of duties had been taken over by Hellenistic Judaism (e.g. Tob. iv. 3-21; Ecclus. vii. 18-35; Ps. Phocylides, *Gnom.* 175-227; Josephus, *C. Ap.* ii. 198-210; Philo, *Decal.* 165-67). The Christian scheme is broadly the same in structure and content, and so it appears that, when the apostolic Church set about working out its practical moral catechesis, it freely plundered existing models, modifying them in details in the light of its own theology and supplying the appropriate Christian motivation.

13 The first sub-division is concerned with the Christian in the state. But it opens with a general charge: **Be subject for the Lord's sake to every human creature.** The Greek represented by the last three words (*pasēi anthrōpinēi ktisei*) is usually rendered either as 'every human institution' (RSV; NEB) or as 'every institution ordained for men' (RSVm, following Hort), but neither version is possible. So far from meaning 'institution', 'ordinance' (AV), or 'authority', the noun *ktisis* always in the Bible signifies 'creation' or, concretely, 'creature'; and there is always the thought of God as Creator behind it. Further, it is inconceivable that the writer should have regarded the state or civil authorities as 'ordinances of men'. These considerations rule out the former of the two customary interpretations. The latter, as well as missing the true import of *ktisis*, puts an intolerable strain on the adjective 'human'. The key to this difficult verse lies in recognizing that the theme of mutual service and submission stated in **Be subject** runs all through ii. 13-iii. 12, the verb itself recurring at ii. 18 and iii. 1 and its underlying idea pervading iii. 7-9. We are thus warranted in taking this opening clause as a general heading to the several sections, with their particular pieces of advice, which follow. *Ktisis* can now be given the only sense which naturally belongs to it in the context, viz. **creature;** the writer is laying it down that the principle of the redeemed Christian life must not be self-assertion or mutual exploitation, but the voluntary sub-

ordination of oneself to others (cf. Rom. xii. 10; Eph. v. 21; Phil. ii. 3 f.). For a similar requirement at Qumran, cf., e.g., 1QS v. 23-25. This exegesis also brings out the point of **for the Lord's sake**. Many commentators refer this to Christ, but it is God who created the world and men; it is therefore out of regard for Him as Creator that we ought to behave humbly towards our fellow-creatures.

Passing from the general to the particular, the writer infers that this principle of voluntary subordination should colour first of all the Christian's attitude to state authorities: **whether to the emperor as sovereign, or to governors as sent under** 14 **his commission.** In the Greek the former officer is described (as in 17) as *basileus* (lit. 'king'), a title which was applied in the East to the client princes whom Rome permitted to reign (in Egypt, Palestine, Syria, Pergamum, etc.), but which belonged *par excellence* to **the emperor** (e.g. Jn. xix. 15; Acts xvii. 7; Rev. xvii. 9; 12; Josephus, *Bell. Iud.* v. 563). He is **sovereign,** i.e. has supreme power concentrated in his hands. In contrast the authority of **governors** (*hēgemones*), i.e. the 'legates' (or, in the case of less important provinces like Thrace and Judaea, 'procurators') and 'proconsuls' who administered the imperial and senatorial provinces respectively, is derivative; they hold it **under his commission** (lit. 'sent through him': strictly correct only in the case of provinces directly under the princeps) with certain specific objects in view, viz. **the punishment of wrongdoers and the commendation of those who do right.** The repression of crime, disorder and injustice is always a function of the state, but no indication is given how it rewards exemplary conduct. It is unlikely, in view of his correspondents' modest social status, that the writer is thinking of public honours (titles, laudatory inscriptions, statues, etc.), which cities in the ancient world tended to bestow relatively freely. In reproducing this axiom (Rom. xiii. 3) he is simply reminding them, in a quite general way, that governments are inclined to look approvingly on well conducted citizens.

The resemblance between ii. 13 f. and Rom. xiii. 1-7, where the point is also made that if you behave decently you will win the applause of the authorities, is obvious but has often been over-pressed. 1 Peter does not explicitly assert, as Paul does, that 'the powers that be are ordained by God', much less that resistance to them is resistance to Him; its statement is much terser, is differently motivated, and is remarkable for the distinction it draws between the princeps and provincial governors. It is therefore hazardous to assume, as many commentators have done, a direct literary relationship. The proper attitude to one's country was (as we have seen) a regular item in conventional classifications of duties, and was apparently included (cf. also 1 Tim. ii. 2; Tit. iii. 1) in Christian adaptations of them. More relevant is the tone of the passage to the date and circumstances of the letter. Granting that the writer was using stock material, it is hard to believe that he would have cast it in a form so favourable to the state at a time (e.g. Trajan's reign) when the imperial authorities as such (local magistrates were different, for when Christians were haled before them in the apostolic age they were usually charged with fomenting disorder, etc.) were actively executing anti-Christian policies. See Introduction, pp. 8-11; 28 f.

15 The writer gives a reason for, and amplifies, what he has just said: **For such is God's will . . .** The Greek construction is ambiguous, for the adverb *houtōs* (**such**: lit. 'so') might refer either back or forward; but the retrospective meaning consorts better with NT usage (cf. also *houtōs* in iii. 5). Thus the drift of the clause might be expressed by such a paraphrase as 'God's will is realized by your being dutifully obedient to the authorities', or (more narrowly) 'by your aligning yourselves with **those who do right**'. On this interpretation the following clause, **that by doing right you should put the ignorance of foolish men to silence,** is not strictly the predicate of **such is God's will,** but is a loosely attached explanatory afterthought which adds a further point: for Christians to conduct themselves in a blameless, public-spirited manner will not only win them esteem from officials, but give the lie to their calumniators. For the verb *phīmoun* (lit. 'muzzle': 1 Tim. v. 18) used metaphorically, cf. Mk. i. 25; iv. 39; Mt. xxii. 34. We have already heard (i. 6) of 'all sorts of painful trials' to which the Anatolian Christians are being subjected; here, as in ii. 12, the curtain is lifted a little, and we find that these consist, in part at any rate, of misrepresentation and slander which proceed, the writer

charitably suggests, from **ignorance,** but which undoubtedly land them, individually and corporately, in embarrassment and danger. The adjective **foolish** (*aphrōn*) is a common LXX description (cf. the Psalms, Wisdom literature—esp. Proverbs) of the arrogant unbeliever who sets himself up against truth and right.

Christians in the primitive Church spoke with assurance of their 'freedom in Christ' (Gal. ii. 4), and the writer evidently senses that his stress on submission to the civil power may arouse disappointment and discouragement. So he hastens to correct any such impression. **Live as free men,** he interjects 16 (in the Greek there is no verb; the nominative adjective **free** stands on its own and, like the participle **using,** is best explained as complementing the preceding injunction). But liberty easily degenerates into licence, and so the liberty of the Christian man calls for careful definition: he must not use it **as a covering for wickedness.** In view of his relationship to God it is always subject to certain constraints, but properly understood these are simply pressures of the divine will which result in his being truly free. Hence the paradox: Christians are **free men,** enjoying a freedom which their neighbours in the world around them cannot know, but what ensures this freedom is precisely the fact that they are **servants of God.**

Again the writer is handling material which was already conventional in the Church. It was commonplace teaching that Christ had brought men freedom (e.g. Mt. xvii. 26; Lk. iv. 18-21; Jn. viii. 32; Rom. viii. 2; 1 Cor. vii. 22; 2 Cor. iii. 17; Gal. v. 1). Through His saving act they are free from the power of the Law, from sin, from the evil forces of the world; the term had become a proud catchword. Freedom, in the sense of the interior independence of the wise man, was of course a favourite theme of contemporary Stoicism, and the Stoic ideal reappears in Hellenistic Jewish writers like Philo (cf. his *Quod omnis probus liber sit*). But the Christian conception had two distinguishing features. First, the Christian's freedom is not the fruit of dogged striving after self-mastery but is the gift of God through grace; and, secondly, it finds its fulfilment in service to God (e.g. Rom. vi. 22; 1 Cor. vii. 21-23) and one's brethren (e.g. Gal. v. 13). Like Paul (Rom. vi. 15) and others (e.g. 2 Pet. ii. 19), our writer is evidently aware of, and quick to guard against, antinomian attempts to misrepresent and abuse it.

17 He then gathers the Christian's social obligations together in a single, four-membered injunction: **Do honour to all, love the brotherhood, fear God, honour the emperor.** While the first imperative is aorist, the other three are present, and this has puzzled commentators. One explanation proposed (so NEB) is that the first serves as a general heading while the others spell out its content; but this must be rejected since (a) it is unlikely that a Greek reader would have attributed this general force to the aorist here; (b) it is incredible that the author intended 'fearing God' to be taken as a particular instance of 'honouring all', or indeed could have included **God** under **all**; (c) it seems clear that **all** denotes mankind, pagans and Jews as well as Christians, as opposed to **the brotherhood**. Probably too much has been made of the change of tenses; though the writer's use of the aorist imperative is generally correct (see, e.g., on i. 13), the subtle nuances of classical Greek were being eroded in the 1st cent. and there are other examples of inexplicable tense variations in imperatives in the NT (e.g. Rom. vi. 13; 2 Tim. iv. 5). As a matter of fact the commands divide neatly into two pairs, with **all** balanced by **brotherhood** and **God** by **emperor**; and they are also arranged chiastically, the second verb having a richer content than the first and the third than the fourth.

The splendid recognition in the first command of the reverence due to personality as such (**all** covers human beings of every race, religion, sex, class, etc.) deserves notice. It recalls *Pirke Aboth* iv. 1 (compiled A.D. 70-170): 'Who is honoured? He who honours mankind', where the reason given is that he thereby honours God. Here the controlling thought (see on 13) is similar, viz. that men are God's creatures. On the other hand, while showing respect to men in general, the readers are bidden to **love the brotherhood**, i.e. their fellow-Christians (the word 'church' nowhere appears in the letter). In the LXX this noun (*adelphotēs*) is found with the meaning 'brotherly relationship', understood either literally (4 Macc. ix. 23; x. 3; 15) or metaphorically (1 Macc. xii. 10; 17). As a collective term connoting a group of society it occurs first in the NT (only here and at v. 9) and is clearly a Christian coinage (Perdelwitz's suggestion that its adoption may have been influenced by the Mithraic term *phratria*, i.e. 'fellowship', is far-fetched and quite unnecessary). The special duty of mutual love (the verb is *agapān*) between Christians is grounded (see on i. 22: 'love of your brothers') on the fact that they are brothers in Christ.

The second pair of commands is modelled on Prov. xxiv. 21; but whereas there one is counselled to 'fear God and the king', here a sharp distinction is drawn between the attitudes appropriate to each. God is to be 'feared' (for this basic religious response, see on i. 17) because He is the Holy One, our Creator and Judge; the civil power is on a different plane, and while it calls for our loyal respect, this is defined by the more general, non-religious term **honour**. Our Lord Himself differentiated (Mt. xxii. 21 and parrs.) between our duties to God and to Caesar, and advised His disciples (Mt. x. 28) to fear only God. A slight but significant difference from Rom. xiii. 7 can be discerned, for Paul explicitly states that both fear (he is, of course, using the word in its non-religious sense) and honour may be due to civil authorities. The divergence from Hellenistic and Oriental ideas is much more striking: cf. Plutarch's story (*Themist.* xxvii. 4) that the Persians reckoned it the fairest of their customs 'to honour the monarch and worship him as the image of the God Who preserves all things'.

Like Rom. xiii. 1-7, as also Mt. xxii. 21; 1 Tim. ii. 1-3; Tit. iii. 1, this passage (inserted in the first instance, no doubt, so as to ensure that the demeanour of the Anatolian converts towards their hostile neighbours might be conciliatory and positive) has had a determining influence on the Church's teaching about the duties Christians owe the state. It is also illuminating for the attitude of the primitive community to the problem—all the more so if it was written when **the emperor** was in fact Nero, whose governors' policies may have brought him popularity in certain provinces, but who was personally execrated in the capital except by the masses with whom he curried favour. Basically it was an OT attitude, which took its rise in early prophecy and was widely, if not universally, accepted by Jews at the beginning of the 1st cent. and even later. Its presupposition was that God, the Creator of the world, was also Lord of history, and so might use pagan powers like Assyria (Is. v. 25-29; x. 5-11) and foreign rulers like Cyrus (Is. xlv. 1) and Nebuchadnezzar (Jer. xxv. 9; xxvii. 6; xliii. 10) as His instruments. Thus we learn from Philo (*Leg. ad Gai.* 157; 355 f.) and Josephus (*Bell. Iud.* ii. 197; *C. Ap.* ii. 77) that sacrifices were regularly offered in the Temple for the emperor and the empire (for similar Christian intercessions, cf. 1 Tim. ii. 1 f.; *1 Clem.* lx. 4-lxi. 2). It was natural that Christian ethical codes should reflect this respect for authority, and indeed the eschatological expectation in which Christians lived in the apostolic age gave them special reasons for regarding the empire as serving a providential purpose (so, according to many, 2 Thess. ii. 6 f.).

7. PRACTICAL ADVICE: (iii) SLAVES
ii. 18-25

(18) House-servants, be subject to your masters with all fear, not only to the ones that are kind and considerate, but also to the harsh. (19) For this is a fine thing, if a man who is suffering unjustly puts up with the pain because of his consciousness of God. (20) For what credit is it if you take it patiently when you do wrong and are beaten? But if when you act rightly and suffer you take it patiently, that is a fine thing in God's sight. (21) For it is to this that you have been called, because Christ himself suffered on your behalf, leaving you a pattern, that you might follow his tracks: (22) who committed no sin, and no deception was found in his mouth; (23) who when he was reviled did not revile in return, when he suffered did not threaten but entrusted his cause to him who judges justly; (24) who himself bore our sins in his body on the tree so that, having broken with our sins, we might live for righteousness: by whose bruise you have been healed. (25) For you were wandering astray like sheep, but have now turned to the Shepherd and Guardian of your souls.

The writer probably assigns priority, and so much space, to slaves (they are, significantly, never mentioned in pre-Christian codes) because a large proportion, perhaps the bulk, of his correspondents belonged to this class. This also explains why they are so often singled out for counsel in the NT (1 Cor. vii. 21; Eph. vi. 5-8; Col. iii. 22-25; 1 Tim. vi. 1 f.; Tit. ii. 9 f.: cf. *Did.* iv. 11; *Barn.* xix. 7). Economically and politically, 1st cent. society was based on slavery, and this was the status not only of artisans, labourers, domestic helps and clerks, but of the majority of teachers, doctors and 'professional' people generally. Legally and in fact the slave was the chattel of his master, whose power over him, though limited to a certain extent by law and custom, was in theory almost absolute. To modern Christians the whole institution seems repulsive, and they are initially surprised and shocked to discover that the apostolic writers never question or criticize slavery as such or deplore the master's right to order his slaves about and punish them. Paul, e.g., not only habitually advises slaves to accept their lot cheerfully (Eph. vi. 5-8; Col. iii. 22-25), but even suggests that, if offered a chance of freedom, they should choose to remain slaves (1 Cor. vii. 21). Understandably he expects Christian masters to show justice, kindliness, indeed brotherly love, to them (Eph. vi. 9; Col. iv. 1; Phm. 16); but there is no hint in his writings of the natural equality of men which we find inculcated, e.g., in contemporary Stoicism. The reason for this conservatism is not primarily, as is often maintained, the early Church's preoccupation with the approaching End, or its fear that, if it encouraged social revolution, it would get embroiled with the authorities and also expose its poorer members to unemployment. Rather it was the burning conviction of these early Christians that, through their fellowship with Christ, they had entered into a relationship of brotherhood with one another in which ordinary social distinctions, real enough in the daily round of life in the world, had lost all meaning (Gal. iii. 28; 1 Cor. xii. 13; Col. iii. 11; Phm. 8-18). Slavery might be, indeed was, inherently wrong, but the NT authors do not seem to have grasped this; they were not so much concerned with natural ethics as with the ethics of the redeemed community.

So the writer instructs **House-servants** to **be subject with** 18 **all fear** to their **masters.** Although the noun he uses to address them (*oiketai*) strictly means 'domestic helps', the persons concerned are in fact slaves. In the original the verb (*hupotasso-menoi*) is not, as we should expect in normal Greek, an impera-tive, but a nominative present participle used for one: for this rabbinic Hebrew idiom, see on i. 14. He does not, we should notice, seek to mitigate the submissive loyalty which slaves should show their masters. As the sequel indicates, it includes the meek acceptance of brutal treatment, and is to be offered **not only to** masters who **are kind and considerate, but also to the harsh** (*skolios*: lit. 'bent', 'crooked'; so of people, figuratively, 'perverse', 'awkward to deal with'). The motive he suggests, however, is a profoundly religious one: their obedience is to be carried out **with all fear.** This does not mean dread of their masters (fear of men is rejected in iii. 14), but rather (cf. the use of 'fear' in i. 17; ii. 17; iii. 2; also the similar command in Eph. vi. 5) awe and reverence for God, in whose sight they accomplish their daily tasks.

19   This idea is elaborated in the next verse, where it is claimed that **this is a fine thing, if a man who is suffering unjustly puts up with the pain because of his consciousness of God.** The opening clause literally reads 'this is a grace', i.e. an act which is intrinsically attractive and thus wins God's approval (cf. the same phrase expanded in 20 below). For this sense of 'grace' (*charis*), so unlike the distinctively Pauline one, cf. Lk. vi. 32-34 (sayings of Christ which, in the view of many, the present passage echoes). In the Bible the term can cover both the gracious action and the appreciation or gratitude which it naturally evokes.

    The following words give a realistic glimpse of the arbitrary ill-treatment to which slaves might be subjected in the ancient world. The writer recognizes that it can be 'unjust', differing in this from, e.g., Aristotle, who maintains (*Eth. Nic.* v. 6. 8 f.) that a man cannot be unjust to his slave since the latter is his property. (A humaner attitude, it may be remarked, prevailed in practice, and in the 1st cent. was encouraged by Stoicism.) Even so, he commends the Christian slave who **puts up with** his painful beating **because of his consciousness of God.** The Greek phrase (*dia suneidēsin theou*) setting out this praiseworthy motive is extremely obscure and has caused commentators a great deal of trouble. The key-word *suneidēsis* normally in the

NT (it is also found in Acts, Paul, the Pastorals, Hebrews)
approximates to the English 'conscience', and this is the sense
it bears at iii. 16; 21 (where see notes). Many therefore argue
that this must be its meaning here: cf. the traditional version
'for conscience towards God' (AV; RV), and E. G. Selwyn's
more sophisticated 'for conscience' sake before God'. Their
difficulty is the genitive **of God** (*theou*), which clearly cannot be
possessive ('God's conscience'). Some seek to explain it as a
genitive of source (conscience is informed by God, and the
slave would have a troubled conscience if he did not endure
patiently), others as a 'genitive of inner reference' (cf. Bengel's
paraphrase: 'the consciousness of a mind which does things
good and pleasing to God even though they please no man');
but these are tortuous expedients which yield unsatisfactory
interpretations.

The awkwardness of the genitive, if *suneidēsis* is assumed to
signify 'conscience', was early appreciated and gave rise to the
insertion of *katharan* ('pure') alongside *theou* in some MSS and
in place of it in others. The correct solution lies in recognizing
that (a) by all the rules of Greek usage the genitive can only
be objective; and (b) *suneidēsis* (lit. 'knowing-with'), while
ordinarily signifying a knowledge shared with oneself (i.e.
moral self-awareness, conscience), can also denote a knowledge
shared with others (so almost certainly at Rom. xiii. 5: cf.
TWNT VI, 914 f.). Thus the puzzling phrase here might be
paraphrased, 'because of the knowledge of God which he and
his fellow-Christians share as members of God's holy people'.
This knowledge in the strength of which the Christian slave
cheerfully bears affliction is not simply knowledge of God's
existence, but awareness of His whole relation to him and
insight into His purpose for His people, as this is expounded
more fully in 21.

Already the idea of Christ as the supreme example of innocent
suffering is forming itself in the writer's mind. So he points out,
by means of a rhetorical question, that it is no **credit . . . if you 20
take it patiently when you do wrong and are beaten.** Some
brazen spirits might be disposed to boast to their fellow-slaves
of their toughness under physical castigation, but boasting
is out of place when the punishment is deserved. The verb

rendered 'beat' (*kolaphizein*: 'strike with the fist') is the one used at Mk. xiv. 65 of the blows given to Jesus at His trial; but although the passion is in the writer's thoughts, his choice of this blunt word from common speech is probably not intended as an allusion to it. As regards rough treatment, the position is radically different **when you act rightly** (again his favourite verb *agathopoiein*: see on ii. 12) **and suffer** (the customary addition of 'for it' here and in 19, as also in iii. 17, is too strong, and brings out rather more than the Greek contains). In a cruel predicament like that meekness and patience are **a fine thing in God's sight.** It is no accident that, instead of using **credit** (*kleos*: 'glory', 'prestige') as in the first half of the verse, he reverts to **a fine thing** (*charis*: see on 19) in the second. Human beings naturally look for fame and reputation from one another, but they cannot expect them as a right from God (Rom. iv. 2), whose favour is granted freely since good works are in fact the result of His grace.

The writer now unfolds the deeper motive implicit in the seemingly strange advice he has been giving. Submissive acceptance of treatment that is patently unfair is a fine and Christian thing precisely because the Lord Himself behaved in that way and the Christian's vocation is to imitate Him. Grounded in His own teaching (Mk. viii. 34 and parrs.), the thought of Christ in His humility, suffering and patience as the model for His followers has left a deep imprint on early Christian literature (e.g. Phil. ii. 5-8; 1 Thess. i. 6; 2 Thess. iii. 5; Heb. xiii. 13; 21 *1 Clem.* xvi. 17; Ignatius, *Eph.* x. 3). So **it is to this,** the writer can say, i.e. to patient and cheerful endurance of maltreatment when you least deserve it, **that you have been called.** As in the NT generally, his reference is to God's saving call in Christ, but just as its end is specified at ii. 9; v. 10, so here he spells out its moral content and purpose (cf. 1 Thess. iv. 7: 'not uncleanness but holiness'; Gal. v. 13: 'freedom'; 1 Cor. vii. 15; Col. iii. 15: 'peace'). In the present context, however, there may also be a fleeting allusion to his correspondents' baptism, in which their calling found sacramental expression.

He proceeds to elaborate his point in a passage (21b-25) which, with its heightened tone and rhythmic parallelisms, bears unmistakable signs of consisting largely of a liturgical citation or citations (cf. i. 18-21 and iii. 18-22 for similar excerpts). The introductory particle **because** (*hoti*), the four times repeated relative pronoun, the sudden transition in 24 from the homiletic 'you' to the first person plural, and above all the contents (cf. esp. the stress on the vicarious nature of Christ's sufferings, which is a theme that is strictly irrelevant to the conduct of slaves) point in the same direction. According to some commentators the whole section is a continuous extract from a hymn, but the opening words, **Christ himself** (lit. 'also': in any case no part of the citation) **suffered on your behalf,** have all the ring of a credal tag (cf., e.g., iii. 18; 1 Cor. xv. 3), and so are almost certainly distinct from the text worked over in 22-25. Some important MSS, we should note, read 'died' (*apethanen*), but **suffered** (*epathen*) is to be preferred. Although at first sight less obvious, it has superior MS support (including Pap. 72), and the scribes who altered it, doubtless so as to conform with the commoner usage (Rom. v. 6; viii. 34; xiv. 9; 15; 1 Cor. xv. 3; etc.), failed to observe that (a) **suffered** suits the argument better, which is about suffering; and (b) in the idiom of the apostolic age (e.g. Mk. viii. 31; Lk. xxii. 15; Acts xvii. 3; Heb. xiii. 12) the Lord's 'suffering' could be taken to include His death. Similarly a number of MSS and versions, again prompted by the conventional formula, read 'on our behalf'. It seems probable that 'our' stood in the original confession, but that the writer, who is still in a hortatory vein, changed it in order to make the citation directly applicable to his correspondents. The reminder that the passion was **on your behalf** no doubt introduces a fresh and deeper motive for imitating Christ, but it is a mistake to press this unduly. The phrase is not brought in to emphasize in any special way the vicarious aspect of Christ's sufferings, but mainly because it was an integral part of the credal sentence quoted.

The next words, **leaving you a pattern, that you might follow his tracks,** clearly belong neither to the credal fragment nor to the hymn excerpt which follows. They are a homiletical gloss, slipped in to drive the writer's moral home with a couple of picturesque, if somewhat discordant, metaphors. The usual rendering 'example' for the first is colourless compared with the rare Greek *hupogrammos* (first found in 2 Macc. ii. 28; as

9

used of Christ, cf. *1 Clem*. xvi. 17), which still has the air of the
schoolroom clinging to it. To judge by Plato, *Prot*. 326d (the
cognate verb), and Clement Alex., *Strom*. v. 8. 49, it originally
connoted an outline tracing of letters to be copied by children
learning the alphabet, or else artificial words containing all the
letters: cf. Origen's description (*De orat*. xviii. 1) of the Our
Father as 'the prayer traced out (*hupographeisan*) by the Lord'.
From this, without losing its classroom associations, it came to
mean a **pattern** or model in general. So too the image conveyed
in **follow his tracks** (cf. Rom. iv. 12; 2 Cor. xii. 18) was much
more alive than the inert English 'follow in his steps' (e.g.
RSV; NEB). The Greek *ichnos* signifies the actual footprint (in
the case of game, the spoor), and in the plural the line of such
footprints; to follow a man's footprints is to move in the direction he is going. Thus the writer's plea is not that slaves should
attempt to reproduce all the particular details of Christ's passion
which he is recapitulating. That is in any case excluded since He
suffered for you, bore our sins, etc. Rather it is that they should
expect to have to suffer, and to suffer without having in any way
earned it, and that they should be ready to exhibit the same
uncomplaining acceptance.

After this short interjection the writer returns to quotation
(22-25). This time it is a liturgical text, possibly a hymn, consisting almost entirely of extracts from or reminiscences of the
fourth of Deutero-Isaiah's Servant Songs (Is. lii. 13-liii. 12),
22 which he applies to his readers' situation. Thus he begins: **who
committed no sin, and no deception was found in his
mouth.** The sentence is taken almost literally from Is. liii. 9,
and in it as in the following verses Christ's passion is interpreted
in the light of the great picture of the Servant of the Lord, with
whom He is identified. The chief (perhaps only) variation from
the LXX (found occasionally in the fathers: e.g. Eusebius, *Dem.
ev*. i. 10. 16) is the substitution of **sin** (*hamartian*) for 'lawless-
ness' (*anomian*). If it is intentional, it brings out quite unambiguously Christ's innocence in relation to God; in the
original the Servant is described as guiltless in relation to other
men. The writer has already hinted (i. 19) at Christ's sinlessness,
which Paul also (2 Cor. v. 21: an echo possibly of the same hymn)
took for granted: so Jn. viii. 46; Heb. vii. 26; 1 Jn. iii. 5. In any

case the words are an impressive reminder to maltreated slaves, when they are tempted to protest their innocence, that Christ their Lord, the Servant whose agony the prophet had foreseen, had been no less blameless.

Turning from Christ's character to His demeanour, the writer recalls, again with an eye to his correspondents' reaction to their persecutors, that he **when he was reviled did not revile 23 in return, when he suffered did not threaten but entrusted his cause to him who judges justly.** According to some (e.g. R. Bultmann), this piece reproduces too faithfully actual incidents of the passion to be part of the text cited; it must be a homiletic insertion of the author's own. But again the careful antitheses, as well as the introductory **who,** connect it with the liturgical context, and it was probably the aptness of its contents which instigated him to incorporate the passage as a whole. While in no sense a quotation, the first two clauses seem inspired by the moving description of the Servant in Is. liii. 7 ('In spite of being afflicted, he does not open his mouth . . . like a lamb dumb before his shearer, he does not open his mouth'), the detail being modified by recollection of the treatment meted out to Jesus (for the insults, cf. Mk. xiv. 65; xv. 17-20; 29-32; for His silence, cf. Mk. xiv. 61; xv. 5; Lk. xxiii. 9). In the third clause **entrusted** (*paredidou*) may have been suggested by Is. liii. 6; 12. While some detect here an echo of the cry from the cross (Lk. xxiii. 46), it is preferable to regard **his cause** as the implied object of the verb (there is none in the Greek) rather than 'himself' (AV; RV): for parallel formulae, cf. Jer. xi. 20; Josephus, *Ant.* iv. 33; vii. 199. The point is, not that the Lord was concerned about His own fate, but that, confident though He was of His righteousness, He preferred to leave its vindication to God rather than take action Himself against His enemies. Slaves driven to despair by misunderstanding and cruelty should do likewise in the knowledge that God **judges justly.** The idea that the Christian should not retaliate, but should leave matters in God's hands since judgment belongs to Him, is a stock element in the primitive catechesis (e.g. iii. 9; Rom. xii. 17-20; 1 Thess. v. 15; Polycarp, *Phil.* ii.—based on 1 Peter).

The variant 'unjustly' (*adikōs*; Lat. *injuste*) instead of **justly** (*dikaiōs*) deserves remark. It appears in the Vulgate but not in any Greek MS, but is very ancient since it is attested by Clement of Alexandria and Cyprian. The unjust judge to whom Christ surrenders Himself is Pilate, and the reading represents an attempt to assimilate the passage even more closely to the record of the passion.

The citation now resumes direct contact with the Servant Song, taking up and expanding the reference to Christ's sacrificial death in 21 above, and incidentally developing ideas of import to all mankind and not just slaves (after all, it had not been originally composed with their special needs in view).

24 Thus **who himself bore our sins in his body on the tree** reproduces, with appropriate modifications, Is. liii. 12, which states that the Servant 'bore the sins of many'. This theme indeed runs through the Song like a refrain (cf. esp. liii. 4: 'he bears our sins and is made to suffer agony for us'). The word translated **tree** (*xulon*: lit. 'wood') is an archaic expression for the cross (properly *stauros*, a term not found in 1 Peter) used in speeches in Acts (v. 30; x. 39; xiii. 29) and in Gal. iii. 13 (quoting Dt. xxi. 23, where it means 'gallows'). Both in classical Greek and in Dt. xxi. 22 f. it had associations with the punishment of malefactors, and as applied to the crucifixion it already contained a theology of the atonement.

Commentators are divided about the exegesis. Many favour such a translation as 'carried up our sins in his body to the tree' (RVm; RSVm; NEB), pointing out that the verb (*anapherein*: cf. ii. 5) is commonly used in the LXX (e.g. Lev. xiv. 20) of bringing a sacrifice to the altar, and that the preposition before **the tree** (accusative case) is *epi*, which with the accusative properly signifies motion towards. But the notion of the cross as such as an altar is absent from the NT (even from Heb. xiii. 10), while that of sin being placed on the altar and slain there is impossible to reconcile with OT conceptions. Others hold that the imagery of the scapegoat (Lev. xvi), on which the high priest put the sins of the people on the Day of Atonement, is in mind, Christ being understood as taking our sins similarly on Himself. It may well be peripherally present, for although the scapegoat was not killed but driven into the wilderness, the dominant idea here is the removal of sin. Various strands from the OT sacrificial system are doubtless intertwined, but on the whole the rendering given above points to the true interpretation. The difficulty of *epi* has been exaggerated, for (a) the strict classical usage was breaking down in late Greek (e.g. Mt. xiv. 25; Rev. xiii. 1, which give accusatives where we should expect genitives), and (b) the idea of having got there, i.e. of motion towards, is in any case latent in **on the tree.** Here, as in Is. liii. 12, 'bearing sins' means taking the blame for sins, accepting the punishment due for them, and so securing their putting away. This is in line with the sense this and similar expressions have in the LXX (e.g. Ex. xxviii. 43; Lev. xxiv. 15; Num. xiv. 33). As already remarked, **our** confirms that this is a liturgical piece currently used in the community. The force of **in his body** is that what Christ did He did as man, sharing our human nature. The implied teaching is that His sufferings and death were vicarious; as our representative He endured the penalties which **our sins** merited.

The further purpose of Christ's death is defined in terms, not of forgiveness or remission of guilt, but of the abandonment of sin; His saving act is a challenge to moral renewal. He suffered **so that, having broken with our sins, we might live for righteousness.** Many translations (e.g. RV; RSV), under the influence of the Pauline theology (e.g. Rom. vi. 10 f.), give 'having died to sins'; but while the verb used (*apogignesthai*) can mean 'die' in appropriate contexts, its original and natural meaning is 'be away from', 'have no part in', 'cease from'. In view of the following **live**, the idea of dying is probably in the background, but the text does not bring it forward in the vigorous way Paul does. The thought has undoubted affinities with the great conceptions which the Apostle unfolds in Rom. vi, but it is independently worked out and less profound; in particular, the distinctively Pauline theology of a mystical union and death with Christ in baptism is only obscurely discernible (see on iv. 1). As in iii. 14, **righteousness** denotes the high standard of moral behaviour expected of Christians. The lesson inculcated is that, Christ having borne the penalty of our sins, it is up to us to relinquish our previous courses and reorientate our lives.

The hymn or liturgical extract closes with language again borrowed from Is. liii: **by whose bruise you have been**

25 **healed. For you were wandering astray like sheep.** The
prophet had written (liii. 5 f.) of the Servant of the Lord: 'By
his bruise we have been healed. We were all wandering astray
like sheep.' It is likely that the first person 'we' stood in the
original text of the citation, as in Is. liii. 5 f.; the writer has substituted the second person so as to adapt the message to the
slaves whom he is particularly addressing. Deutero-Isaiah's
imagery was admirably relevant to their condition, for bruises
(*mōlōps* connoted the weal or discoloured swelling left by a blow
from a fist or whip) were probably frequent in their experience.
There is encouragement for them in the reminder that the Son
of God Himself patiently bore such brutal injuries. But pro-
founder still is the claim, which is the principal theme of the
hymn itself, that Christ's passion was vicariously beneficial;
as a result of His sufferings sinful men have been **healed**,
i.e. restored to health from the wounds which their sins had
inflicted.

In the following clauses too, as above, the text cited must
itself have had the first person, but the writer has altered it to
you, again so as to make the words directly applicable to his
correspondents. As so modified the sentence, in addition to
giving a graphic sketch of Christ as the saviour and defender of
Christians, contains a revealing hint of the Anatolian Christians'
pagan past. Their **wandering astray like sheep** signifies that
they had previously been heathen, while the fact that they **have
now turned to the Shepherd and Guardian of** their **souls**
indicates their conversion. Its main point, however, is to assure
them that, whatever the trials and difficulties confronting them,
they have a trustworthy protector in Christ.

The picture of God shepherding His people recurs in all parts
of the OT (e.g. Gen. xlviii. 15; Ps. xxiii; Is. xl. 11), just as the
metaphor of scattered or shepherdless sheep is regularly applied
to Israel when misguided, discomfited or leaderless (e.g. Num.
xxvii. 17; 1 Kgs. xxii. 17; Ps. cxix. 176; Jer. l. 6). Beginning
with Jeremiah, however, the image acquires a messianic colouring: cf. Jer. xxiii. 3-6; xxxi. 10; Ezek. xxxiv. 23 f. ('I will set over
them one shepherd, my servant David, and he shall feed them');
xxxvii. 24. In the present passage there can be no doubt (cf.
'Chief Shepherd' in v. 4) that **the Shepherd** denotes Christ.

The title, which was to prove richly creative in Christian devotion and art (cf. paintings in the Roman catacombs, early mosaics and sculptures representing the Good Shepherd, etc.), is not applied to Him directly in the synoptic gospels and, apart from 1 Peter, is only found in Jn. x. 11 ff.; Heb. xiii. 20; Rev. vii. 17. Not only the Johannine use, however, but hints contained in such passages as Mt. x. 6; xv. 24 (cf. Ezek. xxxiv); xxv. 32; Mk. xiv. 27 f. (cf. Zech. xiii. 7b) suggest that Jesus spoke of Himself as shepherd in the OT messianic sense. See further TWNT VI, 486-98.

Christ's function as **Shepherd**, which includes ruling the people (e.g. Mic. v. 3: cited in Mt. ii. 6), is related more closely to the readers' situation by the accompanying predicate, **Guardian of your souls**. For **souls** as equivalent to 'yourselves', see on i. 9. The noun translated **Guardian** (*episkopos*) was to become the technical name for the Church's chief ministers ('bishops'), and was already in use as such in some at any rate of Paul's communities (Phil. i. 1). It is interesting to find it used along with the verb 'shepherd' in Paul's address to the elders of Miletus (Acts xx. 28). Here it has no ecclesiastical overtones, but retains its original connotation, viz. 'one who inspects, watches over, protects' (cf. the cognate verb *episkeptesthai*). In the LXX (Job xx. 29; Wis. i. 6) God is described as *episkopos*, while Philo calls Him 'overseer' (*ephoros*) and *episkopos* (*De mut. nom.* 216), and also 'the *episkopos* of the universe' (*De somn.* i. 91).

It is very unlikely that 25b, with its homiletic tone and clear allusion to the readers' conversion and urgent need of a vindicator, belongs to the citation proper. Perhaps the most fascinating aspect of the latter is the Servant Christology which it embodies and which our writer makes his own. According to the Synoptists (cf. esp. Mk. x. 45; xiv. 24 and parr.; Lk. xxii. 37: also Mk. i. 11), it was Jesus Himself who first related the figure of the Servant to the interpretation of His mission. NT scholars have formed very different estimates of this tradition, the more sceptical regarding it as a primitive attempt by the community to work out a scripture-based rationale of the passion, and others holding that it is an authentic and entirely credible reminiscence. Whatever our decision on this, there is no doubt that we have here a very ancient type of Christology which remained popular for a time but soon passed into abeyance. Jesus is actually called 'God's servant' (*pais*: the LXX word) in Acts iii. 13; 26; iv. 27; 30 (all passages where Peter is the speaker, or one of the speakers, as defenders of the Petrine authorship of the epistle are quick to point out); while Is. liii. 7 f. is cited in Acts viii. 32 f. as the key to His person and death. While Paul does not himself exploit the conception, there are possible echoes of it in credal forms or hymns which he reproduces (Rom. iv. 25; 1 Cor. xv. 3; Phil. ii. 5-11). Elsewhere in the NT its influence is discernible at Mt. viii. 16 f. and Heb. ix. 28; and it early found a place in liturgical usage (*Did.* ix. 2 f.; x. 2 f.; *1 Clem.* xvi. 3-14). The strong likelihood that the Servant Christology is of Palestinian origin is confirmed by the fact that in pre-Christian times a messianic interpretation was being read out of Is. xlii. 1 ff. and lii. 13 ff. in Palestinian Jewish circles (see TWNT V, 685-98). Although the atoning effect of the sufferings of the righteous was recognized in later Judaism, this did not extend to the sufferings of the Servant delineated in Is. liii; it was left to Christian faith to perceive that the prophet's vision had been fulfilled in the Messiah.

8. PRACTICAL ADVICE: (iv) MARRIED PEOPLE
iii. 1-7

(1) In the same way, wives, be subject to your husbands, so that if any do not obey the word they may be won over without a word by their wives' behaviour, (2) when they take note of your reverent, pure behaviour. (3) Your adornment should not be the external sort—braiding of the hair, wearing of gold trinkets, putting on of gowns—, (4) but the hidden person of the heart, with the imperishable quality of a gentle, tranquil spirit, which is very precious in God's sight. (5) For that was how in the old days the holy women who hoped in God used to adorn themselves, being submissive to their husbands, (6) just as Sarah obeyed Abraham, calling him her lord. It is her

children that you have become, if you do what is right and let nothing terrify you. (7) In the same way, husbands, show understanding in your marital relations, paying honour to the female as the weaker vessel, and also since you are joint heirs of the grace of life, so that your prayers may not be hindered.

Instructions for family life were regular in household codes (Eph. v. 22-vi. 4; Col. iii. 18-21; 1 Tim. ii. 8-15); and here, as in the advice to slaves, traditional material has been touched up so as to fit the Asian situation. Wives are singled out for mention first because the order is an ascending one (slaves, wives, husbands, the community generally). The greater length of the section assigned to them is due to the large proportion of women in the Asian congregations, and also to the special problems which the fact that many of them had pagan husbands created.

As with slaves, the writer's attitude is conservative, and he gives no hint that he regards the relative status of husbands and **wives** as radically altered by Christianity: **In the same way . . .** 1 **be subject to your husbands.** The opening words are not intended to equate the submissiveness due from wives with that expected from slaves. Rather, as in 7, the Greek adverb (*homoiōs*) harks back to ii. 13, implying that the patriarchal principle of the subordination of the wife to her husband is not a matter of human convention but the order which the Creator has established (so the NT writers generally: e.g. 1 Cor. xi. 3). It applies equally, the writer acknowledges, when the husband is a pagan. In compensation he makes it plain (7) that both sexes share without differentiation in the blessedness of the new life which God bestows, just as Paul affirms (Gal. iii. 28) that at the spiritual level distinctions of sex have been abolished for those who have put on Christ. As in ii. 18 (see note) and iii. 7, the verb (*hupotassomenai*) is the present participle used as an imperative. In the Greek the adjective *idiois* ('own': so AV; RV) appears before **husbands** (so too at 5), but at this stage it had lost its original force, and no special significance should be read into it.

As a particular motive for conjugal submissiveness the writer points out that it may help to commend the faith to pagan husbands. In the Anatolian churches there were evidently frequent cases of men who **do not obey the word,** i.e. the gospel message (see on ii. 8) as expounded either by Christian members of their households or, possibly, by official teachers visiting their homes or preaching at meetings to which they have accompanied their wives. Such people, it is argued, **may be won over without a word,** i.e. without any verbal propaganda, **by their wives' behaviour.** The older translation (AV; RV; but not RSV; NEB) 'without the word' is plainly wrong. The writer is not questioning the part of the gospel in their conversion. It must of course be the converting instrument, but in certain cases the eloquent silence of Christian deportment is its most effective vehicle. The presence of the definite article before the first **word** and its absence before the second in the Greek confirm that a verbal play is intended. The verb rendered 'win over' (*kerdainein*) literally means 'gain', 'make a profit' (so Jas. iv. 13); as a stock missionary term for 'make a Christian', virtually equivalent to 'save', it recurs five times in 1 Cor. ix. 19-22.

'For instruction', Chrysostom remarks (*Hom. in Heb.* xix. 1), 'action carries more weight than speech' (cf. also Philo, *De Ios.* 86). But Augustine's account (*Conf.* ix. 19-22) of the influence Monica had on his father Patricius ('she served her husband as her master, and did all she could to win him for You, speaking to him of You by her conduct, by which you made her beautiful. ... Finally, when her husband was at the end of his earthly span, she gained him for You') provides the aptest illustration of the writer's plea. In the next verse he spells it out in terms which

2 leave no room for misunderstanding: **when they take note of your reverent, pure behaviour** (again *anastrophē*: see on i. 15). For **take note of,** see on ii. 12; there is no suggestion here, any more than there, that the verb used (*epopteuein*) has any vestige of the specialized meaning it acquired in the mystery cults. In the original **reverent** is represented by the prepositional phrase *en phobōi* ('in fear') qualifying **pure behaviour;** what is meant is clearly not that Christian wives should dread their husbands, but that 'godly fear' (cf. i. 17) should be the mainspring of their lives. As their husbands observe their irreproachable conduct (while of course *hagnos*, i.e. **pure,** can mean 'chaste', it is not limited to sexual purity, and here, as in Phil. iv. 8; 1 Tim. v. 22;

Tit. ii. 5; Jas. iii. 17; 1 Jn. iii. 3, has a wider connotation), they will come to acknowledge the divine grace which inspires it.

Next, the writer insists that Christian women should be more concerned about the beauty of their characters than their outward appearances: **Your adornment should not be the ex-** 3 **ternal sort—braiding of the hair, wearing of gold trinkets, putting on of gowns.** Moralists in almost every age have inveighed against the preoccupation of superficial women with dress, coiffure, jewellery, etc.: cf. Is. iii. 18-24 (a scathing and minutely detailed indictment); Test. Reub. v. 5 (outward finery is deception); Philo, *De virt.* 39 f.; Plutarch, *Mor.* 141e ('that adorns a woman which makes her more decorous—not gold, emeralds, scarlet, but whatever invests her with dignity, good behaviour, modesty'); Epictetus, *Ench.* 40; Seneca, *De ben.* vii. 9. The elaboration in hair-styles, make-up, dress and personal jewellery in the 1st and 2nd cents. is eloquently attested by the literature and art of the period. The closely similar admonition in 1 Tim. ii. 9 f. suggests that both passages draw on stock catechetical material, and also that the congregations addressed included a number of well-off women. Later writers (e.g. Clement Alex., *Paed.* iii. 11. 66; Tertullian, *De orat.* xx.; *De cultu fem.* i. 6; ii. 7-13; Cyprian, *De hab. virg.* viii) take these texts literally as a wholesale ban on feminine finery, but the real object of the apostolic authors was a constructive one, to inculcate a proper sense of values. There are hints in the gospels (Mt. vi. 17 f.; Mk. xiv. 6; Lk. xv. 22) that our Lord's attitude on such matters was neither rigorist nor negative.

So our writer argues that the **adornment** appropriate to Christian wives is **the hidden person of the heart, with the** 4 **imperishable quality of a gentle, tranquil spirit.** The whole construction is distinctly clumsy, but he is plainly struggling to contrast interior character with outward appearance. By **hidden person** (lit. 'man') **of the heart** he means the unseen personality (for a rough parallel, cf. Paul's 'inner man' in Rom. vii. 22; 2 Cor. iv. 16), the genitive being either possessive ('the inner person who dwells in the heart') or appositional ('the unseen person, i.e. the heart'). As against the perishable ornaments with which some women deck their bodies, the Christian wife's secret personality should be clothed with (this seems

to be the force of **with**: cf. Jas. ii. 2, where the same preposition
en is used of clothes worn) something **imperishable**, viz. **a
gentle, tranquil spirit.** According to some this is the Spirit of
God which works in the baptized (cf. iv. 14), and they claim that
this is the normal meaning of *pneuma* ('spirit') in the NT, and
point to Paul's expression 'spirit of gentleness' (1 Cor. iv. 21;
Gal. vi. 1). But (a), since this gentle spirit is commended as
pleasing to God, it can hardly be the divine Spirit; and (b) in the
next verse the OT heroines, who had not received the Spirit in
baptism, are held up as models in respect of this very characteristic. So it is on balance preferable to take **spirit** as meaning here
'disposition', 'frame of mind', which is in fact the sense it
probably bears in 1 Cor. iv. 21 and Gal. vi. 1.

'Gentleness' or meekness (*praütēs*) is typical of Christ Himself (Mt. xi. 29; xxi. 5), and occupies a prominent place in NT
ethics (iii. 16; Mt. v. 5; Gal. v. 23; Eph. iv. 2; Col. iii. 12; Tit.
iii. 2; etc.), as also does 'quietness' (*hēsuchia*: 2 Thess. iii. 12;
1 Tim. ii. 11; 12; also 1 Thess. iv. 11). Here, as in ii. 20, the
readers are reminded that the final test of conduct is whether it
wins divine approval: **which is very precious in God's sight.**
Grammatically the neuter relative may be attached to either
imperishable quality or **gentle, tranquil spirit,** but as
spirit is so close to it the latter seems the more natural alternative. The thought behind the passage recalls 1 Sam. xvi. 7:
'Do not look on his appearance . . . for the Lord does not see as
man sees; man looks on the outward appearance, but the Lord
looks on the heart'.

To clinch his argument the writer appeals to revered exam-
5 ples from OT times: **that was how in the old days the holy
women who hoped in God used to adorn themselves,
being submissive to their husbands.** Once again the assumption is that the Church is continuous with, and the appointed
heir of, the OT revelation (cf. i. 1; 10 f.; ii. 9; 11; etc.); hence the
personages of the old covenant are types for those who belong
to the new. The women of Israel were **holy,** not in the sense of
being morally good or saintly, but of being called by God and
inspired by His Spirit (see on ii. 9). They **hoped in God,** i.e.
lived in the faith and expectation of the fulfilment of His
promises (cf. the great roll-call of the heroic figures of Israel in

Heb. xi, esp. xi. 13), as the Anatolian women in their time of trial should be doing. Further, they all exhibited (with persons so hallowed he has no need to go into details) precisely that preference for interior to external adornment and that domestic docility which he has been applauding.

His chief concern seems to be with the latter, for when he leaves generalization and selects a particular and supremely authoritative case, it is **Sarah, who obeyed Abraham, calling** 6 **him her lord.** She was the matron *par excellence* of the Chosen People (cf. Is. li. 2; Heb. xi. 11), and with Rebecca, Leah and Rachel was accounted one of its four mothers (SB I, 29 f.). In the new dispensation, just as Abraham was 'the father of all who believe' (Rom. iv. 11: cf. Gal. iii. 6-29; Heb. ii. 16; vi. 13-15; Jas. ii. 21; *I Clem.* xxxi. 2), i.e. of all Christians, so Sarah could be regarded as their mother, and Christian women in particular were her spiritual daughters. Moreover, scripture represents her as **calling** Abraham **her lord.** The reference is to the story of her amused incredulity at the promise that, despite her barrenness and Abraham's advanced age, she would bear him a son (Gen. xviii. 12: 'After I have waxed old, shall I have pleasure, my lord being old also?'). In fact, this manner of speaking of her husband conformed to conventional Eastern practice, but the rabbis expounded the text as demonstrating Sarah's obedience to Abraham (SB III, 764).

The writer then collects his thoughts together: **It is her children,** i.e. Sarah's spiritual daughters, **that you have become, if you do what is right and let nothing terrify you.** For the Biblical principle of true pedigree based on imitation, cf. Mt. v. 45; Jn. viii. 39; Rom. ix. 6-9: also Philo, *De virt.* 195. The main verb is in the aorist, and thus probably contains a specific reference to the baptism of the women addressed, when in the full sense they became members of the new Israel. In any case the choice of verb ('become') insinuates that they were formerly pagans; had they been Jews, they would have had no need to 'become' Sarah's daughters. The essential condition (this is expressed elliptically in the Greek, the two verbs which follow being present participles) is that they should **do what is right** (again the author's characteristic emphasis on good actions, this time with dutifulness to their husbands no doubt primarily in mind) **and let nothing terrify them.** This latter requirement, set out in words borrowed from Prov. iii. 25, has no connection with the Sarah typology, and is best understood as a direct allusion to the testing situation in which the Asian women are placed (cf. the similar summons to set fear aside in iii. 14). They risked rough treatment at the hands of pagan husbands or neighbours, in all probability both. The Christian woman is expected to stand up to such frightening conditions calmly and courageously.

7   The advice to **husbands** is much briefer; whereas it is assumed that many, almost certainly the majority, of the wives are married to pagans, the men addressed are all Christians (cf. the reference to **prayers** below), and in the circumstances of ancient society their wives and families must normally have conformed too. Hence there is no need to deal with the agonizing problems, and missionary opportunities, of mixed marriages. Nevertheless they too (**In the same way**: see on iii. 1) owe a duty of respect 'to every human creature' (ii. 13). Since they have a natural authority over their wives, it would be inexact to define this as subordination, but the principle requires that they should exercise their authority with proper deference.

Thus they should **show understanding in** their **marital relations.** A literal translation would run, 'Live with [them] according to knowledge', where the verb (*sunoikein*: again a present participle used imperatively) has no expressed object, but 'your wives' is clearly understood (*sunoikein* is similarly used by, e.g., Herodotus, *Hist.* i. 93; iv. 168). Several editors omit the comma after the clause, thus making **the female** the object; but since **the female** (see below) is a generic singular, the resulting expression is odd, and the construction is obliged to play down the emphasis on **the female** which is evident in the Greek. The verb 'live with', as in Ecclus. xxv. 8, covers the wider, day-to-day relations of man and wife, but has special reference to their sexual intercourse. For this reason, probably, Codex Sin. (original reading) prudishly altered *sunoikountes* to *sunomilountes* ('associating together'), thereby eliminating any direct allusion to the physical aspect. By **understanding** (*gnōsis*) is meant Christian insight and tact, a conscience sensitive to God's will. According to 1 Cor. viii. 1-13, Christian *gnōsis* (lit. 'knowledge') consists, not in intellectual superiority, but in understanding sympathy and respect for the weak.

This Christian insight is exhibited in **paying honour to the female as the weaker vessel**. The Greek underlying **the female** is *to gunaikeion*, i.e. the adjective used with the neuter article to form a noun, virtually equivalent to 'the female sex'. In the NT 'weak' (*asthenēs*) can refer either to physical (Mt. xxv. 43; Acts v. 15 f.) or moral and spiritual (Rom. v. 6; 1 Cor. viii. 7-11) weakness; here the former is intended, and there is no innuendo of moral or intellectual inferiority. For the proverbial, though only partially correct, assumption that women have less physical strength than men, cf. Plato, *Resp.* 455e; Philo, *De ebr.* 55; Pap. Oxy. 261, 11-13 ('unable owing to womanly weakness to remain before the court'). The precise sense of **vessel** (*skeuos*) is disputed. According to many the term, which originally signifies 'jar', 'dish', and so 'instrument', something one makes use of, here denotes 'wife', 'sexual partner'. They cite its use in 1 Thess. iv. 4, which in one tradition going back to patristic times has been interpreted as 'take a wife to himself' (RSV: so Moffatt), and also the way the equivalent Hebrew word was employed by the rabbis (SB III, 632 f.; TWNT VII, 361 f.). The latter, however, never in itself connotes 'wife', but only refers to the wife as an instrument; and apart from the doubtful case of 1 Thess. iv. 4 there is no clear example of *skeuos* standing for 'wife'. In this present context there is a further objection to this exegesis, since the statement that woman is the weaker *skeuos* seems to imply that man is the stronger *skeuos*. The alternative is to understand *skeuos* as 'body' (the rendering preferred by most exegetes for 1 Thess. iv. 4: cf. also Irenaeus, *Haer.* i. 21. 5, where the word connotes 'a being'), or perhaps as 'member of the household' (cf. 2 Tim. ii. 20 f.: also Paul's description of the different elements of mankind in Rom. ix. 21-23 as 'vessels of wrath' and 'vessels of mercy'). *Skeuos* and its equivalents (e.g. *aggeion*, i.e. 'vessel', 'receptacle') were regular Greek terms for 'body', the underlying idea being that the soul is contained in the body; and passages like 2 Cor. iv. 7; Philo. *Migr. Abr.* 193; *De somn.* i. 26; Test. Napht. viii. 6; 2 Esd. vii. 88 indicate that this language had become familiar in later Judaism.

On this interpretation **paying honour to the female** etc., while of course including general courtesy and consideration, has definite conjugal implications as well (cf. the choice of 'honour' in 1 Thess. iv. 4). The writer's point is that, in all their relations but particularly their sexual relations with their wives, Christian husbands should not assert their strength arbitrarily and make selfish demands, but should respect their partners' scruples. He adds a second, more specifically religious motive: **since you are joint-heirs of the grace of life.** The translation veils a textual disagreement: for **joint-heirs** some MSS etc. give the nominative *sunklēronomoi*, either in apposition to **husbands** or (more probably) as subject of a fresh clause ('since they are also joint-heirs': cf. the Syrian and Ethiopic versions), others the dative *sunklēronomois*, in apposition to **the female**. Both have strong support, but the latter is probably to be preferred; it may have been altered because of the apparent anomaly of a plural noun in apposition to a generic singular. In either case the broad sense is the same. In **the grace of life** the genitive is epexegetic, the phrase signifying 'the grace which consists in life'. In the new order the natural distinctions between male and female will disappear (Gal. iii. 28).

Finally comes a practical reason why men should behave with Christian consideration towards their wives: **so that your prayers may not be hindered.** In the background lies the principle that a living relationship with God depends on right relations with other people (e.g. Mt. v. 23 f.; xviii. 19-35; 1 Cor. xi. 17-34; Jas. iv. 3), but what makes a more immediate impact is the writer's attitude of reserve to the positive aspect of sexual expression. The reference could be to the prayers of husbands only, but 1 Cor. vii. 5 suggests that those of wives are included. Indeed the whole of 1 Cor. vii. 1-7 is an illuminating commentary on our passage, especially Paul's insistence that self-control in conjugal relations is desirable if prayerful communion with God is to be maintained. For the thought, cf. Test. Napht. viii. 8: 'there is a time for intercourse with one's wife, and a time for abstinence so that one can pray'.

9. PRACTICAL ADVICE: (v) THE COMMUNITY
iii. 8-12

(8) Finally, be all of you of the same mind, full of sympathy and love of your brothers, compassionate, humble-minded. (9) Do not return evil for evil or abuse for abuse, but on the contrary bless; for it is to this that you have been called, that you might inherit a blessing. (10) For 'He who desires to choose life and see good days should restrain his tongue from evil and his lips from talking deceit; (11) he should turn away from evil and do good; he should seek peace and pursue it'. (12) For 'the Lord's eyes are on the righteous, and his ears are open to their prayer; but the Lord's face is against those who do evil'.

Having dealt with selected groups, the monitory section breaks off (it will be resumed at iv. 7-11 and v. 1-5) with some general advice for the community as a whole as regards (a) its internal life and (b) the reaction of its members to their pagan neighbours. The parallelism with Christ's recorded sayings (esp. Mt. v. 5-7; 43-48; Lk. vi. 27 f.) and the close correspondences with hortatory passages in Paul's letters (Rom. xii. 9-19; Eph. iv. 1-3; 31 f.; Col. iii. 12-15; 1 Thess. v. 13-22) and other early Christian documents (e.g. *Did.* i. 3; Polycarp, *Phil.* ii. 2) strongly suggest that the section is built up of traditional catechetical material freely worked over.

So far as (a) is concerned, the proper attitude of Christians towards one another is sketched in five adjectives which illustrate the interweaving of different ethical traditions. First, they are to be **all ... of the same mind,** i.e. divisions of outlook and 8 opinion, natural enough in a heterogeneous group of converts, should be reduced to a minimum. Although the actual adjective (*homophrōn*) is found only here in the NT, Paul uses almost identical language when exhorting correspondents to 'be like-minded' (Rom. xv. 5; Phil. ii. 2), and harmony was for obvious reasons prized in the primitive Church (Acts iv. 32; 1 Cor. i. 10), especially when the environment was hostile. Then they are to be **full of sympathy** (*sumpatheis*: again the sole NT occurrence of the word). This probably denotes, not active compassion for the distressed (that is covered by the fourth adjective), but a readiness to enter into and share the feelings of others (cf. the related verb *sumpathein* in Heb. iv. 15; x. 34).

Both these designate qualities which, while given a larger content by Christianity, were valued in late Greek ethics (for *homophrōn*, cf. Plutarch, *Mor.* 432c; Strabo, *Geog.* vi. 3. 3; Dittenberger, *Or. Graec. Inscr. Sel.* 515, 5: *sumpathēs* is frequent from Aristotle onwards, but cf. Plutarch, *Mor.* 536a; Dittenberger, *op. cit.* 456, 66). The next three represent attitudes which in their richness stem from the gospel revelation (though the second and third are foreshadowed in the OT and at Qumran: e.g. 1QS iv. 2-5). For the first (*philadelphos*: in the Bible only here and at 2 Macc. xv. 14; 4 Macc. xiii. 21; xv. 10), see on i. 22; ii. 17. The writer is not thinking of brotherly love in general, but of the special love which should knit believers in Christ together. For **compassionate** (*eusplagchnos*), cf. Eph. iv. 32; *1 Clem.* liv. 1; Polycarp, *Phil.* v. 2; vi. 1 (all paraenetic catalogues). The adjective is derived from *splagchna*, which originally denotes the internal organs (heart, liver, kidney, etc.) and then, in classical as in later Greek, these organs as the seat of feelings and affections. So in the LXX and NT (e.g. 2 Cor. vi. 12; vii. 15; Phm. 7) it stands for the deepest human emotions, esp. love and compassion, while in the synoptic gospels the verb *splagchnizesthai* is frequently used of being deeply moved or touched. Similarly **humble-minded** (*tapeinophrōn*: only here in the NT) expresses a characteristic directly modelled on Christ (Mt. xi. 29) which soon became a vital element in the Christian ideal of human relationships (cf. esp. Eph. iv. 2; Phil. ii. 3).

So much for the spirit which should animate the community. Though not necessarily, in their context (cf. the theme of Ps. xxxiv, about to be quoted, and iii. 13 ff.) the next words almost certainly define the reaction the writer wishes his readers to
9 make to unfriendly treatment: **Do not return evil for evil or abuse for abuse, but on the contrary bless.** The verbs are again present participles employed as imperatives. The thought and language are strikingly close to Paul's in Rom. xii. 14; 17; 1 Cor. iv. 12; 1 Thess. v. 15; both writers are clearly reproducing an ideal of conduct for persecuted Christians which had

become standard teaching and which drew its inspiration from Christ Himself (e.g. Mt. v. 38-48; Lk. vi. 27 f.). The OT freely recognizes (e.g. Dt. xxxii. 35) that vengeance belongs to God, and discourages one (e.g. Lev. xix. 18; Prov. xx. 22; xxiv. 29) from exacting it oneself; and 2 En. l. 4 lays it down: 'Do not requite [*sc.* with evil] either the neighbour or the stranger, because the Lord will be requiter and avenger on the great day of judgment'. Here we get sorely pressed Christians being invited actually to **bless** their tormentors. In common speech the verb so translated means 'speak well of', 'praise', but in the LXX and NT (e.g. Mt. xxv. 34; Lk. i. 42; vi. 28) stands for 'bless'. The occurrence of **a blessing** in the next clause confirms that this is its sense here.

The construction of this latter, and so its precise bearing, are not immediately clear. If **this** (*touto*) has a forward reference, the sentence propounds a reason why Christians should bless those who injure them: **because** they themselves **have been called** to **inherit a blessing.** In other words, the ground for their goodwill to even their enemies is the mercy they themselves receive from God. But if **this** looks backward (as at ii. 21), the sentence rather holds out a tempting prospect as the motive; we might paraphrase it, 'Bless your insulters (for you were called to bless them) so that you may in turn secure a blessing'. The former seems preferable because (a) the parenthesis which the latter implies is awkward; (b) the similar construction in iv. 6 proves that **to this** can look forward; (c) the thought ('freely you have received, and so give freely') is both better in itself and more in tune with the spirit of the passage. For **inherit a blessing,** cf. Heb. xii. 17, where the expression has its original and proper sense of an heir appropriating his father's blessing. Here the language is metaphorical (for this use of **inherit,** cf. Mt. xxv. 34; *1 Clem.* xlv. 8), but the idea of an inheritance as a free gift which comes to the recipient without his having to merit it remains present.

To clinch his appeal for abstention from retaliation, the writer, following his usual practice, inserts some lines from the OT: **He who desires to choose life and see good days** 10 f. **should restrain his tongue from evil and his lips from talking deceit; he should turn away from evil and do**

good; he should seek peace and pursue it. The source of the quotation is Ps. xxxiv. (12-16), which he has already cited more than once (see on ii. 3) and whose theme (the Lord will rescue the afflicted who trust in Him) is of a piece with the encouragement he wants to give his readers. He has made some verbal changes in the LXX version, which reads, 'Who is the man desiring life, longing to see good days? Restrain your tongue . . . Turn away from evil . . . Seek peace . . .'. More important, he has greatly deepened the sense, giving the key-words a strongly eschatological colouring. In the LXX, as in the Hebrew, **life** and **good days** properly refer to man's earthly existence and the temporal satisfactions (prosperity, good reputation, longevity, freedom from disaster, etc.) which it can bring to those who conduct themselves with becoming prudence. Here they stand for eternal life (cf. 'life' in 7), 'the salvation ready to be revealed in the last time' (i. 5), which is in fact the content of that 'blessing' the Anatolian Christians are to inherit (9), and the prospect of which should prompt them to bless rather than abuse their detractors. The verb rendered **choose** (*agapān*) is usually translated 'love', but it can also have the meaning 'strive after', 'prefer' (cf. Wis. i. 1; Lk. xi. 43; Jn. iii. 19; xii. 43; 2 Tim. iv. 8; 10), and this fits better here.

12   The rest of the citation—**the Lord's eyes are on the righteous, and his ears are open to their prayer; but the Lord's face is against those who do evil**—exactly reproduces the LXX text of the Psalm. It develops the antithesis between doing good and doing evil set out in 11, which is one of the writer's stock themes (e.g. ii. 14-16; 20; iii. 9); and with its reference to God's readiness to listen to the prayers of **the righteous** when they suffer, it holds out comfort to the readers. Perhaps significantly, the concluding words of the verse in the LXX, 'to destroy the memory of them from the earth', have been omitted. In the original **those who do evil** specifically denotes the wicked, but as he interprets and applies the phrase the writer gives it a more general sense. It is his Christian correspondents whom he has been warning against evil doing, i.e. intemperate reaction to persecution, and so the drastic threat in the additional clause would be somewhat out of place.

(13) Who then is going to harm you if you are devoted to what is good? (14) But if indeed you should suffer because of your upright behaviour, you are blessed. Have no fear of them and do not be alarmed, (15) but sanctify the Lord Christ in your hearts. Be always ready to make your defence to everyone who asks for an account of the hope that is in you, (16) but with gentleness and reverence, maintaining a good conscience, so that in cases where you are abused those who vilify your good behaviour in Christ may be put to shame. (17) For it is better to suffer when doing right, if such be God's will, than when doing wrong.

We have now reached the main section of the letter, which continues right up to the paragraph of farewell greetings. The trials and dangers of the young Asian churches, which have so far been the ever-present background but have only been occasionally (i. 6 f.; ii. 12; 15; 19 ff.; iii. 9) brought into the open, now move onto the centre of the stage. To encourage his readers to stand firm, the writer develops a number of interwoven strands of thought: the idea that the innocent man can face suffering with confidence; the basis of this confidence is Christ's victory and the privilege of sharing His passion; the imminence of the End, when righteous suffering will receive its reward.

The section opens with a rhetorical question: **Who then is** 13 **going to harm you if you are devoted to what is good?** The transition seems abrupt, but in fact the question draws the logical conclusion from the preceding verses, which have touched on the attacks made on Christians (9) and have promised that, so far from suffering **harm**, the man who avoids evil and does good (11: cf. **devoted to what is good**) will inherit life and good days. The verb **harm** (*kakoun*) picks up 'evil' (*kaka*) in the line above. That this exegesis gives the correct sequence of thought is confirmed by the particle *kai* (lit. 'and') with which the question is introduced. The rendering **then** is much to be preferred to 'And' (RV), 'Now' (RSV), or 'Besides' (E. G. Selwyn), for what we have is a fine example of the (primarily Semitic) use of the particle to preface an apodosis, with or without the protasis expressed, with the sense 'under the circumstances just set forth', or 'in the light of what has been said' (cf. Mk. x. 26; Jn. ix. 36; xiv. 22; 2 Cor. ii. 2).

For **devoted to what is good** (lit. 'zealous of good'), cf. Tit. ii. 14 ('zealous of good deeds'); Acts xxi. 20 ('zealous of the Law'); xxii. 3; Gal. i. 14. The thought of the verse finds a close parallel, with exactly the same key-verb in the question, in LXX Is. l. 9 ('Behold, the Lord will help me: who will harm me?'), a text which may have been in the writer's mind. He is, of course, using **harm** in a rather special sense. He is not deluding his correspondents with the idea that, if their conduct is beyond reproach, they will escape abuse, maltreatment, physical injury; he has already conceded the possibility in ii. 20. His point is that, whatever disasters strike the man of faith, they cannot touch the integrity of his personality or injure him in the ultimate sense. The confidence is thoroughly Jewish and runs through the OT (e.g. Ps. lvi. 4; cxviii. 6) and NT (e.g. Mt. x. 28; Rom. viii. 31); but an excellent pagan parallel is Socrates's remark to his judges (Plato, *Apol.* 41d): 'No harm can befall a good man, either when he is alive or when he is dead, and the gods do not neglect his cause'.

He feels able to go further still in his reassurances. Not only 14 can maltreatment do them no ultimate hurt, **but if indeed** they **should suffer because of their upright behaviour,** they **are blessed,** and so should reckon themselves highly privileged (cf. Lk. i. 48). His words contain an echo of Christ's own promise (Mt. v. 10), 'Blessed are those who are persecuted for righteousness' sake', which the Church evidently found comforting when menacing forces gathered round it. As in ii. 24, the word for **upright behaviour** is *dikaiosunē* (lit. 'righteousness'), used in the Hebrew (cf. 'righteous' in 12) rather than the specifically Pauline sense. In the Greek **should suffer** is in the optative (*paschoite*), a mood which is virtually obsolete in the NT and the popular speech of the time, but which a stylist with some rhetorical education might be expected to employ with care. If pressed, it might point to what the writer conceives of as a remote contingency ('if you were to suffer . . . you would be blessed'). Because of this it has been claimed that the atmosphere here differs markedly from that of iv. 12 ff., where persecution is not a hypothetical threat but is actually taking place. The apparent discrepancy is the chief plank in the case for regarding iv. 12-end as separate from the body of the letter.

This analysis is to be rejected for several reasons. (a) There are no solid grounds for supposing that the situation has deteriorated in iv. 12 ff. (see Introduction, pp. 7-9). The following verses, as well as i. 6, the advice to slaves and the ominous background of these earlier chapters, make it plain that the Asian Christians were just as much exposed to real persecution at the time they were written. (b) In neither section is the picture one of Christians continuously undergoing concrete ill-treatment; in both it is of an environment charged with suspicion and hostility which has erupted, and is liable at any moment and in any place to erupt again, in painful incidents. This risk, always imminent but for the most of the time a threat rather than an actuality, it itself sufficient to explain the optative. But (c) a further reason for its presence may be detected in the logic of the writer's line of thought. This verse is closely tied to the preceding one, where he has in effect declared, 'No one can possibly hurt you if you are devoted to goodness'. Now, as if conscious that this may sound (as it is) unrealistic, he qualifies his statement by adding, 'Nevertheless, if your devotion to goodness should land you in trouble, you should count it a privilege'. We should note that, while the theme of iv. 12 ff. is suffering as a Christian, suffering **because of your upright behaviour** is spoken of both here and in 17 (cf. ii. 20) as a distinct possibility to be reckoned with. In view of the writer's ready admission (ii. 14) that the role of provincial governors is to applaud such conduct, it is very unlikely that he is envisaging state persecution.

Still further to brace his readers' morale, he inserts, suitably adapted, some words from Is. viii. 12 f.: **Have no fear of them and do not be alarmed, but sanctify the Lord Christ in** 15 **your hearts.** The LXX text on which he is drawing reads: 'Be not terrified with the fear of him, and do not be alarmed: sanctify the Lord himself, and he himself shall be your dread'. In the Hebrew original the prophet and his disciples are warned not to share the fears of the populace ('fear ye not their fear') or count holy what they count holy, but to regard the Lord of hosts as holy and fear Him alone. The Greek translator seems to have misunderstood the first part of the passage and, substituting 'fear of him' for 'their fear', to have taken it as an exhortation to the citizens of Jerusalem not to be afraid of the king of Assyria. As applied by our writer, the utterance lends itself admirably to the Asian Christians' plight. Literally rendered, the first clause reads: 'Do not fear with their fear' (*ton phobon autōn* is a cognate accusative: the plural 'their' has been restored), and it might be more natural to understand 'their' ('of them' in the Greek) as a subjective genitive, translating, 'Do not share their fear' (which in fact is the sense of the Hebrew). But in the context the genitive must be taken as objective: 'do not be afraid of them', i.e. your persecutors.

Instead of being terrified by human beings, the readers are admonished to **sanctify the Lord Christ** (the reading 'God' of some MSS is a mistaken correction) **in** their **hearts**. Some (RV; RSV) prefer the rendering 'sanctify Christ as Lord', pointing out that the word-order in the Greek might suggest that 'Lord' has the force of a predicate. They may be right; but since the author is adapting the LXX 'sanctify the Lord [i.e. Yahweh] himself', it seems more natural to construe **Christ** (*ton Christon*) as appositional, intended to clarify the reference of **the Lord.** By **sanctify** he does not, of course, mean 'make holy', but 'acknowledge as holy' (cf. Is. xxix. 23; Ezek. xx. 41; Ecclus. xxxvi. 4: also 'hallowed be thy name' in Mt. vi. 9). He adds **in your hearts** (lacking in the LXX) because the heart is the seat of the deeper emotions, the place where fear would reside, but where faith and reverence should have their home. The verse has a bearing on 1 Peter's Christology, for as in ii. 3 the title 'the Lord', which in the Hebrew original denotes God, is unhesitatingly attributed to Christ.

The courage which springs from deep-seated reverence for Christ shows itself in a readiness to testify to Him when one is attacked. So the Asian Christians are enjoined: **Be always ready to make your defence to everyone who asks for an account of the hope that is in you.** It is hard to decide whether the situation envisaged is a police-court interrogation or a more informal inquiry either by a hostile group or by individuals. In favour of the former is **defence** (*apologia*), which often has the technical meaning 'legal defence against a charge' (Acts xxv. 16; xxvi. 2; 2 Tim. iv. 16); **account** (*logos*), since 'to give an account' (e.g. iv. 5; Rom. xiv. 12) has a juridical flavour; and perhaps the reference to a blameless conscience in the next verse. The experiences of Paul at Philippi, Thessalonica and Ephesus (Acts xvi. 19-40; xvii. 6-10; xix. 24-40) illustrate the kind of actions and charges that might be brought in the apostolic and sub-apostolic age, and it is improbable that many in the Anatolian congregations had the advantage which Paul had of being a Roman citizen. Against this, however, (a) we must set the extreme generality of **always** and **everyone who asks**; the latter at any rate conjures up something much more ordinary and everyday than court cases can have been. (b) While **defence** and **account** can have a specifically legal connotation, they by no means necessarily do. For *apologia* meaning an informal explanation or defence of one's position, cf. 1 Cor. ix. 3; 2 Cor. vii. 11; while our very expression 'ask for an account' (*logon aitein*) is found in Plato, *Polit.* 285e, with the sense 'request and explanation of something'. (c) 'Requesting an account concerning the hope . . .' hardly squares with what we should expect to have been a magistrate's interest and procedure, but does aptly describe the inquiries, sceptical, abusive or derisive, of ill-disposed neighbours.

The phrase should therefore probably be taken as general and comprehensive, though not of course as excluding questions asked in court. For the advice, cf. R. Eleazar's remark (*Pirke Aboth* ii. 18): 'Be alert to learn the Torah so as to be able to answer an Epicurean'. We note that, as at i. 3; 21, **hope** is for the writer a conception of primary importance, expressing as it does a cardinal aspect of the gospel. Grammatically **that is in you** could mean either 'that pervades and sustains the Christian community' or 'that is in the heart of each of you', but the latter seems to suit the context better.

The readers, however, are to explain and defend their beliefs **with gentleness and reverence.** The former noun defines 16 the attitude (see on iii. 4) they should adopt to their critics; it should have no trace of truculence or pride, but should be marked by that Christian meekness which (we may suppose the author to imply) is more likely to commend the gospel to the suspicious-minded. The latter reminds them of their responsibility to God; the Greek word (*phobos*) means 'fear', and as at i. 17; ii. 17; iii. 2 connotes, not fear of men, but awe and **reverence** for God. It is important, too, that they should maintain **a good conscience** if their witness is to be effective. Here **conscience** (*suneidēsis*), in contrast to ii. 19, falls within its normal NT range of meaning. Borrowed by primitive Christianity from popular Greek thought but with its connotation enriched, it stands basically for a man's inner awareness of the moral quality of his actions (e.g. Rom. ii. 15; ix. 1; 2 Cor. i. 12), although it can also pronounce on the actions of others (e.g. 2 Cor. v. 11). The expression 'good (or clear, pure) conscience' is also found in iii. 21; Acts xxiii. 1 (cf. xxiv. 16); 1 Tim. i. 5; 19; iii. 9; 2 Tim. i. 3; Heb. xiii. 18, and seems to have been almost stereotyped. Primarily it signifies the consciousness of freedom from guilt and of having nothing to hide, but it often seems to carry much deeper implications, and the psychological aspect is less prominent than in the English word. At baptism the Christian undergoes a transformation (Rom. xii. 2), having his mind renewed by the influx of the Holy Spirit so that he is enabled to understand what is God's will as well as to carry it out. The Spirit is thus the principle which informs his conscience, and a 'good conscience' is characteristic of the baptized man who lives in the Spirit.

If such is their demeanour, the effect may well be **that in cases where** (for this translation of *en hōi*, see on ii. 12) **you are abused those who vilify your good behaviour in Christ** will **be put to shame.** Here again the impression one gets is not of formal proceedings before a governor's court, but either of taunting by individuals or mobs or of trumped-up charges before a local magistrate's court. Two points, one textual and the other theological, call for note. (a) Instead of the passive **you are abused** (*katalaleisthe*), several important MSS etc. give the active (indicative or subjunctive) 'they abuse [you]' and add 'as evil-doers' (*hōs kakopoiōn*: genitive). This makes a smoother sentence, but has probably been modelled on ii. 12 with the object of improving the construction (*katalalein* is normally followed by a genitive object, and the passive does not occur in the Bible). (b) While both the term **behaviour** (*anastrophē*: cf. i. 15; 18; ii. 12; iii. 1; 2) and the stress on conduct as a persuasive form of witness are characteristic of the writer, the formula **in Christ** (so too v. 10; 14) is undoubtedly a Pauline trait. It occurs some 164 times in the Apostle's writings, and since it is found nowhere before him it is probably his creation. It reflects his conviction that the Christian, by virtue of his faith, is mystically united with Christ, and that all Christians are one in Him (e.g. Rom. vi. 11; xii. 5). Although the writer gives it here a distinctive nuance, to insinuate that the excellence of his readers' manner of life is rooted in their relationship with Christ, his use of it betrays the impact of the Pauline theology in his circle.

He winds up his counsel with a general statement: **it is better 17 to suffer when doing right, if such be God's will, than when doing wrong.** It repeats a principle which he has already laid down (ii. 20) in a more particular context for slaves, and which has parallels in the finer ethics of paganism: cf. Socrates's splendid paradox (Plato, *Gorg.* 508b) that 'to act unjustly is worse, in so far as it is more disgraceful, than to be treated unjustly'. Here, however, it is reinforced by the Christian idea of Providence. When wrongdoers suffer, they are in no position to complain, for in a universe ordered by divine justice their crimes merit punishment. When well-doers suffer, they have the satisfaction of knowing that their suffering is not the moral consequence of their well-doing, even if it is their good actions which have brought their enemies' hostility down upon them. Indeed, in so far as they can discern God's hand in their afflictions, Christians have a ground for rejoicing (ii. 14; iv. 13). The verb in **if such be God's will** is optative, and once again, as at 14 above, several critics have argued that this implies that suffering is still only a hypothetical possibility for his readers. The argument, however, is even less convincing here than there, for (a) 'if God will' (the Greek has the solemn-sounding expansion 'if the will of God will') was, as in English, a devout cliché in Greek in which the conditional element might be minimal; (b) as phrased the statement is a general proposition, in which the use of the optative is in any case entirely appropriate;

(c) it requires little or no reading between the lines to deduce from, e.g., ii. 12 and ii. 18-20 that some at any rate of the readers are already the victims of misunderstanding, abuse and bullying.

11. CONFIDENCE BASED ON CHRIST'S VICTORY OVER EVIL

iii. 18-22

(18) For Christ also died once for all for sins, the just on behalf of the unjust, in order to bring us to God, being put to death in the flesh but made alive in the spirit: (19) in which he also went and made his proclamation to the spirits in prison (20) who once upon a time refused obedience, when God's patience waited in the days of Noah during the building of the ark, in which a few (eight persons in fact) were saved through water: (21) which thus prefigured now saves you too, [I mean] baptism—not the removal of filth from the body, but the pledge to God of a good conscience—through the resurrection of Jesus Christ, (22) who has gone into heaven and is at God's right hand, with angels, authorities and powers made subject to him.

In iii. 13-17, while speaking more and more openly about the harsh realities of persecution, the writer has been urging the Asian Christians to face their ordeal fearlessly and indeed with cheerful confidence. Now he sketches the sure basis of their confidence: this is nothing less than the victory which Christ has won, by His death, resurrection and ascension, over the forces of evil, the fruits of which Christians share as a result of their baptism.

There is wide agreement that, like i. 18-21 and ii. 21b-24, this section has, in part at any rate, been pieced together out of liturgical, hymnic or catechetical material. This is supported by 18 (a) the tell-tale particle **For** (*hoti*: cf. i. 18; ii. 21b), which reads like the introduction to a quotation; (b) the concise style, heightened tone and antithetical structure; (c) the inclusion of ideas (e.g. the atoning effect of Christ's death) which go beyond the strict requirements of the argument; and (d) the nature of the contents, which consist of basic items of the primitive kerygma. Scholars are divided, however, as to the extent of the hymn or creed and its relationship to other liturgical scraps in the letter. Some (e.g. Bultmann) would include 19; some (e.g. Bultmann; Boismard) would link it, in different ways, with the antithetical couplet at i. 20. The element of sheer guesswork in such reconstructions makes them of doubtful value, and we should probably be content with limiting the fragment cited to 18 and 22. In any case 19-21, with its prosaic and even laborious style, leaves the impression of being the author's own composition, embodying however in 21 a catechetical extract on baptism. His clumsy style may be due to the difficulty of welding these different elements together.

So he begins: **For Christ also died once for all for sins, the just on behalf of the unjust, in order to bring us to God.** It is important to be clear about the movement of thought. The first clause does not (as many assume) attach what follows exclusively to the preceding verse, as if the writer were referring his readers (as he did in the similarly worded sentence in ii. 21) to Christ as the pattern of innocent suffering; here there can be no question of Christ as an example, since His act was unique and redemptive. Rather the clause and the section it introduces look back to, and seek to justify, the teaching contained in the whole paragraph iii. 13-17: when unjustly persecuted the readers can count themselves blessed (iii. 14), for through baptism they participate in the victory Christ has won over the evil powers whose agents their earthly adversaries are.

There are several textual variants in this verse, but most of them (the addition of 'our' after **sins** in some Latin and Syriac texts and certain Latin fathers; the insertion of 'on our behalf' or 'on your behalf' by some MSS) are only attempts to give precision to the somewhat vague original. More significant is the fact that, instead of **died** (*apethanen*), which is supported by the great majority of MSS, Pap. 72 and the versions, a number of MSS headed by B, K and P give 'suffered' (*epathen*). There is no doubt that on textual grounds the claims of **died** (RSV; NEB) are overwhelming. On the other hand, it is held by many

that the sense requires 'suffered', which may have been altered
to **died** partly under the powerful influence of the Pauline
parallel in Rom. vi. 10, and partly because later scribes correctly
felt that the reference must be to Christ's death but failed to
notice that in the vocabulary of early Christianity 'suffer'
included this (see on ii. 21). They point out that the relationship
of the verse both to iii. 13-17, where suffering but not death is
the theme, and to iv. 1 leads us to expect 'suffered' here; and
further that to say that **Christ also died** seems to imply that
the Asian Christians were being killed, of which there is no
evidence in the epistle.

Against this we can argue that it was precisely the desire to
harmonize the verb with the verbs used in iii. 13-17 and iv. 1
that tempted scribes to substitute 'suffered' for the original
died. The fact is that **died** is, in view of the writer's predilection
for 'suffer', the more difficult reading and as such would have
strong claims even without the weight of MS testimony. We
may suspect that left to himself he would have opted for
'suffered', but wrote **died** because it stood in the liturgical texts
he was citing. The other difficulties, which centre on **also** (*kai*),
disappear when the true logic of his argument is grasped. As
has already been remarked, he is not in effect saying: 'You are
suffering innocently, but be of good cheer: Christ also suffered
innocently'; but rather: 'In your sufferings you are in fact
blessed and triumphant, for Christ also after seeming defeated
in His ordeal is triumphant and enthroned in glory'.

If **died** is the correct reading, our hymn or creed embodies
much the same formula as the credal excerpt in 1 Cor. xv. 3
(cf. Gal. i. 4; Heb. x. 12). Here, however, the preposition used
(*peri*) literally means 'concerning'; it is found also in similar
contexts at Rom. viii. 3; 1 Thess. v. 10; 1 Jn. ii. 2; iv. 10. In the
LXX the phrase 'concerning sin' (*peri hamartias*) is a common
description of the sin-offering (e.g. Lev. v. 6; 7; vi. 23; Ezek.
xliii. 21). The emphatic **once for all** (*hapax*) recalls the similarly worded statement in Rom. vi. 10: cf. its repeated use in
Hebrews (vii. 27; ix. 12; 26; 28; x. 10). As in the latter passages,
it highlights the absolute sufficiency and unique value of
Christ's sacrifice. So **the just on behalf of the unjust** crystallizes in a pregnant phrase at once its vicarious character and the

innocence of the Redeemer, both points which have been expounded at length in the earlier citation at ii. 21-24. The title **the just** (cf. its use of Christ in Acts iii. 14; vii. 52; xxii. 14) may possibly echo the similar description of the Servant in Is. liii. 11. A good commentary on the paradox of the innocent dying for the guilty is provided by Rom. v. 6-10.

The object of Christ's once-for-all death is **in order to bring us** (*hēmas*) **to God.** Several MSS (B; C; Pap. 72; etc.) read 'you' (*humas*), but **us** has better MS authority and also fits more naturally into a liturgical unit to be recited by the congregation generally. It could be argued that, as at ii. 21, the writer might have adapted the original **us** to suit the context, but there he was using an admonitory tone which is not in place here. To explain the imagery some editors appeal to the mystery cults, in which the saviour-god was represented as passing through death and leading the initiates by the hand into the presence of the supreme God. Such conceptions, however, were far removed from the writer's thought-world, and it is unnecessary to have recourse to them. In itself **bring us to God** simply means 'bring about (more accurately, restore) our right relationship with God', a relationship which has been interrupted by sin. So Paul, using the kindred noun *prosagōgē*, declares (Rom. v. 1 f.) that we have peace with God through Christ, through whom 'we have access to this grace' (cf. Eph. ii. 18; iii. 12). For a Greek-speaking Jew reared on the OT the verb 'bring to' (*prosagein*) was steeped in rich associations (cf. TWNT I, 131-34). It could denote bringing a person before a tribunal or presenting him at a royal court, or (both in classical Greek and the LXX) the ritual act of bringing sacrifice to God (e.g. Ex. xxix. 10; Lev. i. 2), or again (esp. LXX) the consecration of persons to God's service (e.g. Ex. xxix. 4; 8; xl. 12; Lev. viii. 24; Num. viii. 9 f.). The first seems out of place in the present context, but there may have been a blending of consecratory and sacrificial associations in the writer's mind.

It is of course impossible to reconstruct his theory of the way in which Christ's death had redemptive effect. As in ii. 21-24, he is repeating ready-made, traditional formulae, not struggling to work out a theology. The stress in both passages, however, on the death of the guiltless on behalf of the guilty, so characteristic of primitive Christian thought, can be paralleled in a striking way in later Judaism, which in post-Maccabean times developed the doctrine that the sufferings and death of God's righteous servants have atoning value. We can see this taking shape in 2 Macc. vii. 37 f., while in 4 Macc. vi. 28; ix. 24; xii. 17 f.; xvii. 22 the idea that God will be merciful to His people for the sake of the blood of His saints is unambiguously stated, often in language very like that of the NT. Similarly at Qumran the community was convinced that it could expiate the sins of others by suffering and the observance of strict rectitude (e.g. 1QS v. 6 f.; viii. 2 f.; 6; ix. 4; 1QSa i. 3). It was accepted in the later teaching of the rabbis that the suffering and death of the righteous could make atonement for Israel.

The formulary ring is distinctly audible in **being put to death in the flesh but made alive in the spirit.** Two parallels which immediately spring to mind are Rom. i. 3 f. ('descended from David according to the flesh, designated Son of God in power according to the spirit of holiness') and 1 Tim. iii. 16 ('who was manifested in the flesh, vindicated in the spirit'), which are generally acknowledged to embody credal and hymnic scraps respectively. Here the contrast, even more vivid in Greek as a result of the *men—de* construction, is between Christ's death and resurrection, and the hymn is repeating the primitive credal affirmation that He died and was raised to life again (e.g. Rom. viii. 34; 1 Cor. xv. 3 f.). The verb for 'make alive' (*zōopoiein*) is thus virtually synonymous with 'raise from the dead' (*egeirein*), as in Rom. iv. 17; viii. 11; 1 Cor. xv. 22; 36 (so also Jn. v. 21).

The connected antithesis **flesh—spirit** demands careful handling if we are to enter into the writer's thought-forms. In the patristic age it was inevitably interpreted in terms of the currently accepted Greek division of human nature into two 'parts', one material and one spiritual. Thus **flesh** stood for Christ's body, and **spirit** either for His soul (e.g. Origen, *C. Cels.* ii. 43; Hilary, *Tract. in cxviii ps.* xi. 3; Cyril Alex., *Frag. in 1 Pet.*) or, more precisely, for His divinity in union with His human soul (e.g. Epiphanius, *Haer.* lxix. 52; Augustine, *Ep.* clxiv. 17-21). This exegesis, or some variant of it, has been generally held both at the Reformation epoch and in modern times, although its adherents are obliged either to take **being brought to life in the spirit** as equivalent to 'being kept alive in His immortal soul (or divine nature)', or to imply that His immortal soul (or divine nature) died and was then revived. In fact the flesh-spirit distinction which we meet in the NT, and particularly in Paul (whose ideas and language have evidently influenced the credal text here cited), is completely OT in inspiration and has nothing to do with the Greek, ultimately Platonic, dichotomy of soul and body (see TWNT VI, 387-453; VII, 98-151: also the discussion in W. J. Dalton, 124-34). As in Rom. i. 3 f.; 1 Tim. iii. 16, **flesh** and **spirit** do not here designate complementary parts of Christ, but the whole Christ regarded from different standpoints. By **flesh** is meant Christ in His human sphere of existence, considered as a man among men. By **spirit** is meant Christ in His heavenly, spiritual sphere of existence, considered as divine spirit (see on i. 11); and this does not exclude His bodily nature, since as risen from the dead it is glorified. The datives are datives of reference, and the credal excerpt is affirming the paradox that, regarded as man, Christ was done to death, but, regarded as eternal spirit, that same Christ in the fulness of His being, His body of course included, has been restored to life by God's power. Indeed, it is as thus risen and glorified that He 'brings us to God'.

Having established this point, the writer breaks away momentarily (he will come back to it in 22) from his liturgical text in order to introduce two further considerations which will help to reassure his anxious correspondents. The first consists of a brief sketch, which will be filled out in 22, of the triumphant activity of the risen Christ, while the second presents a summary explanation of baptism, as a result of which the Asian Christians participate in Christ's victory over the evil powers and their earthly representatives. That these three verses are, from the point of view of literary structure, an intrusion is shown (a) by the relative **in which** followed by **also**, which suggests that the 19 writer is supplementing his liturgical source with further ideas which have occurred to him as relevant; (b) by the abrupt switch from solemn liturgical language and balanced antitheses to a diffuse, prosy and even cumbersome style; and (c) by the topics treated, which are not of the kind that, as far as we know,

normally figured in primitive kerygmatic material. But if they
are in this sense an interpolation, so far as their contents are
concerned they cohere closely with the writer's main objectives.

19 f. So he begins: **in which he also went and made his
proclamation to the spirits in prison who once upon a
time refused obedience ... in the days of Noah.** These and
the following verses present the most difficult and controversial
problems in the letter, but we may be reasonably confident
about the opening words. First, the proposed insertion of
'Enoch' (*Enōch*) after **in which ... also** (*en hōi kai*), on the
assumption that it dropped out through haplography, may be
dismissed as a brilliant but untenable guess. Popularized by
J. Rendel Harris, it has convinced several distinguished
scholars, but is unsupported by any MS evidence, and in the
light of our fuller understanding of the text can be shown to be
quite unnecessary. Secondly, while there has been much dispute
about **in which,** there can be no real doubt that it refers back to
in the spirit as antecedent. The argument (E. G. Selwyn) that
it must be a vague resumptive phrase, as at i. 6, since there is no
other example in the NT of an adverbial dative (here **in the
spirit**) serving as antecedent to a relative pronoun, has to face
the fact that this is how the ancient commentators, to whom
Greek was a native language, unhesitatingly took it. The alternative proposed ('in which process', 'in the course of which')
leaves its precise relation to the two preceding participles un-
explained; nor can the use of *en hōi* ('in which') at i. 6; ii. 12;
iii. 16; iv. 4 be advanced as a parallel, for in those passages no
single noun stands out as the obvious antecedent as **spirit** does
here. The meaning must therefore be, 'in which, i.e. in His
spiritual mode of existence, as spirit'. Thirdly, **also** should not
be attached closely to **the spirits in prison,** which it immediately precedes in the Greek; this would imply that they are the
second recipients of Christ's **proclamation,** but there has been
no hint of earlier recipients, and indeed no previous talk of a
proclamation by Christ at all. The adverb must be intended to
bring out that the writer is about to mention yet another aspect
of Christ's activity **in the spirit** which he deems relevant. The
first, clearly, is His resurrection from death, which results in
our being brought to God; the second is that proclaiming to the

imprisoned spirits which we must now proceed to examine.

Here we are confronted with four interlocking problems, concerned with (a) the identity of the imprisoned **spirits,** (b) the location of their **prison,** (c) the direction of the journey Christ **went,** and (d) the nature and content of His **proclamation.** The older patristic solution, which starts with Clement Alex. (*Adumb. in 1 Pet.* iii. 19 f.; *Strom.* vi. 6. 44-46) and has had a fresh run of popularity in modern times, connects the episode with Christ's Descent to Hell—a Jewish-Christian doctrinal development which quickly established itself in the common tradition (e.g. Ignatius, *Magn.* ix. 2; Justin, *Dial.* lxxii. 4; Irenaeus, *Haer.* iii. 20. 4; iv. 22. 1; 27. 2; Cyril of Jerusalem, *Cat.* iv. 11; xiv. 17-19). According to it, the **spirits** are Noah's sinful contemporaries, or else those Jews and Greeks who lived before the incarnation, to whom, in the underworld, Christ preached in the interval between His death and resurrection. This solution, however, soon lost favour with the fathers because it could be taken to imply the possibility of conversion for sinners in the next world (the very reason which has commended it to liberal Protestants), and the prevalent interpretation in the Latin West (also with the stricter Reformers) since Augustine (*Ep.* clxiv. 14-17) has been that Christ, pre-existing in His divine nature (cf. i. 11), preached to Noah's contemporaries in the person of Noah while they were still alive, imprisoned in sin and ignorance. Neither of these explanations has ever been thought entirely satisfactory (e.g. why should Noah's contemporaries be singled out to hear the gospel? Can **in prison** bear the highly metaphorical sense 'imprisoned in sin'?), and both have to face the objections (i) of failing to notice the linkage between 19 and 22; (ii) of reducing the whole section to a digression without any apparent relation to the author's message of hope and encouragement; and (iii) of crediting him with a Hellenistic flesh-soul dichotomy he does not seem to have accepted (see on i. 9: also on 18c above). In any case there is a growing conviction among scholars that, if the obscurity of the passage is to be cleared up and its relevance appreciated, the key must be sought in the myth of the sin and condemnation of the rebellious angels of Gen. vi. 1-4, which fascinated the imagination of late Jewish apocryphal writers, and

which must have been as familiar to the author and his readers
as to the authors and readers of Jude and 2 Peter (cf. Jud. 6;
2 Pet. ii. 4). The text which is most illuminating is 1 Enoch, a
compilation which has exercised a great influence on the NT,
which in certain Christian circles was regarded as inspired (see
further on Jud. 15), and which relates with picturesque detail
how the revered Enoch (for his prestige in the eyes of 1st cent.
Christians, cf. Heb. xi. 5) was sent by God to announce their
doom to the fallen angels.

Thus (a) it is highly improbable that **spirits** denotes the
spirits of dead human beings. If it does, the expression 'spirits
who refused . . .' is, to say the least, strange; we should have
expected 'spirits of those who refused . . .'. In any case this noun
pneuma, alone and without qualification, occurs nowhere else in
the NT with this sense (in Heb. xii. 23 it has a defining genitive).
Normally in the NT (e.g. Mt. xii. 45; Lk. x. 20; Heb. i. 14) it
stands for supernatural beings, good or bad; and when undefined
by a genitive this is its usual meaning in the extra-biblical Jewish
literature, esp. 1 Enoch (e.g. x. 15; xiii. 6; xv. 4-12; xix. 1). If
this applies here too, the case becomes strong for identifying
the spirits . . . who . . . refused obedience with the 'sons of
God' or wicked angels who, according to Gen. vi. 1-4, lusted
after the daughters of men and fathered giant children on them.
In later Jewish literature the story of their misbehaviour and
dreadful condemnation was avidly dwelt upon and richly embroidered (e.g. 1 En. x-xvi; xxi; Apoc. Bar. lvi. 12f.; Jub. v. 6;
6QD ii. 18-21; 1QGnApoc. ii. 1; 16). In particular we should
note (i) that their misdemeanour was specifically defined as
disobedience, for they had 'transgressed the commandment of
the Lord' (1 En. xxi. 6: cf. cvi. 13 f.); (ii) that their place of
punishment is called a prison (1 En. xviii. 14; xxi. 10); (iii) that
the corruption of mankind and consequently all human sin are
traced back to them and their leader Azazel (1 En. x. 8); and
(iv) that even after their sentence they continue their evil work
by means of their 'spirits', defiling men and luring them to
idolatry (1 En. xix. 1: cf. xv. 9-12). An at first sight insuperable
objection to this interpretation might be that **the spirits** are
said to have disobeyed **in the days of Noah,** for the transgression of the 'sons of God' presumably took place ages before

the Flood. All its force vanishes, however, when we notice that, because of the way the one narrative is dovetailed with the other in Gen. vi, the two events became inextricably connected in the uncritical minds of the apocryphal writers (e.g. 1 En. cvi. 13-18); indeed one of them (Test. Napht. iii. 5) actually describes them as contemporary.

This brings us to our second (b) and third (c) problems. So long as **the spirits** were taken to be the souls of dead people, it was perhaps natural to assume that **prison** (*phulakē*) denoted the nether world, or in Jewish parlance Sheol, despite the fact that the abode of the dead is nowhere else depicted as a gaol in Biblical or extra-canonical literature. Some students who reject the traditional exegesis and concede that **the spirits** are the rebellious angels still insist on this explanation. Admittedly differing, and sometimes conflicting, accounts of the place where the victims were confined are found in the apocryphal books. In Jub. v. 6, e.g., they are certainly bound 'in the depths of the earth', a tradition reproduced in Rev. xx. 1-3; 1QH iii. 17 f. In 1 En. xiii. 9; xiv. 5 (Eth.), however, their place of punishment is 'on the earth', not under it; while in 1 En. xxii. 1-3; lxvii. 4 its situation is 'in the west'. On the other hand, in 1 En. xviii. 12-14 the prison is an abyss at the end of heaven 'which had no firmament of the heaven above, and no firmly founded earth beneath it'. This picture is elaborated in the early-1st cent. 2 Enoch (Alexandrian Jewish), which presupposes the conception of a plurality of heavens (in this case seven) which made a strong appeal to late Jewish and early Christian circles and of which echoes can be overheard in the NT. According to this, both the world of the dead and the world of spirits, good and evil, are now located above the earth, and Enoch relates (2 En. vii. 1-3) how he came across the apostate angels, tormented and weeping, in the second heaven. A similar account is found in Test. Lev. iii. 2. If it seems difficult to determine where our writer placed them, the context points decisively to the upper regions. First, it is natural to regard Christ's journey as taking place after His being **made alive in the spirit**; and if these words denote His resurrection, the journey must be His ascension. Secondly, while the verb translated **went** (*poreuesthai*) could conceivably be used of descending to the nether world, it is nowhere so used in the NT, and such a verb as *katabainein* ('go down') would be more suitable. Thirdly, the present verse can hardly be dissociated from 22, where precisely the same word (*poreutheis*) undeniably denotes His ascension (cf. Acts i. 10 f.).

Finally, we have to inquire (d) what Christ's **proclamation** (or 'preaching': RV; RSV) consisted in. The Greek verb is *kērussein* (cf. *kērux*: 'herald'), which basically means 'cry aloud', 'announce', 'proclaim'. Two LXX passages which are relevant are Is. lxi. 1 ('announce release to captives and recovery of sight to the blind') and Jon. iii. 2; 4 (of Jonah's proclamation of approaching destruction to Nineveh). In the NT it acquires, and in most cases carries (with or without the object specified), the technical Christian sense of 'preach the gospel'. Nevertheless, even where this connotation is to the fore, the fundamental meaning remains 'proclaim', 'announce' (TWNT III, 702), and on a few occasions the verb is used without any reference to the gospel (e.g. Lk. xii. 3; Rom. ii. 21; Rev. v. 2). We are therefore not obliged to understand the writer as stating that Christ proclaimed the gospel to the wicked angels with a view to their conversion. Such an exegesis has attractions on general grounds, but can hardly be squared with (i) his mention in 22 of their subjection, (ii) his purpose of bracing his readers' morale, or (iii) the parallel he is evidently drawing between the post-resurrection activity of Christ and the legendary mission of Enoch. This mysterious figure, who had 'walked with God' and whom 'God took' (Gen. v. 24), was for him, it would appear, a type of Christ, and his allotted task had been to declare, not forgiveness, but doom to the apostates. Viewing Christ as the new Enoch, he must have understood His **proclamation to the spirits** as His triumphant announcement that their power had been finally broken.

The relevance of this in the context, as a message which will stiffen the confidence of the Asian Christians as they face insults and attacks, is obvious. The message is underlined by his emphatic reminder that the wicked **spirits** had **refused obedience.** The verb so translated (*apeithein*) is, significantly, the very same verb he has used more than once already (ii. 8; iii. 1: cf. ii. 7 and his equation of faith with 'obedience' in i. 2; 14; 22) of the contumacy of pagans who reject the gospel. In other words, his readers can reflect that the neighbours who badger and bully them are merely reproducing the rebellious character-istics of the demonic powers whose agents they are, and will surely share their destruction. Both his general world-view and his way of envisaging Christ's work were widely shared by the NT writers (cf., e.g., Mark's gospel, esp. iii. 23-26), and not least by Paul. He would agree with the Apostle (e.g. Gal. iv. 3; 8 f.; Eph. ii. 2; vi. 12) that before Christ's coming the world and human lives had been dominated by 'spiritual hosts of wicked-ness in the heavenly places', but that by His cross and resur-rection (cf. Eph. i. 20-22; Col. ii. 15) Christ had triumphed over them gloriously.

His second object in this interpolation (see p. 151 above) is to impress on his readers their participation in Christ's victory, and his mention of **the days of Noah,** introduced no doubt 20a for this very purpose, opens the door for him. The Flood, a favourite topic for imaginative exploitation in Jewish apocalyp-tic, was eagerly seized on by 1st cent. Christians as prefigurative, sometimes of the eschatological judgment (e.g. Mt. xxiv. 37-39; 2 Pet. iii. 3-10, where see notes), but sometimes also, like the crossing of the Red Sea (e.g. 1 Cor. x. 1 f.), of baptism, the sacrament in which solidarity between themselves and Christ was established. This latter typology, which was to be richly elaborated by the fathers and in the liturgy (cf. esp. the Latin rites for Holy Saturday), has its roots in the ideas underlying this passage, and was inevitably suggested by the amazing and gratuitous preservation by means of water, amid the destruction of a world alienated from God, of a chosen remnant of men and women who had preferred to listen to Him. Noah himself was acclaimed by Judaism as the pattern of righteousness (Ezek. xiv. 14; 20; Wis. x. 4), with whom God had made eternal covenants (Ecclus. xliv. 17 f.), and the inaugurator of a new race of mankind (Philo, *De Abr.* 46). For primitive Christianity, simi-larly, he was the prophet of righteousness whom God had spared with a few like him when he had annihilated the wicked world (e.g. 2 Pet. ii. 5), the man who heeded God's warning, saved his family, and thus was the type of 'the righteousness which comes by faith' (Heb. xi. 7).

The parallelism between the age of the Flood and the present age is hinted at in the reminder that **God's patience** then **waited.** This is an obscure allusion to the Lord's statement in Gen. vi. 3: 'My spirit shall not abide in man for ever, for he is flesh; but his days shall be a hundred and twenty years'. In the original this defines the duration of human life, but the rabbis understood it of the respite which, in His merciful forbearance, God granted to sinners in Noah's time to see if they would repent (*Targ. Onk.*; *Pirke Aboth* v. 2). For God's long-suffering, cf. Rom. ii. 4 f.; 2 Pet. iii. 9 (see note). The point of dwelling on it here is not, as some believe, to reverse the accepted view of Judaism (e.g. Mishnah, *San.* x. 3) that there was no hope of repentance and restoration for sinners drowned by the Flood, but rather to suggest that, while God has been equally patient with the Asian Christians' adversaries, He has met with an equally negative reaction. The addition of **during the building of the ark** is intended to throw **God's patience** into relief: it continued throughout the entire laborious operation. Later the ark was to be expounded as a type either of the cross (the wood on which Noah was carried to safety: Justin, *Dial.* cxxxviii. 2) or of the Church (e.g. Tertullian, *De bapt.* viii. 4; Cyprian, *De cath. eccl. unit.* vi), and the latter idea is almost certainly present here in embryo.

20b   The baptismal typology now begins to become explicit: **in which** (i.e. in the ark) **a few (eight persons, in fact) were saved through water.** In the Greek **in** is *eis* (lit. 'into'), but this is not really an example of the breakdown of the correct use of prepositions in late Greek; rather *eis* conveys the double sense of going into the ark and so being saved in it. The **eight persons** (*psuchai*: lit. 'souls'—for this sense of *psuchē*, see on i. 9: cf. also Gen. xlvi. 15; Ex. i. 5; Lev. vii. 27; xxiii. 29; Acts ii. 41; vii. 14; xxvii. 37) are, of course, Noah himself, his wife, his three sons (Shem, Ham and Japheth), and their wives. To the writer, as to the early Church in general, they seemed to fore- shadow Christians both in their obedient response to God's word and in their rescue from destruction, and for this reason he deliberately stresses their fewness: the thought of it should give courage to his readers, who must have been painfully con- scious of their own position as a tiny minority. But there is probably a deeper significance in his mention of the number **eight**. For Christians this number designated the eighth day, i.e. the day on which Christ rose from the dead and on which the believer entered the Church by baptism, customarily administered early on Easter, the eighth day *par excellence*. This symbolism, which was to become widely accepted and which even dictated the octagonal shape of ancient baptisteries, was already in full swing by the middle of the 2nd cent. (e.g. Justin, *Dial.* cxxxviii. 1).

Noah and his family **were saved** from God's judgment, thereby anticipating the blessed privilege of baptized Christians; but there has been much discussion about **through water,** chiefly because if **through** (*dia* with the genitive) is given its instrumental sense, it is not immediately clear how they were preserved by means of the flood-waters, since they owed their lives rather to the ark. Some therefore prefer to take **through** in a local sense (*dia* can have this too), paraphrasing the clause by 'were brought to safety by passing through water', or even calling in aid the rabbinical midrash, based on Gen. vii. 7, that Noah hesitated until the water rose to his knees and so had to wade **through** it to the ark. Admittedly the verb (*diasōizein*) tends to favour the latter type of explanation, for it can mean 'bring through safely' (e.g. Plato, *Resp.* 540a; Thucydides, *Hist.* iv. 113; Wis. xiv. 5), but it is likely that the writer is consciously using **through** in both senses at once. The instrumental sense must be present in some degree in his mind, for in the very next sentence he declares that water is the instrument of our salvation too (cf. Hermas, *Vis.* iii. 3. 5: 'Your life was saved through water, and will be saved'). The difficulty of Noah's being saved **through water** has been exaggerated. It was no doubt paradoxical that the water which drowned his contemporaries should have preserved him (Josephus remarks on the similar paradox of Moses's preservation 'through the sea': *Ant.* ii. 347), but preserve him it did at least in the sense of buoying up the ark and carrying it to safety. Christians were just beginning to work out the comparison between the waters of the Flood and the water of baptism (cf. Tertullian, *De bapt.* viii. 4), and if anything were delighted by such paradoxes without bothering about precision of detail.

21   The writer proceeds to spell out what he is getting at: **which thus prefigured now saves you too, [I mean] baptism.** While the drift of the sentence (that Christians are now saved by water, of which the water that saved Noah was the 'type') is clear enough, its construction is so taut and difficult that the comparatively unblemished state of the text is a matter of surprise. Actually there are only two variants which call for note, the first being the replacement in a number of inferior cursives (but no uncials) of **which** (*ho*: neuter nominative) by 'to which' (*hōi*: neuter dative), and the second the omission of the relative altogether by several MSS, including Codex Sin. and Pap. 72. Both yield the general sense, 'In fulfilment of this, baptism now . . .'; but in each case (leaving aside the extremely weak MS support) the resulting Greek is so easy that, if it was the original reading, one cannot imagine how it ever came to be altered. As the text stands, **which** has **water** in the previous verse as its antecedent, with the adjective translated **thus prefigured** (*antitupon*) qualifying it so as to indicate that the water of baptism is not the identical water which saved Noah but the sacramental water to which it pointed forward. The writer adds **baptism,** and although his construction is clumsy he clearly means it to be appositional; his purpose is partly to make his meaning absolutely plain (in this he has not been markedly successful), and partly to prepare the way for the summary explanation of the significance of the sacrament which he is about to insert.

The key-term *antitupos* is of critical importance for both primitive and later Christian thinking. The 'antitype' is what corresponds to, or is the counterpart of, the 'type' (*tupos*). In Acts vii. 44; Heb. viii. 5, which refer to Ex. xxv. 40, the 'type' is the perfect archetype or model of which the earthly representations are imperfect replicas; so in Heb. ix. 24 the 'sanctuary made with hands' is a 'mere copy (*antitupa*) of the true one'. More directly relevant, however, is the alternative NT usage, according to which 'type' denotes a person, thing, practice or event in the past which imperfectly foreshadows a more perfect and richer reality (the 'antitype') to come. So for Paul Adam is the 'type' of Christ (Rom. v. 14), and the experiences of Israel in the wilderness find their true fulfilment both in the Christian sacraments and in the doom awaiting apostate

Christians (1 Cor. x. 1-11). It is in this sense that, according to our author, the water of the Flood prefigures that of baptism. This method of reading the OT, which is presupposed in the NT and was to be ingeniously exploited by the fathers, had plenty of precedent in the OT itself and in later Judaism (cf., e.g., the contemporary Qumran commentary on Habakkuk), and is in fact founded on the conviction that one and the same God is at work in history, bringing the same purpose to ever fuller realization in the succession of personages and events.

Strictly the writer should at this point have added: **through the resurrection of Jesus Christ.** In his thinking these words are closely attached to **saves,** for it is his doctrine (cf. i. 3), in line with that of Paul (Rom. vi. 4-11; Col. ii. 12 f.) though expressed in different language, that baptism depends for its efficacy on Christ's resurrection. He wishes, however, to high-light the ethical implications of the sacrament, and so he thrusts in a brief characterization of it, at once negative and positive. On the one hand, it does **not** consist in **the removal of filth from the body.** At first sight this looks like a denial that its function is to cleanse the body, either literally or ceremonially, with water, but there are difficulties about this explanation. First, it is hard to believe that such a view of baptism needed refuting (but against this cf. Tertullian, *De res. mort.* xlviii. 11: 'The soul is not sanctified by the washing, but by the answer'). Secondly, if such was his intention, we should expect him to have written 'not only', for baptism (as is freely stated in Heb. x. 22) is clearly in one sense a washing. Thirdly, the Greek noun trans-lated **removal** (*apothesis*) is a surprising one to use of removing dirt by *washing*; both it and its cognate verb *apotithesthai* (see on ii. 1), in their basic connotation, suggest a physical putting away, like the taking off of clothes or of some integument (2 Pet. i. 14: its only other instance in the NT). It has accordingly been proposed (by W. J. Dalton, 215-24—taking up hints of W. Estius and E. G. Selwyn) that the phrase in fact refers to circumcision. Its actual wording, including the choice of *apothesis*, aptly describes circumcision, for in the OT the foreskin is a symbol of uncleanness (e.g. Jer. iv. 4) and 'uncircumcised' is a term of abuse implying impurity (e.g. 1 Sam. xvii. 26; 36; Jer. ix. 26); in Jewish tradition, too, the foreskin is an unclean part of the body (SB IV, 31-37; Philo, *De spec. leg.* i. 2-7). Christians in the apostolic age were conscious of a typological relationship between circumcision and baptism; the latter was 'a circumcision made without hands' (Col. ii. 11). If this exegesis is, as seems probable, correct, we may infer that the writer is excerpting a primitive baptismal catechesis in which the Christian sacrament, with its profound interior moral dedication, is contrasted with the ritual **removal** of purely external, physical **filth** which marked its type in the OT dispensation. The technical *apothesis* (see on ii. 1) may have been deliberately chosen to emphasize that the baptismal 'putting off' concerns something far more radical and spiritual than the discarding of a despised portion of flesh.

On the other hand, baptism has its positive aspect: it is **the pledge to God of a good conscience.** The key-word here, translated **pledge** or 'engagement', is *eperōtēma*, and this term itself, as well as **good conscience** and the exact relation of the two expressions, have been endlessly debated. *Eperōtēma*, like the kindred verb *eperōtān*, fundamentally means 'question', 'inquiry'; hence RV's 'interrogation of a good conscience'. No plausible sense, however, can be extracted from this; and as there are a few cases (Ps. cxxxvii. 3; Mt. xvi. 1) of *eperōtān* signifying 'make a request for', many attribute that meaning to the noun here (cf. TWNT II, 685 f.). So the commonest rendering today is 'prayer', 'appeal'—either 'appeal to God for a clear conscience' (RSV: objective genitive), or 'appeal made to God by a good conscience' (NEB: subjective genitive). Any such exegesis, however, falls under suspicion, for (a) there is no evidence, theological or liturgical, that baptism, either in the 1st or in subsequent centuries, was envisaged from the human side as a prayer or 'appeal'; (b) it relies exclusively on the two or three instances of *eperōtān* meaning 'request', overlooking the fact that *eperōtēma* itself nowhere bears this sense but is found with another, more suitable one; (c) it ignores the one or two precious patristic comments on the text which survive.

The following are the chief considerations favouring the rendering adopted. (a) There is abundant evidence, mainly papyrological and well assembled, e.g., by B. Reicke (*The Disobedient Spirits*, pp. 182-85), that *eperōtēma* was a technical term for making a contract (Lat. *stipulatio*), and specifically could denote the undertaking given by one of the parties in answer to the formal question addressed to him. (b) We also know that in the early Church baptism was viewed as a contract, the all-important feature being the assurances (about belief, etc.) demanded and the undertakings given (see J. N. D. Kelly, *Early Christian Creeds*, ch. 2). Naturally the detailed evidence begins with the end of the 2nd cent., but the contractual idea was intrinsic to the rite from the beginning, and the NT itself contains hints of the role played by questions and answers (e.g. Acts viii. 37; Rom. x. 9; 1 Tim. vi. 12; Heb. iv. 14—at Qumran those joining the community submitted to a similar procedure: e.g. 1QS v. 8-10). (c) There can be no doubt that among the baptismal undertakings was a repudiation of the immoralities of paganism and acceptance of the Christian way of life, later to be formalized in the renunciation of Satan. Writing *c.* 150, Justin tells us of such a promise (*1 Apol.* lxi. 2: cf. Tertullian, *De spect.* v), and it is implied in the pre-baptismal catechesis reflected in the NT (see on ii. 1). (d) The explanations of our text given by Cyril Alex. (*Hom. pasch.* xxx. 3) and Ps. Oecumenius (PG cxix. 560: 10th cent., but crystallizing the Greek exegetical tradition) are in line with this.

The question remains whether we should treat the genitive as subjective ('a pledge proceeding from a good conscience') or objective ('the pledge to maintain a right moral attitude'). The latter accords much better with the ancient conception of baptism, witnessed to as much in the NT as in the fathers, as involving a decision to make a clean break with the past (could the unbaptized pagan be said to have 'a good conscience'?). It also agrees closely with the kind of teaching we find in, e.g., Heb. x. 22-24, with its stress on objective purification bearing its fruit in positive Christian living, and brings out, much more forcibly than the mention of a subjective feeling of innocence could, the essence of the undertaking the Christian makes in the sacrament. By **a good conscience** the writer means (as at iii. 16: cf. Heb. xiii. 18), not a psychological awareness of rectitude, but the sound moral disposition or attitude which the man who is conscious of his duty to God possesses.

With the mention of **the resurrection of Jesus Christ** the credal or hymnic passage resumes, and we have the stylized

22 affirmation that He **has gone into heaven and is at God's right hand.** Such texts as Acts vii. 56; Rom. viii. 34; Eph. i. 20; Col. iii. 1 are proof that Christ's heavenly session very early became an article of faith. To reach the divine presence, however, He had to ascend (**has gone:** *poreutheis*—the same participle as in 19b) through those spheres between earth and highest heaven in which, according to the picture of the cosmos accepted by latter-day Judaism, Paul, etc., a hierarchy of supernatural powers (specified in Col. i. 16 as 'thrones or dominations or principalities or authorities') was installed. These, it is clear, are the enemies of God, allied with the rebellious angels and with 'the prince of the power of the air' (Eph. ii. 2), and the hymn confidently adds that they have been forced to submit to Christ's supremacy: **angels, authorities and powers made subject to him.** The technical names for these malefic beings are derived from late Jewish speculation, and the same triumphant theme of Christ's victory over them finds expression, with interesting variations, in 1 Cor. xv. 24 (where it is placed at the End); Eph. i. 21 (as here); Phil. ii. 10; Col. ii. 15 (where it is won on the cross). The imagery is inspired by Ps. cx. 1 ('The Lord said to my Lord, "Sit at my right hand until I make your enemies your footstool"'), which was given a messianic interpretation in rabbinical circles (SB IV, 1, 452-65). Thus the Asian Christians are given a renewed assurance that the evil powers whose agents their calumniators and persecutors are have already had their power shattered.

12. THE BAPTISMAL LIFE

iv. 1-6

(1) Since then Christ has suffered in the flesh, you too should arm yourselves with the same thought, that he who has suffered in the flesh has finished with sin, (2) so that you may no longer live your remaining time in the flesh in accordance with the passions of men but with God's will. (3) For the time that is past has been sufficient for accomplishing what the pagans wish to do, living in sensualities, passions, intoxications, revelries, drunken

parties, and lawless idolatries. (4) In this they are astonished that you no more rush with them into the same
dissolute profligacy, and they vilify you; (5) but they will
give account to him who stands ready to judge living and
dead. (6) For this is why he was preached to those who
are dead also, in order that they might be judged in the
flesh in the eyes of men, but might live in the spirit in the
eyes of God.

His liturgical citation with its catechetical insert concluded,
the writer continues his argument, inviting his readers to apply
to themselves, in the light of their baptism, the principles
operative in Christ's passion and subsequent triumph over evil.
If their baptism is not explicitly mentioned (but see below), it is
implied in the vigorous contrast between the new life they are
called to live and the shameful past they have abandoned—a
contrast in which we can overhear the renunciation they made
when they accepted 'the undertaking to maintain a right
attitude'. The whole aim of the paragraph, with its four times
repeated 'in the flesh', is to reinforce the Asian Christians' confidence by impressing on them that, as a result of the baptismal
mystery, they can obtain a victory over their persecutors parallel
to that which, as already described, Christ has won over the
malefic powers which control them.

So he begins: **Since then Christ has suffered in the flesh.** 1
He is looking back in the first instance to iii. 18, with its mention
of Christ 'being put to death in the flesh', but his thought, as
the sequel shows, embraces the whole activity of Christ described above of which the crucifixion was the prelude, as well
as the teaching given about baptism in iii. 21. There is some MS
support for the addition of 'on behalf of us' (or 'of you') after
in the flesh, but it is clearly an interpolation; as a stock formula
its insertion is understandable, but it has no logical place in the
argument. The verb 'suffer' was used specifically of Christ's
sacrificial death in certain strata of the NT, as we saw at ii. 21,
and also in certain very early Christian texts (e.g. Ignatius,
Smyrn. ii; *Barn.* vii. 11; Old Roman Creed).

In the light, then, of Christ's passion he urges his readers
that they **too should arm themselves with the same**

thought. The picture of Christians putting on armour or equipping themselves with weapons for their struggle against evil is a Pauline cliché (Rom. vi. 13; xiii. 12; 2 Cor. vi. 7; x. 4; esp. Eph. vi. 11-17), and probably reflects the atmosphere of the baptismal catechesis. By **the same thought** (*ennoia*) he means the same attitude of mind or guiding conviction as Christ had (cf. Phil. ii. 5), viz. that death 'in the flesh' issues in life 'in the spirit' and the resulting overthrow of the sinful powers. Armed with this **thought,** the Asian Christians can face their critics and adversaries confidently. As **too** and **the same** show, he is assimilating the experience of the baptized Christian with the death, resurrection and triumph of Christ.

The remainder of the verse presents two difficulties. The first and relatively minor one concerns the connection of the clause **that he who has . . .** with the preceding clause and, more particularly, the meaning of the introductory particle (*hoti*). According to the rendering adopted, *hoti* is explicative and the clause spells out the content of **the same thought.** Most editors, however, prefer to translate *hoti* by 'for' or 'because', regarding the clause as stating a reason for the advice just tendered, or even as a pure parenthesis. Both constructions give an admissible sense, but the former reads more naturally in the Greek (for an exact parallel, cf. Philo, *De praem. et poen.* 42); it also does justice both to the repetition of **has suffered in the flesh** and to **has finished,** which bind the clause closely with 1a and 2 ('no longer') respectively. Commentators are deterred from accepting it because it seems to represent Christ also as having **finished with sin** and therefore, by implication, as having been a sinner. But this latter inference does not necessarily follow. The writer is suggesting no more than is stated elsewhere in the NT, viz. that, sinless though He was (ii. 22: cf. 2 Cor. v. 21; etc.), Christ came 'in the likeness of sinful flesh' (Rom. viii. 3), identifying Himself with sinful men and bearing their penalty (ii. 24), and indeed subjecting Himself for a time to the powers of evil (1 Cor. ii. 8). The verb has a passive rather than a middle force, meaning in effect 'is freed from the domination of sin'. A final decision, however, must depend on our solution of the second, and larger, of the two difficulties, viz. our understanding of the clause itself.

A widely canvassed exegesis interprets this as affirming the cleansing power of bodily suffering. Sin, it is presupposed, has its seat **in the flesh,** and when the flesh has suffering inflicted on it sin is progressively overcome; hence the sufferer is **finished with sin.** The saying, therefore, whether taken as epexegetic of **this thought** or (as by most of this school) as a parenthesis, is an exhortation to the readers to imitate Christ by putting up cheerfully with brutal physical maltreatment, even when it is undeserved, and striving to do good, secure in the knowledge that it will eradicate their sinful tendencies. For the belief that suffering has a purgative effect on the spirit appeal is made to such texts as 1 En. lxvii. 9; 2 Macc. vi. 12-16; Apoc. Bar. xiii. 10; lxxviii. 6, or in the NT 1 Cor. v. 5. But this explanation raises serious doubts. (a) In the Greek **suffered,** like **suffered** in 1a, is an aorist participle, and **has finished** is in the perfect tense; they designate therefore a definite experience in the past and the state resulting from it, and are ill adapted to express a general aphorism. (b) The claims advanced for suffering on this view are surely extravagant, for while it disciplines a man and can improve his character (it can also maim it), it does not remove him from sin. None of the texts cited as illustrations says anything approaching this, and indeed the NT doctrine is that it is the redemption of Christ, made effective through faith and baptism, which frees us from sin. (c) If **suffered** in 1a denotes Christ's death, we should expect **suffered** to denote death in some sense here too, but the letter does not elsewhere represent the Asian Christians as facing actual martyrdom; in the present passage the only suffering they are depicted as undergoing is vilification. (d) There must be a parallelism between the Christian's experience in 1b and Christ's, but the writer cannot be implying that He too was purified in character by His passion.

An altogether different approach (A. Strobel: *Theol. Zeitschrift* xix, 1963, 412-25) which merits consideration identifies him **who has suffered in the flesh** with Christ Himself, rendering *hoti* by 'because' and treating the clause as giving the ground for the advice in 1a. This is the only exegesis which satisfactorily explains the singular **he who . . .**; if the reference is to the addressees, the more natural construction would be either the plural 'those who . . .' or some phrase like 'whoever has . . .'. The obvious difficulty, of course, is how we are to understand the statement that Christ **has finished with sin,** but a solution might be provided of the kind sketched in the paragraph before the last. 'To finish with' (*pauesthai*), it should be noted, does not necessarily imply active personal participation in that with which one **has finished** (e.g. Diodorus Sic., xvii. 56. 4; Plutarch, *Mor.* 593e; Diogenes Laert., vi. 2. 69). Thus the meaning of the obscure expression might be that by His death Christ has been freed from the sinful powers under whose sway, by identifying Himself with sinful mankind, He had placed Himself.

On the other hand, the baptismal overtones of the passage and its close logical linkage (cf. the emphatic **then** at the beginning) with iii. 18-22 strongly suggest that the writer has the readers' baptismal status in mind here. If so, 'suffer' is to be taken figuratively as referring to the Christian's death in baptism. Though he does not share the Pauline mysticism in all its fulness, his thought runs very close to Paul's in Rom. vi. 1-12 (see on ii. 24), with its claim (vi. 7) that through his baptismal death the believer is delivered from the slavery of sin. The idea was not exclusively Pauline, for in 1 Jn. v. 18 f. we find the same affirmation that 'everyone who has been born of God does not sin', as also the same contrast between Christians and the world, the former being 'of God' and the latter lying in the power of the evil one. Indeed it is implicit in the primitive conception that the candidate's renunciation of sin (see on iii. 21) is an integral element in the baptismal act. This exegesis, which discloses the writer's acquaintance with the Pauline theology but not with Romans directly (the discrepancy of language rules that out), views the sentence as expounding the content of **this thought,** viz. that by his death in baptism the Christian is emancipated from the forces of evil exactly as Christ was by His physical death; but while in general supplying an admirable sense it presents one or two awkward features, such as the singular participle with the definite article (not in itself insuperable) and, much more perplexing, the bold expression **suffered in the flesh** for the mystical death of baptism. Perhaps a satisfactory account of the latter might be (a) that **suffered,** which in any case is equivalent to 'died' when used of Christ, has been chosen because of the need for a phrase exactly parallel to the one used in 1a; and (b) that the addition of **in the flesh** is in both cases a by-product of the domination of the whole pericope iii. 18-iv. 6 by the tension between 'flesh' and 'spirit', the former being the sphere of man's mortality and sinfulness, and the latter denoting the new life upon which Christ and, with Him, the Christian enter as a result of the resurrection.

The writer proceeds, with a few vigorous strokes, to sketch for his readers the practical objectives of thus realizing what is involved in Christ's victory and their own sacramental separation from sin: it is **that you may no longer live your remain-** 2 **ing time in the flesh in accordance with the passions of men but with God's will.** Once again (i. 14; 18; ii. 1; 9 f.; 24 f.: cf. Eph. iv. 22-24; Tit. iii. 3 ff.; Heb. x. 32) he underlines the familiar antithesis between the two periods into which baptism bisects a man's life. Before regeneration he is governed by sensuality and worldliness (for **desires**, see on i. 14; ii. 11: **men** seems to carry a pejorative flavour, as 'the world' frequently does in the Fourth Gospel); once he has become a Christian, he is guided by **God's will.** The curiously worded **your remaining time in the flesh** is more than a simple paraphrase of 'the rest of your earthly lives'. It contains a reminder, warning but also encouraging, that the End is close at hand (cf. iv. 7). So at Qumran (QpHab vii. 7-12) the teaching was given that special merit would be gained by those 'whose hands do not slacken in the service of truth when the final age delays for them'. And the point of **in the flesh** is that, although the readers have 'suffered in the flesh' in baptism and have thus proleptically entered upon life 'in the spirit', they have still a spell to live **in the flesh** before the End is fully manifested.

The writer then elaborates and drives home his allusion to their pre-Christian existence by urging that **the time that is** 3 **past has been sufficient for accomplishing what the pagans wish to do.** His language must imply that they themselves had previously been pagans, not Jews, and that they had been converted to Christianity as adults. In Greek, as in English, **sufficient** or 'enough' (*arketos*) can be used ironically with the clear innuendo 'more than enough' (e.g. *Anth. Pal.* ix. 749: cf. Isocrates, *Paneg.* 167; Ezek. xliv. 6; xlv. 9). In the

original **what the pagans wish . . .** literally means 'the wish of
the pagans', the expression being consciously set against **God's
will** in 2 above. The catalogue of misconduct which follows—
**living in sensualities, passions, intoxications, revelries,
drunken parties, and lawless idolatries**—closely resembles
those in Rom. xiii. 13 f. and Gal. v. 19-21 (note the prominence
of sexual and alcoholic excesses in all three, and the stress on
idolatry here and in Gal. v. 20), as well as having points of contact with late Jewish texts (e.g. Ass. Mos. vii. 3-10) and the
Dead Sea Scrolls (e.g. 1QS iv. 9-11). The material is therefore
probably stock (this is confirmed by the inelegant repetition of
desires from 2), but (as esp. at Rom. xiii. 13 f.) is worked up in
such a way as to convey a graphic impression of the sexuality,
heavy drinking and disorder which were as characteristic of
many social parties in the towns of Asia Minor in the 1st cent.
as they are of similar celebrations in the permissive west today.

4   **In this,** the writer continues, **they are astonished that you
no more rush with them into the same dissolute profligacy, and they vilify you.** In the opening phrase (*en hōi*:
lit. 'in which') we have another example of a favourite turn we
have met at i. 6 and ii. 12 (see notes). The relative is neuter, and
is attached loosely to the whole thought of the preceding sentence; one might paraphrase, 'In regard to this, i.e. your abandonment of pagan social habits, they are astonished . . .'. The
verb **rush with them** vividly conjures up the euphoric stam-
pede of pleasure-seekers. Equally vivid is **dissolute profligacy**
(*tēs asōtias anachusis*: lit. 'overflowing, or flood, of dissipation').
The noun **profligacy** is associated with drunkenness in Eph.
v. 18; the cognate adverb (*asōtōs*) is used to describe the Prodigal
Son's 'riotous living' in Lk. xv. 13. Not unnaturally, the pagans'
surprise and bewilderment at the refusal of their former companions to fling themselves into the 'dolce vita' soon change to
indignation (cf. the very similar reaction of the wicked to the
righteous man so eloquently delineated in Wis. ii. 12-16), and
so **they vilify you.**

    In much the most strongly supported text this verb is not
in the present indicative (as the translation suggests) but the
present participle (*blasphēmountes*). This latter is slightly awkward, and the much less well attested substitution of the finite

verb (*kai blasphēmousin*: 'and they vilify') results from a misguided attempt to achieve stylistic smoothness. The verb itself
(*blasphēmein*) can mean either specifically 'speak profanely of
God or sacred things', 'blaspheme' (e.g. Mt. ix. 3; Rom. ii. 24)
or, more generally, 'speak slanderously of someone', 'calum-
niate', 'denigrate' (e.g. Rom. iii. 8; 1 Cor. x. 30; Tit. iii. 2).
Some choose the former meaning here, rendering the participle
almost as an interjection, 'Blasphemers!'. In the context, however, and in the light of the writer's references (ii. 12; iii. 16) to
the scandalous imputations brought against Christians, the
word much more naturally denotes the abuse in which the
pagans' astonishment finds a crude outlet: not that the former
meaning is excluded, since from the Christian point of view
insults against God's people are insults against God (e.g. Mt.
v. 11; Acts ix. 4). There is plenty of evidence, from pagan as
well as Christian sources, that it was precisely the reluctance of
Christians to participate in the routine of contemporary life,
particularly conventionally accepted amusements, civic cere-
monies, and any function involving contact with idolatry or
what they considered immorality, that caused them to be hated,
despised and themselves suspected of illicit practices.

The Asian Christians, however, can face misrepresentation
and calumny with stern optimism: their detractors **will give an 5
account to him who stands ready to judge living and dead**
and will receive (it may be inferred) the sentence they deserve.
The End, as the writer is about to emphasize (iv. 7), is close at
hand and will usher in the final judgment (the judge is even now
ready), which will be universal, embracing both all who are
still alive and all who have already died; these latter will be
raised from the grave (1 Cor. xv. 51 f.). The expression 'the
living and the dead' with the noun or verb 'judge' was one of
the earliest tags to harden into a stereotyped formula, and very
soon ensconced itself in primitive credal material (e.g. Acts x.
42; Rom. xiv. 9; 2 Tim. iv. 1: cf. *Barn.* vii. 2; Polycarp, *Phil.* ii.
1; *2 Clem.* i. 1). In all these quasi-credal passages the reference
is to Christ's Second Coming and to those who are physically
alive or dead when that event takes place, and this unquestionably applies to the present text too. The suggestion that it
denotes the judgment of those who are spiritually alive or dead

is far-fetched and unnatural. It is practically certain, too, in spite of i. 17; ii. 23, that the judge is to be identified with Christ. Though God is occasionally (Rom. ii. 6; iii. 6; xiv. 10) spoken of in the NT as judging the world, its normal teaching is that this function is exercised by Christ, to whom God has committed it (e.g. Mt. xxv. 31-46; Lk. xxi. 34-36; Acts x. 42; xvii. 31; 1 Cor. iv. 4 f.; 2 Tim. iv. 1), and this is invariably the meaning of this stereotyped formula.

Prompted by his mention of Christ's role as judge, i.e. as punisher of the wicked and vindicator of the faithful, the writer adds a further consideration which he knows will brace his
6 readers' spirits: **For this is why he was preached to those who are dead also, in order that they might be judged in the flesh in the eyes of men, but might live in the spirit in the eyes of God.** As this is a very obscure statement which has perplexed commentators, it is proper to point out that in the original the verb rendered **he was preached** (*euēggelisthē*) has no subject expressed; hence it might be impersonal, bearing the sense 'the gospel was preached' (AV; RV; RSV; NEB), and the implication might be that Christ Himself was the preacher. Further, the repeated preposition translated **in the eyes of** (*kata*) is ambiguous; many prefer to render it 'according to' (AV; RV) or 'after the manner of', 'like' (RSV). Most students are agreed, however, that the first of the two balanced clauses in 6b (in the Greek the construction is *men—de*) should be taken concessively, the resulting sense being 'that though judged . . ., they might live . . .'. It is also practically certain that the enigmatic **be judged in the flesh** denotes the condemnation implied in dying. Death is not merely the natural termination of life, but according to the Bible teaching (Rom. v. 12; vi. 23: cf. Gen. ii. 17; iii. 19; Wis. ii. 24) gives expression to God's judgment on sin.

According to one influential school of thought, the main verb is impersonal ('the gospel was preached'), and the verse is to be understood as a reference to Christ's Descent to Hell and His proclamation there of the good news *either* (a) to the dead generally (so many liberal theologians, attracted by the implied enlargement of the scope of salvation), *or* (b) to the souls of the OT saints (so many Roman Catholic scholars since the 16th cent.; this view had for them the dogmatic advantage of not leading to universalism). As a result of this preaching, though they have undergone the physical death which is the lot of sinful men, these souls are given the possibility of eternal life. The sequence of thought, it is argued, is in (a) that, if Christ is to judge the dead as well as the living (as iv. 5 affirms), they must in fairness all have had a chance of hearing the gospel; in (b) that while in the strict sense the OT saints did not need conversion, it was fitting that they should hear the gospel. A close rival of this type of explanation has been the theory (e.g. Clement Alex., *Adumb. in 1 Pet.* iv. 6; Cyril Alex., in PG cxxv. 1237-40; Augustine, *Ep.* clxiv. 21) that 'the dead' here denotes, not the physically dead, but the spiritually dead (for this use of *nekros*, i.e. 'dead', cf. Eph. ii. 1; Col. ii. 13). The argument, according to this, is that God's judgment extends to all (iv. 5), and rightly so; for even the spiritually moribund, or alternatively those who have gone to their graves with their sins (like the mocking persecutors of iv. 4 f.), have had the gospel preached to them in their lifetime, and so had the opportunity of making the right decision.

This latter explanation can hardly be maintained unless **dead** in 5 also means 'spiritually dead'; the noun is identical in both verses and must have the same connotation in both, and we have already seen that in 5 it almost certainly refers to the physically dead. In any case the aorist verb **was preached** points to a definite occasion; if the statement were a general one about the availability of the good news to sinners, we should have expected the present tense 'is preached'. Interpretations of the former type derive some of their plausibility from taking it for granted that the Descent has already been mentioned in iii. 19, and this is proportionately weakened if we accept (see note) that that verse contains no allusion to it at all. In any case the assumption that iii. 19 and iv. 6 deal with the same event is entirely arbitrary and, in view of the fact that the former speaks of 'spirits' (i.e. either disembodied souls or supernatural beings) and the latter of 'dead persons', with no suggestion of disembodiment, most improbable. More substantial, however, are the objections which cluster round their proposal that *euēggelisthē* means 'the gospel was preached by Christ'. (a) Since Christ is described in 5 as judging, the switch from the active to the passive is distinctly odd; if He is the preacher too, one would have expected 'this is why he preached'. (b) This switch is all the more suspicious since a strictly impersonal passive is exceedingly rare in the NT, the only real parallel being provided by Rom. x. 10. (c) Christ is very rarely the subject of the verb 'preach the good news' (*euaggelizesthai*—middle) in the NT (only Lk. iv. 18; 43; viii. i; xx. 1 in the gospels), and then only when He is alive on earth. (d) On the other hand, the verb often has Christ, or some other equivalent term, as the object of the preaching (Acts v. 42; viii. 35; xi. 20; xvii. 18; Gal. i. 16), and the almost identical verb 'preach' (*kērussein*) is used personally in the passive with Christ as subject (1 Cor. xv. 12; 2 Cor. i. 19; 1 Tim. iii. 16). Almost invariably 'preaching the gospel' is an activity carried out by Christian evangelists, always in this world. These two last considerations suggest that **he was preached** is much the most natural translation.

Perhaps the chief weakness, however, of these theories is that they fail to connect this at first sight enigmatic sentence with the writer's overriding motive. In fact its words are closely tied to what precedes (observe **For** and **also**); and yet, if they are to be interpreted along the lines proposed, it is hard to see what comfort they could give to the readers in their trying situation. For this reason, over and above its intrinsic plausibility, much the most attractive solution (so F. Spitta; J. Moffatt; E. G. Selwyn; W. J. Dalton; etc.) is one which identifies **those who are dead** with members of the communities addressed to whom Christ had been **preached,** who as a result became Christians, but who have since died. They were of course alive when the message was proclaimed to them, and so the description of them as 'the dead' may sound incongruous; but (a) it is no odder in Greek than the statement in English, say, that Prime Minister Wilson was taught economics at Oxford, and (b) the writer has in any case chosen it because it picks up **dead** in 5. It is well known that in the apostolic Church, with its eager anticipation of the Second Coming, the deaths of believers caused intense worry and heart-searching, for they seemed to have been cheated of the fulfilment of their hopes. So Paul in 1 Thess. iv. 13-18 exerts himself to assure his readers that, when the Lord comes, Christians who are still alive will have no advantage over those who have died beforehand. In an environment of persecution and social ostracism the problem must have been accentuated for the Asian churches. They may well have been exposed to scoffing questions from pagan neighbours, and anxious ones from one another, 'What is the gain of your having become Christians, since you apparently die like other men?' The writer's answer is that, so far from being useless, the preaching of Christ and His gospel to those who have since died had precisely this end in view, that although according to human calculation they might seem to be condemned, they might in fact enjoy eternal life.

This explanation, which is in harmony with the eschatological expectation pervading the letter, so far from being an irrelevant digression, is firmly built into the argument. Thus **this is why** (*eis touto*), as in iii. 9, refers forward, being the antecedent of **in order that they . . . For,** on the other hand, looks back to the preceding verse, where the writer's chief interest is not in the all-embracing scope of Christ's judgment (**living and dead** is a standardized formula), but in the judgment as such, involving as it will the vindication of the good as well as the punishment of the wicked. The point of **For,** therefore, is not to suggest reasons why Christ should judge the living and the dead, but rather to draw out and underline an aspect of His judgment which will comfort and sustain the Asian Christians, viz. that because He is a righteous judge their converted brothers who have died have not believed in Him in vain. The particle **also** (*kai*) is in keeping with this. It is understandable that the writer and his readers should have had Christ preached to them, for they presumably will experience the Parousia; the problem is why He should have been proclaimed **also** to people who were to die before His Coming. In **that they might be judged in the flesh in the eyes of men** we can overhear the derision of pagan sceptics, which must have stirred anxious doubts in the Christian friends of the deceased (cf. the striking parallel in Wis. iii. 2-4: 'In the eyes of the foolish they [the righteous] seemed to have died . . . in the sight of men they were punished'). Similarly the balancing clause affirms that Christ's judgment will give the lie to such mockery and doubts; despite having since died, they will, because of their acceptance of the gospel, **live in the spirit in the eyes of God**. For like faith in the vindication of the righteous, cf. Wis. iii. 1-9; v. 15. Finally the antithesis **flesh-spirit** pointedly looks back to iii. 18; Christ's experience of 'being put to death in the flesh but made alive in the spirit' becomes through baptism the experience of all Christians, not excluding those who have already undergone physical death. As Paul explained the matter (Rom. xiv. 8), 'whether we live or whether we die, we are the Lord's'. Elsewhere (1 Cor. xv. 51-53) he describes how, when the End comes, the Christians who have already died (i.e. 'the dead' here) and those who are still alive will both share in the victory, but all alike will have to 'be changed' and assume an imperishable mode of existence; in the present writer's idiom, they will **live in the spirit.**

13. CHRISTIAN LIFE AS THE END APPROACHES
iv. 7-11

(7) But the end of all things is at hand. So be self-controlled and keep clear-headed for your prayers. (8) Above everything, keep your love for one another at full strength, for love covers a multitude of sins. (9) Practise hospitality towards one another without grumbling. (10) Use whatever gift each has received in service to one another, as responsible stewards of God's manifold grace. (11) If a man speaks, let it be as God's oracles; if a man renders service, let it be as from strength which God supplies: so that in everything God may be glorified through Jesus Christ, to whom belong glory and power for ever and ever. Amen.

The judgment of which the writer has been speaking is, 7 however, imminent: **the end of all things is at hand**. This addition of **But** is intended to bring out the force of the particle *de*, which is overlooked in most translations but which in fact links this section closely with the preceding one. In the Greek

is at hand (*ēggiken*) is almost 'has arrived': cf. esp. Mk. i. 15; Rom. xiii. 12. The conviction expressed was universal in the primitive Church (e.g. Rom. xiii. 12: 'the night is far gone, the day is at hand'; 1 Cor. vii. 29: 'the appointed time has grown very short'; Heb. x. 25: 'you see the day drawing near'; 1 Jn. ii. 18: 'it is the last hour'), but is particularly intense and vivid in 1 Peter (i. 4 f.; 8-12; 20; iv. 17). The consummation is described as **the end of all things** because, according to primitive Christian thinking, history would reach its climax and heaven and earth as we know them would pass away. The prospect has its terrifying aspect, but is full of exciting hope for God's elect.

In the NT the approach of the End is regularly (e.g. Mt. xxiv. 45-xxv. 13; Mk. xiii. 33-37; Rom. xiii. 11-14; Phil. iv. 4-6; Heb. x. 23-31; Jas. v. 7-11; 1 Jn. ii. 18; Rev. xxii. 12) interpreted as a challenge to watchfulness and irreproachable behaviour. So here the writer appeals to his readers: **be self-controlled and keep clear-headed for your prayers.** His use of the former verb (*sōphronein*: 'be sober-minded', 'keep a cool head') perhaps conveys a hint that they should not get excited by the proximity of the End or allow it to upset the routine of their lives: cf. Paul's remarks in 1 Thess. iv. 11; 2 Thess. ii. 2. For the second verb (*nēphein*: lit. 'be sober'), see on i. 13; the Lord had counselled prayer in the hour of crisis (Mt. xxvi. 41), and an unclouded mind is necessary for it. The last days are to be days of surprise, catastrophe and testing, and the writer's picture, in this and the following verses, of the quiet confidence, mutual support and reliance on God which Christians should exhibit is remarkably like Paul's in 1 Thess. v. 1-10; 1 Cor. vii. 29-31.

So like Paul in Rom. xiii. 8-10; 1 Thess. v. 8; 15, he requests that in these critical, expectant days they should **keep** their **love** 8 **for one another at full strength.** This is to come **Above everything** (*pro pantōn*), a stock expression from ethical catechesis which is found also in Jas. v. 12, a passage (v. 7-12) which sounds a similar eschatological note and presents several correspondences with iv. 7-11. The adjective translated **at full strength** is *ektenēs* (see on i. 22b, where the adverb is coupled with the verb 'love'), and is clearly predicative. His teaching about the primacy of love reflects primitive Christian thinking (e.g. 1 Cor. xiii. 1-13; Gal. v. 13 f.; Jas. ii. 8; 1 Jn. *passim*), which itself was nourished on our Lord's own sayings (Mk. xii. 30-33; Jn. xiii. 34 f.; xv. 12-17).

He reinforces his advice by loosely quoting Prov. x. 12: **for love covers a multitude of sins.** His version is closer to the Hebrew original than to the LXX; and since his practice is to draw on the latter for OT citations, it is evident that the saying had become proverbial by the time it reached him. As a matter of fact it is found frequently and with varying applications in early Christian writings: e.g. Jas. v. 20 (in part); *1 Clem.* xlix. 5; *2 Clem.* xvi. 4; *Didasc.* ii. 3. 3 (attributed to Christ). In the Hebrew the meaning is that love, unlike hatred which stirs up strife, conceals and passes over faults in silence (cf. 1 Cor. xiii. 7; Test. Jos. xvii. 2); and some opt for that exegesis here (so probably *1 Clem.* xlix. 5). But this fails to do justice to the urgent eschatological overtones of the verse. It is much more likely that the writer's point is that at the coming judgment his readers will receive mercy for their own sins (of which he has been constantly reminding them: i. 14; ii. 1; 11 f.; iv. 1-4) provided in the meantime their mutual love does not falter. Forgiveness is God's free gift, and there is no suggestion of its being merited; but the gospel teaches (Lk. vii. 47) that he who loves much has many sins forgiven him and that at the final assize (Mt. xxv. 31-46) what will be decisive will be the love, or lack of love, we have displayed in our actions. This is the sense in which, e.g., *2 Clem.* xvi. 4; Tertullian, *Scorp.* vi. 11; Origen, *Hom. in Lev.* ii. 4 (citing them alongside Lk. vii. 47) understand the words. Prov. x. 12 is rarely commented on by the rabbis, but when it is it repeatedly has the same meaning read into it as we are attributing to it here (SB III, 766). For the growth of the (potentially dangerous) notion that works of charity help to secure forgiveness, cf., e.g., *1 Clem.* l. 5; *Did.* iv. 6; *Barn.* xix. 10; Polycarp, *Phil.* x. 2.

A particularly important and appreciated outlet for mutual
9 charity was **hospitality**; so the Asian Christians are bidden to **Practise hospitality towards one another without grumbling.** The lack of a network of decent hotels for ordinary people was one of the most striking social-economic differences between the ancient world and the modern, with the result that readiness to provide board and lodging for friends and other

suitably sponsored travellers was even more highly esteemed than it is today. There was a great deal of coming and going in the early Church (cf. the journeys of apostles, evangelists, teachers, carriers of letters, etc.), and in such a close-knit community it was natural that visitors should be put up by fellow-Christians. So the Lord's praise for entertaining guests was treasured (Mt. xxv. 35; Lk. vii. 44-47; xi. 5-10; xiv. 12-14), and admonitions to be hospitable figure prominently in early writings (e.g. Rom. xii. 13; Heb. xiii. 2; 3 Jn. 5-8; *1 Clem.* x-xii; Hermas, *Mand.* viii. 10). The more affluent members of congregations placed accommodation at their disposal for meetings (Rom. xvi. 5; 1 Cor. xvi. 19; Col. iv. 15), and there are hints that the entertainment of visitors ranked high among the responsibilities of church officials (1 Tim. iii. 2; Tit. i. 8; Hermas, *Sim.* ix. 27. 2). The addition of **without grumbling** has a sharp tang of realism about it. Then as now guests could overstay or otherwise abuse their host's welcome (cf. the regulations specifically drafted to obviate this in *Did.* xi-xiii; also the Italian proverb: 'A guest is like a fish—after three days he stinks'), and a reminder that hospitality can be an exasperating chore, to be shouldered cheerfully if it is to be worth while, is in place.

More generally, the readers are exhorted, as the End approaches, to **Use whatever gift each has received in service** 10 **to one another, as responsible stewards of God's manifold grace.** Since **each** (cf. 1 Cor. xii. 7) has some **gift,** the writer cannot be thinking exclusively either of the specifically 'pneumatic' gifts (talking with tongues, prophesying, etc.) which attracted much attention in the apostolic age or of distinctive tasks of ministers, but of any capacity or endowment which can be employed for the benefit of the community. His words recall Rom. xii. 6-8, where Paul enumerates as 'gifts' (the same noun *charisma*) not only prophecy, but care of the needy, teaching, preaching, alms-giving, administration, and acts of mercy. Like the Apostle, he takes the view that everything a man possesses, whether it is an extraordinary spiritual faculty or merely some humdrum aptitude, is on trust to him from God and so ought to be expended for the good of his fellow-Christians. Hence individuals are, as it were, **stewards,** a term (*oikonomos*) which denoted (e.g. Lk. xii. 42; xvi. 1-8) the slave who was responsible for managing a man's property or household and for distributing their wages, food, etc., to its members. In this case the treasure to be handed out is nothing less than **God's manifold grace,** i.e. the bounty which God freely bestows and which is infinitely variegated in the forms it takes. For **manifold** cf. i. 6, where the same adjective (*poikilos*) is translated 'all sorts of'. As in 1 Tim. iii. 5; 15, the local church is, by implication, pictured as a household.

He then gives two examples of specialized activities in the community, suggesting that those who exercise them should consider themselves as in fact agents of God's grace. Thus **If a man speaks, let it be as God's oracles.** The reference is not to conversation or discussion generally, nor (as many commentators suppose) to those forms of ecstatic utterance ('glossolalia', etc.) which Christians in the apostolic age found so exciting, but rather to routine functions like teaching and preaching. The verb is *lalein*, which we find elsewhere with precisely this connotation (e.g. Acts x. 44; Rom. vii. 1; 2 Cor. ii. 17; iv. 13; Phil. i. 14). These, too, though lacking the outward tokens of Spirit-possession, should be regarded (he implies) as in the true sense charismatic, for what the Christian spokesman enunciates, if he is faithful, is God's word; he does not simply repeat the divine message, but God speaks through him. As Paul expressed it (2 Cor. v. 20), 'God makes his appeal through us', contending (1 Thess. ii. 13) that what he preaches should be received 'not as the word of men but as what it really is, the word of God'. For **God's oracles** (*logia*: a word used in classical Greek and the LXX for divine utterances), cf. Acts vii. 38; Rom. iii. 2.

In exactly the same way, **if a man renders service, let it be as from strength which God supplies.** Here the verb (*diakonein*) is the same as the one used in 10 above (**Use . . . in service**), but while its connotation there is general, it now designates specific forms of service, ministerial or social, in the community. 'Service' (*diakonia*) was a key-word in the primitive Church, and Paul remarks (1 Cor. xii. 5) that 'there are varieties of services'. These ranged from the administration of alms and the relief of bodily needs (e.g. Acts vi. 1; xi. 29; 2 Cor. ix. 12) to the leadership of the community, whether by apostles and prophets (e.g. Acts i. 17; Rom. xi. 13; 1 Tim. i. 12) or by more routine officials (e.g. Col. iv. 17; 2 Tim. iv. 5). The parallelism with **If a man speaks** suggests that here too the writer has the activities of ministers primarily in mind. His argument is that, if the minister's or the Christian man's contribution to the common life is to be effective, he ought to rely, when making it, not on his own human resources, but on God's help. Any worthwhile **strength** he has comes from God, who is at work in him, 'inspiring both the will and the deed' (Phil. ii. 13: NEB). The Greek verb rendered **supplies** (*chorēgein*: cf. *epichorēgein* in 2 Pet. i. 5; 11) originally denoted providing a choir for a public festival at one's own expense, and thus suggests supplying lavishly and without stint.

This section, while differing in eschatological perspective, has several points of contact, in wording and substance, with Rom. xii. 4-8, but none sufficiently close to warrant our assuming a literary relationship. Like Paul, our writer is freely reformulating traditional hortatory material. And since giving glory to God is fitting on 'the day of visitation' (see on ii. 12), he concludes by reminding his readers that their motive for behaving in the ways he has described should be **so that in everything God may be glorified through Jesus Christ.** They give glory to God when they heartily acknowledge that whatever service they offer the community, in charitable good works, edification or anything else, is in fact the overflowing of His abounding goodness. But, strictly, it is not men, or anything human effort achieves, that can promote God's glory; this comes about only **through Jesus Christ,** whose servants they are. The binitarian formula (cf. i. 3a) is liturgical and stereotyped (cf. Rom. xvi. 27; Jud. 25), but the idea is probably present that Christ is the mediator of the gifts and graces mentioned. It is through Him that the new people of God has been founded, and through Him (ii. 5) that it offers acceptable spiritual sacrifices.

After this powerful climax the writer inserts a doxology: **to whom belong glory and power for ever and ever. Amen.** Almost certainly the relative pronoun refers to God, not Jesus Christ. Proximity might suggest the latter, but the noun **glory** takes up and echoes **be glorified** in the preceding clause; it would be anomalous, too, if glory were to be attributed *to*

Christ immediately after the statement that God is glorified *through* Him. Interesting parallels are provided by *1 Clem.* xx. 12; l. 7, where we have doxologies which almost certainly are directed to God in spite of the fact that in each case 'through J.C. our Lord' precedes the ascription. In the Greek there is no verb representing **belong,** and some consider a prayer ('be': AV) more appropriate than a statement. But (a) we nowhere find an optative in doxologies in the NT; (b) where the verb is given (e.g. Rom. i. 25; 2 Cor. xi. 31) or can be inferred (Jud. 25: see note), it is indicative; (c) the indicative coheres admirably with the NT conviction that God's glory and honour are His by right. We notice that this doxology differs from the Pauline ones, which normally (e.g. Rom. xi. 36; Eph. iii. 21; Phil. iv. 20) ascribe only 'glory' to God, by the addition of **and power** (*kratos*: 'might', 'sovereignty'). This is found in doxologies in 1 Tim. vi. 16; Jud. 25; Rev. i. 6; v. 13, and probably emphasizes (very suitably in the context of our writer's purpose) the irresistible might which ensures God's triumph over every evil force. The **Amen** is regular after doxologies in the OT (e.g. Neh. viii. 6; Ps. xli. 13; LXX 1 Esd. ix. 47) and the NT (e.g. Rom. i. 25; Gal. i. 5; Phil. iv. 20; 1 Pet. v. 11) alike. It is a liturgical formula signifying devout assent, 'So be it' or 'So may it be'.

Why does the writer introduce a doxology at this point? According to some (see below: also Introduction, pp. 18; 20), because this is the end of what was originally an independent document. In its only plausible form, however, this depends on the highly improbable theory that the bulk of 1 Peter is a baptismal address. If it is a genuine letter, as the Commentary so far has attempted to show, a doxology makes a very unlikely finale to it. There are only three cases in the NT (Rom. xvi. 27; 2 Pet. iii. 18; Jud. 25) of an epistle concluding with a doxology; and in the first of these it is almost certainly a liturgical insertion. Doxologies are frequently found in the body of NT and early Christian letters (there are no fewer than ten in *1 Clement*), normally as expressions of the author's awe and devotion after some statement or outburst underlining the majesty of God or Christ. This is the sufficient explanation of the presence of one here; and indeed, having been anticipated by **may be glorified** above, it comes in more smoothly and naturally than most.

14. JOY AND CONFIDENCE IN PERSECUTION
iv. 12-19

(12) Dear friends, do not be surprised at your fiery ordeal, which comes upon you for your testing, as though something strange were happening to you. (13) But rejoice in so far as you are sharing Christ's sufferings, so that you may rejoice with exultation also at the revelation of his glory. (14) If you are insulted for the name of Christ, you are blessed, because the Spirit of glory and of God rests upon you. (15) For let none of you suffer as a murderer or a thief or a malefactor, or as a mischief-maker; (16) but if as a Christian, a man should feel no disgrace, but should glorify God in this name. (17) For the time has come for the judgment to begin with the house of God; and if first with us, what will be the end of those who do not obey the gospel of God? (18) And if the righteous man is saved with difficulty, where will the impious and sinful man appear? (19) Therefore those too who suffer according to God's will should, in active well-doing, entrust their souls to their faithful Creator.

This paragraph develops and reinforces the theme of suffering which came into the open as early as i. 6 f. and has been central from iii. 13 onwards, reiterating the promise that those who inflict it are already marked out for destruction. Because of the apparent break between 11 and 12 (there is no connecting particle), the doxology in 11, the more urgent note they detect here, and the impression they form that we are now for the first time confronted with actual as opposed to hypothetical persecution, many scholars conclude that iv. 12-end must be either a distinct document from the rest of the epistle, or possibly an appendix composed on the receipt of news of the outbreak of a pogrom or for the benefit of particular communities involved in one. For a discussion of the persecutions and a defence of the unity of 1 Peter, see Introduction, pp. 5-11; 20. Points which should be noted here are that (a) the doxology in 11 does not read like a conclusion (see note); (b) there is nothing significant in the

absence of a connecting particle in a hortatory clause like 12 (cf.
ii. 11; 13; etc.); (c) the admittedly intensified tone is entirely
natural as the writer gathers together his message; and (d) the
close linkage of this section with the foregoing one is confirmed
by such touches as the use in both of the same, rather uncommon verb 'be surprised' (iv. 4 and 12), the repetition from iv. 11
of the idea of glorifying God in iv. 16, and the strongly eschatological atmosphere pervading both, with the same threat of
judgment (cf. iv. 5 and iv. 17 f.) for the Asian Christian's persecutors.

12   The writer begins his renewed exhortation by addressing his
readers, as in ii. 11 (see note), as **Dear friends.** He uses the
expression deliberately so as to remind them that in all their
anxieties and troubles they belong to a fellowship whose members are knit together by love. He pleads: **do not be surprised
by your fiery ordeal, which comes upon you for your testing, as though something strange were happening to you.**
The main verb is exactly the same one (*xenizesthai*) as he has
used in iv. 4, and is itself taken up in the adjective **strange**
(*xenos*) which follows. From this it is clear that it does not
denote 'a paralysing shock' (F. W. Beare) so much as bewildered astonishment; he is giving the same advice as the author
of 1 Jn. iii. 13: 'Do not be surprised if the world hates you'. It
was a poignant problem to Christians in the apostolic age,
especially those who had emerged from a Gentile background,
that they should be misunderstood, disliked and subjected to
insults and ill-treatment, when they knew themselves to be
striving to carry out God's will. The gospels provide evidence
of the comfort and support they found in our Lord's explicit
warnings (e.g. Mt. v. 11 f.; Mk. xiii. 9-13; Jn. xv. 18-20).

The vivid noun **fiery ordeal** (*purōsis*) by which the writer
describes their painful experiences properly means 'burning',
'firing', and so secondarily (a) 'exposure to the action of fire',
as in cooking (e.g. Aristotle, *Prob.* xxi. 12) or surgery (e.g.
Antyllus, in Oribasius Med., xliv. 20. 42); (b) the testing or
purifying of metals by fire (e.g. Prov. xxvii. 21); (c) 'destruction
by fire' (e.g. Josephus, *Ant.* i. 203: of Sodom). In the LXX the
cognate verb *puroun* frequently connotes the refining of metals
by fire (e.g. Ps. lxvi. 10: cf. Rev. iii. 18) or, metaphorically, the

testing of people (e.g. Jdt. viii. 27). In the NT the noun is only used, apart from here, at Rev. xviii. 9, where it refers to the burning of Babylon. In selecting it the picture in the writer's mind is the one predominant in the OT of the purifying of metal by fire. As the explicative clause **which comes upon you for your testing** confirms, he is harking back to his doctrine, set out in i. 6 f., that the sufferings his readers have to undergo should be viewed as a divinely ordained trial of their faith and discipleship. The claim often made that the language suggests a sharper, more immediate onslaught which has suddenly descended on the communities, or some of them, is without foundation. The imagery of fire, like the doctrine of testing by suffering, does no more than reproduce ideas already used at i. 7; while the present imperative **do not be surprised,** and the present participles rendered **comes upon** and **were happening,** seem to presuppose an enduring situation rather than an unexpected crisis.

So far from being bewildered or upset, the writer goes on to argue, the Asian Christians should **rejoice in so far as** they 13 **are sharing Christ's sufferings, so that** they **may rejoice with exultation also at the revelation of his glory.** Here again we get the same paradox of exultation in suffering set against the backcloth of the Lord's triumphant Parousia which we met at i. 6 f. (see notes). Earlier he has taught them that imitation of Christ in His suffering is their Christian vocation (ii. 21), and that through their baptism they participate in His death (iv. 1). Their seemingly distressing experiences, he now declares, are of a piece with this, and in fact amount to **sharing Christ's sufferings.** They should not therefore cause them surprise or disheartenment, but rather joy, a joy which will have its even more rapturous counterpart and fulfilment (cf. **also**) when the End finally comes and they find themselves sharing in the **glory** of their Lord. For **at the revelation . . .,** cf. i. 7; 13. The thought underlying the verse finds striking parallels in Mt. v. 11 f. (cf. 'rejoice and be glad'); Lk. vi. 22 f. (cf. 'rejoice . . . your reward is great in heaven'); Heb. x. 32-39; xi. 26; xiii. 13 f.; Jas. i. 2 f.; but esp. in the Pauline letters, e.g. Rom. viii. 17 ('provided we suffer with him that we may be glorified with him'); 2 Cor. i. 5-7; Phil. iii. 10 f. (cf. 'participation in his

sufferings . . . resurrection from the dead'); 2 Tim. ii. 11 ('if we
have died with him, we shall also live with him'). It is questionable, however, whether, as many maintain, a direct influence of
the Apostle's theology is to be detected here. These ideas about
the sufferings and ultimate vindication of the believer were, it
is apparent, commonplace in primitive Christianity, and Paul
himself elaborates them in distinctive ways of his own not
represented here, e.g. viewing his sufferings as part of the travail
of the whole inanimate creation (Rom. viii. 18-25), or again as
complementary to those of Christ (Col. i. 24).

14   Nor does the glorification which suffering brings belong to
the distant future: **If you are insulted for the name of Christ,
you are blessed,** i.e. here and now. This further assurance
recalls, and doubtless ultimately stems from, our Lord's own
promise in Mt. v. 11; Lk. vi. 22. Passages like these, and Mt. x.
22; Mk. xiii. 13; Lk. xxi. 17; Jn. xv. 21; Acts ix. 16; xv. 26;
xxi. 13; Rev. ii. 3; iii. 8, indicate that to suffer, or be persecuted,
'because of' or 'on behalf of' or 'in' Christ's name were almost
technical expressions in the apostolic Church. In this formula
'name' is not to be pressed; it is an idiom, and 'in the name of'
is virtually equivalent to 'on account of', 'because of'. We may
compare, e.g., Mk. ix. 37, where the Lord speaks of receiving a
child 'in my name', i.e. 'for my sake'; also the rabbinical use of
le-shem ('for the name of') with the meaning 'for the sake of'.
Texts like Acts v. 41 ('suffer dishonour for the Name'); 3 Jn. 7
('they set out for the Name') are not true parallels, representing
rather an extension of the usage with stress on the name of
Christ as such. The verb 'insult' (*oneidizein*), it should be noted,
is a favourite one in the LXX (esp. the Psalms) for reproaches
heaped on God and His saints by the wicked, and in the NT
becomes associated, with its cognates, with the indignities and
maltreatment which Christ had to endure (Mt. xxvii. 44; Rom.
xv. 3; Heb. xi. 26; xiii. 13).

The reason why they are already **blessed** is **because the
Spirit of glory and of God rests upon** them (the addition of
'and of power' after **glory** has very strong, ancient support from
leading MSS and versions, and may be correct). In other words,
they already (cf. i. 8: 'you . . . exult with joy . . . full of glory'),
through the grace of the Spirit and as the crown of their suffer-

ings, participate in the divine glory (see on i. 7) which, according to the NT (i. 7; v. 4; 2 Cor. iv. 17; Col. iii. 4; etc.), the faithful will enjoy at the final consummation. Already that **glory,** spoken of in the OT (e.g. Ex. xxxiii. 9 f.; xl. 34 f.; Is. lx. 1-7; Hag. ii. 7) as manifesting itself in the pillar of cloud or in other ways, is breaking in on the Church, and is being imparted by a special anointing of the Spirit to Christians who suffer for their Lord and bear His reproach. For the early Christian belief that God's Spirit is bestowed on the persecuted, cf. the saying of Christ in Mt. x. 19 f. and the report (Acts vii. 55: cf. vi. 15) that Stephen, whose face was 'like an angel's face', was 'full of the Holy Spirit' at his martyrdom and 'saw the glory of God'. The later accounts of martyrdoms show how long this ancient idea persisted in the Church (e.g. *Mart. Polyc.* ii. 2; *Pass. Perp. et Fel.* i. 3; Eusebius, *Hist. eccl.* v. 1. 29; 34).

In part the wording is inspired by LXX Is. xi. 2 ('and the Spirit of God shall rest upon him'). But while the broad meaning of the sentence is reasonably clear, the Greek is bafflingly difficult to construe, and it is possible that the original text (copyists very soon began altering it) is lost. As the text stands, we have the neuter definite article with the genitive 'of the glory' (*to tēs doxēs*) followed by **and,** and then a second neuter definite article with **Spirit of God** (*to tou theou pneuma*). The article may be repeated so as to give emphasis: 'the Spirit of the glory—yes, the Spirit of God'. In both cases, on this assumption, it is one and the same Spirit, the genitives denoting its possessor and source, which is first (because of the mention of **glory** in 13) described as 'the glory', and then for purposes of clarification as 'God'. Admittedly the reduplicated article is cumbersome, but this is the best sense that can be made of the sentence. An alternative explanation is that two distinct subjects are required, and so we should take 'the of the glory' as a substantival phrase equivalent to 'the presence of the glory', i.e. the Shekinah; but the precedents quoted for this use of the bare article (Mt. xxi. 21; 1 Cor. x. 24; Jas. iv. 14; 2 Pet. ii. 22) are instances of a well recognized usage which is of dubious relevance here. The motive, too, for this curious periphrasis, alleged to be reverence, is odd in view of the writer's readiness to speak of the divine glory elsewhere.

A number of MSS, including practically all the cursives, Cyprian, the Sahidic version, etc., add the sentence: 'Among them it is blasphemed, but among you it is glorified'. The subject is either the Spirit or, more probably, the name of Christ; the insertion is an unnecessary, but clearly very ancient, gloss.

So far in this paragraph the writer has been advancing two considerations to fortify his readers' courage: (a) these trials of theirs should be accepted as God's way of testing them; but in addition (b) they should be a ground for positive exultation since people who suffer for Christ already share in the glory of the End. Now, to guard against possible misunderstanding, he

15 f. interjects a qualification: **For let none of you suffer as a murderer or a thief or a malefactor, or as a mischief-maker; but if as a Christian, a man should feel no disgrace, but should glorify God in this name.** The opening particle **For** (*gar*) looks back to and is explicative of **for the name of Christ** in 14; the blessing there mentioned of course does not extend to those whose rough treatment is punishment for manifestly guilty conduct. The first three classes of evil-doers read like a stock list, and this is perhaps borne out by the repetition of **as** (*hōs*) before the fourth, which may indicate an after-thought addition to the list. Both Tertullian (*Scorp.* xii. 3) and Cyprian (*Test.* iii. 37) render **malefactor** (*kakopoios*) by 'maleficus', and since this Latin noun occasionally (Lactantius, *Inst.* ii. 16. 4; Jerome, *In Dan.* ii. 2; *Cod. Theod.* ix. 16. 4) connotes 'magician', 'sorcerer', some (so NEB) maintain that this must be the sense intended here (cf. 2 Tim. iii. 13, where *goēs* may have it), especially as **murderer** and **thief** designate specific crimes. But there is no evidence either that *kakopoios* ever bore this meaning or that Tertullian and Cyprian thought it did ('maleficus' is a literal transposition of *kakopoios* into Latin, and its normal meaning is simply 'wrong-doer'), and the more general **malefactor** is definitely preferable in view of the writer's use of the noun and related verb at ii. 12; 14; iii. 17.

Much heavy weather has been made over *allotrioepiskopos* (**mischief-maker:** so RSV). Some have proposed the translation 'agitator', arguing that it is probably an improvisation of the writer's to designate proletarian revolutionary activity, while others have conjectured that it might stand for either 'spy' or 'informer' (TWNT II, 617-19). These are all fanciful guesses, based on the assumption that, like the first three nouns, this word must point to an actionable offence; but the unexpected second **as** seems to differentiate it and introduce a fresh category. As a matter of fact, while exceedingly rare, *allotrioepiskopos* is used by the 4th cent. Epiphanius (*Ancor*. xii. 5) with the clear sense of 'interfering with someone else's business'. He almost certainly uses it a second time (*Haer*. lxvi. 85. 6) with the similar, more technical meaning 'one who has purchased the right to act in another man's property'. We can only speculate what kind of meddling the writer has in mind (excessive zeal for making converts? causing discord in family or commercial life? over-eager denunciation of pagan habits ?prying curiosity?), but he plainly regards it as disreputable. This exegesis agrees with that of Theophylact (cf. PG cxxv, 1214).

Scholars have been needlessly exercised by this list. Is it conceivable, they have asked, that he should have reckoned with the possibility that the members of the freshly converted, ardent Asian communities would be charged with murder, theft, etc.? So, to put the matter in perspective, they have reminded us that Christians in the apostolic age were not all saints: Paul had to deal with a case of incest at Corinth (1 Cor. v. 1-8), and more than once (e.g. 1 Cor. v. 9-13; vi. 9-11; Eph. iv. 28; v. 3-12) found it useful to warn his correspondents against contact with, or relapse into, immoral behaviour. All this is very true and realistic, but in fact they are missing the writer's point. He is not naming these sins because he seriously supposes people are likely to commit them (the possibility exists, of course, but that is not the issue here). The first two at any rate come from a stock catalogue, and his object in citing them is simply to underline, with a rhetorical flourish, the world of difference between paying a penalty when you are guilty of a misdemeanour and paying a penalty which you deserve (a point he has already made in a more specialized context in ii. 20). The more heinous the examples of the former he selects, the more effective his argument. Probably the only item he is really in earnest about is **mischief-maker** (we can readily imagine an over-enthusiastic convert creating disturbance by crude defiance of accepted customs), and this is why he highlights it by inserting the second **as**.

It is of course disgraceful to incur punishment for such mis-conduct, and a Christian should be ashamed if caught in such a situation; there is no question of glory then. But the position is totally different if he is called upon to suffer **as a Christian**, i.e. not on the ground of any specific act of wickedness, but simply of being **a Christian**. This term (*Christianos*: the reading *Chrestianos* found in Codex Sin. is interesting in view of the occurrence of the name 'Chrestus' in Suetonius, *Claud*. xxv, and may be original) is found in the NT, apart from this verse, in Acts xi. 26; xxvi. 28: the former text records that adherents of the new religion were first so called at Antioch (*c*. A.D. 45). It occurs in *Did*. xii. 4 and several times in Ignatius's letters, while Tacitus (*Ann*. xv. 44) and Suetonius (*Ner*. xvi) write as if it were in popular use at Rome at the time of the Neronian persecution (64). Pliny (*Ep*. x. 96. 1-3) vouches for its currency *c*. 110. In such a predicament **a man should feel no disgrace**; on the contrary, he **should glorify God in this name**.

As with **for the name of Christ** in 14, a literal translation of the Greek underlying **in this name** has been deliberately adopted so as to present the facts fairly to English readers. The exact interpretation of the phrase has been much discussed. In the view of some it looks back to **for the name of Christ,** and **this name** is 'Christ'; but this is to be rejected, if only because (a) **this** must surely have a more immediate reference, and (b) we have seen that in 14 **name** is not strictly the name 'Christ'. The more usual view is that it refers to **Christian, this name** being in fact the description 'Christian'. But we still have to explain what is intended by 'glorifying God **in** this name'. The most plausible suggestions are that the believer gives glory to God either by his manner of living up to the name or boldly witnessing to it, or simply 'by virtue of bearing the name'. E. G. Selwyn, who offers the latter paraphrase, argues that **in** (*en*) may be instrumental, but more probably connotes 'the sphere in which'. Neither of these, it must be confessed, gives an entirely convincing account of the construction, and the former at any rate seems to read more into the words than the argument would lead us to expect. There is, however, an idiomatic use of 'name' (*onoma*) which may throw light on the difficulty. In Mt. x. 41 f., e.g., 'in the name of a prophet/

disciple' is equivalent to 'as being in the category of prophet/ disciple', i.e. 'because he is . . .'; while, still more relevantly, in Mk. ix. 41 the curious expression 'in the name that you are Christ's' means 'on the ground that you are Christ's'. From secular Greek we have, e.g., Pap. Oxy. i. 37, 17 (49 A.D.), where 'in the name of free-born' means 'on the ground that it [a foundling] is free-born'; Josephus, *Ant.* xii. 154, where 'in the name of a dowry' means 'under the heading of a dowry'; and numerous instances in papyri (cf. Liddell and Scott, *s.v.*) of 'name' bearing the sense (derived from accountancy) of 'to the account of', and so 'under the heading of'.

It seems more than likely, then, that it is a construction of this type that is employed here. If so, the Greek behind **in this name** should be rendered either 'in this capacity', i.e. in his capacity as a Christian, or 'on this account', i.e. because he is called upon to suffer as a Christian. The former version overlaps with Selwyn's, but rests on a more accurate syntactical analysis. In favour of the latter are (a) the fact that a number of later MSS give the variant reading *en tōi merei toutōi* (i.e. 'on this account': cf. AV's 'on this behalf'), an undoubted gloss but one which reveals both that Greek-speaking copyists did not find the meaning so obvious as many modern scholars do, and how in fact they understood it; and (b) its agreement with the writer's attitude to suffering as the ground for exultation and so for giving glory to God. In neither case is **this name** to be identified with 'Christian' strictly. In the latter it has nothing to do with 'Christian'; while in the former a legitimate para- phrase would be 'in his standing as a Christian'.

Not unnaturally, these lines have been ransacked for clues to the nature of the Asian Christians' plight, and also to the date. For the claim that they represent Christianity as a capital offence in the eyes of the state and presuppose an official persecution, roughly contemporary with, or only slightly earlier than, the one described by Pliny in his famous letter (*Ep.* x. 96) to Trajan *c.* 110, see Introduction, pp. 28-30. Here we may note the following points. (a) If capital charges had been envisaged, we should have expected a less vague, comprehensive term than **suffer.** This is the verb used through- out the epistle to cover a whole range of maltreatment of which bullying by unsympathetic masters and slanderous abuse are typical instances, and while we need not doubt that court proceedings of some kind may be included, we need not (see on 15) deduce from the mention of murder and theft that they are of a capital nature. (b) Since 'suffering as a Christian' develops directly out of 'being insulted for Christ's sake' (an expression without any judicial overtones), the writer would surely have given some clearer indication had he been switching his thoughts now to trials and martyrdom. (c) If 'suffering as a Christian' really does stand for being executed for the faith, it is amazing that a man of his outlook should have used such a weak expression as 'let him not feel ashamed' (*mē aischunesthō*). Such language would, of course, be appropriate enough if he were thinking of humiliating treatment like being jeered at, bemobbed, even beaten up or dragged before local magistrates on petty charges. (d) It is unwarranted to interpret **suffer as a Christian** as necessarily implying that Christianity as such has become a capital offence. It probably counted as one, following the precedent set by Nero (Tertullian, *Ad nat.* i. 7. 9), from 65 onwards when it was forced on the attention of the authorities; but in the context of 'being insulted for Christ's sake' the phrase probably means no more than having to endure the obloquy, ostracism and occasional violence which the despised name brought on its bearers. In so far as court cases are in view, the words are of course consistent with Christianity being the charge. But it is at least equally possible that, while the victims were arrested and denounced as Christians, the charges brought against them were more specific, e.g. provoking disturbances, interfering with local customs. (e) In general it may be questioned whether the situation implied differs in any important respect from those conjured up by the experiences of, e.g., Paul at Philippi, Thessalonica and Ephesus (Acts xvi. 19-40; xvii. 5-10; xix. 24-40), or presupposed in the primitive synoptic tradition (e.g. Mk. xiii. 9-13) as the lot of the apostolic Church.

Reverting now to the eschatological theme which runs through the whole section (cf. iv. 5; 7), the writer spells out the reason
17 (**For**: the particle *hoti* is explicative) why the Asian Christians should, paradoxically, give glory to God in their tribulations: **the time has come for the judgment to begin with the house of**

God. In other words, agonizing and inexplicable though they may appear, these trials are the preordained opening phase in the unfolding of God's plan for the End. A preparatory judgment and purification are indipensable, and the prophets (Jer. xxv. 29; Ezek. ix. 6; Mal. iii. 1-6) had foretold that a start would be made with the chosen people, indeed with the sanctuary and the priesthood. The apostolic Church took these ideas up, believing (Mk. xiii. 8-13) that, as 'the beginning of travails', Christians would have to face hatred, brutality and imprisonment; while Paul develops a variant of this by teaching (1 Cor. xi. 31 f.) that their chastening here and now is salutary since it exempts them from being 'condemned along with the world'. As in ii. 5, the Church is pictured, not as a 'household' (RSV; NEB), but (as Ezek. ix. 6, which is in the writer's thoughts, shows) as God's temple or sanctuary.

Encouraging though this is, however, it is only a fraction of the story. If God's judgment is ordained to start with His chosen people, it is certainly not going to stop with them: **and if first with us, what will be the end of those who do not obey the gospel of God?** These, of course, are the readers' hostile neighbours and persecutors; their lack of faith is characterized, as in ii. 8; iii. 1, as disobedience, just as faith is identified as obedience in i. 2; 14; 22. The doom in store for them, the writer implies, will indeed be frightful: no glorious denouement, as for Christians who suffer faithfully, but utter destruction. Though less circumstantial, his message is the same as Paul's, who assures his distressed correspondents (2 Thess. i. 5-10) that 'God deems it just to repay with afflictions those who afflict you', and that when Christ is revealed from heaven they will be granted rest from their pains, while the punishment meted out to 'those who do not know God and do not obey the gospel of our Lord Jesus Christ' will consist in 'eternal destruction and exclusion from the presence of the Lord'. A common pattern of teaching underlies both.

To drive the contrast home, he cites LXX Prov. xi. 31: **And 18 if the righteous man is saved with difficulty, where will the impious and sinful man appear?** In the original context the subject under discussion is the temporal welfare of the two types of men, but the writer transposes the moral to the plane of eschatology. Even **the righteous man,** he points out, meaning the faithful Christian, will only be **saved** on the day of judgment **with difficulty**; the foretaste of judgment which his readers are already experiencing is proof of that. He has none of the starry-eyed optimism of some modern Christians, but shares the stern outlook of the apocalyptic discourses attributed to our Lord Himself (e.g. Mk. xiii. 19 f.). But if God's elect have to pass through such hazards and trials, the reflection that should stiffen their resolution and redouble their courage is that words cannot describe the irreparable fate awaiting **the impious and sinful,** i.e. those who reject the gospel and, more particularly, the Asian Christians' adversaries.

Having thus eloquently sketched the blessedness of righteous suffering and the awful fate of those who inflict it, he draws his
19 conclusion: **Therefore those too who suffer according to God's will should, in active well-doing, entrust their souls to their faithful Creator.** In the Greek, as in this literal rendering, the meaning is somewhat obscured; to bring it out, the elliptic **those who . . . God's will** needs to be paraphrased as 'those who suffer, since (or if) God wills their suffering'. The force of **too** (*kai*: in the sense of 'also') is not altogether clear. According to some, the particle, which they prefer to translate 'also', really goes with **should . . . entrust,** the imperative introducing a fresh injunction. This is attractive, but its position seems to suggest that it is emphatic and qualifies **those who . . .** If this is correct, the thought intended is that, while people exempt from suffering will naturally commit themselves to God, **those who suffer** should do so **too,** for their suffering is providentially ordered. That his correspondent's afflictions are all part of God's plan is one of the writer's constant themes (i. 6; ii. 15; iii. 17; v. 6). So too is his insistence on **active well-doing** (*agathopoiïa*), which throughout the letter he regards as the fruit of the baptismal life, the comportment appropriate in a hostile environment for Christians awaiting the End (e.g. i. 15; ii. 12; 15; 20; iii. 6; 13; 17).

By **souls** (*psuchas*: see on i. 9) he means little, if anything, more than 'themselves'. It is a mistake to overhear a deliberate distinction between soul and body and a hint that, while the readers may have to see their *bodies* done to death, they can be confident that God will preserve their *souls*. Martyrdom is not envisaged, for he expects them to go on living normal lives and to be energetic in practical charity. The verb **entrust** (*paratithesthai*), it has often been pointed out, is the one used, according to Lk. xxiii. 46, by the dying Jesus of committing His spirit to God; but the writer is not so much recalling this detail of the passion as independently echoing Ps. xxxi. 5. It is a graphic term connoting entrusting something valuable to someone for safe-keeping; for its use elsewhere of commending to God, cf. Acts xiv. 23; xx. 32. In the light of this we perceive the proper nuance of **faithful**: God is a reliable depository Who can be trusted. His faithfulness is the basic motive for Christian hope in the NT (e.g. 2 Tim. i. 12; ii. 13; Heb. x. 23). The description of Him as **Creator** (*ktistēs*) is noteworthy. Though frequent in the LXX, Apocrypha, Philo, etc. (TWNT III, 999-1034), this is its sole appearance in the NT. The title may have been chosen here 'because it involves power which is able, and love which is willing, to guard His creatures' (C. Bigg).

15. INSTRUCTION TO LEADERS AND FAITHFUL

v. 1-5

(1) So I appeal to the elders among you—I who am a fellow-elder and witness to Christ's sufferings, who am also a partaker in the glory which is going to be revealed: (2) Tend the flock of God in your charge, exercising your oversight not under constraint but willingly, as God would have it, not for shameful gain but eagerly, (3) not as domineering over the charges allotted you, but making yourselves examples to the flock. (4) So when the Chief Shepherd is manifested, you will receive the unfading garland of glory. (5) In the same way, you younger people should be subject to your elders. All of you, however, should gird yourselves with humility towards one another, for 'God is opposed to the arrogant, but gives grace to the humble'.

With his powerful appeal in iv. 12-19 the writer's message of encouragement is almost, but not entirely, concluded; he is to make a further mention of tribulation in v. 6-9. At first sight the present verses seem to consist of traditional exhortation, rather more personal than anything we have had before, and critics have queried whether their logical position would not have been in the section ii. 13-iii. 9 devoted to advice to the several groups in the community. They also sense a lack of connection with the preceding section, and are inclined to

1 treat the particle **So** (*oun*: replaced in many MSS by the definite article *tous*, linking **elders** with **among you**) as merely transitional. Others point out that it may refer back to 'active well-doing' in iv. 19, the object of the clause being to indicate specific forms of this in which elders ought to engage; but while on the right lines, this latter explanation is too narrow, and overlooks the fact that 'active well-doing' applies to the Asian Christians generally and covers the whole range of charitable goodness. Actually the paragraph is much more closely integrated both with what precedes and with what follows (cf. 'therefore' in 6) than is commonly allowed. The writer has deliberately placed his special instructions to leaders and the community as a whole here because, in the testing situation with which all his previous exhortations have been concerned, effective and disinterested pastoral leadership and mutual respect between members are absolutely indispensable. **So** underlines that the counsel which follows is the practical corollary of the advice and encouragement he has been trying throughout to give.

He begins then: **I appeal to the elders among you.** In contrast to 5 below, where its primary meaning at any rate is 'older people', **elders** (*presbuteroi*) here denotes the officials who acted as pastoral leaders of the congregations. The most detailed picture of such leaders in the NT comes in the Pastorals, but it is evident that the apostolic Church very early appointed suitable persons, selected no doubt partly on grounds of seniority and experience, for this important responsibility in the local communities. So Paul speaks of 'those who labour among you and are over you in the Lord and admonish you' (1 Thess. v. 12), and of 'persons who lend assistance and exercise rule' (1 Cor. xii. 28: cf. Rom. xii. 8); in Phil. i. 1 he calls them 'overseers (*episkopoi*) and deacons'. The Pastorals apart, 'elders' are not mentioned by that name in the acknowledged Paulines, although Acts xiv. 23 represents the Apostle as 'appointing elders in every church'. The title is applied in Acts to the leaders of the Jerusalem church (in association with the apostles: xv. 2-xvi. 4; with James: xxi. 18), and of the Ephesian church (xx. 17-38); cf. also Jas. v. 14 ('the Elder' in 2 Jn. 1; 3 Jn. 1 seems a different kind of personage, while the 'twenty-four elders' of Rev. iv; v; etc. raise special problems). The type of organization implied as well as the name was already well established in Judaism, for every Jewish settlement, in the Diaspora no less than in Palestine, was supervised by a board ('sanhedrin': in Greek *gerousia*) composed of elders under a president with responsibility for finance and the corporate life generally (for the 'elders' at Qumran, cf. 1QS vi. 8 f.). There is little doubt that the primitive Christian communities, which even in pagan districts usually started from an ex-Jewish nucleus, tended to take over the presbyteral organization which they found ready to hand, modifying it to suit their special needs and evolving theological conceptions.

The present reference is too casual and fleeting to enable us to form any very clear-cut idea of the administrative structure of the Asian churches. It is evident, however, from 2 that the elders' functions include leadership, pastoral supervision, and disciplinary and financial responsibilites. They seem therefore to correspond broadly to the ministers vaguely referred to by Paul in the passages cited above, and to those more circumstantially described in the Pastorals. Although it is difficult to judge on the basis of such fragmentary evidence, the impression left is of a relatively early stage in the evolution of church government. For example, there seem to be no distinctions among ministers (as in the Pastorals), still less an articulated hierarchy such as we find in Asia Minor very early in the 2nd cent. (Ignatius), and no hint that they are custodians of the sound tradition of doctrine.

In order to add weight to his charge the writer strikes a personal note which underlines his authority, but also raises in a tantalizing way the problem of his identity (see Introduction, pp. 30-33). Is he Peter himself, or some disciple who has assumed Peter's mantle? In any case he first describes himself as **a fellow-elder,** intending the Asian elders to understand by this that the great Apostle shoulders the same responsibilities as they and can sympathize with their difficulties. So far from making much of his overriding apostolic status, he plays it down and ranks himself with the local church leaders, much as Ignatius speaks (*Eph.* ii. 1; *Magn.* ii. 1; *Philad.* iv. 1; *Smyrn.* xii. 2) of the deacons of the churches as his 'fellow-servants'. According to some, this self-effacement is most naturally explained as an unconscious token of Petrine authorship.

Next, he reminds them that he is a **witness** (*martus*) **to Christ's sufferings.** The obvious and straightforward interpretation of this might seem to be that he has been an eyewitness (for this sense of *martus*, cf. Mk. xiv. 63; Acts vii. 58; 2 Cor. xiii. 1) of the Lord's passion, and as such is qualified to hold up His patient endurance of suffering as an example (cf. ii. 21-23). But although many understand the phrase so, we should hesitate to follow them. Not only is the motive alien to the context, but Peter could hardly be described as having been in any strict sense a spectator of the passion. Properly speaking, *martus* denotes one who testifies rather than an eye-witness, and it is frequently applied in the NT (e.g. Lk. xxiv. 48; Acts i. 8; xxii. 15) to people who proclaim, and so bear witness to, Jesus. In several passages (e.g. Acts xxii. 20; Rev. ii. 13; xvii. 6) we observe it acquiring the further implication of suffering for one's testimony to Christ. Later, of course, as the Christian technical vocabulary developed, the noun came to stand by itself with the meaning 'martyr', but this usage is not found in the NT, where the idea of testifying to Christ always remains the dominant one (cf. TWNT IV, 492-500). Is the writer then grounding his right to a respectful hearing on the fact that he is a preacher of Christ crucified, who throughout his letter (i. 11; 19; ii. 21-24; iii. 18-iv. 1; 13) has constantly dwelt on the Lord's sufferings? This exegesis is admirable so far as it goes, but more far-reaching overtones must be recognized in the phrase if justice is to be done to the close connection between it and the following clause which the Greek construction (cf. **who am also**) and the parallelism between **witness** and **partaker** demand. It is highly probable that, as at iv. 13, the thought in the writer's mind is the correspondence between sharing Christ's sufferings and sharing His glory. In other words, he is claiming (as Luther and Calvin perceived) to be a **witness to Christ's sufferings** in the deeper sense of himself suffering for his testimony. Moreover, his manner of expressing himself (in the Greek the definite article before **fellow-elder** applies to **witness** too, and the force of **fellow-** is carried over to the second noun) implies that in his sufferings as a missionary and teacher of the faith he is at one with the Asian elders in their present tribulations.

Thus he can claim, thirdly, that, as a **witness to Christ's sufferings**, he is (again like the Asian elders) **also a partaker in the glory which is going to be revealed.** Some would interpret this as an allusion to Peter's presence at the Transfiguration, and the author of 2 Peter (i. 16-18), who envisaged that mysterious event as an anticipatory disclosure of the glory of the Parousia, undoubtedly took it so. But had this been the meaning (the wording is not favourable to it), we should have expected some more precise reference to the circumstances and some definite indication that the experience had happened in the past; in fact, though no participle is expressed, the time intended is much more naturally understood as present or future. Undoubtedly the writer is thinking of the divine glory which has been given to Christ (i. 11; 21; iii. 22) in His resurrection, ascension and session at God's right hand, and which will **be revealed** (cf. iv. 13), i.e. manifested in its fulness for the benefit of His faithful followers, at His Second Coming. He pictures himself as partaking, like his correspondents, of that glory in the present; for while its full manifestation belongs to the future, he holds (cf. esp. iv. 14) that, with the End so close at hand, those who suffer for Christ already enjoy a foretaste of it.

For his charge he incorporates a piece of stock exhortation for ministers; it is revealed as such by the contents of 2 f., which find close parallels in late Jewish and early Christian literature, and even more by its exceptionally formal structure (cf. esp. the three careful antitheses, with the contrasting adverbs or participial clauses introduced in each case by the same negative and adversative particles). Its burden is: **Tend the flock of 2 God in your charge.** The imperative is the ingressive aorist (*poimanate*: was it perhaps the present *poimainete* in the original code?), suggesting that the situation demands energetic action. The thought of God's chosen people as His **flock** is deeply rooted in the OT (e.g. Ps. xxiii; Is. xl. 11; Jer. xxiii. 1-4; Ezek. xxxiv. 1-10); while in Ps. Sol. xvii. 45 (1st cent. B.C.) the Messiah is represented as 'shepherding (*poimainōn*) the Lord's flock in faith and righteousness'. In the NT the imagery of shepherding is occasionally applied, as here, to the community leaders (Jn. xxi. 15-17; Acts xx. 28), but only in one place (Eph. iv. 11) are they actually designated 'shepherds', and even here the word is not a fixed title of office. The nearest analogy comes from Qumran, where we read (6QD xiii. 9) of the 'mebaqqer', or overseer, sustaining the people 'as a shepherd his flock'. Early in the 2nd cent., though without losing its vigorous symbolism, the noun becomes a conventional description of the bishop (Ignatius, *Philad.* ii. 1; *Rom.* ix. 1) or of ministers (Hermas, *Sim.* ix. 31. 5 f.).

It is desirable, especially in these times of trial, that the elders should exercise their **oversight** in the right spirit, and this is defined in three carefully chosen antitheses. It is difficult to decide whether the participle which introduces them, translated **exercising your oversight** (*episkopountes*), belongs to the original text or not. It is not syntactically necessary, adds nothing to the sense, and is omitted by Codex Sin., B, the important cursive 33, and the Sahidic version. Many explain it as interpolated under the influence of 'Shepherd and Guardian' (*episkopos*) in ii. 25. It is supported, however, by Pap. 72, A, and the Old Latin, Syriac and Bohairic versions; and there is a great deal of evidence in early literature (e.g. Acts xx. 28; the passages of Ignatius cited above) for the almost routine combination of the nouns or verbs for 'shepherding' and 'overseeing'. The fact that our writer has already juxtaposed them at ii. 25 is proof that they were associated in his mind. It is conceivable that if *episkopountes* is original (as the translation presupposes), it was omitted because the verb later came to mean 'function as a bishop', and this seemed to scribes incongruous in an address to 'elders'.

First, supervision should be exercised **not under constraint but willingly, as God would have it.** (The last clause, in

Greek *kata theon*, is lacking in some MSS, but should probably be retained since its subsequent intrusion is hard to explain.) The language seems to presuppose that being an elder is a recognized position to which one is appointed. It also clearly implies that the right people sometimes needed pressure to be brought upon them to accept office; we can only guess the reasons for their reluctance (a natural shrinking from the responsibilities involved, the desire to avoid the dangers to which church officers were exposed, etc.). Much the same concern inspires the hope expressed in Heb. xiii. 17 that leaders will carry out their tasks 'with real joy and not with groaning'; so too 1 Tim. iii. 1 seeks to overcome the hesitations of unwilling candidates for the ministry. The clause **as God would have it** is to be taken closely with **willingly**; the elders are to serve, not for their own satisfaction in the job, but as glad volunteers in God's service. This idea of voluntary self-dedication finds interesting parallels in later Judaism (e.g. 1 Macc. ii. 42: 'everyone who offered himself willingly for the Law'), and especially at Qumran, where the sectaries were all 'volunteers' (1QS i. 7; 11; v. 1; 6; etc.) and the priests in particular 'willingly pledged themselves' to fulfil the community aims (1QS v. 21 f.).

Secondly, Christian leaders should watch over their flock **not for shameful gain but eagerly.** Apparently the eldership brought opportunities of profit, and it has been conjectured that some system of remuneration (cf. 1 Tim. v. 17 f.) was already in force. We recall that Paul upheld (1 Cor. ix. 7-11) the right of apostles and others to be supported by the churches, though declining (2 Cor. xii. 13-17) to take advantage of it himself. Probably more relevant, however, is the fact that the finances and poor relief of the communities were in the hands of the elders or overseers, and the temptation to abuse one's trust and make a profitable business out of it was very real. Similar warnings against an interest in money or private gain are a commonplace in primitive codes about ministers (1 Tim. iii. 3; 8; Tit. i. 7; 11; *Did.* xv. 1; Polycarp, *Phil.* v. 2), and these often use the very word (*aischrokerdēs*: 'sordidly greedy of gain') employed adverbially here. The adverb opposed to this (*prothumōs*), translated **eagerly** above, is, to judge by the use of the corresponding adjective and noun in the LXX, Philo, etc. (TWNT VI,

694-700), an extremely strong one; it expresses enthusiasm and devoted zeal.

The third antithesis, at least in its negative half, is extra-
3 ordinarily obscure: **not as domineering over the charges allotted to you.** There is no doubt that the writer is warning elders against abusing their authority; following the Lord's own prescription, they are to serve their subordinates rather than 'lord it over them' (Mk. x. 42 has the very same verb *kata-kurieuein* as we find here) in the manner of pagan rulers. Our problem is to determine exactly what kind of autocratic be-haviour he has in mind, and more particularly what he intends by the plural (*klēroi*) translated **charges allotted to you.** In the LXX, Philo, etc., and also in the NT, this noun means (a) 'lot' (for 'cast lots' cf. Mk. xv. 24; Acts i. 26); (b) 'something assigned by lot'; and so (c) 'portion', 'share' (e.g. Acts viii. 21; xxvi. 18: all idea of lots in the literal sense has disappeared, but the notion of something one has not worked for but has received from God remains). Of the many conjectures put forward ('funds earmarked for the community and the elders'; 'plots of land assigned to the elders'; etc.) the most widely favoured is that the term here denotes the spheres of duty, or portions of the whole flock, allocated to the care of the elders severally. The suggestion is that each has his own group, or 'parish', within the community for which he is pastorally responsible.

This gives an excellent sense both in itself and in relation to the next clause, and for that reason has been provisionally adopted. There are, however, at least two difficulties which it raises, for we have no evidence elsewhere either of *klēros* signifying a group within the whole congregation or of con-gregations being organized in this fashion. Further, we know that the term later acquired the meaning 'ecclesiastical office' (cf. Hippolytus's statement in *Trad. apost.* iii. 5 that the bishop's prerogative includes 'bestowing *klēroi*': also ix. 7), the way for this being prepared by the primitive practice of casting lots for church leaders (Acts i. 26). At Qumran, it appears, the 'mebaqqer' (6QD xiii. 12), or earlier the priests (1QS v. 20-24; vi. 22; ix. 7), had the task of assigning to newcomers their rank or standing, this being determined by lot. It has therefore been attractively argued (W. Nauck, ZNTW xlviii, 200 ff.) that, as the present section embodies traditional elements, it is best explained as forbidding church leaders to take a high-handed line of their own in allocating offices and functions (e.g. those listed at iv. 10 f.) and push it through on the sole basis of their own authority regardless of the real interest of the community.

Whatever the true interpretation, the writer is convinced that there must be nothing **domineering** in the elders' attitude; rather they should make themselves **examples to the flock.** The context (cf. 5b: also ii. 13-iii. 12 with its emphasis on submission to one another) makes it clear that the spirit he wishes to see pervading the community, and which the elders should take the lead in displaying, is one of mutual humility. So Paul, in order to influence people, prefers not to assert his authority but to make himself an example (2 Thess. iii. 9). And if the Asian leaders carry out their tasks with proper enthusiasm, integrity and humility, they can be sure of obtaining their reward when the End, now imminent, dawns: **when the Chief Shepherd is 4 manifested, you will receive the unfading garland of glory.** Christ has already been described as 'Shepherd' in ii. 25 (see note); the title **Chief Shepherd** (*archipoimēn*: a NT hapax, but attested in pre-Christian papyri; also Test. Jud. viii. 1), i.e. 'master shepherd', delicately reminds the elders that they are His delegates, and hints at His right to call them to account and, if appropriate, reward them for their discharge of their duties. In a similar way the description of Christ in Heb. xiii. 20 as 'the great Shepherd of the sheep' underlines His uniqueness in comparision with all the other shepherds of Israel, especially Moses (cf. LXX Is. lxiii. 11), who have preceded Him. The verb 'to be manifested' (*phanerousthai*), used at i. 20 (cf. 1 Tim. iii. 16; Heb. ix. 26) of His incarnation, is also applied to His Second Coming at Col. iii. 4; 1 Jn. ii. 28; iii. 2.

For **you will receive,** cf. i. 9, where the same verb (*komizesthai*) is used; it is almost a routine term (Eph. vi. 8; Col. iii. 25; Heb. x. 36; xi. 13; 39) for appropriating the promised eschatological reward (or penalty). In the NT the meed of the faithful is frequently depicted as a **garland** or crown: 1 Cor. ix. 25 ('an imperishable garland'); 2 Tim. iv. 8 ('the crown of righteousness'); Jas. i. 12 ('the crown of life'); Rev. ii. 10 ('the crown of life'); iii. 11; iv. 4. In Greek cities it was customary to

bestow a crown, possibly of precious metal but more often of
ivy, bay or wild olive, on athletes victorious in the games or on
citizens who had rendered distinguished public service. This is
the background of 1 Cor. ix. 25, but it is unlikely to have been
operative here or, say, in the passages from Revelation. We
should note that the expression 'crown of glory' is found in Is.
xxviii. 5; Jer. xiii. 18; Ecclus. xlvii. 6; Test. Ben. iv. 1; 1QS iv. 7;
1QH ix. 25, and that the crown imagery became extremely
popular in the Wisdom literature (Prov. iv. 9; xii. 4; xiv. 24;
xvi. 31; xvii. 6; Ecclus. i. 11; 18; vi. 31; xv. 6; xxv. 6; Wis. v. 16).
The fact that this passage, and also 2 Tim. iv. 8; Jas. i. 12; Rev.
ii. 10, speak of the crown as the prize for suffering and endurance probably points to a common paraenetic tradition. The
genitive **of glory** is epexegetic: the crown in fact consists of the
divine glory which will encompass the faithful Christians at
Christ's Coming. For **unfading** (*amarantinos*: lit. 'that does not
wither': so *amarantos* in i. 4; of wisdom, Wis. vi. 12), cf. 1 Cor.
ix. 25: the Christian's **garland** is contrasted with perishable
earthly ones (e.g. Is. xxviii. 1; Lam. v. 16; Wis. ii. 8).

5   **In the same way,** the exhortation continues, **you younger
people should be subject to your elders.** Commentators
have been puzzled by **In the same way,** wondering, e.g., in
what way the deference due from junior members is supposed
to resemble the attitude expected of leaders. To resolve this
difficulty while also eliminating that caused by having to take
presbuteroi as denoting office-bearers in 1 and older persons
here, some have proposed that the word translated **younger
people** (*neōteroi*) really means subordinate ministers, i.e.
deacons. If this is accepted, we have in v. 1-5a, logically
arranged, instructions first to elders or overseers (*episkopoi*)
about their duties to the congregation, and then to deacons
about their duties to elders. Unfortunately for this exegesis, no
parallel to this use of *neōteros*, in itself improbable, can be found
in the Bible (*neaniskoi*, i.e. 'young men', in LXX Ex. xxiv. 5
hardly counts) or early Church. These difficulties disappear
once it is recognized that 5a is a detached fragment of the community code paraphrased in ii. 13-iii. 9 which the writer has
transferred here for reasons of his own. **In the same way**
(*homoiōs*) is the conventional link between successive items

which we noticed at iii. 1 and 7; while the theme is the identical one of proper subordination (the verb *hupotassesthai* is the one used at ii. 13; 18; iii. 1; 5) to one's superior in the natural order. In the ancient world the division of society into older people and younger (cf., e.g., 1 Tim. v. 1 f.; Tit. ii. 6; Philo, *Quod omnis prob.* 81—of the Essenes: 'they sit in appointed places . . . the young men below the old') was just as much taken for granted as the division into men and women, free men and slaves, etc. The transition from 'elders' (= officials) in 1 to 'elders' (= older men) here is nothing like so hard as is alleged, for the leaders were naturally chosen from the older age-group of the community, and the term *presbuteros* had not yet acquired a fixed technical meaning; we have precisely the same switch from one sense to the other in 1 Tim. v. 1 and 17.

This Christian subordination, however, is not to be confined to one section of the Church: **All of you . . . should gird yourselves with humility towards each other.** The passage from particular groups to the community as a whole is characteristic (cf. iii. 8). The translation adopted assumes that a full stop should be placed after **your elders,** but it has been questioned whether this is correct. In the Greek the next clause opens with (literally) 'and all to one another' (*pantes de allēlois*), and if we take these words as beginning a new sentence, 'to one another' seems to be left standing on its own. Hence some attach 'and all to one another' to the previous sentence, as is quite possible in the Greek, the resulting composite admonition being: 'Younger people, be subject to your elders, and all of you to one another'. This rearrangement has certain attractions, and may be right; but we should note that (a) it is really unnecessary, since in the arrangement commonly adopted *allēlois* does not in fact stand on its own but is a perfectly respectable dative of relation (we might paraphrase, 'All of you, in your relations with one another . . .') constructed both with **All of you** and the verbal phrase following; and (b) it has the disadvantage of making the next sentence commence without any connecting particle in the Greek, which is less acceptable here than, say, at ii. 13; iv. 12; etc., where in each case a new admonitory section begins.

The injunction receives a striking comment from 1QS v. 23-25: '. . . that they may all obey each other, the lower the higher . . . They shall reprove each other in truth and humility and loving charity one towards another'. For humility, cf. iii. 8: also 1 Cor. iv. 6; Phil. ii. 3-11. In the NT we sometimes come across the figure of 'clothing oneself' with fine qualities (Col. iii. 12) or of donning them like armour (Rom. xiii. 12; 1 Thess. v. 8), but here the imagery seems deliberately designed so as to suggest self-effacement or even menial service. The verb tranlated **gird** is the rare, working-class *egkombousthai*, first found in the comic playwright Apollodorus of Carystus (*c.* 300 B.C.), which derives from *egkombōma*, i.e. the apron or overall which slaves fastened in front of their sleeveless vest (*exōmis*) to keep it clean when at work. In using it to describe the way the Asian Christians should 'gird on humility', the writer seems to be hinting that they should imitate the Lord, who tied a towel about Himself in order to wash His disciples' feet. Though fundamentally an attitude of mind, **humility** (*tapeinophrosunē*) should find expression in practical action.

To back his teaching he appeals to scripture: **for 'God is opposed to the arrogant, but gives grace to the humble'.** As previously (ii. 21; iii. 18; iv. 8), he uses **for** (*hoti*) to introduce the theological ground for his ethical counsel. The citation, with **God** substituted for 'the Lord' in the original, is from LXX Prov. iii. 34; it states an idea which the whole OT accepts as axiomatic (e.g. 1 Sam. ii. 7 f.; Ps. xviii. 27; xxxi. 23; cxlvii. 6; Ezek. xvii. 24; Ecclus. x. 14 f.), and which is splendidly proclaimed in the Magnificat (Lk. i. 51-53). The fact that the text reappears, in the same wording but in a different setting and with a different moral, in Jas. iv. 6 almost certainly points to its having been incorporated in the catechetical or liturgical tradition (see below).

16. ENCOURAGEMENT TO HUMILITY AND WATCHFULNESS

v. 6-11

(6) Humble yourselves therefore under God's mighty hand so that he may exalt you at the appointed time, (7)

**casting all your anxiety on him, for he cares about you.
(8) Be sober, be watchful. Your adversary, the Devil, is
prowling around like a roaring lion seeking someone to
devour. (9) Resist him, firm in your faith, realizing that
the same kinds of suffering are being accomplished for
your brotherhood in the world. (10) But the God of all
grace, who has called you to his eternal glory in Christ,
after you have suffered a short while, will himself restore,
establish, strengthen and settle you. (11) To him belongs
dominion for ever and ever. Amen.**

The closing section, the greetings apart, consists of loosely
connected pieces of exhortation; it is direct and personal in tone,
and embodies traditional catechesis, probably also a liturgical
echo or two, adapted to sustain the Asian readers in their
critical situation. The correspondences between the whole
pericope, including 5 above, and Jas. iv. 6-10 (cf. the citation of
Prov. iii. 34; the demand for submission to God; the evocation
of the Devil and the order to resist him; the assurance that if one
'humbles' oneself before God He will 'exalt' one; the fervent
note) are remarkable. So the proposal (M. E. Boismard) that we
should detect in both the outline traces of yet another hymn (for
others in 1 Peter, cf. i. 3-5; ii. 22-25; i. 20 with iii. 18. 22), this
time focussed on God rather than Christ but having the baptismal ceremony (the renunciation of Satan?) as its setting, has
much to commend it.

The writer begins by drawing a practical lesson (cf. **there-** 6
fore: *oun*) from the text of Proverbs he has just cited. Since
God bestows His favour on the humble-minded and humility,
basically, is the attitude which recognizes the divine sovereignty,
he can logically urge: **Humble yourselves . . . under God's
mighty hand so that he may exalt you at the appointed
time** (cf. Jas. iv. 10). As always, his attention is concentrated on
his readers' afflictions; he is suggesting that, if they accept them
humbly as God's providential chastisement and testing (cf. his
teaching in i. 6; iii. 17; iv. 19), they will find themselves vindicated at the last. **God's mighty hand** is a bold picture much
favoured in the OT (Ex. iii. 19; vi. 1; xiii. 3; 9; 14; 16; Dt. ix. 26;
29; Jer. xxi. 5; Ezek. xx. 33 f.; etc.), being applied particularly to

His deliverance of Israel from Egypt. Equally characteristic of the OT is the contrast between humbling (*tapeinoun*)and raising up (*hupsoun*): e.g. 1 Sam. ii. 7 f.; Ezek. xvii. 24 (for the NT, cf. Mt. xxiii. 12; Lk. i. 52; xiv. 11; xviii. 14). Here the 'exaltation' consists in the reversal of the readers' present misfortunes, their triumph over their detractors and their participation in the divine glory, and this will be brought about **at the appointed time.** This expression paraphrases the enigmatic *en kairōi* (lit. 'in time'), which in classical Greek can mean (e.g. Thucydides, *Hist.* iv. 59; vi. 9) 'at the opportune time' or (e.g. *ib.* i. 121) 'in our good time'). But in the NT *ho kairos* acquires eschatological overtones, meaning 'the time of crisis', 'the last time', 'the time of the End' (e.g. Mt. viii. 29; Mk. xiii. 33; Lk. xxi. 8; 1 Cor. iv. 5). This is clearly its force here; it is equivalent to 'in the last time' (*en kairōi eschatōi*) of i. 5, i.e. the time of the Parousia, and indeed in some MSS it is glossed by the insertion (after ii. 12) of 'of visitation' (*episkopēs*).

The admonition **Humble yourselves . . .,** however, has yet 7 to be completed; the clause which follows, **casting all your anxiety on him, for he cares about you,** is integral to it. Most modern translations (RSV; NEB; etc.) render the verb by an imperative ('Cast . . .'), thereby appearing to imply that this is an additional, separate injunction. In the Greek, however, it is a participle and should be construed closely with **Humble yourselves.** The true Christian attitude is not negative self-abandonment or resignation, but involves as the expression of one's self-humbling the positive entrusting of oneself and one's troubles to God. The participial phrase derives straight from Ps. lv. 22 (LXX: 'Cast upon the Lord your anxiety, and he will sustain you: he will never allow the righteous to stumble'); while in the second half of the verse there is an echo of Wis. xii. 13 ('For neither is there any God but thou, who carest for all'). The passage recalls, and probably depends on, the community's remembrance of our Lord's advice (Mt. vi. 25-34) not to be worried or anxious since God is aware of our needs. An apt comment is Augustine's grateful cry (*Conf.* iii. 11. 19): 'O You Who are good and almighty, You Who care for each one of us as for one, and for all of us as for each'.

But trust in God and His loving protection needs to be supplemented by unrelaxed self-control and alertness; so the next admonition rings peremptorily: **Be sober, be watchful.** The 8 writer has stressed the importance of the former attitude in i. 13 (see note) and iv. 7; watchfulness and sobriety are similarly coupled in 1 Thess. v. 6, and were plainly a recurrent motif of primitive teaching (Mt. xxiv. 42; Lk. xxi. 34-36; Rom. xiii. 11 f.; 2 Tim. iv. 5). They are all the more urgently called for at the present juncture because **Your adversary, the Devil, is prowling around like a roaring lion seeking someone to devour.** The imminence of the End, prominent everywhere in the letter, is the backcloth of the scene. Christian apocalyptic, like Jewish, envisaged this as a period when the powers of evil would be particularly active and the elect would consequently be exposed to extraordinary trials (e.g. Mt. xxiv. 4-28; 2 Thess. ii. 3-12; 2 Tim. iii. 1-9). The Asian Christians could observe the fulfilment of these terrifying surmises in the cruel treatment which seemed to descend so arbitrarily upon them and which, we may conjecture, tempted many of them to apostasy.

Both **adversary** and **Devil** represent the Hebrew *Sātān* (lit. 'opponent', sc. of God and all who belong to Him). The former term (*antidikos*) strictly signifies 'opponent in a law-suit' (Prov. xviii. 17), and so comes to connote 'enemy' in general (Esth. viii. 11); it is nowhere used in the LXX to translate *Sātān*. The latter (*diabolos*) means 'calumniator', 'accuser' (Ps. cix. 6), and is the regular LXX rendering of *Sātān* (1 Chron. xxi. 1; Job i and ii; Zech. iii. 1—where Satan appears as the inciter or accuser of men). The conception of Satan developed late in Hebrew thought, owing much to Persian influence, but it crops up frequently, with rich elaborations, in the apocryphal books and rabbinical literature. In the NT he is the tempter, the rebellious prince of evil, the antichrist and perverter of God's purposes, the vicious power to whom He allows temporary domination over the world (e.g. Jn. xiv. 30; 1 Jn. v. 19). It is he who is the mainspring of the Asian Christians' tribulations, and so the writer strives to put them on their guard against him. He is pictured as **prowling around** (cf. Job i. 7, where he himself reports that he has been 'walking up and down on the earth') **like a roaring lion.** The guess that this graphic image may have been inspired by the lions which often figured in Oriental representations of the mother-goddess Cybele, the object of great veneration in Asia, is too fanciful to be entertained seriously. The Psalmist's description (xxii. 13) of his enemies attacking him 'like a ravening and roaring [the same participle *ōruomenos* in the LXX] lion' points to a much more likely source. The persecutors of God's saints are often likened to lions in the Scrolls (1QH v. 9; 13 f.; 19; 4QpNah i. 5 f.; 4QpHos i).

The Devil is **seeking someone to devour.** There is a variant reading here, for some authorities (including Codex Alex., Pap. 72 and the Syriac version) give the third person singular subjunctive *katapiei* instead of the infinitive *katapiein*, the resulting sense being 'whom he may devour'; but this is probably an attempt to ease an unusual construction. The verb itself (*katapinein*) properly means 'drink down', but can be used of an animal swallowing its prey (Jon. ii. 1; Tob. vi. 2; Josephus, *Ant.* ii. 246). This is probably the sense here, although some point to 1QH v. 7: 'lions that . . . drink the blood of the valiant'. In any case the Devil's object, the vigorous metaphor stripped away, is to destroy the Asian Christians, undermining their morale by the harsh treatment they are receiving from his agents and so driving them to deny the faith.

This interpretation is confirmed by the counter-advice the
9 writer now gives: **Resist him, firm** (*stereoi*: 'compact', 'solidly built', and so 'steadfast') **in your faith.** By **faith** (there is an article in the Greek) he means, not 'the faith', i.e. the belief of Christians (for this use, cf., e.g., 1 Tim. i. 19; vi. 21; 2 Tim. ii. 18), nor simply 'faithfulness', but rather 'your positive faith and trust in God'. Paul has much the same thought when he urges the Colossians (i. 23) to 'continue firmly fixed and steadfast in your faith'. The counsel is well illustrated by Rev. xii. 9-11, where 'the devil is said to have been overcome by faithful testimony and fearless devotion unto death' (A. M. Stibbs). As was remarked above, the charge 'Resist the Devil' appears in Jas. iv. 7, and there are also points of contact ('stand against the wiles of the Devil'; 'resist'; 'stand fast') in Eph. vi. 10-13. The common pattern suggests that these are unlikely to be coincidences; it seems probable that resistance to the Devil and standing steadfast were stock motifs of the pre-baptismal instruction. We recall that the solemn renunciation of Satan was

to become a dramatic incident in the fully developed baptismal ceremony (e.g. Hippolytus, *Trad. apost.* xxi. 9; Cyril of Jerusalem, *Cat. myst.* i. 2-9), and this kind of teaching may well have provided its seed-bed.

A powerful motive for courageous resistance is the sense of solidarity with others, and so the writer adds pointedly: **realizing** (sc. as you do) **that the same kinds of sufferings are being accomplished for** (i.e. are being laid upon) **your brotherhood in the world.** This is an almost literal rendering of an extremely clumsy (e.g. Greek readers will notice the odd placing of **your** in the original) and difficult piece of Greek. The alternative often preferred, viz. 'knowing how to pay the same meed of suffering (or pay the same tax of suffering) as your brethren', is inacceptable because (a) it gives a very strained and artificial sense; (b) it depends on the mistaken notion that the verb translated 'realize' (*eidenai*: lit. 'know') cannot, when it means 'know that', be followed as here by an accusative-infinitive construction but must have a *hoti* clause dependent on it (Lk. iv. 41 alone refutes this; but cf. also *I Clem.* lxii. 3); and (c) it fails to observe that the infinitive verb (*epiteleisthai*), when used in the active, always in the LXX and NT properly connotes 'carry through to the end', 'accomplish', 'fulfil', and that where sacrificial overtones are present they are incidental and supplied by the context (see TWNT VIII, 62 f.). It is natural to take it as passive here, and the clause might be paraphrased by, 'realizing as you do that your brothers in the world are having to put up with the same ill-treatment as yourselves'. Like Phil. i. 30, the remark gives a vivid little glimpse of the close relations which widely separated churches maintained with one another in the 1st cent. and of their friendly concern for each other's fortunes.

The expression **for your brotherhood in the world** also calls for discussion. On the exegesis given above the case (dative) is a 'dative of disadvantage'. As regards **your brotherhood,** we are at first surprised that the writer did not employ the simpler and more natural-sounding 'your brothers . . .', but he has already shown his fondness for the collective term *adelphotēs* (ii. 17: cf. his stress on 'brotherly love' at i. 22; iii. 8). It has the advantage here of quietly emphasizing the solidarity between the numerous and widely scattered little Christian communities. The precise nuance of **in the world** is more debatable. According to most, **the world** (*ho kosmos*) has the straightforward significance 'inhabited world', 'earth', as in 2 Macc. iii. 12 (the Temple is honoured 'in the whole *kosmos*'); Mt. iv. 8; Mk. xiv. 9; Rom. i. 8; 1 Cor. xiv. 10; etc. On this view the writer, with a touch of understandable exaggeration perhaps, is pointing out that sufferings like these are the lot of Christians everywhere in the world. Others, however, argue that *kosmos*, as frequently in the NT (e.g. Jn. viii. 23; xviii. 36; 1 Cor. iii. 19; Gal. vi. 14; 1 Jn. v. 19), stands for the world as an order organized against God. Thus the writer's point would be that suffering is inseparable from the experience of Christians while they are in the world (so NEB: cf. esp. Jn. xvi. 33). This is possible, but very unlikely; had he wanted to express this idea (of which there is no evidence elsewhere in the letter), he could surely have done so in a less roundabout, not to say tortuous manner. His appeal to what is happening to other Christians, and his use of the collective **brotherhood,** strongly suggest that he is seeking to encourage his readers, not by highlighting the inevitability of suffering in this life, subject as it is to the powers of evil, but by setting their experiences in Asia Minor in the perspective of the experiences of the world-wide Church.

The main letter ends with a solemn assurance that they have One on their side who is more than a match for their worst adversary (cf. Jas. iv. 7 f.): **But the God of all grace, who has called you to his eternal glory in Christ, after you have suffered a short while, will himself restore, establish, strengthen and settle you.** Much of the language seems stereotyped, and it is useful to compare the similar texts in 1 Thess. v. 23 f.; 2 Thess. ii. 16 f.; Heb. xiii. 20 f. For **God of all grace,** cf. Paul's 'God of all consolation' (2 Cor. i. 3), and the expression 'manifold grace' in iv. 10; the meaning is that God bestows help sufficient for every occasion and emergency. God's call has earlier been a characteristic theme (e.g. i. 15; ii. 9; 21); here its goal is depicted as being the sharing of the elect in His own **eternal glory** (cf. iv. 13; v. 1, where the glory is Christ's). This calling is **in Christ** (see on iii. 16); it seems better to take these words with **has called** than with **glory.** And the

glory is **eternal,** an adjective which pointedly marks the contrast with the brief, transitory trials the Asian Christians at present have to put up with. The assurance that these will be short-lived exactly reproduces (cf. the same word *oligon*, i.e. **a short while** in both passages) that given at i. 6.

The permanent vindication and blessedness which God will ensure for them are hammered home in four powerful verbs in the future indicative; some MSS, influenced by the optatives found in similar passages elsewhere (Heb. xiii. 21; 1 Thess. v. 23), give them in the optative, but this is a misguided attempt at improvement which eliminates the vigorous confidence of the original. Both **restore** (*katartizein*: 'put in order', 'make complete': cf. 1 Cor. i. 10; 2 Cor. xiii. 11; Gal. vi. 1; Heb. xiii. 21) and **establish** (*stērizein*: Lk. xxii. 32; Rom. xvi. 25; 1 Thess. iii. 2; 13; 2 Thess. ii. 17; iii. 3; Jas. v. 8) belong to the technical paraenetic vocabulary. Together they promise the firmness and courage which the harassed minority urgently needs. This is the sole occurrence of **strengthen** (*sthenoun*) in Biblical or secular Greek, although *sthenein* ('be strong', 'be able') is frequent in the latter and is found in 3 Macc. iii. 8. A number of MSS (Codd. A and B; several cursives; the Latin versions) omit **settle** (*themeliōsei*: lit. 'found', 'set upon a firm foundation': cf. Ps. cii. 25; Mt. vii. 25), but the majority, including Pap. 72, support it; its insertion is hard to explain if we assume that it was originally absent.

As is fitting after such an eloquent affirmation of the divine succour, a doxology is added: **To him belongs dominion for 11 ever and ever. Amen.** It is similar to, though shorter than, the doxology at iv. 11 (see note), confining itself to emphasizing the mighty power of God on which the reassurances in the paragraph are based.

17. PERSONAL GREETINGS

v. 12-14

(12) I have written you this short letter by Silvanus, our faithful brother as I account him, exhorting you and testifying that this is God's true grace. Stand fast in it. (13) She

**who is in Babylon, elect like you, sends you her greetings,
as does my son Mark. (14) Greet one another with the kiss
of love. May peace be with all you who are in Christ.**

These closing verses, striking a personal note and containing
the greetings which both convention and brotherly courtesy
required in Christian correspondence, raise in a tantalizing way
the problem of the authorship and date of the letter. Taken at
their face value, they can be read as implying that, like Paul in
many of his letters (1 Cor. xvi. 21; Gal. vi. 11; Col. iv. 18;
2 Thess. iii. 17), Peter had employed a secretary to write out, or
in this case probably to draft, the body of the letter, but at the
last moment took the pen into his own hand to insert the farewell messages. On the view that the epistle is post-Petrine, they
have been represented as a skilful improvisation, pieced together
perhaps out of actual reminiscences, which the pseudonymous
author has contrived, on the model set by Paul, so as to create
an air of verisimilitude. For the wider considerations on which
a decision must be based, see Introduction, pp. 30-33

12   So the writer states: **I have written you this short letter by
Silvanus.** This proper noun (*Silouanos*) seems to be the
Latinized form of the Aramaic *She'īlāh* (i.e. 'sent'), the Greek
version of which was *Silas*. It seems fairly certain, on any
hypothesis, that the name is intended to refer to the prophetically
gifted Silas whom the Jerusalem church sent to Antioch (Acts
xv. 22-34), and whom Paul later selected as his companion on
his 'second missionary tour' (Acts xv. 40-xviii. 5: mentioned by
name nine times). If so, he is also to be identified with the
Silvanus whom the Apostle speaks of as a fellow-preacher of the
gospel (2 Cor. i. 19) and as joint-author of certain letters
(1 Thess. i. 1; 2 Thess. i. 1). We are entitled to infer that he was
a person of considerable standing in the apostolic Church, and
this is perhaps hinted at in the comment, **our faithful brother
as I account him.** Any fellow-Christian was, in the language
of early Christianity, a **brother**, but in the NT the context
sometimes suggests that the term carries a more specialized
sense, viz. 'brother in office', 'fellow-apostle' (e.g. 1 Cor. i. 1;
2 Cor. i. 1; ii. 13; Eph. vi. 21; Col. i. 1; iv. 7; Phm. 1).

The expression **by** (*dia* with the genitive) **Silvanus** may hold the key to the secret of the letter. It has been held to mean (a) that Silvanus, as was regular practice in antiquity, was to act as its bearer (cf. Acts xv. 23, where 'having written by their hand . . .' indicates that the persons mentioned were given the letter to deliver, not that they had penned it); or (b) that Silvanus was the amanuensis who up to this point has taken the letter down from the author's (Peter's?) dictation; or (c) that Silvanus had been responsible for drafting the letter on the author's (Peter's?) behalf and on his instructions. As regards (a), such passages as Ignatius, *Rom.* x. 1; *Philad.* xi. 2; *Smyrn.* xii. 1; Polycarp, *Phil.* xiv. 1 confirm that the formula 'write by X.' could in Greek signify 'despatch a letter with X. as its carrier', although the more normal idiom was 'send by X.' or something of the sort; but this exegesis seems ruled out in the present case by **short** (a more literal rendering would be 'I have written briefly'), which requires us to take 'write' in the strict sense of actually writing or drafting rather than the enlarged sense of transmitting. We should equally exclude (b) on the ground that we can hardly envisage Silvanus, Paul's collaborator in writing to Thessalonica, serving as a dictation clerk, which was a role too modest for so important a figure. Everything in fact points to (c) as the correct explanation, and it is strikingly supported by a letter of the late-2nd cent. bishop Dionysius of Corinth (in Eusebius, *Hist. eccl.* iv. 23. 11) to the Roman church referring to *1 Clement* (sent from Rome to Corinth *c.* 95) as 'your earlier letter to us written by (*dia*) Clement'. Clearly Dionysius implies by this phrase that in writing the epistle Clement was expressing in his own words the views of the Roman church.

We may conclude, then, that the historical Silvanus either is, or is represented as being, the drafter of 1 Peter. This latter alternative leaves one wondering why the real author resorted to this further refinement of disguise: it is easy to imagine a second-generation Christian fathering his own work, in good faith and in harmony with conventional practice, on the great Apostle, but why complicate his fiction by dragging in Silvanus? If the former alternative is correct, the question of course still remains open whether Silvanus drafted the letter (a) at the request of Peter and to set out his ideas, or (b) on his own or the Roman church's initiative after the Apostle's death, convinced that he was faithfully transmitting the kind of message the revered leader would have wished to convey. If (a), we can readily appreciate the force of **our faithful brother as I account him.** The words are the Apostle's certificate to Silvanus's fitness, on the basis of his faith and devotion, to act as his spokesman, and **I account** (*logizomai*), which means rather more than 'I think', 'in my opinion', and expresses firm conviction (e.g. Rom. iii. 28; viii. 18; 2 Cor. xi. 5), retains its full force. If (b), we have the problem of explaining how Silvanus could be responsible for such a flattering testimonial to himself. One possibility is that on this hypothesis the fiction was bound to be transparent, since Peter's death must have been widely known, and these words, inserted at the instance of the Roman church, would be read as its express confirmation of Silvanus's reliability as an interpreter of the Apostle's mind.

Whoever he is, the writer describes his letter as **short,** which some have found strangely inapt, having regard to its 105 verses. But the author of Hebrews uses almost the same expression (xiii. 22) of his own much lengthier composition. The formula is in fact one of conventional politeness (so too, e.g., Ignatius, *Rom.* viii. 2; *Polyc.* vii. 3); letters were expected to be brief (e.g. Isocrates, *Ep.* ii. 13; viii. 10; Pliny, *Ep.* iii. 9. 27; Demetrius, *De eloc.* 228; 231; 234; Jerome, *Ep.* lvii. 8; lxviii. 2), and the writer is deprecating having had to compress so large a subject into such a comparatively restricted space.

Actually he manages to summarize his message with admirable succinctness: he has been **exhorting** his correspondents **and testifying that this is God's true grace.** The former participle (*parakalōn*) aptly covers the ethical instruction which fills so much of the letter, and also the summons to bear persecution with fortitude and hope which rings through every line of it. By **this . . . grace** he means that blessed glorification upon which his readers are soon to enter (i. 13: cf. i. 10), but of which they already enjoy a foretaste (e.g. i. 6; ii. 5; 10; iv. 14) through their status as God's elect people and their participation in Christ's sufferings. With all the authority at his command he has been **testifying** (*epimarturōn*: a strong verb which implies that his testimony carries weight) that this grace is **true,** i.e. authentic and to be relied upon. The Asian Christians need this assurance, for the troubles they are passing through might well make them doubtful that God's promises would be fulfilled.

So he bids them **Stand fast in it** (lit. 'in which stand'). In the original **in it** is *eis hēn* ('into which'), i.e. the preposition *eis*, which properly denotes motion towards, has replaced the correct *en* ('in', of rest). This is the only instance in 1 Peter (as we saw, the use of *eis* at iii. 20 does not really count), and almost the only one in the NT epistles, of the confusion of *eis* with *en* which was becoming common in popular Greek. It is tempting to regard it as a tiny fragment of evidence confirming that a different hand composed this postscript. Apart from this, the clause presents a textual difficulty which has an important bearing on its meaning. The great majority of MSS, including Pap. 72, read *eis hēn stēte*, in which the verb is aorist subjunctive or imperative and which yields the translation printed above. Several other authorities, however (K; L; P; many cursives; some versions), read instead *eis hēn hestēkate*, which means 'in which you stand'. As *stēte* is much the better attested reading, and much the more difficult to make sense of, and as *hestēkate* looks suspiciously like the product of assimilation to Rom. v. 2; 2 Cor. i. 24, the majority of editors adopt the former and translate as above. Admittedly, however, the abrupt imperative is awkward, and the acceptance of this construction leaves **this** hanging in the air; 'this grace' almost asks to be defined by a relative clause, and 'in which you stand' would fill this gap admirably. While agreeing that *stēte* must be correct, one is attracted by the suggestion (M. Zerwick, *Analysis Philologica Novi Testamenti Graeci*: Romae, 1953) that the author may have confusedly used it for *hestēkate*, intending the sense of the latter.

The next sentence, **She who is in Babylon, elect like you,** 13 **sends you her greetings,** is at first sight somewhat cryptic. First, who is the lady referred to? Some Protestant commentators in the past liked to identify her as the wife whom Peter 'took around' with him (1 Cor. ix. 5: cf. Mt. viii. 14) and whom tradition (Clement Alex., *Strom*. vii. 11. 63) saluted as a martyr. But this is in the highest degree improbable; the writer would surely have named her or indicated her identity by some less roundabout phrase. The parallels 'the elect lady' and 'your elect sister' in 2 Jn. 1; 13 confirm that this is a picturesque description of the local church from which the letter was written. This community is **elect like you** (*suneklektē*, i.e. 'co-elect') because, like the Asian churches addressed (i. 1; ii. 9), it has received and responded to God's saving call. The fact that Codex Sin., a few cursives, the Vulgate and the Peshitta inter-polate the noun 'church' (*ekklēsia*) shows that this was the meaning attributed to the words in antiquity.

Secondly, to what locality does **Babylon** point? Strabo (*Geog.* xvii. 1. 30) and Josephus (*Ant.* ii. 315) mention a military strongpoint of this name, the headquarters of a Roman legion, in the Nile Delta near Old Cairo; but although tradition con-nects Mark (see next clause) with Egypt, we have no evidence that this place, which was hardly more than a garrison post, was an early centre of Christianity, nor is it likely either that Peter visited it or that a pseudonymous writer would have thought it plausible to locate him there. The famous Babylon in Meso-potamia might seem the most obvious candidate. According to Josephus (*Ant.* xviii. 371-379), however, the Jewish population had been forced to abandon it in Claudius's reign (A.D. 41–54); it was declining rapidly in the 1st cent., and when Trajan visited it in 115 he found little but ruins (Cassius Dio, *Hist.* lxviii. 30). A missionary stay there by the Apostle of the circumcision (ac-companied, moreover, by some astonishing coincidence, by Mark and Silvanus) seems therefore hard to credit, and the complete absence of local traditions attesting one reinforces these doubts.

The key to the problem, in the view of most critics, lies in the fact that in the 1st cent. 'Babylon' was becoming in Jewish and Christian circles a symbolical title for Rome. For the prophets (e.g. Is. xiii; xliii. 14; Jer. l. 29; li. 1-58) the name had denoted the proud, immoral, godless city which dominated their world, and it was natural for later Jews to see this as the type of the Rome they knew and which embodied these very characteristics. So we find Rome referred to as 'Babylon' in the rabbinical literature (SB III, 816) and in apocalyptic writings contem-porary with or slightly later than 1 Peter (Apoc. Bar. xi. 1; lxvii. 7; Orac. Sib. v. 143; 159). For specifically Christian examples, cf. Rev. xiv. 8; xvii. 5; 18; xviii. 2; etc. So here, it is argued, **She who is in Babylon** simply means 'the church at Rome'; and two cursives actually substituted 'Rome' for **Babylon.**

This exegesis is thus very ancient; and Eusebius, without explicitly adopting it himself, reports (*Hist. eccl.* ii. 15. 2: cf. 'they say . . .') that it was current in his day. So far as it goes, it is almost certainly correct, although we should reject the suggestion that the writer chose **Babylon** as a code-name for Rome so as to throw dust in the eyes of police censors; the contents of his letter, with its reiterated appeals for exemplary and submissive behaviour, were not likely to disturb such officials, even if they were interested in it at all. Nor should we infer that his use of the cryptogram implies that he viewed the Roman empire as such as the arch-persecutor of Christianity. The deeply respectful attitude he reveals to the emperor and the imperial authorities in ii. 13-17 rules this out, and in any case he is not thinking of the Roman empire but of the city of Rome. It is **Babylon** in his eyes, as apparently in the eyes of other Jews too, because it is the capital of the pagan world, the notorious centre of affluence and sensuality; possibly too, if the letter dates from after the Neronian persecution, because it has been the scene of the martyrdom of God's saints. It seems probable, however, that other motives too criss-cross with these in his mind. The name 'Babylon' conjures up the idea of the Dispersion, and the thought of Christians as 'aliens and temporary sojourners' in this world has never been far from his thoughts (i. 1; 17; ii. 11). So the church in Rome is **in Babylon** because Rome is its place of exile.

Some would take a further step and argue that, once the presence of this idea is admitted, we can scarcely evade the question whether **Babylon** is intended to designate any specific locality at all. Reading Ps. cxxxvii. 1, the Jew of the Dispersion could identify 'the waters of Babylon' with whatever place in the world he was obliged to make his home. Hence a satisfying paraphrase of **She who is in Babylon, elect like you,** might be, 'the Christian community here, which like you is elect and like you is in exile from our true home'. There would thus be no reference to Rome or any other place in this verse, and while the letter might still emanate from Rome the case for this would have to be argued (as it can be: see Introduction, pp. 33 f.) on other grounds. After all, there was no need to mention the place of origin since it can have been no secret from the Asian

THE FIRST EPISTLE OF PETER

Christians. It is worth pointing out that there is not a single example among the NT letters of the author, when adding his closing greetings, expressly naming the church from which he was writing. The argument has been attractively developed (cf. K. Heussi, *Die römische Petrustradition in kritischer Sicht*, 1955, pp. 36-41; M. E. Boismard, 'Une liturgie baptismale', 1957, p. 181), but just fails to carry conviction. The tone of the valediction, with its naming of particular individuals, leads us to expect a reference to a particular locality too; and the fact that Rome became so early known figuratively as **Babylon** is bound to have great weight. Moreover, **She who is in Babylon** seems to distinguish the community from which the letter is sent from those which will be receiving it, but if **Babylon** is given an exclusively allegorical meaning without any local reference at all, they are all alike **in Babylon.**

The local church thus **sends you her greetings,** and **my son Mark** joins in them. On any hypothesis this must be John Mark, the evangelist, who in the early days had been a member of the Jerusalem community and in whose home Peter had been a familiar visitor (Acts xii. 12-17). He had set out with Paul and Barnabas on their 'first missionary tour', but for reasons which failed to satisfy Paul turned back (Acts xii. 25; xiii. 13; xv. 36-39). Years later he was at Paul's side during his imprisonment in Rome (Col. iv. 10; Phm. 24; 2 Tim. iv. 11), where his old family friend Peter almost certainly worked and met his glorious end. According to trustworthy tradition (Papias in Eusebius, *Hist. eccl.* iii. 39. 15), he attached himself to the Apostle, deriving much of the material for his gospel from him and thus becoming his 'interpreter' (*hermēneutēs*). The description **my son** aptly reflects the relationship of trust and affection between the older Christian leader and his younger disciple.

Thus these scraps of personal information fit neatly together; they have the ring either of historical veracity or of extremely skilful contrivance. After conveying his church's salutation, the

14 writer then bids his correspondents **Greet one another with the kiss of love.** Paul concludes several of his letters (Rom. xvi. 16; 1 Cor. xvi. 20; 2 Cor. xiii. 12; 1 Thess. v. 26) with a similar request, using however the rather less personal, perhaps more liturgical expression 'holy kiss' (substituted here in several

cursives and versions, including the Vulgate). The practice
evidently established itself very early for Christians, as a token
of their affectionate spiritual ties, to embrace one another at the
community meeting. It was entirely Christian in origin, without
precedent in the synagogue; and the appropriate moment, we
may conjecture, was either the climax of the act of worship or
some other significant point, e.g. after the reading out of a
weighty communication from an apostle. By the middle of the
2nd cent., according to Justin (*1 Apol.* lxv. 2), the 'kiss of peace'
was a regular feature in the Sunday eucharist at Rome; and it
has retained its place, modified in various ways, in the great
traditional eucharistic rites down to the present day.

Finally comes a blessing which recalls i. 2: **May peace be
with you all who are in Christ.** For the meaning of **peace,** a
routine Hebrew salutation here enriched by a Christian colouring, see on i. 2. The prayer with which Paul concludes his letters
is normally for 'grace' (Rom. xvi. 20; 1 Cor. xvi. 23; 2 Cor.
xiii. 13; Gal. vi. 18; Eph. vi. 24; Phil. iv. 23; Col. iv. 18; 1 Thess.
v. 28; 2 Thess. iii. 18; 1 Tim. vi. 21; 2 Tim. iv. 22; Tit. iii. 15;
Phm. 25), but he can on occasion (Rom. xv. 33; 2 Cor. xiii. 11;
Gal. vi. 16; Eph. vi. 23; 2 Thess. iii. 16) add a reference to
'peace' to his good wishes. For the present form, cf. 3 Jn. 15.
The persons addressed are described as being **in Christ,** the
suggestion being that the blessed **peace** which the writer prays
may be theirs is grounded in their relationship with Christ. As
in iii. 16 (where see note), the formula implies that as the result
of baptismal regeneration the believer has moved into a new
sphere of existence: he is united with Christ and shares His
risen life.

INTRODUCTION TO 2 PETER AND JUDE

1. CANONICITY

BECAUSE of their close relationship, it is advantageous and indeed necessary to treat 2 Peter and Jude together for introductory purposes. The first point about them which calls for comment is their place in the NT. Modern readers are sometimes uneasy about this, being disappointed by the one-sided emphasis and general mediocrity (as they tend to describe it) of 2 Peter, and put off by Jude's almost unrelievedly denunciatory tone; they find their preoccupation with eschatology, expressed uncompromisingly in the imagery of Jewish-Christian apocalyptic, uncongenial. In the 16th cent. too, when the new spirit of inquiry on the one hand and Protestant concern for the purity of the gospel on the other were prompting Christians to take a fresh look at the canon, both letters came under critical scrutiny. Although the final verdict went in their favour, scholars like Erasmus and Calvin were fully alive to, and affected by, the doubts which were arising about their authenticity. Jude was relegated by Luther to the appendix of his September Testament (1522), with no number in the table of contents; while the Catholic Cajetan and the Protestant Oecolampadius were united in reckoning both epistles as of secondary authority.

In the early Church their respective fortunes were markedly different. Quite apart from the tacit respect accorded to it by 2 Peter (see §2), Jude seems to have been widely popular in the 2nd cent., being acknowledged as scripture c. 200 in Rome (Muratorian Canon), Africa (Tertullian, *De cult. fem.* i. 3), and Alexandria (Clement: in Eusebius, *Hist. eccl.* vi. 14. 1). After that it fell under a cloud, and Origen, who himself welcomes it (*In Matt.* x. 17) as 'packed with sound words of heavenly grace', implies (*ib.* xvii. 30) that some people rejected it. Eusebius bears this out, classing it (*Hist. eccl.* vi. 13. 6; 14. 1) among the books that were contested, the reason apparently

223

being (Didymus, PG xxxix, 1811-18; Jerome, *De vir. ill.* iv) its predilection for apocryphal books like 1 Enoch. In spite of this Athanasius included it in his famous canon of 367 (*Ep. fest.* xxxix: PG xxvi, 1437), and henceforth its position was generally assured, although the Syriac-speaking churches (as we should expect, in view of their conservative development of the canon) did not fall into line until the beginning of the 6th cent., when the Philoxenian recension was published.

By contrast no NT document had a longer or tougher struggle to win acceptance than 2 Peter. In the west, notwithstanding the illustrious name it bore, it seems to have been unknown or at any rate ignored until the second half of the 4th cent., and even then Jerome reports (*De vir. ill.* i) that many discarded it because of its difference of style from 1 Peter. Recognition first came to it in the east, for its presence in the early Coptic version (*c.* 200) and in Greek in Papyrus 72 (early 3rd cent.) suggests that it belonged to the canon that was taking shape there. Yet even Origen, while frequently citing it (if we can trust Rufinus's Latin translation) under the name of Peter, frankly admits (*In Ioann.* v. 3) that it is a disputed work. Eusebius is aware of these doubts and himself treats it (*Hist. eccl.* iii. 3. 1-4; 25. 3) as inauthentic and so uncanonical. The recension of Lucian of Antioch did not contain 2 Peter, and classic Antiochenes like John Chrysostom and Theodore of Mopsuestia made no use of it. Again it was the Alexandrian Athanasius who set the seal of approval on it by listing it in his festal canon (367), and following him Basil, Gregory of Nazianzus and Epiphanius cite it as authoritative. Its clear teaching about 'sharing the divine nature' (i. 4) and about the Church as the proper custodian of scripture (i. 20 f.) may have helped to secure it a passport. It appears in the Latin canon of the synod of Carthage (397), but the hesitations of the Syrian churches were not overcome until the start of the 6th cent.

The ancient Church had its own criteria for assessing a book's suitability for the canon. High among them was presumed apostolic authorship, and the evidence of Jerome and others makes it plain that most of its reservations about 2 Peter (a work which was widely read and contained teaching, as we have noted, of indisputable orthodoxy) were precisely on this score. Present-day, like Reformation, misgivings have very different grounds; let it be granted that, judged against the rest of the NT, both epistles are somewhat lacking in quality. But this admission should not tempt us to underrate their religious value, still less their importance for our understanding of primitive Christianity. As with some other parts of the NT, their presuppositions and manner of expression may not commend them to modern people, and Luther was right that the gospel message does not shine very luminously through them. Even so both contain passages which even those who go by subjective impressions must concede reveal remarkable spiritual insight and power. The problems they wrestle with, too, are real and obdurate: in particular, the tension between law and liberty in Christian ethics is as live an issue today as it apparently was in the 1st and early-2nd cents. And their warning of divine judgment, 2 Peter's interest in the Second Coming, and the appeal they both make to the teaching of the Lord and His apostles as the decisive touchstone, are as challenging to a Church hypnotized by the fashionable claims of secularism and confused by conflicting voices, as when they were first written down.

2. MUTUAL RELATIONSHIP

The close relationship between the two epistles is evident from their startling resemblances in subject-matter, vocabulary and phrasing, and even order of ideas. It is brought out most convincingly by a comparison of 2 Pet. ii. 1-18 and Jud. 4-16, where both are inveighing against trouble-makers and bringing virtually indistinguishable charges against them. The imagery they use to describe these people, and often the very words (including several uncommon ones), are the same. In both letters the errorists are castigated as followers of Balaam, and in both the doom in store for them is likened to the fate of the rebellious angels and that of the Cities of the Plain. But the points of contact extend beyond these central sections. The reminder in Jud. 17 f. that the Lord's apostles had foretold the emergence of 'scoffers' is matched by an almost identical reminder in 2 Pet. iii. 1-3. Both letters, too, have the habit of addressing their recipients as 'dear friends'; and there are unmistakable verbal correspondences between 2 Pet. i. 1 f.; 5; 12; iii. 14; 18 and Jud. 1 f.; 3; 5; 24; 25.

How are we to account for this relationship? A theory which some scholars have found tempting is that both epistles are drawing on a common source, which might be 'a sermon pattern formulated to resist the seducers of the Church' (B. Reicke). One point advanced in favour of this is the fact that, for all their close correspondences, actual verbal agreement is rare; the only clauses which are identical are 2 Pet. ii. 17b and Jud. 13b. Another is the vague, very general character of the polemic in the central sections; the heretics are drawn in silhouette, with the content of their teaching only obscurely hinted at. These considerations are certainly significant, but a fatal objection to a solution on these lines is that the parallels are not confined to the denunciatory blocks. There is indeed hardly anything in Jude which does not reappear in some form in 2 Peter, so that the supposed common source must have been to all intents and purposes identical with it. Apart from adapting this material, the writer's own contribution must have been limited to adding the prescript and the short pericope 19-23, and one wonders why he thought this worth the trouble.

We are therefore left with two alternatives, that Jude is dependent on 2 Peter or 2 Peter on Jude; and the argument against a common source tells with equal weight against the former. It is also difficult to understand why, if he had the whole of 2 Peter before him, the author of Jude restricted his borrowings so drastically (it surely contained much else that he could have exploited profitably), and why he speaks vaguely (17) of 'the apostles of our Lord' instead of mentioning Peter by name. The tendency in the early Church was in any case towards enlargement rather than curtailment, and not only is 2 Peter much the longer tract but over and over again, when the correspondences are analysed, its version is found to be more elaborate and verbose than Jude's (cf., e.g., ii. 1-3 and Jud. 4; ii. 4 and Jud. 6; ii. 15 and Jud. 11a). The counter-pleas that, whereas 2 Peter tends to speak of the false teachers in the future tense (ii. 1-3; iii. 3), Jude uses the present, and that the statement in Jud. 4 about their condemnation 'long ago' may be a reference to 2 Peter's prophecies, rest on a misunderstanding of the passages concerned. Except on the improbable hypothesis that 2 Peter is authentic, its resort to the future tense is a palpable literary artifice, and we shall discover that the prophet of 'long ago' is in fact Enoch.

For reasons like these the priority of Jude is all but unanimously accepted today; and a closer inspection of the text serves to confirm 2 Peter's secondary character. In a general way Jude is a more spontaneous and vigorous piece of writing, and also harsher in tone. Again, both catalogue examples (mostly the same ones) from Biblical history, but while Jude is careless of their correct chronological order, 2 Peter observes it scrupulously. Both appeal to these incidents in order to emphasize God's severity in dealing with sinners, but 2 Peter softens the denunciatory tone by introducing reminders of His graciousness towards righteous men like Noah and Lot. Finally their atttitudes to scripture suggest that 2 Peter is the later document. On the one hand, while Jude freely draws illustrations from 1 Enoch and the Assumption of Moses, even quoting (14 f.) the former, 2 Peter condenses or cuts out these features with a consequent loss of picturesque detail and even, on occasion (see on ii. 11), intelligibility; plainly he has stricter views on the OT and is reluctant to employ apocryphal books. On the other hand, his manner of speaking about Paul's letters (iii. 16) betrays his awareness that an embryonic NT canon is beginning to be recognized. His at first sight curious failure to reproduce the exact wording of Jude is to be explained, in part at any rate, by the fact that he is a self-conscious stylist with a passion for opulent diction; but it is also possible that he did not have the earlier trait on his desk before him as he wrote, but preferred to trust his memory.

3. CHARACTER AND AIMS

Jude and 2 Peter (like 1 Peter) are commonly called 'catholic' or 'general' epistles, by which are meant (cf. the definition in the 6th cent. *De sectis* ii. 4: PG lxxxvi, 1204) circulars addressed to the Christian world at large as opposed to letters sent to particular communities or individuals; but this description is somewhat misleading, though less so of the latter than the former. It is true, of course, that their addresses are couched in general terms, without any indication of a specific destination (2 Pet. iii. 1 might appear to contradict this, but see note), and that neither contains any personal messages or greetings. These peculiarities no doubt explain the designation they have borne from the early centuries; Athanasius (*Ep. fest.* xxxix), e.g., speaks of 'seven so-called catholic epistles'. It is obvious, however, that both writers were instigated to take up their pens by outbreaks of misconduct and false teaching which they considered pernicious, and it is difficult not to believe that these crises affected, at any rate in the first instance, particular churches or regions. Jud. 4 specifically alludes to 'certain' interlopers who are undermining the faith; and the graphic sketch in Jud. 12 of their misbehaviour at the love-feasts seems drawn from life. The epistle is in any case relatively early (see §4), and we may question whether the idea of Christendom as a whole had taken shape at the time it was written. The attitude of the author of 2 Peter is rather different, for he undoubtedly represents himself as the Apostle and his message (e.g. i. 12-15) as having ecumenical import. But he too seems to betray personal acquaintance with his correspondents (cf., e.g., his reference to recent converts in ii. 18), and some of the errors he combats, especially scepticism about the Parousia, are sufficiently clearly defined to imply a concrete situation.

In content and manner the two epistles, despite much overlapping, show marked differences. Apart from a few short sentences at the beginning and end, Jude is a straightforward polemical tract, wholly taken up with exposing pseudo-Christians and their scandalous misdemeanours. Its style is vigorous and colourful; and the author, who deploys a rich vocabulary, writes smooth-flowing, excellent Greek interspersed with occasional semitisms. His background is Jewish-Christian, and he is well versed in the OT and its traditional, often legendary interpretation known as *haggadah*, and also in apocalyptic literature, which he freely exploits. 2 Peter's tone is less even, revealing violent alternations of mood, and its Greek, more Hellenistic in flavour, tends to be tortuous, ungainly and at times pretentiously elaborate in the 'Asiatic' manner. An interesting feature is the writer's familiarity with, and readiness to use, the language and ideas of Hellenistic religion (e.g. i. 3-7;

16). His aims, too, are at once more complex and more constructive. Faced with a situation in part resembling Jude's, he incorporates with adaptations the whole of its diatribe; but in addition he finds it necessary to deal with entirely fresh errors, notably about the Second Coming and the interpretation of scripture. More positively, he wants to portray the Christian eschatological hope against the backcloth of the final cosmic conflagration (a trait unique in the NT), and to encourage his readers to rise to the moral heights their vocation demands. A further motive is disclosed in the way he invests his tract with the character of a last will and testament (see on i. 13-15); he wishes it to be read as Peter's farewell message to the churches.

Both writers are satisfied that the apostolic faith is the absolutely sure bulwark against error; and, as we shall see, it is precisely this conviction which impels the writer of 2 Peter to assume the guise of the Apostle. As regards the false teachers, 2 Peter, as we have already noted, is greatly concerned to reaffirm, in face of the jeering of doubters who are unsettling ordinary Christians, the certainty of Christ's Second Coming and of the catastrophic end of the world, and to furnish credible reasons for the delay in their realization. Another disquieting tendency which it seeks to counter (i. 20 f.; iii. 15 f.) is the individualistic exploitation of scripture in support of doctrines which are anathema to the official Church. These issues apart, the deviations from traditional Christianity attacked in the two pamphlets seem broadly the same, with significant differences of emphasis; but since their approach is largely denunciatory and negative, it is difficult to define them as precisely as we could wish. Some contend that the attempt is in any case futile, since what we have before us is a 'portrait-robot de l'hérétique' (C. Spicq); but while much of the abuse is generalized, the picture which emerges from it, though shadowy, has a recognizable outline. Two preliminary points which can be safely made are the following. First, the scepticism about the Parousia which worries 2 Peter is not a distinct heresy, but seems (cf. iii. 3 f.) to be somehow connected with the other deviations we are about to summarize. Secondly, in both cases the troublemakers are not schismatic groups but work inside the communities (Jud. 4; 2 Pet. ii. 14), and indeed their disgraceful behaviour at fellowship meals (Jud. 12; 2 Pet. ii. 13) is singled out for rebuke.

The allegations made against them are both doctrinal and moral, and while they are probably closely linked it is the latter which the two writers press home most persistently. Over and over again we hear of the errorists' licentiousness, sensual dissipations and sexuality, and cupidity; their propaganda and example are evidently having a corrupting influence (2 Pet. ii. 18 f.) and are creating factions among their fellow-Christians (Jud. 19; 2 Pet. ii. 1). Much of this should probably be discounted as conventional diatribe, but a point which comes out clearly is that their shameful practices are based (if one may so express it) on a principle. They believe they are entitled to behave in these uninhibited ways because they participate in God's grace (Jud. 4) and enjoy the freedom of the sons of God (2 Pet. ii. 19). If this interpretation is correct, their heresy includes what is technically known as antinomianism, which has been a recurrent phenomenon in Christian history since apostolic times (see notes on Jud. 4; 2 Pet. ii. 9) down to the present day, which springs from a variety of roots and can take a multitude of forms, but of which the essence is the assumption that the truly spiritual man, in virtue of his privileged relationship with God, is emancipated from the ethical restrictions, obligations and standards (particularly in matters of sex) which bind ordinary mortals.

The strictly doctrinal charges are more elusive, and (as the Commentary will show) the key-texts present baffling problems of exegesis. First, the errorists are accused in Jud. 4 (but see note) of denying God and Christ, and in 2 Pet. ii. 1 of denying 'the Master who bought them', i.e. Christ; but in neither case is it made clear whether this denial was practical, consisting in the repudiation of Christian morality, or involved unorthodox theological views as well. If the latter (as is tentatively argued in the notes), we still have no inkling of the respects in which, e.g., their Christology was defective. Secondly, according to many the implication of Jud. 4; 8; 25 is that the strict monotheism of this group at any rate was open to suspicion. This interpretation (see notes) may well be correct, but it remains extremely doubtful whether this entitles us to conclude, as some have done, that they supported the doctrine of a Demiurge or inferior creator-God. Thirdly, the trouble-makers are undoubtedly guilty (Jud. 8; 2 Pet. ii. 10) of abusing angelic powers, but what precise form this presumption took (the attitudes of the two writers seem to be different) remains a mystery.

Lastly, there is the question of their relationship to Gnosticism—that amorphous complex of religious, astrological, mythological and philosophical notions which, influenced probably by heterodox Judaism and setting a premium on salvation by 'knowledge' (*gnōsis*), confronted the 2nd cent. Church with formidable problems, but was already infecting certain communities and areas (e.g. Colossae) in Paul's lifetime. Several passages in the letters leave a strong impression that the movements criticized had a Gnostic colouring. We notice, e.g., the hints in Jude that the sectaries are recipients of esoteric revelations (8) and regard themselves as pneumatics (19), and in 2 Peter the insinuation that 'knowledge' of Christ is the true *gnōsis* (i. 3; 8; etc.) and the reference (i. 16) to 'cunningly devised fables'. Such a colouring is entirely consistent both with their doctrinal shortcomings, so far as we can identify them, and with their ethical libertinism; for some brands of classic Gnosticism were to disparage the body and to consider any actions performed with it as morally indifferent. We are therefore probably justified in overhearing in these letters the opening shots in the fateful struggle between the Church and Gnosticism which was to feature large in the 2nd cent. We should be on our guard, however, against exaggerating their anti-Gnostic traits, for the form of Gnosticism, more precisely 'Gnosis', in view is evidently a very primitive, incipient one, with no trace, e.g., of the hierarchies of aeons or other important tenets of the mature 2nd cent. systems.

4. AUTHORSHIP AND DATE: JUDE

According to Jud. 1, this epistle was written by 'Judas . . . brother of James'. Both these names were exceedingly common in Biblical times, and both crop up in several connections in the NT. There is, e.g., the Judas who is mentioned in Mk. vi. 3 as one of the brothers of Jesus (James, Joses and Simon being the

16   231

others); and, in addition to Judas Iscariot, Luke's list of the Twelve (vi. 16; Acts i. 13) comprises an apostle described as 'Judas of James'. A 'Judas called Barsabbas' was one of the two 'leading men' whom the church at Jerusalem assigned as companions to Paul on his journey to Antioch (Acts xv. 22). James was if anything an even more popular name. According to the synoptists, the Twelve included both James the son of Zebedee and brother of John, and James the son of Alphaeus, and we know (Acts xii. 2) that the former was executed by Herod Agrippa I in 44. As already stated, one of the Lord's brothers was called James, and he later became prominent as leader of the Jerusalem church (Acts xv. 13; Gal. i. 19). We also hear (Mk. xv. 40; Mt. xxvii. 56) of a 'James the younger' (lit. 'the small'), whose mother Mary was one of the women who watched the crucifixion from a distance, and of the James whom Luke (vi. 16) refers to as related to the apostle Judas. Finally there is the author of the Epistle of James, unless we are persuaded that he is in fact either the Lord's brother or the apostle.

It is of course conceivable that the reference in Jud. 1 is to persons otherwise completely unknown to us, but this is intrinsically improbable. The way the description is framed seems to imply that, at the time the letter was written, James at any rate would be recognized by the readers as a familiar, indeed important figure. If this is accepted, there are strong grounds for identifying Judas or Jude with the Lord's brother of that name. The only remotely plausible alternative (Judas Barsabbas, and the Jude whom *Const. apost.* vii. 46 and Eusebius, *Hist. eccl.* iv. 5. 3, record as one of James's successors in the see of Jerusalem, can be dismissed as unsupported guesses) is the apostle Judas, but a fatal objection is that, correctly translated, Luke's elliptic formula means 'son of James', not 'brother of James'. Further, the patent implication of Jud. 17 is that the author does not count himself as an apostle. We know next to nothing about the Lord's brother Jude, but a fragment of the 2nd cent. chronicler Hegesippus (in Eusebius, *Hist. eccl.* iii. 19. 1-20. 6) relates a curious incident about his two grandsons. The morbidly suspicious emperor Domitian (81–96), hearing of their Davidic descent and fearful that they might entertain dynastic ambitions, had them haled before him personally for

examination. He soon discovered that they were simple agri-
cultural workers, owning only a few acres of land between them,
and that the only kingdom they were interested in was not of
this world. So he let them go free, 'despising them as persons
of no account'.

It is more difficult to decide whether this Jude himself composed the epistle, or whether it has been fathered on him
pseudonymously. Many scholars are satisfied that he did, and
the possibility cannot be ruled out. The date might be thought
an obstacle, for Jud. 17 clearly looks back to the apostles as
belonging to the past; but against this certain features of the
tract (which is, as we have seen, prior to 2 Peter) would be
consistent with its composition, say, in the seventies of the 1st
cent.: one thinks, e.g., of its free use of uncanonical books, and
of the very early type of Gnosticism presupposed. Jude was
probably younger than James, who was stoned to death by the
Sanhedrin in 62 (Josephus, *Ant.* xx. 200), and might easily have
been alive and active a decade or so later. Paul's statement about
'the Lord's brothers' in 1 Cor. ix. 5 may be evidence that he
engaged in missionary work; if so, it was only natural that, like
Paul himself, he should write to his converts when he learned of
the perils threatening their faith. The Jewish-Christian background and tone of the letter tell in favour of this hypothesis,
as does the writer's partiality for apocalyptic writings. It was
precisely in the humble, God-fearing circles in which our Lord's
family moved that this kind of literature enjoyed a vogue. If we
are surprised that Jude should have said nothing about his
kinship with Jesus, his silence is readily explained, as Clement
of Alexandria (*Adumb. in ep. Iud.*) perceived centuries ago, as
due to understandable humility and reserve.

The case has considerable weight, but the counter-arguments
it provokes are perhaps weightier. The author is probably, but
not necessarily, a Jewish Christian, but in any case he is a
Hellenized one with a cultivated Greek style. The text shows no
signs of being a translation, and while a Galilean like Jude must
have spoken Greek fluently, it is not easy to imagine him handling the language with such art. If he worked as a missionary,
we should expect it to have been among the Aramaic-speaking
population of Palestine; but the recipients of the letter appear to

have been Gentile Christians with a Greek cultural background. It is in any case unlikely that they were converts from Palestinian Judaism, for the Gnostic libertinism attacked cannot have had much attraction for people brought up to reverence the Law. Phrases, too, like 'the faith . . . delivered once for all the saints' (3), and the appeal (17) 'to remember the words spoken before by the apostles of our Lord J.C.', scarcely sound natural on the lips of Jude. Nor, since James was commonly known as 'the Lord's brother', does there seem any sound reason (*pace* Clement) why Jude should have denied himself this description; its avoidance by some later Christian writer for reasons of reverence is much more comprehensible. Finally, while it is just possible that the letter was drafted in Jude's lifetime, a rather later date such as 80–90, or even nearer the end of the century, would fit all the circumstances much better.

If it is pseudonymous, we can only speculate about the unknown author's motive for putting it out under the name of Jude. According to some its choice was particularly apt in a pamphlet designed to rebut Gnostic trends, for we now know from the *Gospel of Thomas* (cf. also *Acts of Thomas* 39) that Jude was honoured in certain Gnostic circles as the Lord's twin-brother, to whom He had imparted special revelations. But to follow this line of thought not only magnifies the problem of the self-description '*servant* of J.C. and *brother* of James', but involves reading back into the 1st cent. the fanciful theorizing of 2nd cent. Gnosticism. The most likely clue is the emphatic mention of James, whose name the writer evidently knew to be venerated by his prospective readers. Since everyone was aware of James's martyrdom in 62, he may have judged it appropriate to write under the name of his obscurer but still respected brother; the NT and tradition, of which the Hegesippus story is a sample, witness to the esteem in which the Lord's brethren generally were held. On any hypothesis of authorship, however, the tract must have originated in Palestine, for it was there that Jude probably worked and that his and James's names were highly regarded. For the same reason its destination is likely to have been some community or group of communities, Greek-speaking and Gentile in origin but attached to the Jewish-Christian wing of the Church, somewhere in Palestine or Syria.

5. Authorship and Date: 2 Peter

Scarcely anyone nowadays doubts that 2 Peter is pseudonymous, although it must be admitted of the few who do that they defend their case with an impressive combination of learning and ingenuity. The author certainly represents himself as the Apostle, starting off with a greeting from 'Symeon Peter', recalling his presence as an eye-witness at the Transfiguration (i. 16-18) and his receipt of a private communication from the Lord about his imminent death (i. 14), affirming in a clear allusion to 1 Peter that this is his second epistle (iii. 1), and speaking of Paul as his colleague (iii. 15). But several considerations combine to cast suspicion on these over-eager protestations. First, the central section of the epistle is a recasting of Jude, and the rest of it is studded with other borrowings from the same source; but the earliest possible date for Jude is (as we have just seen) the early seventies of the 1st cent., i.e. well after Peter's death in Nero's anti-Christian pogrom (c. 64). Secondly, while his acquaintance with Jewish *haggadah* (cf. ii) makes it probable that the writer was a Jewish Christian, he also had a close familiarity with Hellenistic religious and philosophical culture which the one-time Galilean fisherman is hardly likely to have possessed. Thirdly, he lets it out that he lived at a time when the first Christian generation had passed away (iii. 4), and when a collection of Paul's letters had been compiled (iii. 15 f.). Fourthly, his concern for the orthodox interpretation of scripture (i. 20 f.; iii. 15 f.) and for the apostolic tradition (e.g. ii. 21; iii. 2) smacks of emergent 'Catholicism' rather than of first-generation Christianity. Fifthly, if the epistle really is the product of Peter's pen, the slowness and reluctance of the Church, especially at Rome, to accord it recognition present a serious problem.

These difficulties are enormously enhanced if 1 Peter is accepted as authentic. It has indeed been argued (A. Q. Morton, *The Authorship and Integrity of the New Testament*, 1965), on the basis of cumulative sum analysis on the computer, that the two works are linguistically indistinguishable, but most readers of Greek would agree that this conclusion illustrates the limitations of the method. In general the style of 2 Peter is more highly coloured, effusive and pompous than that of its predecessor; it slips readily into iambic rhythms, its choice of words is bookish and artificial and its constructions laboured; and while particles of liaison, hebraisms and participles are much rarer, the article is more frequent and the proportion of hapaxes markedly higher (the highest in the NT). There are also important theological discrepancies between the two letters, and even where their themes overlap they tend to be expressed in different terms (e.g. 1 Peter speaks of 'the revelation of J.C.', 2 Peter of 'the Parousia' or 'the day of the Lord'; 1 Pet. i. 9 of 'the salvation of your souls', 2 Pet. i. 11 of 'entry into Christ's eternal kingdom'). These facts were noted long ago by Jerome, who remarks (*Ep.* cxx. 11) that they 'are divergent in style, character and structure of words'; but his theory that they are to be accounted for by a change of amanuensis fails to explain the altogether different atmosphere of the two writings.

We must therefore conclude that 2 Peter belongs to the luxuriant crop of pseudo-Petrine literature which sprang up around the memory of the Prince of the apostles. Apart from it we know of the highly popular *Apocalypse of Peter* (*c.* 135), which the Muratorian Canon accepts as scripture while recognizing that its position is disputed, the widely read *Preaching of Peter* (early 2nd cent.), the docetic *Gospel of Peter* (*c.* 190), and the legendary *Acts of Peter* (2nd half of 2nd cent.); and still more writings with Peter's name attached have come to light among the finds at Nag Hammadi. 2 Peter was studied and used by the author of the *Apocalypse of Peter*, and is probably the earliest of the group (just as it is certainly much the finest in quality), although it may possibly be contemporary with the *Preaching*. Its author is familiar with 1 Peter, which he accepts without question as authentic and authoritative, and professes to be writing a sequel to it; indeed (as G. H. Boobyer has demonstrated), he takes up and develops several points in the earlier work. Its exact date is not easy to determine. It is obviously later than Jude, but not necessarily much later; the false teaching and moral deviations dealt with are to a large extent the same, and while the writer evidently regards Jude with respect, he does not mention it by name in spite of its claim to be by 'the brother of James' or treat it as scripture. As has already been mentioned, the type of Gnosticism envisaged is much simpler than the mature forms current in the mid-2nd cent., and very similar doubts about the Parousia are complained about in *1 Clement* (*c.* 95: see on iii. 4). All in all, 100–110 is a date with which most of the relevant data concur, although some prefer to place it slightly earlier and others rather later.

Egypt has been conjectured as its place of origin, mainly on the grounds that it obtained its earliest and firmest recognition there and was so speedily pounced upon by the author of the *Apocalypse of Peter*, which is probably of Egyptian provenance. In the absence of any internal evidence this seems a reasonably likely solution. The question of its destination depends, of course, on the prior decision whether it is likely to have been originally (a) a 'catholic epistle', i.e. a homily for Christendom as a whole dressed up in the guise of a letter, or (b) a genuine piece of correspondence. The latter (see §3) does not exclude the possibility that the writer expected his message to reach a wider audience. On the assumption that it is correct, some have opted for Palestine as the area in which the troubled churches were placed, others for Asia Minor on the ground that they must be identified with those for which 1 Peter was intended (iii. 1), others still (notably J. B. Mayor) for Rome in view of the writer's remark in iii. 15 about Paul's writing 'to you' and their belief that his reference is to Romans. This last must be discounted, partly because of the lack of any evidence elsewhere pointing to Rome as the address, but mainly because it rests on a misunderstanding of the passage concerned. The discussion is not really very profitable, but if we are satisfied that the writer had some particular communities in view, we are bound to conclude that his statement in iii. 1 was most likely to carry conviction if they were situated somewhere in Asia Minor. That they consisted of Gentile Christians seems apparent from the whole tone and atmosphere of the letter.

SELECT BIBLIOGRAPHY TO 2 PETER AND JUDE

COMMENTARIES

The editions of C. Bigg, A. Charue, C. E. B. Cranfield, J. Felten,
R. Franco, Fr. Hauck, R. Knopf, A. R. C. Leaney, R. Leconte,
J. Moffatt, B. Reicke, K. H. Schelkle, J. Schneider, C. Spicq, J. W. C.
Wand, H. Windisch (rev. by H. Preisker), and G. Wohlenberg listed
on p. 35. In addition the following:

A. E. Barnett and E. G. Homrighausen, *The Second Epistle of Peter
and the Epistle of Jude* (Interpreter's Bible. London, 1957).

G. H. Boobyer, 'II Peter' and 'Jude' (*Peake's Commentary on the
Bible*. London, 1962).

J. Chaine, *Les Épîtres catholiques* (Études Bibliques. Paris, 1939).

M. Green, *The Second Epistle General of Peter and the General Epistle
of Jude* (Tyndale NT Commentaries. London, 1968).

M. R. James, *2 Peter and Jude* (Cambridge Greek Testament. Cambridge, 1912).

J. B. Mayor, *The Second Epistle of St. Peter and the Epistle of St. Jude*
(London, 1907).

A. Plummer, *St. James and St. Jude* (Expositor's Bible. London, 1891).

E. M. Sidebottom, *James, Jude and 2 Peter* (Century Bible. London, 1967).

STUDIES AND ARTICLES

L. W. Barnard, 'The Judgement in II Peter iii' (*Expository Times*
lxviii, 1958).

W. Bieder, *Die Vorstellungen von der Höllenfahrt Jesu Christi* (Zürich, 1949).

J. Boehmer, 'Tag und Morgenstern? Zu 2 Petr. i. 19' (ZNTW xxii, 1923).

G. H. Boobyer, 'The Verbs in Jude 11' (*New Testament Studies* v, 1959).

'The Indebtedness of 2 Peter to 1 Peter' (*NT Essays: Studies in
Memory of T. W. Manson*: ed. A. J. B. Higgins. Manchester, 1959).

H. Braun, *Spätjüdisch-häretischer und frühchristlicher Radikalismus*
(Tübingen, 1957).

J. Chaine, 'Cosmogonie aquatique et conflagration finale d'après la
Secunda Petri' (*Revue Biblique* xlvi, 1937).

F. H. Chase, 'Jude, Epistle of', and 'Peter, Second Epistle of' (Hastings' *Dictionary of the Bible*, Vols. II and III. Edinburgh, 1899
and 1900).

238

SELECT BIBLIOGRAPHY

J. T. Curran, 'The Teaching of 2 Peter i. 20' (*Theological Studies* iv, 1943).

W. Foerster, 'Eusebeia in den Pastoralbriefen' (*New Testament Studies* v, 1959).

T. F. Glasson, *Greek Influence on Jewish Eschatology* (London, 1961).

E. M. B. Green, *2 Peter Reconsidered* (Tyndale Monographs. London, 1961).

D. Guthrie, *New Testament Introduction*, Vol. III (London, 1962).

E. Käsemann, 'An Apologia for Primitive Christian Eschatology' (*Essays on NT Themes*, ch. viii. Eng. trans., London, 1964).

R. Mayer, *Die biblische Vorstellung vom Weltbenbrand* (Bonn, 1956).

E. Molland, 'La thèse "La prophétie n'est jamais venue de la volonté de l'homme" (2 Pierre i. 21) et les Pseudo-Clémentines' (*Studia Theologica* ix, 1955).

S. Rappaport, 'Der gerechte Lot' (ZNTW xxix, 1930).

K. H. Schelkle, 'Spätapostolische Briefe als frühchristliches Zeugnis' (*Festschrift J. Schmid*. Ratisbon, 1963).

J. Schmitt, 'Pierre (Deuxième épître de)' (*Dictionnaire de la Bible*, Supplément vii. Paris, 1966).

P. E. Testa, 'La distruzione del mondo per il fuoco nella seconda epistola di san Pietro' (*Rivista Biblica* x, 1962).

THE EPISTLE OF JUDE

1. ADDRESS AND GREETING

1-2

(1) Jude, servant of Jesus Christ and brother of James, to those who are called, beloved in God the Father and kept safe for Jesus Christ: (2) May mercy, peace and love be multiplied to you.

The letter opens with a greeting of the conventional Jewish pattern adapted to Christian usage. Though much shorter, it has the same basic plan and broadly the same content as that of 1 Pet. i. 1 f. (see note). The writer's name is given as **Jude** 1 (*Ioudas*): for his identity, see Introduction, pp. 231-234. The intention seems to be to impress on the recipients that he is not some obscure, otherwise unknown individual in the apostolic Church, but the brother of the Lord mentioned in Mk. vi. 3; Mt. xiii. 55.

This is reinforced by two descriptive labels which clearly have the object of indicating which Jude is meant (the name was extremely common in contemporary Judaism), and of underlining his authority. First, he is a **servant** (lit. 'slave') **of Jesus Christ**. As in Jas. i. 1 and 2 Pet. i. 1, the formula probably reflects the influence of Paul, who employed it occasionally in letter-openings (Rom. i. 1; Phil. i. 1), though himself preferring the word-order 'Christ Jesus' (the change to **Jesus Christ** in the Catholic Epistles is a byproduct of their later date). Its origins lie in the OT, in which members of God's chosen people, the devout, or, more specifically, religious leaders like Moses and David, are called 'servants of God'. In the NT this latter title is in retreat as applied to Christians (but cf. Tit. i. 1: also 1 Pet. ii. 16, where it is used quite straightforwardly), its place being taken by the more characteristic and appropriate 'servant of Jesus Christ' (e.g. Rom. i. 1; 1 Cor. vii. 22; Eph. vi. 6). The underlying thought is that, having been rescued by Christ from slavery to sin and death, Christians now belong wholly to Him as His slaves. As a self-designation, however, the title has a specialized significance: it connotes one who is charged to labour in Christ's service, i.e. His authorized minister and representative. Examples are Rom. i. 1; Phil. i. 1, where it is either linked with or substituted for a reference to Paul's role as an apostle; and Gal. i. 10; Col. iv. 12; Jas. i. 1; 2 Pet. i. 1, where it envisages primarily ministerial activity or office (see TWNT II, 264-80). So here the implication is, not simply that **Jude** is a Christian, but that he is a recognized leader with a claim to speak and be listened to.

Secondly, he is **brother of James.** To mention a man's father is natural enough, but why his brother? There is no parallel in the NT, and the expression only makes sense if **James** is a prominent person whose identity will be immediately recognized. This fits in with his being the James who was the eldest of the Lord's brothers (Mk. vi. 3), whom Paul acknowledged as one of 'the pillars' (Gal. ii. 9), and who was leader of the Jerusalem church for many years (Acts xii. 17). As a matter of fact, James and Jude, the Lord's brethren, are the only pair of brothers bearing these names of whom we hear in the NT. If this James is meant, the reference to him makes it absolutely clear who **Jude** is supposed to be as well as underlining his authority. Both these ends would, of course, have been achieved by describing him directly as 'the Lord's brother' (as Paul describes James in Gal. i. 19: cf. 1 Cor. ix. 5). If the letter really comes from Jude, it is hard to see why he did not use such language. The fact that it is carefully avoided is a pointer to pseudonymity. Whoever was the true author wrote at a time when reverence for the Saviour might have made a claim to blood relationship seem presumptuous.

The persons addressed are simply characterized as **those who are called** (*tois . . . klētois*). The fact that no particular locality is named has led scholars to infer, without sufficient justification, that the epistle was meant to be a 'general' one, i.e. addressed to worldwide Christendom. This is unlikely in view of its brevity and the distinctive nature of the errors castigated, and in any case it contains hints that the author had a specific emergency affecting a particular community or communities in mind (see Introduction, pp. 227 f.). The verbal adjective **called** (*klētos*) had come to be used almost as a noun, to all intents and purposes synonymous with 'a Christian', as early as Paul's time (Rom. i. 6 f.; viii. 28; 1 Cor. i. 24: cf. Rev. xvii. 14). The reason is that the idea of God's 'call' (see on 1 Pet. ii. 9) was a vivid personal experience to every Christian; he knew that as a result of it he had passed from sin and death into the redeemed life which Christ bestows.

A glimpse of what this means is given in the two participial phrases which are attached. As Christians the addressees are, first, **beloved** (*ēgapēmenois*) **in God the Father**—AV, following a number of MSS, reads 'sanctified' (*hēgiasmenois*), but this clearly represents a correction, inspired by 1 Cor. i. 2, of a superficially difficult text. What the writer means by this is, not that they are loved by himself with a love rooted in God, but rather that they are loved by God and that His love enfolds them. As a result of being called, they have fellowship with Him, and in that fellowship experience His love. This is the sense demanded not only by the Pauline parallels (Col. iii. 12; 1 Thess. i. 4; 2 Thess. ii. 13), but also by the coordinate phrase following, which speaks of an objective aspect of God's action on them.

Secondly, they are **kept safe for Jesus Christ,** i.e. for His Coming and for the kingdom He will establish. When the great day arrives, they will have no need to be afraid. For the idea, cf. 1 Thess. v. 23. The participle here, it should be noted, like **beloved** above, is in the perfect tense, the suggestion being that they not only were once, but continue to be, objects of God's love and care. Although his point cannot become clear until we have read further, the writer is veiledly contrasting the love and security in which his readers are wrapped with the tragic condition of the unfortunates he is about to denounce.

The absence of mention of the Holy Spirit has struck some as surprising; 1 Pet. i. 2 stands in marked contrast. But the two-membered, or binitarian, dogmatic framework, based on God the Father and Jesus Christ (e.g. Rom. iv. 24; 1 Cor. viii. 6; 1 Tim. ii. 5 f.; vi. 13 f.), is as characteristic of the NT as the three-membered, and persisted well into the 2nd cent. (e.g. Ignatius, *Magn.* viii. 2; Irenaeus, *Haer.* iii. 1. 2; 4. 2). While our author seems to favour it (4b—but see note; 25), its use implies neither ignorance nor depreciation of the role of the Spirit (cf. 19; 20).

2 The address is followed, as was customary in ancient letters, by good wishes for the recipients: **May mercy, peace and love be multiplied to you** (or 'be yours in fullest measure'). For the form, especially the traditional Jewish **be multiplied,** see on 1 Pet. i. 2. It differs slightly from Paul's, his prayer being usually for 'grace and peace from God our Father and the Lord Jesus Christ', but approximates to 1 Tim. i. 2; 2 Tim. i. 2; 2 Jn. 3 ('grace, mercy, peace'). Evidently the formula became standardized, for we come across it in almost identical terms ('grace, peace and love from God the Father and our Lord J.C. be multiplied') in *Mart. Polyc.* praef. (*c.* 156), which was probably written in complete independence of Jude.

According to some, the prayer draws out ideas latent in 1, **mercy** being the effective action of God's call, **peace** the serenity of soul which springs from the assurance of being **kept safe,** and **love** the charity appropriate to people who are themselves **beloved.** But since **mercy** is clearly God's objective gift, it seems arbitrary to give the other two terms a subjective interpretation; all three surely denote coordinate aspects of God's grace. As often in the NT (e.g. Rom. xv. 9; Tit. iii. 5), **mercy** refers primarily to God's saving action in Christ; as in 21, it probably carries eschatological overtones also, hinting that He will be merciful at the judgment. For Christians **peace,** too (see on 1 Pet. i. 2), stands not so much for the interior tranquillity of believers as for their reconciliation with God, which Christ has brought about by His death and resurrection, and their resulting preservation at the final denouement. Similarly **love** in such a context as this is primarily 'the love of God in Christ Jesus our Lord' (Rom. viii. 39: cf. v. 8); it is this love which makes men children of God (1 Jn. iii. 1), and in so far as it is **multiplied to** them they abide in it, and their joy becomes full (Jn. xv. 11).

(3) Dear friends, although I was making every effort to write to you about our common salvation, I have found it necessary to write to you with an appeal to struggle for the faith which has been delivered once for all to the saints. (4) For certain persons have smuggled themselves in, who were long ago marked out for this condemnation—ungodly people, who pervert the grace of our God into licentiousness and deny the only Master and our Lord Jesus Christ.

His brief greeting concluded, the writer plunges at once into the circumstances which have instigated him to write his letter. He has felt impelled to do so, he explains, by alarm at the threat offered to the Church's traditional teaching by innovators of doubtful orthodoxy and morality. But if this much is clear, the exact import of the participial clause introducing **I have found it necessary** is not easy to disentangle. According to the rendering adopted above (so too NEB), it had been his earnest intention **to write to you about our common salvation,** i.e. (presumably) to prepare a general and positive presentation of the faith for their benefit, but this project had been interrupted by the urgent need to deal with a particular critical situation. On the other hand, many scholars fail to detect in his words any implication of a change of plan. The **common salvation,** they point out, is virtually synonymous with **the faith which has been delivered once for all,** and the two clauses are not antithetical but complementary; all the writer is saying is that, 'being very eager to write to' his correspondents (so RSV), he has been constrained to do so by the emergency. Both exegeses make good sense and are syntactically possible: but in favour of the former it may be urged (a) that the latter makes the sentence unnecessarily laboured and repetitive; (b) that the difference of tense between the two infinitives **to write** (the first is present, the second aorist) seems to distinguish a general intention which fell short of accomplishment from a concrete action carried through; and (c) that the structure and wording of the sentence suggest the contrast between a general essay on the faith and a peremptory exhortation to defend it. If we accept the former exegesis, it is fruitless to speculate whether the writer ever fulfilled his original plan or not. The picture presented, incidentally, is entirely lifelike, and coheres well with the view taken in the Introduction (p. 228) that Jude is not a general homily but a genuine letter directed at a particular situation.

For the affectionate **Dear friends** (*agapētoi*: lit. 'loved', picking up **beloved** in 1b but with the emphasis this time on the writer's rather than God's love), see on 1 Pet. ii. 11. By **our common salvation** some think he means the salvation which he, a Jewish Christian, and they, Christians of Gentile extraction, share alike; but in the absence of any other reference in the letter to such a distinction this seems artificial. Almost certainly the expression means 'the salvation which all we Christians share in common'. It brings out the corporate nature of salvation as understood by Judaism, with its consciousness of being the people of God, and even more vividly by Christianity, with its conviction of fellowship in Christ. This was one of the most characteristic differences between it and Hellenistic piety, in which salvation (cf. esp. the mystery cults) tended to be a private experience of the individual. On the other hand, we can sense a marked divergence between the writer's conception of 'salvation' (*sōtēria*) and that found, e.g., in 1 Peter and the Pauline letters. In the former (i. 5: see note) we read of 'a salvation which is all ready to be revealed in the last time', and in the latter too (e.g. Rom. v. 9; xiii. 11; 1 Cor. v. 5; Phil. i. 28; 2 Tim. ii. 10) the eschatological aspect is normally very much to the fore. By contrast **our common salvation** seems to stand for something in which Christians participate here and now; it is almost equivalent to 'our common Christianity'.

In **I have found it necessary** the Greek verb is aorist (*eschon*: lit. 'I had'—almost 'received'—'the necessity'), thus standing in contrast to the present continuous participle **making every effort** and lending support to the exegesis of 3a defended above. He has been driven to **appeal** to his readers **to struggle for** their religion (the noun is in the dative, and while this case could denote either the person against whom or the instrument with which one fights, here it obviously denotes the cause on behalf of which one fights: cf. Plutarch, *Mor.* 1075d). The verb (*epagōnizesthai*: only here in the NT) is exceptionally strong, and the picture originally conjured up by it and its cognates is not of warfare but of athletics, a wrestling match or some other contest at the games. The metaphor is more alive and vivid in the Pastorals, which speak of 'the noble contest of faith' (1 Tim. vi. 12) and of Paul's fighting 'the noble match' (2 Tim. iv. 7 f.). In his acknowledged letters the Apostle draws on the arena, stadium or battlefield to drive home the rigorous demands of the Christian life (1 Cor. ix. 24-27; Eph. vi. 10-17) or of the apostolic vocation itself (Col. i. 29). There is nothing specially Christian, however, about this imagery. Greek writers (e.g. Plutarch, *Mor.* 593de) never tire of comparing the life of virtue to the strenuous training and toilsome encounters of athletes; while in the literature of Hellenistic Judaism the struggle which the pious have to sustain in this world is constantly described in picturesque, often consciously athletic language (e.g. Wis. iv. 2; Ecclus. v. 28; 2 Macc. xiii. 14; 4 Macc. xi. 20; xvii. 10-16; Philo, *Agric.* 102; 119). Often, however, as in the present verse, the underlying imagery has completely faded or been transposed into that of actual warfare, and a legitimate parallel is provided by the Qumran sect, which conceived of the Sons of Light, i.e. the elect community, as engaged in deadly battle with the Sons of Darkness (cf. 1QM).

Here the cause which needs defence is **the faith which has been delivered once for all to the saints.** This is an extremely important expression which, taken in conjunction with **our common salvation** above, adds precision to our author's conception of Christianity. Clearly **the faith** is not the believing man's response to Christ (the *fides qua creditur*), but is to be concretely understood as the *fides quae creditur*, i.e. the message or body of saving beliefs accepted as orthodox in the Church. Moreover, it **has been delivered,** i.e. handed down, committed and entrusted, with the idea of transmission in the Church included, **once for all** (*hapax*: cf. its use again at 5) **to the saints** (*tois hagiois*: lit. 'the holy ones'—see on 1 Pet. i. 15 f.), i.e. in the idiom of primitive Christianity (Acts ix. 32; Rom. viii. 27; xv. 26; etc.) to the members of the Church. In other

words, Christianity is viewed as a system of revealed teaching
which is by its very nature unalterable and normative (this is
the force of **once for all**). It is not immediately clear whether
its authoritative source is thought of as God Himself or the
apostles; but the latter seems the correct interpretation (cf. 17)
since in the NT the agents for the 'delivery' or transmission of
doctrine are always human beings (e.g. Lk. i. 2; Acts xvi. 4;
Rom. vi. 17; 1 Cor. xi. 2; 2 Thess. ii. 15; iii. 6; 2 Tim. ii. 1 f.).

These notions are by no means alien to the earlier strata of
the NT, for it is evident that the idea of tradition, of the gospel
as an authoritative message committed to and handed down in
the Church, was integral to Christianity from the start. An
analysis of Paul's letters, e.g., reveals how packed with traditional material they are; and he too is prepared to use 'faith' in
the objective sense of the content of belief (e.g. Rom. x. 8; Gal.
i. 23; vi. 10), appeals to tradition (e.g. 1 Cor. xi. 23; xv. 1), and
commends loyalty to the authorized teaching (Rom. xvi. 17;
1 Cor. xi. 2). Nevertheless it cannot be denied that, with the
passage of time and the emergence of 'heretical' doctrines, the
emphasis on this traditional and normative aspect steadily
increased. It becomes much more pronounced, e.g., in the
Pastorals (e.g. 1 Tim. i. 3; iv. 6; 2 Tim. ii. 2; iv. 3 f.; Tit. i. 9),
whether these are works of Paul's old age or by a later hand.
The present passage, in itself succinct but backed up by the very
similar 'your most holy faith' in 20, seems to presuppose an
even more formalized view of the Church's message as a clearly
defined and authoritatively transmitted deposit.

What makes this call to rally to the defence of the orthodox
4 apostolic faith necessary? Because **certain persons have smuggled themselves in** who are distorting and eroding it. There
is a contemptuous ring in **certain persons** (*tines anthrōpoi*: cf.
Paul's use of *tines* in Gal. i. 7; ii. 12); the writer has particular
individuals in mind, but there is also probably an intentional
contrast with **the saints** in the previous verse. The verb
smuggled themselves in, or 'wormed their way in' (NEB:
pareiseduēsan, though supported only by Codex Vat., is to be
preferred to *pareisedusan*, which represents a correction to conform with more ordinary usage), indicates that these are interlopers (possibly itinerant trouble-makers, like those mentioned

by Ignatius, *Eph.* vii. 1; ix. 1) who have installed themselves in the communities. They are trying to disseminate their hetero-dox views rather than form a separatist sect (it is clear from 12 that they are working inside the church), and the writer's obvious anxiety betrays that they are making some impression. The situation resembles that of Gal. ii. 4, where Paul speaks of 'false brothers secretly brought in, who slipped in to spy out our freedom . . . so that they might bring us into bondage'. In-novators like these, perverting what the 'official' Church considered the authentic teaching and upsetting people, seem to have been a constant worry in the 1st as well as the 2nd cent.: cf. 2 Cor. xi. (with its reference in 5 to 'these superlative apostles'); Phil. iii. 2 ('Look out for the dogs, look out for the evil-workers . . .'); 2 Tim. iii. 6 ('those who make their way into households and capture weak women'); 2 Pet. ii; 1 Jn. iv. 1 ('many false prophets have gone out into the world'); 2 Jn. 7 ('many deceivers . . .'); 3 Jn. 9 ('Diotrephes, who likes to put himself first').

So eager is the writer to warn his readers against these people that, even before mentioning the nature of their error, he angrily interjects that they **were long ago marked out for this condemnation,** i.e. they are men already in effect damned with whom good Christians associate at their peril. The **con-demnation** (*krima*: 'judgment') is obviously the terrible fate which awaits them, but **this** is puzzling. According to some, it is backward-looking, its reference being to 3b, where the heretics' defeat by the defenders of orthodoxy is darkly hinted at; but the effort of imaginative deduction required for this is excessive. Alternatively the adjective must look forward, as at 1 Pet. iii. 9 (see note); but again a clear and precise, and reason-ably near, point of reference is lacking: their final conviction is formally stated in 15, but this is too remote. The most plausible explanation is that the sentence is carelessly composed, **this condemnation** pointing forward in a loose, non-specific way to the stern penalties God has in store for sinners like them which the writer is going to describe in 5-7 and 15 and which already preoccupy his imagination.

There is also a puzzle about **long ago marked out.** NEB, it may be noted, renders the Greek (*palai progegrammenoi*) by 'whom Scripture long ago marked down', presumably on the basis of the use of the same verb ('whatever was written in former days') at Rom. xv. 4, but the specific meaning 'scripture' which Paul reads into it there is peculiar and ordinarily it carries no reference to sacred texts. The once popular suggestion that the writer is recalling the prophecy of doom pronounced on false prophets and teachers at 2 Pet. ii. 1-3 must be rejected, if only because most are now convinced that Jude antedates 2 Peter. So must the more recent theory that he may be thinking of similar prophecies by the apostles (cf. 17), whether in scripture (e.g. Paul's warning to the Milesian elders at Acts xx. 29 f.) or elsewhere, for (a) such an allusion would be incomprehensible without further elucidation, and (b) he would in that case scarcely have written *palai*: the adverb, which normally means **long ago,** can colloquially denote a short interval, but this colloquial usage seems inappropriate here. We have therefore to decide between two competing interpretations. First, the writer's point may be that these 'modernists'' names have been **long ago** written down or recorded in the heavenly books in which, according to Jewish conceptions, God enters each individual's destiny for good or ill (Ps. lxix. 28; cxxxix. 16; Is. iv. 3—lit. 'written unto life'; Jer. xxii. 30; Dan. vii. 10; Mal. iii. 16), and which fascinated the imagination of Jewish apocalyptic writers (cf. esp. Test. Ash. vii. 5; Apoc. Bar. xxiv. 1; 1 En. lxxxix. 62-71; cvi. 19; cviii. 7). On this see SB II, 169-74; III, 840; TWNT I, 772. Alternatively, the idea of heavenly books may be a false trail, the reference being simply to the clear denunciation of evil-doers and blasphemers set out in the OT and other hallowed writings (including 1 Enoch) and specifically illustrated by the warnings about to be recounted in 5-7, 9 and 14 f. Either of these exegeses is acceptable, but the advantage seems to lie with the former, which incidentally is that of Clement of Alexandria (*Adumb. in ep. Iud.*: 'praedestinati erant in iudicium'). (a) The writer has a special familiarity with 1 Enoch, quoting 1 En. i. 9 at 14, and the heavenly books figure largely in that work. (b) This interpretation is supported by the verb (*prographein*), which has the technical sense of entering the names of proscribed persons on a list (e.g. Polybius, *Hist.* xxxii. 5.12; 6.1; Lucian, *Tim.* 51: cf. also 1 Macc. x. 36, where it con-

notes enrolment in an army), and which with the preposition
'to' or 'for' can mean 'proscribe' (Appian, *Bell. civ.* iv. 1. 1).
(c) The idea of names entered in heavenly books was current
among NT writers (e.g. Phil. iv. 3; Rev. xx. 12). The only
serious objection is that *palai*, translated **long ago,** normally
designates a point or points in far-back time, i.e. in human
history (e.g. Heb. i. 1), not the pre-temporal counsel of God
(as Clement Alex. and John Calvin took the meaning to be).
But this latter notion seems in any case out of place; the text
does not require a pre-temporal insertion of the names in the
books, and indeed we are not informed when they were entered.

After these preliminaries the writer launches out into a brief
but pregnant description of these dangerous interlopers. They
are, he protests, **ungodly people,** and he then proceeds to
spell out the content of this rather general characterization in
two parallel clauses. First, they **pervert the grace of our God
into licentiousness.** By **grace** (*charita*: this unusual accusative
in place of *charin* deserves note) he means 'the glorious liberty
of the children of God' (Rom. viii. 21: cf. 2 Cor. iii. 17) which
the Christian enjoys as the result of the forgiveness of his sins,
his emancipation from the Law, and his adoption to sonship. The
noun translated **licentiousness** (*aselgeia*), as in Greek ethics,
stands for sensuality or debauchery (e.g. Mk. vii. 22; Eph. iv.
19; 1 Pet. iv. 3), sometimes more specifically for sexual indulgence (Rom. xiii. 13; 2 Cor. xii. 21; 2 Pet. ii. 2; 7; 18). The
insinuation seems to be that they are guilty of antinomianism
of the kind against which Paul repeatedly warns his correspondents (Rom. iii. 8; vi. 1; 15; Gal. v. 13: cf. 1 Pet. ii. 16 and note;
2 Pet. ii. 19; Rev. ii. 24), and which itself resulted from a misunderstanding or twisting of his own teaching about God's
grace and man's justification by faith, not works of the Law.
Allied with a dualistic doctrine which disparaged the body,
antinomianism was to be characteristic of certain forms of
2nd cent. Gnosticism (cf. esp. the detailed account given by
Irenaeus, *Haer.* i. 6. 2-4: cf. Hippolytus, *Ref.* vi. 19; Clement
Alex., *Strom.* iii. 30), and it is possible that the errorists criticized
here are incipient Gnostics; 19 (see note) tends to support this.
But the arrogant, in the last resort blasphemous, assumption
that one's privileged status in the faith puts one above the

morality which binds ordinary people is liable to manifest itself in every age and in the context of a variety of presuppositions.

The second charge is that they **deny the only Master and our Lord Jesus Christ,** i.e. both God the Father and Christ (so RVm; RSVm; NEBm). The alternative translation, 'deny our only Master and Lord, Jesus Christ' (AV; RV; RSV; NEB) is equally possible linguistically, and the decision between them is not easy. The fact that there is a definite article before **only Master** and none before **our Lord J.C.** might seem to suggest that the whole complex expression applies to a single person, but this argument cannot be pressed: the article is often omitted before 'God', 'Lord', and the like (5 below; Eph. v. 5; 2 Thess. i. 12; 1 Tim. v. 21; Tit. ii. 13). A weightier point is that 2 Pet. ii. 1, which is modelled on this phrase, evidently understood **Master** as referring to Christ; but the ambiguity must have been as real and puzzling soon after it was written as it is today. The following are considerations in favour of the rendering adopted. (a) Both **only** (*monos*) and **Master** (*despotēs*), as used in an early Christian text, and especially as used together, naturally suggest God. 'Only God', 'only Master', and the like were almost standard formulae, in Jewish as well as Christian writings, for expressing their distinctive monotheism as opposed to polytheism or Caesar-worship (e.g. 25 below; Jn. v. 44; xvii. 3; Rom. xvi. 27; 1 Tim. i. 17; Josephus, *Bell. Iud.* vii. 323; *Ant.* xviii. 23; Philo. *Mut. nom.* 22); while **Master** nowhere else in the NT, 2 Pet. ii. 1 apart, denotes Christ, but was a regular description of God, especially in texts with a liturgical or formulary note (e.g. Lk. ii. 29; Acts iv. 24; Rev. vi. 10; *1 Clem.* lix. 4; lx. 3; lxi. 1 f.; *Did.* x. 3; Justin, *1 Apol.* lxi. 3). (b) The description of Christ as *both* **Master** *and* **Lord** is pleonastic and unprecedented. (c) The writer, as we have noted on 1, seems to have a predilection for two-membered formulae. (d) There is a remarkable parallel, in wording and sense, in 1 En. xlviii. 10 ('they have denied the Lord of Spirits and his Anointed') which, in view of his acquaintance with that work, may well have prompted his choice of one here. It is worth noting that several MSS and the Syriac version understand the verse in this way, inserting 'God' after **Master.**

How do they **deny** God and Christ (or Christ)? According to many, simply by their moral depravity, which is tantamount to a denial since, instead of obeying them (or Him), they have chosen to follow a course of life condemned by the gospel. For a parallel, cf. Tit. i. 16 ('they confess they know God, but deny him by their deeds'). But in view of the writer's concern for doctrinal purity in 3, the charge he is to advance in 8, and his emphasis on 'the only God' in 25, it is tempting to infer that their denial involved some kind of falsification of belief as well. We may compare 1 Jn. ii. 22 f., where 'denying' the Father and the Son connotes a defective Christology. This surmise is supported by the hints elsewhere in the letter (cf. esp. 19) that these people had Gnostic leanings, for with its distinction between the Supreme God and the Demiurge, or creator-God, and its disparagement of matter Gnosticism offered a standing threat to strict monotheism and the reality of the incarnation. There is no direct allusion, however, to these characteristic features in the letter, and while some kind of distortion of basic monotheism and Christology seems implied, the evidence available is too scanty for us to be able to form any precise picture of the form it took.

3. THREE NOTORIOUS EXAMPLES

5-7

(5) I should like to remind you—you who have been informed of all things once for all—that after the Lord had saved his people out of the land of Egypt, he next time destroyed those who did not believe; (6) and that he has kept under darkness in eternal chains, awaiting the judgment of the great day, the angels who did not keep their dominion but abandoned their proper dwelling-place: (7) just as Sodom and Gomorrah and the surrounding cities, which practised immorality in the same way as these and lusted after different flesh, stand out as an example, undergoing as they do a punishment of everlasting fire.

Having summarized the errors of the innovators, the writer wishes to leave no doubt whatsoever (he has to steady the resolution of wobblers) that a terrible punishment is in store for them. So he selects three classic illustrations of the way God has treated those who, having enjoyed His favour, prove rebellious and abandon themselves to wantonness. He starts off, however, with an apology for recalling truths which they already know

5 full well: **I should like to remind you—you who have been informed of all things once for all.** Similar complimentary references to the recipients' knowledge are frequent in NT letters (Rom. xv. 14; 1 Thess. iv. 9; 2 Pet. i. 12; 1 Jn. ii. 21; 27); also in early Christian letters outside the NT (*1 Clem*. liii. 1; *Barn*. i. 2 ff.; Ignatius, *Eph*. iii. 1; viii. 1). The present example, however, has a deeper significance than conventional politeness. The addressees 'know everything' (*panta*); their knowledge extends beyond the cautionary stories from sacred history about to be cited, and includes the fulness of God's revelation, all that a Christian can need. Further, this saving knowledge has been acquired **once for all** (*hapax*, as at 3: this is its true position in the clause, although some important MSS, in order to make an easier reading, place the adverb after **that** in the following clause). Tradition, with the associated concepts of 'remembering' and 'reminding' (e.g. Lk. xxiv. 8; Jn. xii. 16; xiv. 26; Rom. xv. 15; 1 Cor. xi. 2; 2 Tim. ii. 8; 14; Tit. iii. 1; 2 Pet. iii. 1f.), is an essential element in OT and NT religion, grounded as it is in God's saving acts in history (see TWNT IV, 678-82); but here, as in 3b, we have a sharper insistence that the apostolic faith is a complete whole which has been definitively given to men and cannot be altered. As in 1 Jn. ii. 20 f., there is probably also a hint in 'you know everything' that that faith, and not the teaching of the errorists, is the true and final *gnōsis*.

The first illustration is God's destruction in the desert of the faithless Israelites whom He had earlier rescued from captivity: **after the Lord had saved his people out of the land of Egypt, he next time destroyed those who did not believe.** Although the translation represents what is almost certainly the true text, there are important variant readings. First, as stated above, some MSS, including Codex Sin., transfer *hapax* ('once') from the previous clause to this one, their motive being in part to ease the awkward **next time** (see next paragraph); but *hapax* means 'once only', not 'once in a series', and the balancing of 'faith once for all delivered' by 'you who know all things once for all' is unmistakable. Secondly, instead of **the Lord** (*kurios*, with or without the definite article), some authorities (including Clement Alex., a corrector of C, and the Philoxenian Syriac) give 'God' (*ho theos*). Others (Origen, Codex Alex. and Codex Vat., several cursives and early versions) offer the much more interesting 'Jesus' (*Iēsous*); while Pap. 72 conflates the two traditions and reads 'God Christ' (*theos Christos*). Some critics favour 'Jesus', pointing to (a) the possibility that it may have been intended as 'Joshua' (so NEBm), or alternatively (b) the eagerness of Christian writers even in the apostolic age to recognize the pre-existent Christ as active in OT events (Jn. xii. 41; 1 Cor. x. 4; 9 *var. lect.*; Heb. xi. 26; 1 Pet. i. 11—see note); but this is hardly likely to have been the original reading. As regards Joshua, it was not he who brought the Israelites out of Egypt and then destroyed them. As regards Christ, He who punished the murmurers in the desert is declared in the next verse to have imprisoned the fallen angels, and there is no evidence of Christ having been credited with this; 2 Pet. ii. 4 explicitly ascribes the action to God. Much the most probable solution is that **the Lord** (*kurios*, probably without the article) represents the original text, the writer meaning by it God (as in 9), but that in certain circles, under the influence of the interest in the pre-existent Christ just mentioned as well as of the typology Joshua/Jesus, this was increasingly interpreted as denoting Jesus, who is most frequently designated 'Lord' in the NT. Cf. Justin, *Dial.* cxx. 3, who speaks of 'Jesus, who also led our fathers out of Egypt', and elaborations of the same idea in Clement Alex., *Paed.* i. 60. 3; Origen, *Hom. in Ex.* xi. 3; *In lib. Iesu nave hom.* i. 1.

To return to the illustration of God's vengeance, the story is set out in full in Num. xiv. 1-38; xxvi. 64 f.: for its later exploitation as a warning, cf. Ps. xcv. 10 f.; Ecclus. xvi. 9 f.; 1 Cor. x. 1-13; Heb. iii. 7-iv. 10. Because they lacked faith in Moses's power and God's promises (Num. xiv. 11; Dt. i. 32), i.e. **did not believe,** the people 'murmured', and as a punishment all aged twenty years and upwards perished of plague except Joshua

and Caleb, who alone survived to enter the promised land. The
initially puzzling **next time** represents the Greek *to deuteron*,
lit. 'the second time'. As God only **saved his people** once out
of Egypt and only once destroyed them then, scholars have
tried to eliminate the difficulty by bringing in the sacking of
Jerusalem in A.D. 70. According to some, 'the second time' is to
be construed with **had saved,** this second saving being the
rescue of the Christian community in the holy city in 70;
according to others, it is to be taken with **destroyed,** this
second destruction being the wiping out of the Jews in the city
who refused to acknowledge the Messiah. Both exegeses, however, are extremely forced, unnecessary, and out of touch with
the writer's thinking: the retribution meted out in the desert to
the chosen people was a stock example which lay ready to hand.
Clearly 'the second time' goes with **destroyed**; the earlier
occasion is not explicitly indicated, but is implied in the reference to the Lord's rescuing His people out of Egypt. We might
paraphrase 'the second time' by 'when next He intervened in
Israel's history'.

6   As his second illustration the writer holds up the fate of **the
angels who did not keep their dominion but abandoned
their proper dwelling-place.** These are 'the sons of God'
who, according to Gen. vi. 1-4, yielded to the attractions of 'the
daughters of men' and formed unions with them. In later
Jewish speculation, which Jude is following, the legend was
developed and elaborated in fantastic detail (for references, see
note on 1 Pet. iii. 19), the 'sons of God' being identified (so even
Codex A of the LXX) as angels; and this richly embroidered
version of the brief narrative in Genesis was, it may be remarked, taken up and readily adopted by early Church fathers
(e.g. Justin, *2 Apol.* v. 3; Irenaeus, iv. 36. 4; Tertullian, *De
idol.* ix. 1; *De cult. fem.* i. 2; *Apol.* xxii. 3; Clement Alex., *Paed.*
iii. 2. 14; *Strom.* iii. 7. 59). These heavenly beings possessed a
dominion (*archē*: this noun could mean 'beginning' or 'first
estate', as AV renders it, but this is quite out of place here)
granted them by God, and indeed in the NT they appear with
such titles as 'principalities' or 'principalities and powers'
(Rom. viii. 38; Col. ii. 15: the Greek for 'principality' is *archē*),
or even 'world-rulers' (Eph. vi. 12). The basis of this was the

belief that the nations of the world had been assigned to them
(LXX Dt. xxxii. 8), and the whole course of the universe, the
sun, moon, stars, etc., placed under their supervision (e.g. 1 En.
lxxii-lxxxii). Thus they had **their proper dwelling-place,**
which is described in 1 En. xii. 4 (cf. xv. 3; 7) as 'the high
heaven, the holy, eternal place'; but those of their number who
'lusted after the daughters of men' (two hundred in all, according to 1 En. vi. 6) committed the sin of abandoning this as
well as failing to keep **their dominion.**

As a punishment God **has kept** them **under darkness in
eternal chains, awaiting the judgment of the great day.**
Their penalty is again not mentioned in Gen. vi. 1-4, but is set
out in full detail in several passages of 1 Enoch, which is plainly
the writer's main source (his text has several correspondences
with surviving fragments of the Greek version: for his actual
citation of it, see on 14). These indeed provide the best commentary on the present verse, esp. xii. 4-xiii. 1: ' "Enoch, thou
scribe of righteousness, go, declare to the Watchers of the heaven
who have left the high heaven, the holy eternal place, and have
defiled themselves with women . . . "You have wrought great
destruction on the earth; and you shall have no peace or forgiveness of sin" . . . And Enoch went and said, "Azazel [their
leader], thou shalt have no peace: a severe sentence has gone
forth against thee to put thee in bonds".' Also x. 4-6: 'And
again the Lord said to Raphael, "Bind Azazel hand and foot,
and cast him into the darkness . . . And place upon him rough
and jagged rocks, and cover him with darkness, and let him
abide there forever, and cover his face so that he may not see
light. And on the day of the great judgment he shall be flung
into the fire".' According to the usual interpretation, the
darkness is that of the nether world (cf. 'nether darkness' in
RSV), and it is true that in classical authors the Greek word
(*zophos*) is applied to the gloom of Hades. But the place of con-
finement of the fallen angels is much more likely (cf. 2 En. vii.
1-3; Test. Lev. iii. 2: see note on 1 Pet. iii. 19) to have been the
second heaven as conceived of in late Jewish, early Christian
cosmology. For the formula **the great day,** i.e. the End, cf.
1 En. x. 6 (cited above); xxii. 11: also Acts ii. 20; Rev. vi. 17;
xvi. 14.

Some scholars observe a significant resemblance between this account (and its parallel in 2 Pet. ii. 4) and Hesiod's narrative (*Theog.* 713-35) of the punishment of the Titans, pointing out that these too were bound in chains (*desmoi*, as here) and consigned to darkness (*zophos*, as here) in Tartarus (cf. the verb *tartaroun* in 2 Pet. ii. 4). It may be doubted, however, whether any useful conclusions, least of all about possible literary influences, may be deduced from these data. The linguistic resemblances are slight and unimportant (e.g. *desmos* is the natural word for 'chain'), and the myth of the rebellion of superhuman beings against the gods and their subsequent punishment reappears with numberless ramifications in the legends of the east.

An essential ingredient in the angels' wickedness, over and above treachery to their high responsibilities, was (as later Judaism saw it: e.g. 1 En. xii. 4) the unbridled sexual passion which motivated it. It is therefore likely, and in keeping with his remarks elsewhere (4b; 10; 16), that the writer finds the modernists guilty of sexual excesses too. This is borne out by 7 his third illustration (cf. **just as**), drawn from the behaviour and subsequent doom of **Sodom and Gomorrah and the surrounding cities** (Admah and Zeboiim, according to Dt. xxix. 23; Hos. xi. 8—a fifth, Zoar, was spared at Lot's intercession: Gen. xix. 20 ff.), **which practised immorality in the same way as these** (i.e. the fallen angels: **these** is masculine, and so cannot refer to **Sodom and Gomorrah,** which are treated as feminine) **and lusted after different flesh.** The Biblical narrative (Gen. xix. 1-25, esp. 5-9) describes the licentiousness of the men of Sodom (not, however, of Gomorrah etc.: tradition probably attributed the same vices to all the cities alike because they shared the same fate), and particularly their eagerness to have sexual relations with the two angels whom Lot was entertaining. This being the allusion here, many have interpreted **lusted after different flesh** (*heteras sarkos*) as meaning 'indulged in sodomy'. The Greek, however, does not tolerate this: it simply states that the **flesh** they desired was **different** (these good angels appeared in human form, but their **flesh** presumably was **different** in kind), whereas in homosexuality, as J. Chaine (*ad loc.*) aptly remarks, 'the natures are only too alike'. The solution lies in recognizing that, while the writer is singling out the Cities of the Plain as examples of immorality, his attention is focussed not so much on their unnatural conduct (for this, cf. Rom. i. 24; 27) as on the close parallel between their behaviour and that of the wicked angels. Both had made their sin even more appalling by lusting after **different flesh**—the angels because, spiritual beings though they were, they had coveted mortal women, and the Sodomites because, though only human beings, they had sought intercourse with angels. It is probably legitimate (see on 8) to infer that he is snidely accusing the innovators of homosexual practices.

As a result the unhappy cities **stand out as an example, undergoing as they do a punishment of everlasting fire.** The alternative rendering, 'stand out as an example of everlasting fire, undergoing punishment', is grammatically possible but gives a less satisfactory sense: they are an example, but not strictly an example of everlasting fire. Their destruction (more particularly Sodom's) became a proverbial object-lesson of God's vengeance on sin: Is. i. 9; Jer. xxiii. 14; Ezek. xvi. 48-50; Am. iv. 11; Test. Napht. iii. 4; iv. 1; Test. Ash. vii. 1; 3 Macc. ii. 5; Mt. x. 15; xi. 24; Rom. ix. 29. According to tradition (e.g. Josephus, *Bell. Iud.* iv. 483-5), they were situated at the southern end of the Dead Sea, and the desolate aspect of this region, with bituminous exhalations, hot springs and deposits of sulphur, seemed to testify to the **everlasting fire** which had consumed them and which (so Philo, *Abr.* 140 f.) 'still continues to burn'. Thus the present tense of **stand out** (*prokeintai*) and the adjective **everlasting** are intended to impress on readers that the appalling effects of the catastrophe are still visible for all to see and note with dread. So Wis. x. 7, speaking of 'the five cities', reports: 'Evidence of their wickedness still remains—a continually smoking wasteland, plants bearing fruit that does not ripen, and a pillar of salt standing as a monument to an unbelieving soul'; while Philo can write (*Vit. Mos.* ii. 56): 'Thunderbolts then . . . hurtled from heaven and burned up both the impious population and their towns; and even down to the present day the visible tokens of the indescribable disaster are pointed out in Syria—ruins, cinders, brimstone, smoke, and murky flames which continue to rise as from still smouldering fire'.

4. A MORE CIRCUMSTANTIAL DENUNCIATION

8-13

(8) Notwithstanding these men too, in similar fashion, in their dreamings pollute their bodies, and at the same time set authority at nought and revile the glorious ones. (9) But the archangel Michael, when he was at odds with the devil, disputing about Moses's body, did not presume to pronounce a reviling judgment against him, but said, 'May the Lord rebuke you'. (10) But these men revile whatever they do not understand, while they are brought to destruction by those things which they know in a purely natural manner like brute beasts. (11) Woe to them! For they have walked in the way of Cain, have abandoned themselves for profit to Balaam's error, and have perished in Korah's rebellion. (12) These are people who at your love-feasts, hidden rocks, carouse with you, brazenly looking after themselves—waterless clouds scurrying before the winds, late autumn trees bearing no fruit, dead twice over and uprooted; (13) wild waves of the sea tossing up their shameful deeds as foam; stars straying from their courses for whom the murky gloom of darkness has been reserved for ever.

After these terrifying illustrations of God's judgment, the writer returns to direct attack, specifying three forms of wickedness of which the false teachers are guilty. His fondness for groups of threes (cf. 5-7; 11) is interesting. The section is 8 closely linked with what precedes not only by **Notwithstanding** (*mentoi*: to bring out the force of this one might paraphrase, 'in spite of the dreadful fate of the three groups just mentioned'), but even more by **too** and **in similar fashion**. In the Greek this latter adverb (*homoiōs*) stands first in the sentence, and must therefore be taken as assimilating the behaviour about to be criticized to that of the Sodomites. The participle rendered **in their dreamings** (*enupniazomenoi*: though something of a paraphrase, 'as a result of their dreamings' brings out the sense

260

better) has divided commentators. According to one school, it goes closely with **pollute their bodies,** denoting the polluting physical effects of erotic dreams (cf. AV's 'filthy dreamers': also Clement Alex., *Adumb. in ep. Iud.*: 'qui somniant imaginatione sua libidines'). The construction, however, suggests that it should cover all three of the following clauses. LXX usage points to the true exegesis, for in Dt. xiii. 2; 4; 6; Is. lvi. 10; Jer. xxxiv. 9; xxxvi. 8 the same verb 'dream' (*enupniazesthai*) is applied to false prophets and their like. The false teachers are therefore 'dreamers', not in the sense that they indulge in wishful thinking, but because they have ecstatic visionary experiences, or claim to have them, and seek to justify their doctrines and practices on the strength of these. Cf. Col. ii. 18: 'taking his stand on visions'. The 4th cent. Epiphanius (*Pan. haer.* xxvi. 3), who compiled a dossier of Gnosticism, reports that some Gnostics did precisely this.

The writer then comes to his charges. The first is that they **pollute their bodies** (lit. 'the flesh', echoing **flesh** in 7b). We have already heard in general terms of their **licentiousness** (4); here their conduct is defined more precisely through being connected (cf. **in similar fashion**) with that of the inhabitants of Sodom and Gomorrah. While sexual immorality in general is clearly indicated, a specific reference to homosexual activities can hardly be excluded. The writer did not single these out in 7, being more concerned about the Sodomites' demand for intercourse with angels (the errorists are presumably innocent of this); but any reference to the Sodomites must have conjured up the type of misbehaviour for which they had become proverbial (cf. SB III, 785 f.).

In the translation the next two charges have been prefaced by and **at the same time.** These words have been inserted in order to bring out a nuance which is manifestly intended in the Greek but of which most renderings lose sight, viz. the balancing of the first clause, introduced as it is by the particle *men*, against the two following clauses introduced by *de*. The point is important, for the two latter clauses hang closely together, the sins of presumption which they describe being contrasted sharply with the fleshly indulgence mentioned in the first (see note on 10).

The second charge, **they set authority at nought,** has also been the subject of discussion. We may dismiss at once the suggestion that it means 'flout the ecclesiastical (or civil) authorities'; for (a) the noun used (*kuriotēs*: 'lordship', 'sovereignty'), which is non-classical, only acquires this sense, if at all, in Byzantine times and does not seem to have it in any early Christian text, and (b) the manifest implication of 11 is that these 'revilings' concern matters the errorists 'do not understand'. In the NT *kuriotēs* is only used, apart from this passage and 2 Pet. ii. 10 (which is dependent on it), at Eph. i. 21 ('far above every rule, authority, power, *dominion*') and Col. i. 16 ('whether thrones or *dominations* or principalities or authorities'), where by common consent it denotes a class of angelic powers; this is confirmed by 1 En. lxi. 10; 2 En. xx. 1; Test. Sal. D. viii. 6. Hence many commentators conclude that this must be its significance here, and find support in the following clause, which (as we shall see) accuses the false teachers of insulting angels. Against this, however, it must be objected (a) that the repetition of virtually the same charge in both clauses is unexpected and improbable; and (b) that the use of *kuriotēs* with this sense in the singular is difficult, since where it denotes angelic beings it is always in the plural or implies a plural reference. More positively, the two other sins mentioned bear a loose relation to two of the sins enumerated in 5-7, one being concerned with the flesh and the other with angels, and so we look here for something to balance the defiance of 'the Lord' shown by the Israelites in 5. Thus we seem obliged to take the word in what is after all its basic sense, i.e. as the abstract noun from 'Lord' (*kurios*), equivalent to 'lordship', 'divine sovereignty'. There are examples of this meaning in early Christian literature outside the NT. *Did.* iv. 1, e.g., speaks of *kuriotēs* as the majesty of the Lord God, and Hermas, *Sim.* v. 6. 1 of *kuriotēs* as the lordship of the Son of God; while in patristic Greek the noun connotes an essential and distinctive characteristic of deity. According to our interpretation of 4, this 'rejection of the lordship' will be either practical, consisting in the errorists' libertinism, or theological, but the latter is much the more likely (see note on 4). Even so, we can only speculate whether it affects their doctrine of God or their Christology, or (this on the whole seems more probable) both.

The third charge, that they **revile the glorious ones,** is less ambiguous, in spite of the initial strangeness of **glorious ones** (*doxai*: lit. 'glories'). This term cannot, any more than **authority** above and for much the same reasons, designate community leaders: this is quite out of keeping with the context, and there is no plausible instance of its bearing this sense (in Diodorus Sic., *Bib. hist.* xv. 58. 1, sometimes cited, it simply connotes 'public reputation', not public office and still less office-bearers). In the light of the context (cf. 9) and 2 Pet. ii. 10 f., which borrows from this verse, there can be no doubt that it here denotes a class of angelic beings; and this usage of the noun is supported by LXX Ex. xv. 11. 'Glory' (*doxa*) originally stands for the numinous radiance which belongs to God Himself (e.g. Ex. xxiv. 16 f.; xxxiii. 18-23; Ps. xix. 1), but later the angels who surround Him come to be regarded as sharing in it (cf. Philo, *Spec. leg.* i. 8. 45: 'by thy glory I understand the powers which keep watch around thee'). So we hear of 'cherubim of glory' in Heb. ix. 5, 'angels of glory' in Test. Lev. xviii. 5, and 'powers of glory' in Test. Jud. xxv. 2. The leap to calling angels 'glories' *tout court* cannot have been a very difficult one.

As a Jewish Christian, sharing the intense interest in angels which characterized later Judaism, the writer has a properly deferential attitude towards **the glorious ones.** The parallelism between them and Satan in 9, as well as the fact that the angels in 2 Pet. ii. 10 f. seem to be evil, has persuaded some that he must view them here in an unfavourable light. But (a) this is neither likely nor necessary: the contrast intended is even more impressive if the impudence shown by mortal men to good angels is matched by the restraint of the prince of angels towards a discredited angel. (b) The juxtaposition of **the glorious ones** with **authority,** and the writer's evident disgust that the former should be insulted, only make sense if they are beings deserving of reverence. In any case the distinction between bad and good angels is misleading and can be overpressed. The angels were heavenly powers, appointed by God to carry out important functions in the governance of the universe and for the protection of men, and while offering them divine worship was clearly blasphemous (Col. ii. 18), it was

appropriate to treat them all with respect and awe. According to
Irenaeus (*Haer*. i. 25. 1 f.), certain 2nd cent. Gnostics despised
the angels, believing them to have been the agents of the
inferior creator-God in bringing the universe into existence.
There are no grounds for attributing such advanced views to
the errorists, but angels evidently figured in their speculations
and their disrespect for them may be an indication of embryonic
Gnosticism. Scholars have conjectured that they may have im-
puted faults to these celestial powers, or mocked their supposed
authority, or sneered at them as the mediators of the moral law
(Acts vii. 53; Gal. iii. 19) they themselves repudiated; but these
are only guesses.

Their presumption, 'Jude' points out, stands in glaring con-
9 trast with the modesty and restraint exhibited by even **the
archangel Michael,** who on a famous occasion, **when he was
at odds with the devil, disputing about Moses's body, did
not presume to pronounce a reviling judgment against
him, but said, 'May the Lord rebuke you'.** In the Bible
Michael is one of the chief angels, the name meaning 'Who is
like God'; the title **archangel**, found in the NT only here and
at 1 Thess. iv. 16, reflects the classification of angels in grades
in later Judaism, which came to recognize four, six or seven
archangels. He is mentioned in Dan. x. 13; 21; xii. 1 ('the great
angel'); 1 En. xx. 5; xl. 4-9; 2 En. xxii. 6; xxxiii. 10; Ass. Mos.
x. 2; Rev. xii. 7; Hermas, *Sim*. viii. 3. 3, where he is thought of
as the guardian angel of the Jewish people and the antagonist
of the Devil (in Rev. xii. 7 his role, by an appropriate trans-
ference, becomes that of the protector of the Church in its
struggle against the dragon). For **the devil,** see on 1 Pet. v. 8.

As far as we can reconstruct it, the ancient legend to which
the writer is alluding was to the effect that, when Moses died,
Michael was deputed to bury the body, but the Devil did his
best to prevent him, claiming that as lord of the material order
the corpse was his and then, faced with Michael's refusal,
threatening that he could accuse Moses (it was part of his office
to accuse men before God) of having murdered the Egyptian
(Ex. ii. 12). The archangel, however, instead of responding with
a reviling judgment (this rendering of *krisin blasphēmias* fits
the context better than 'a judgment on his reviling'), committed

the responsibility for rebuking him for his insolence to God, using a mild imprecation which actually comes from Zech. iii. 2, and proceeded to bury Moses with his own hands. For details, see TWNT IV, 858; 870. The story does not appear in scripture, which merely records (Dt. xxxiv. 6) that 'he [i.e. the Lord] buried him in the valley in the land of Moab opposite Beth-peor; and no man knows the place of his burial to this day'. To eliminate the offensive anthropomorphism the LXX alters the verb to the plural 'they buried'; and Philo (*Vit. Mos.* ii. 291) relates that 'immortal angelic powers buried him'. According to several early Christian writers (Clement Alex., *Adumb. in ep. Iud.*; Origen, *De princ.* iii. 2. 1; Didymus Alex., *In ep. Iud. enarr.* —PG, xxxix, 1815; Gelasius of Cyzicus, *Hist. eccl.* ii. 20. 7), our writer is quoting the legend in the form it appears here from the Assumption of Moses, which he must have regarded as authoritative. This was a composite Jewish apocalyptic work by a Pharisaic quietist, written in Hebrew or Aramaic in the first quarter of the 1st cent. but soon translated into Greek. A substantial fragment survives in a Latin translation, but the sections dealing with the death and burial of Moses are missing from this.

After his brief digression, the author returns to 8 and draws out the deeper reasons for the errors, the first carnal and the other two spiritually presumptuous, criticized there. Once again he begins with a contemptuous **these men** (*houtoi*), which he takes up from 8a and will repeat with mounting bitterness at 12, 14, 16 and 19; as an introductory formula, often but not always pejorative in tone, it is frequent in apocalyptic (e.g. 1 En. xlvi. 3; 2 En. vii. 3; xviii. 3; Rev. vii. 14; xi. 4; xiv. 4). Their flouting of lordship and angels, he argues (**revile** clearly picks up **reviling** of 9 and **revile** of 8, but covers the 'setting at nought' of 8 too), is not the result of their having any superior knowledge (is there a veiled attack here on 'Gnostic' pretensions?); on the contrary, it is their habit to **revile whatever they do not understand.** As he is going to explain in 19, they cannot claim to have the Spirit. An illuminating commentary is provided by 1 Cor. ii. 7-16, esp. 10 and 15 f., where Paul declares that the unspiritual man has no clue to the mysteries of God; in the present case the mysteries in question are the divine majesty and the true status of angelic beings. On the other hand, while preening themselves on matters about which they are really ignorant, **they are brought to destruction by those things which they know in a purely natural manner like brute beasts.** He admits, in other words, that there is a field in which they can claim to be experts, but it is the field of physical experience. He is looking back to his remark in 8a about their polluting their bodies and is thinking, as in his reference in 4b to their 'licentiousness' and in 16 to their 'following their own passions', of their sexual misbehaviour. This kind of knowledge or expertise he can dismiss as **purely natural** (the Greek adverb is *phusikōs*: 'naturally'), i.e. physical or material, comparing it to that of **brute beasts.** Little wonder that **they are brought to destruction** by it. The threat contained here is not of physical disease and death, nor even of moral and spiritual deterioration, but of God's condemnation when the day of judgment comes.

Once again 'Jude' turns to the OT for examples with which to compare the errorists, and selects three notorious characters (we observe again his predilection for triads) whose wickedness brought them disaster, including exclusion from a place in the world to come. A similar fate awaits their present-day counterparts, and any of the readers who is so foolish as to be deluded
11 by them. **Woe to them!**, he exclaims, using an imprecation of doom which is found in 1 Cor. ix. 16, frequently in the gospels, and repeatedly in 1 Enoch (esp. xciv-c). First, **they have walked in the way of Cain,** i.e. their conduct (for *poreuesthai*, lit. 'go' or 'walk', of behaviour or manner of life, cf. 16; 18; Ps. cxix. 1; Lk. i. 6; 1 Pet. iv. 3; etc.) resembles his. What looms largest in modern people's minds about Cain is that he slew his brother and was the first murderer; so the point of the likeness has often been found in the allegation that they inflict spiritual or moral death on their Christian brothers. In contemporary Judaism, however, he was 'a child of the Evil One' (1 Jn. iii. 12) and personified a much wider spectrum of iniquity. For Philo (*De post. Cain.* 38 f.; *Migr. Abr.* 75; *Quod det. pot. ins. sol.* 32; 48; 78) he is the great lover of self, the rebel against God who relies on his own resources, the instructor and leader of men who give themselves over to godlessness and sensuality and are

266

doomed to eternal corruption. Josephus similarly (*Ant.* i. 52-66) treats him as the embodiment of violence and lust, greed and blasphemy in general. So in the Jerusalem Targum (on Gen. iv. 7) he is the first cynic to say, 'There is no judgment, no judge, no future life; no reward will be given to the righteous, and no judgment will be imposed on the wicked'. Heb. xi. 4 reflects this tradition, by implication attributing lack of faith to him. There was a 2nd cent. Gnostic sect (Irenaeus, *Haer.* i. 31. 1; Epiphanius, *Haer.* xxxviii. 1. 1-3), we should note, who called themselves Cainites because they regarded the God of the OT as responsible for the evil of the world and therefore exalted those who are recorded as having resisted Him (e.g. Cain, Esau, Korah). So in likening the innovators to Cain 'Jude' is painting a picture of their godlessness, moral irresponsibility, and ultimate damnation in as lurid colours as he can.

Secondly, they **have abandoned themselves for profit to Balaam's error.** For the verb (passive of the Hellenistic *ekchunein*: lit. 'pour out'), cf. Ecclus. xxxvii. 29; Test. Reub. i. 6; Ignatius, *Philad.* v. 1; Plutarch, *Vit. Anton.* xxi. 1: here it expresses plunging into or wallowing in. Modern students tend to be at first taken aback by the inclusion of Balaam in this company, for on their reading of the Bible he appears in a distinctly favourable light as the prophet who declined to prophesy otherwise than as the Lord had commanded him. Such indeed is the older OT tradition as found in Num. xxii-xxiv; Josh. xxiv. 9 f.; Mic. vi. 5. According to the later tradition, however, it was as a result of Balaam's advice that the Midianites caused the Israelites to lapse into idolatry (Num. xxxi. 16), in revenge for which Balaam himself was slain (Num. xxxi. 8). This was the version on which later Judaism seized (e.g. Philo, *Vit. Mos.* i. 264-300 and the rabbinic exegesis of Numbers: SB III, 771; 793). Further, while in the older stories (e.g. Num. xxii. 18; xxiv. 12-14) Balaam consistently refused the bribes offered him by Balak if only he would curse Israel, the later tradition represented him as yielding to them (Dt. xxiii. 4; Neh. xiii. 2; Rev. ii. 14; Philo, *Vit. Mos.* i. 268; *Migr. Abr.* 113 f.; Josephus, *Ant.* iv. 118: for his covetousness, cf. SB III, 771). He thus became the prototype of unprincipled people who will not shrink from any enormity for monetary gain and who, like him (*Pirke Aboth* v. 29), are doomed to hell.

Clearly this is the view the writer takes of Balaam's character, and he condemns the errorists as his disciples. The Greek noun translated **error** is *planē*, which can mean either 'going astray' or 'leading astray'. So **Balaam's error** can be understood either in a passive sense (i.e. they are victims of the weakness which seduced him) or in an active sense (i.e. they seduce others in the same way as he did). The verb, suggesting that they have been debauched, and the context, which implies that they are conducting themselves as he did, supports the former. Evidently they sought to make money (cf. **for profit:** also 16b) by their propaganda, an unsavoury trait which they shared, apparently, with other innovating teachers criticized in the NT (1 Tim. vi. 5; Tit. i. 11: cf. *Did.* xi. 5 f.), and which recalls the anxiety of leaders of the apostolic Church that its ministers should be clear of any such imputation (2 Cor. xii. 14-18; 1 Tim. iii. 3; Tit. i. 7; 1 Pet. v. 2—where see note).

Thirdly, they **have perished in Korah's rebellion.** The reference is to Korah, the son of Izhar, who, with Dathan and Abiram and two hundred and fifty members of the congregation of Israel, mutinied against Moses's and Aaron's leadership and sought to get hold of a share in the priesthood themselves. According to the Biblical narrative (Num. xvi. 1-35), a terrible vengeance befell them: the earth opened and swallowed up Korah, Dathan and Abiram and their households alive, while fire from heaven consumed their two hundred and fifty fellow agitators. They too counted as flagrant examples of blasphemous insubordination and of the swift penalty awaiting it (Num. xxvi. 10), and later tradition (Mishnah, *Sanhed.* x. 3) taught that they were among those who would have no share in the resurrection. The choice of Korah is probably not fortuitous, but may indicate that the false teachers have been defying the church overseers and sowing unrest and division among the community members.

In the Greek the verb **have perished** (*apōlonto*) is aorist, and some have taken this as meaning that the destruction which is coming to them is already taking visible effect in their moral corruption. Much more probably, however, the past tense is a dramatic way of saying that their fate is already settled.

They are already lost to the church, and their doom will be ratified at the judgment. On the other hand, all three verbs in the verse are in the aorist, and it has been proposed (G. H. Boobyer) that they should all be understood as expressing, by different images, the divine punishment on the innovators: 'they have gone to destruction by the way Cain went to it, they have fallen to ruin by Balaam's error, etc.' This is just possible lexically, and has certain attractions; but it undoubtedly puts a strain on the first two verbs. The first (*poreuesthai*), e.g., can certainly be used as a euphemism for going to one's death (e.g. Lk. xxii. 22; *I Clem.* v. 4), but when the subject of discussion is morality its normal meaning (see p. 266, and cf. 16; 18 below) is 'conduct oneself', 'behave', and this is its much most natural sense when used, as here, with 'way' (e.g. 1 En. xcix. 10; *Barn.* xix. 2; Hermas, *Mand.* vi. 1. 2).

At this point the writer leaves the OT and with a few colourful strokes characterizes the disruptive elements. **These are 12 people who at your love-feasts, hidden rocks, carouse with you.** For the disparaging **These,** repeated from 8 and 10, see on 10a. Apparently the 'ungodly' errorists are full members of the church and as such can participate in its common repasts or *agapai* (this is the earliest recorded occurrence of the noun with this sense). These were suppers, religious in character and representing a primitive Christian adaptation of Jewish practice (cf. the *chaburah* meals; also for the Qumran sectaries, 1QS vi. 2-8; 1QSa ii. 17-22), which in the early Church gave expression to the brotherly love (hence the word) binding the community together. They were held in the evening at the conventional time, were real meals intended to satisfy hunger, and in the earlier period were, in some places at any rate, closely linked with the eucharist. 1 Cor. xi. 17-34 provides a lively glimpse of what might happen at a feast of the latter type; the *agapai* which seem to be mentioned in Acts ii. 46; *Did.* ix f.; *Ep. apost.* (c. 160) xv were also linked with the eucharist. In the 2nd cent., however, the *agapē* seems to have become everywhere independent of the eucharist: Ignatius, *Smyrn.* viii. 2 (probably); Pliny, *Ep.* x. 96. 7; Tertullian, *Apol.* xxxix; Minucius Felix, *Octav.* xxxi; Hippolytus, *Trad. apost.* xxvi. Nothing in the present passage indicates whether the meals in question were directly connected with the eucharist or not. On either assumption, however, they must have had profound religious significance, and the writer's complaint is essentially the same as Paul's in 1 Cor. xi. 20 ff., viz. that the false teachers ignore this and exploit the *agapē* as an occasion for gluttony and selfishness, if not worse. The addition of **with you** (this brings out the force of the prefix *sun* in the participle *suneuōchoumenoi*, lit. 'feasting with') suggests that their unseemly behaviour is all the more shocking because they indulge in it at common meals with their fellow-Christians, and also hints that these latter, unless they are careful, may be infected by it. Many prefer the translation 'together' (RSV), i.e. 'with one another', partly because it cuts out any idea of the ordinary members of the congregation 'carousing', and partly because both **looking after themselves** and 19 (see note) seem to imply that the errorists kept themselves to themselves. But the rendering adopted seems to bring out the real point of the charge, viz. that in spite of their misguided views and behaviour they still take part in community gatherings.

As a result he can describe them as **hidden rocks,** meaning that at these meals they are liable to undermine the faith and decent comportment of their fellow-Christians much as submerged reefs can wreck shipping. The noun used (*spilades*: in the sing. *spilas*) is common in Greek of all periods from Homer (cf. *Od*. iii. 298, relating how Menelaus's ships were broken by the waves on the *spilades*) to denote rocks in the sea close to the shore and covered with water, and so dangerous to vessels. So the *Etymologicum Magnum* (*c*. 1000?) defines it, while Josephus (*Bell. Iud*. iii. 420) uses it of rocks jutting into the sea and barring the port of Tel Aviv. There is some very slight evidence that the identical word could mean 'stain', 'blemish', being thus equivalent to the more usual *spilos*, and many commentators (so too RSV; NEB) prefer to take it in this sense here. They find support in 2 Pet. ii. 13, which is plainly modelled on this verse and gives *spiloi* (i.e. 'stains'), and in the Vulgate translation *maculae* (i.e. 'stain-spots'). Their decision is hard to understand, for **hidden rocks** gives an excellent sense, harmonizes admirably with the writer's penchant for vigorous imagery drawn from nature (see 12b-13), and agrees with patristic exegesis (Ps. Oecumenius in PG cxix, 716). In any case the noun *spilades* (feminine) stands in apposition, as do all the nouns in 12b and 13, to 'those who [masculine] feast'; thus a translation such as 'these are hidden rocks, or blemishes, at your love-feasts, carousing . . .' misrepresents the writer's construction.

A variant reading calls for a brief remark. Instead of *en tais agapais humōn* (i.e. **at your love-feasts**), which is read by the majority of MSS including Pap. 72, certain MSS give *en tais apatais humōn* or *autōn* (i.e. 'in your deceptions' or 'in their deceptions'). The latter noun *apatais* should probably be read at 2 Pet. ii. 13 (where see note), but in view of the context, the rarity of the word itself and the intrinsic difficulty of *apatais* (not to mention the weight of MS evidence), *agapais* is undoubtedly correct here. Its alteration to *apatais* may have been due either to the influence on later scribes of 2 Pet. ii. 13 or to uneasiness at the idea of scandalous heretics like these participating in the church's sacred repasts. This account further explains the variants *humōn* and *autōn*, for once *apatais* had been accepted the inappropriateness of *humōn* must have become apparent.

The writer adds a further touch to his picture: **brazenly looking after themselves** (lit. 'shepherding themselves', 'pasturing themselves'). It is not wholly clear whether he is thinking of their selfish preoccupation with their own interest in general, or more specifically of their conduct at the *agapai*. The context and choice of verb make the latter much the more probable interpretation. Like the affluent at Corinth (1 Cor. xi. 20-22), they tuck in shamelessly without attending to the needs of their poorer brothers. For the thought, cf. Ezek. xxxiv. 8 ('the shepherds have fed themselves and have not fed my sheep'); also LXX Prov. xxix. 3 ('He who pastures [the same verb *poimainein*] prostitutes will lose his wealth'). The adverb **brazenly,** we should note, might go equally well with **carouse** (so RSV; NEB). Since we have already linked **hidden rocks** with the latter, the balance of the clause is better if we take it with **looking after**; so construed it serves to highlight the selfishness of their behaviour.

'Jude' then piles up, without regard for their mutual congruity, four colourful images which reveal his feeling for nature and are intended to expose from different angles the uselessness, perniciousness and approaching damnation of the false teachers. All four nouns stand loosely in apposition to **people who . . . carouse.** First, they are **waterless clouds scurrying before the winds.** The traveller in Syria and Jordan, Lebanon and Israel is often exasperated by heavy clouds which fail to dissolve in rain and only augment the excessive heat. The suggestion is that the errorists are all show and no substance; they have nothing to give to those who are so foolish as to listen to them. Very similarly the man who talks big of presents he never bestows is compared in Prov. xxv. 14 (*N.B.* the Hebrew text: mostly Jude's reminiscences are of the LXX, but occasionally of the original—so Ezek. xxxiv. 8 above) to 'clouds and wind without rain'.

Secondly, they are **late autumn trees bearing no fruit, dead twice over and uprooted.** Again the general suggestion is that they are sterile and have nothing to offer, being rotten through and through, and as such have been discarded; but the analysis of the image calls for care. Thus commentators are divided on the precise bearing of the adjective rendered **late autumn** (*phthinopōrinos*). The majority argue that **late autumn** denotes the very end of the time of harvest, when any tree that is at all healthy might be expected to bear ripe fruit; a tree which is **bearing no fruit** then must indeed be useless, fit only (like the fig-tree in our Lord's parable in Lk. xiii. 6-9) to be cut down. But this exegesis ignores the facts (a) that in south Mediterranean and near east countries the harvest normally falls well before **late autumn,** the season for it being designated in Greek not *phthinopōron* but *opōra* (strictly, late summer); (b) that ancient writers (e.g. Plutarch, *Mor.* 735b) describe the **late autumn** (*phthinopōron*) as the season when trees shed their leaves, while Herodotus (*Hist.* iv. 42) speaks of it as the time of winter sowing: not a season, in other words, when fruit would be expected at all. It is much more likely, therefore, that to a 1st cent. reader the picture conveyed by **late autumn trees** would be of branches bare and leafless, with all growth sapped, at the approach of winter. If this is correct, the adjective **bearing no fruit** (*akarpa*) is added so as to spell out the full significance of their condition: they are trees from which, sapless and sterile as they are, no fruit can be looked for.

The next two epithets are arranged in gradation with their predecessors and elaborate the attack contained in them: these **trees** to which the false teachers are likened are **dead twice over** (*dis apothanonta*) **and uprooted.** As regards the former, a tree can presumably be designated 'twice dead' in the sense, first, of being sterile, and then, secondly, of being actually life-less. But the writer is less interested here in arboriculture than in the objects of his diatribe, and his language about trees should not be pressed. The exact application of his metaphor to these latter is more important, and it needs some unravelling. One common explanation is that the errorists, having been dead once through their sins but made alive by Christ in baptism (Col. ii. 13), have now through their backsliding and virtual apostasy reverted to death (cf. Heb. vi. 4-8; 2 Pet. ii. 18-22). In itself this is reasonably acceptable, but we may doubt whether such a recondite exegesis would have been the first to occur to the original readers, especially as the notion of 'the second death' was perfectly familiar, in an eschatological context, to 1st cent. Christians versed in Jewish apocalyptic (cf. Rev. ii. 11; xx. 6; 14; xxi. 8). The first death was of course the physical death which all men undergo, the second the final destruction of the wicked in the next world. For the rabbinical background of the idea, see SB III, 830 f. (esp. the Jerusalem Targum on Dt. xxxiii. 6: 'Let Reuben live in this age and not die the second death, in which the ungodly die in the world to come'). This interpretation is attractive here, for the writer's mind moves in that world of ideas and is obsessed with the coming judgment (cf. 4; 5-7; 14 f.). Either he is graphically treating the physical death and subsequent damnation of the errorists as accom-plished facts (cf. his use of **have perished** in 11b) or, as seems more probable, he is suggesting that, spiritually and morally dead as their sterility shows them now to be, they are already marked down for 'the second death' when the day of judgment comes.

With **uprooted** he develops his simile of fruit-trees which have proved failures. Such trees were commonly torn up by the roots and disposed of by burning (Mt. iii. 10; vii. 19; xv. 13; Lk. xiii. 6-9; Jn. xv. 2-6). As applied to the errorists the par-ticiple again anticipates, and treats as already sealed, the destruction which ultimately awaits them. Just possibly, however, it also insinuates that they are no longer in any true sense members of the community, since God has effectively separated them from it.

In his last two images 'Jude' turns from the futility of the errorists as teachers to their moral degeneracy. First, they are

13 **wild waves of the sea tossing up their shameful deeds as foam.** The extraordinarily vivid picture must reflect Is. lvii. 20 (the Hebrew text, not the LXX): 'the wicked are like the tossing sea . . . its waters toss up mire and dirt'. Scraps of filth and debris collect in foam and are cast up on the foreshore; and in the same way the false teachers spread everywhere traces of their corruption and impurity. The adjective **wild** (*agrios*: it is used of waves in Wis. xiv. 1) may be intended to glance at their lack of self-control. Secondly, they are **stars straying from their course for whom the murky gloom of darkness has been reserved for ever.** At first sight the reference might seem to be to meteors or shooting stars which flash across the night sky, only to plunge eventually into darkness, but this is to overlook the scientific-religious conceptions of antiquity. In fact (see TWNT VI, 251), as the Greek adjective (*planētēs*) he uses with **stars** indicates, he is thinking of the planets. The ancients did not understand their apparently irregular movements, which seemed to violate the perfect order of the heavens established by God, and these were accordingly attributed, in a complex of myths going far back in Oriental folkore, to the disobedience of the angels (hence the masculine **for whom**) controlling them. As a punishment these latter were imprisoned, according to 1 En. xviii. 13-16; xxi. 1-10, in a fiery abyss **for ever.** The false teachers resemble them because they too, as a result of rebellion and sin, have gone off course, and while pretending to give light in fact lead people astray (there is a play of words between *planētai*, i.e. 'wandering stars', and *planē*, i.e. 'deception' in 11). For the fiery gaol of Enoch's vision the writer has substituted **the murky gloom of darkness** (*ho zophos tou skotous*), borrowing the idea and wording from 6b (where *zophos* is used). The 2nd cent. apologist Theophilus of Antioch, who we have no reason to think was acquainted with Jude, develops exactly the same thesis in *Ad*

Autol. ii. 15. 47-49, pointing out that righteous, law-abiding men are like the fixed stars, but 'the stars which move about from place to place and are called planets are the type of men who separate themselves from God, abandoning the law and its commands'.

5. THE PROPHECY OF ENOCH

14-16

(14) It was with reference to these that Enoch, too, who was seventh from Adam, prophesied, saying, 'See, the Lord has come with his holy myriads (15) to execute judgment on all and to convict all the ungodly of all their deeds of ungodliness which they have committed and of all the despiteful things which, ungodly sinners, they have spoken against him'. (16) These are grumblers who complain of their lot and who follow their own desires, and their mouth utters bombastic words; they flatter individuals for the sake of advantage.

The writer rounds off his attack by an appeal to prophecy. So far he has pointed ominously to the ruin that has overtaken notorious sinners, and has voiced his own conviction that the errorists are already in effect doomed; now he shows that their punishment has in fact been authoritatively predicted. As he puts it, **It was with reference to these that Enoch, too, . . . 14 prophesied.** Later Judaism regarded Enoch, the mysterious figure who 'walked with God' and whom 'God took' (Gen. v. 24), as the model of righteousness and God's special friend; taken up to heaven, he is the guardian of all the celestial treasures and knows all secrets and mysteries. For the Christian understanding of him as the type of Christ, see on 1 Pet. iii. 19. In the line of patriarchs he **was seventh from Adam** (i.e. sixth by our method of counting: for his genealogy, cf. Gen. v. 4-20; 1 Chron. i. 1-3), and this is his stock description (e.g. 1 En. lx. 8; xciii. 3; Philo, *De post. Cain.* 173: cf. also rabbinic texts in SB III, 787). Seven being the most sacred number and the sign of God's grace (cf. the Sabbath), the stress on his being **seventh** had the effect of enhancing his authority and the weight of his words.

He **too . . . prophesied . . . with reference to these.** This last word *toutois* is in the dative (lit. 'to' or 'for': a curious use of the case, but the sense is obvious), and refers contemptuously (see on 10a) to the libertinists. Many prefer to construe **too** (*kai*) with **these,** immediately before which it stands in the Greek, and argue that the writer's point is that Enoch's prophecy was directed at the present-day errorists as well as at his own contemporaries. The underlying assumption, however, that a prophet spoke in the first instance to his own generation is more modern than ancient; and as a matter of fact Enoch himself is represented (1 En. i. 2) as explicitly stating that his vision relates 'not to this generation, but to a remote one in the future'. Examples of the displacement of this particle are by no means rare in the NT, and it is tempting to assume one here. Certainly 'with reference to these too' does not give a very good sense, for the writer's thought seems more logically expressed by such a paraphrase as, 'Further, there is a prophecy of Enoch's aimed directly at these people'.

The prophecy which follows is a fairly close citation of 1 En. i. 9, a passage which happens to survive in both the Greek and the Ethiopic versions. Our text agrees in the opening words more closely with the latter, but in the remainder with the former; perhaps we may infer from this that the writer read the book in Greek rather than in the Semitic original. While literary dependence is certain, it is likely that he is quoting from memory. The context describes a vision of the holy and eternal God coming forth to bestow blessing on His elect and pronounce doom on the wicked. 'Jude' has introduced **the Lord,** which does not appear in the original, and a Christian reading or hearing the phrase must have taken it to refer to Christ, Who the early Church knew was expected to come escorted by angels to judge the world (Mt. xxv. 31). The verb rendered **has come** (*ēlthen*: aorist) is a 'prophetic preterite', analogous to the aorists employed at 14 and intended to underline the certainty of God's action by dramatically envisaging it as already accomplished. For **his holy myriads,** i.e. the tens of thousands of angels or 'holy ones' who accompany God, especially in judgment, cf.

Dt. xxxiii. 2; Dan. vii. 10; Zech. xiv. 5; Mt. xxv. 31 (of Christ); Heb. xii. 22. As the visionary sees it, the Lord (or Holy Great One, as He is called in the original) at His coming **will execute** 15 **judgment on all**: as the context shows, this is a **judgment** of condemnation, and **all** denotes all the wicked. In particular, He will **convict the ungodly of all their deeds of ungodliness . . . and of all the despiteful things. . . they have spoken against him.** The deliberate repetition of **ungodly** (*asebeis*) and its derivatives should be noted; the writer has used it already at 4 with considerable emphasis, and will use the related noun 'ungodlinesses' again at 18, and it thus crystallizes his view of the heretics. 1 Enoch is full of denunciations of 'the ungodly', and this must have attracted his attention to the prophecy. The division of their sins into sins of deed and sins of word is also characteristic of 1 Enoch, which while continually harping on social injustice (xciv. 6-9; xcvi. 4-8; etc.), idolatry (xcix. 7-9) and transgressions of the Law (v. 4), repeatedly mentions arrogant and insulting language which is derogatory to God's majesty (e.g. v. 4; xxvii. 2; ci. 3).

Clearly the writer has a profound respect for the heterogeneous collection (the various parts of which it is composed all appear to date from the last two centuries B.C.) of supposed revelations imparted to Enoch which we know as 1 Enoch (see on 6; 13). This should not occasion surprise, for the prestige of the work stood enormously high at the time he wrote. For the use made of it in late Jewish and early Christian literature, see R. H. Charles, *Apocrypha and Pseudepigrapha* II, 177-84; its popularity in Judaism has been confirmed by the discovery of numerous Aramaic fragments of it at Qumran. Though regarded with reserve in certain quarters (e.g. 2 Peter: see Introduction, p. 227), it was treated as scripture by several early Christian writers (e.g. *Barn.* xvi. 5; Tertullian, *De idol.* xv. 6; Clement Alex., *Ecl. proph.* iii); and, as the Ethiopic version indicates, it must have been in the Greek Bible which was taken to Abyssinia when that country was christianized in the 4th cent. It was only with the dawn of that century that it began to fall into disfavour and neglect, and Jerome reports (*De vir. ill.* iv) that Jude was rejected by many precisely because of the appeal it makes to the witness of this 'apocryphal' book; it is finally condemned in *Const. apost.* vi. 16. 3 (*c.* 380). The writer's use of **prophesied** implies that he regarded 1 Enoch as the work of the patriarch himself and therefore, in view of the latter's privileged position as the recipient of divine revelations, as inspired.

His quotation finished, 'Jude' develops his attack on the false teachers in the light of it. **These,** he exclaims, **are grumblers who complain of their lot and who follow their own passions.** As in Enoch's prophecy, their misdeeds are divided into sins of word and sins of action. As regards the former, the two terms used in the original, **grumblers** (*goggustai*: hapax in the NT) and the adjective 'malcontent' (*mempsimoiroi*: also NT hapax), go closely together, the literal meaning of the latter being 'blaming their fate'. According to many commentators, the charge is that the false teachers are insubordinate, grumbling against and repudiating the authority of the church's appointed leaders; while others detect a reference to the existential discontent which, Gnostics as they are, they feel at the imprisonment of their spark of light in material bodies. Both these exegeses, however, are wide of the mark. Both Enoch's prophecy (cf. **despiteful things . . . they have spoken against him**) and the LXX use of 'grumble' (*gogguzein*: see TWNT I, 727-38) and 'grumbling' (*goggusmos*) in such passages as Ex. xvi. 7-12; xvii. 3; Num. xiv. 27-29; xvii. 5; 10, make it certain that it is the errorists' truculent attitude towards God that is being censured. Dissatisfied with their lot, they complain bitterly against Providence, and so doing reveal their lack of faith. The adjective 'malcontent' may be an echo of Ass. Mos. vii. 7. Philo, it may be observed, uses (*Vit. Mos.* i. 181) the related verb *mempsimoirein* of the Hebrews who 'murmured' in the wilderness, and this was understood as directed not just against Moses and Aaron as leaders but against God (e.g. Num. xiv. 27-29).

The parallel charge that the errorists **follow** (lit. 'walk according to': see on 11a) **their own desires** is easier; the reference must be either to their sensuality (cf. 4; 8; 10) or to their greed for gain (cf. 11 and **advantage** below), or, as is most probable, to both. As in 1 Pet. i. 14 (see note), **desires** (*epithumiai*), which can be a morally neutral term, carries a dis-

approving note. These, it is evident to the writer, issue in the
deeds of ungodliness which Enoch predicted so accurately.
But his diatribe is not finished: **their mouth,** he adds, **utters
bombastic words.** Exactly the same expression (*lalein huperogka*) is used in Theodotion's version of Dan. xi. 36 of Antiochus
Epiphanes's blasphemous utterances against God, and probably
lies behind the Latin translation ('os eorum ingentia loquetur')
of Ass. Mos. vii. 9: 'Jude' may have got it from the latter work,
with which (see on 9) he was acquainted. The reproach of using
proud, insolent language is also found in 1 En. v. 4; xxvii. 2; ci. 3.
These passages, taken in conjunction with the accusations of
denying or repudiating divine authority in 4 and 8, make it
probable that the phrase **bombastic words** is intended to
designate, not so much their boastful talk about themselves, as
their presumptuous and arrogantly expressed doctrines about
God.

   Although the translation conceals the break, the clause **and
their mouth . . . words** is in the Greek a parenthesis which
interrupts the syntactical structure. This is taken up again in the
following participial clause, which also lays bare a further un-
attractive trait in the errorists: **they flatter individuals for
the sake of advantage.** A more literal rendering would be
'they admire, or do honour to, faces'. This is an expression, not
found elsewhere in the NT, which is fequently employed in the
LXX to translate the Hebrew idiom *nāsā' pānîm*, 'take, or raise,
a man's countenance', i.e. do honour or show favour to him
(e.g. Gen. xix. 21; Dt. x. 17; xxviii. 50; 2 Chron. xix. 7; Job xiii.
10; xxii. 8). The formula had its origin in the Oriental custom,
when someone prostrated himself by way of greeting, of 'raising
his face', i.e. making him rise from the ground, in token of
welcome. An alternative, rather better LXX rendering was
'accept the countenance' (e.g. Lev. xix. 15; Job xlii. 8; Mal. i.
8; 9). The original imagery of prostration and lifting in welcome
soon disappeared, and both expressions tend to have the
pejorative sense of 'show favouritism towards' or 'curry favour
with'. They regularly occur in the constant OT protests against
singling out the rich and powerful for favour and the poor and
weak for unjust treatment (e.g. Lev. xix. 15; Dt. x. 17; Prov.
xxiv. 23; xxviii. 21; Ecclus. iv. 22), and the point is often made

that God is 'no respecter of persons' (lit. 'countenances') (e.g.
Dt. x. 17; 2 Chron. xix. 7; Acts x. 34).

All such partiality or favouritism is sharply condemned in
Jas. ii. 1-9. But it is precisely this fault, viz. courting the rich
and influential members of the community to the neglect (we
may presume) of the weaker and more modestly endowed, of
which, the writer seems to be suggesting, the innovators are
guilty; and their motive is the shoddy one of **advantage**. We
can hardly avoid linking this with the reference to their cupidity
in 11. Almost exactly the same complaint is set out in Ass. Mos.
v. 5, where we read: 'In those days they will admire the persons
[*mirantes personas*: the exact Latin equivalent of *thaumazontes
prosōpa* here] of the rich and will accept gifts': additional evidence of 'Jude's' close familiarity with that work. If we are
tantalized by our inability to give precision to the picture, we
can console ourselves with the reflection that some at any rate
of these charges, as the language in which they are expressed
reveals, are traditional and that the substance behind them, as
opposed to the three or four more specific accusations, may not
have been very dreadful.

6. EXHORTATION TO THE FAITHFUL

17-23

**(17) But you, dear friends, should remember the words
which were spoken before by the apostles of our Lord
Jesus Christ, (18) how they said to you, 'In the last time
there will be scoffers, following their own ungodly
desires'. (19) These are the people who set up divisions,
worldly-minded, lacking the Spirit. (20) But you, dear
friends, building yourselves up on your most holy faith
and praying in the Holy Spirit, (21) keep yourselves in the
love of God, looking forward to the mercy of our Lord
Jesus Christ unto eternal life. (22) On some have pity, the
ones who are still hesitating—(23) save them by snatching them from the fire; but on others have pity with fear,
hating the very clothing which has been contaminated by
the flesh.**

While this new paragraph is closely linked with the preceding one (cf. the antithesis between **But you** and **These** in 16), its 17 tenor is altogether different. In 5-16 the writer's object was to expose the errorists and threaten them with certain destruction; here it is to reassure his fellow-believers. His words convey a vivid impression of the dismay and bewilderment which the emergence of novelties in belief and behaviour created in the late-1st cent. Church. His plea is that there is no cause for dejection, since the apostles themselves have given an unambiguous forecast of precisely these alarming developments. Good Christians should rather regard these dangers as a challenge to stand fast by the apostolic witness and give compassionate help, in whatever ways are appropriate, to their unsettled brothers.

So he urges his correspondents to **remember the words which were spoken before by the apostles of our Lord Jesus Christ.** Who are these **apostles** to whose predictions he directs them? Without going into the detail of a complex problem, we may say in a general way that in the NT the term can stand for either a narrower or a wider circle: the former consisting of the Twelve and certain others of special rank, like Paul and Barnabas, and the latter comprising commissioned messengers or missionaries of the communities (e.g. Rom. xvi. 7; 2 Cor. viii. 23; Phil. ii. 25). Some have argued that it must have the latter sense here, and claim that **they said to you** in 18 implies that they had carried the gospel to the readers. This usage, however, is rare and soon disappears. There is, moreover, a solemn note in **the apostles of our Lord Jesus Christ** which almost compels us to take it as referring to the apostolic college in the strict sense. This interpretation also harmonizes with our author's general viewpoint, according to which (see on 3) the faith is a body of teaching authoritatively handed down in the Church. We should observe (a) that he does not include himself among **the apostles,** just as he does not call himself one in his prescript; and (b) that while **spoken before** does not necessarily imply 'spoken long ago' but merely 'spoken prior to the events predicted', the whole tone of the verse leaves the impression that **the apostles** constituted a revered group belonging to an earlier generation.

In the next verse the writer recalls what **they** [the apostles] 18

said to you. As remarked above, these words have been pressed to mean that the communities addressed had actually been visited and evangelized by the apostles in question. This is, however, a most improbable interpretation, if only because the latter are not mentioned individually or in general terms, but are spoken of as a close-knit group ('*the* apostles . . .'). The writer's point is that, when the apostles uttered their message, they addressed it to all generations of Christians, his own correspondents included. This message, he states, contained the prophecy that **'In the last time there will be scoffers, following** (lit. 'walking according to': see on 11a) **their own ungodly desires.** There is no single passage in the writings which have come down under the apostles' names which corresponds exactly with this except 2 Pet. iii. 3, which we have reason to believe to be later than and dependent upon this very verse, and which itself does not claim to be an original utterance by an apostle but a summary of the predictions of the prophets and the Lord's apostles. The writer, it is clear, is not thinking of any specific statement by the apostles or any single apostle, but of a characteristic element in the teaching of the apostolic Church. Warnings against the imminent rise of false teachers and the confusion and peril they are certain to cause are in fact a constant theme of 1st cent. propaganda (e.g. Acts xx. 29 f.; 1 Tim. iv. 1-3; 2 Tim. iii. 1-5; iv. 3: cf. also *Did.* xvi. 3). Faced with internal difficulties, the early Church found support and reassurance in such warnings, as also in the belief that the Lord Himself had predicted the rise of impostors who would lead the faithful astray (Mk. xiii. 5 f.; 21 f.).

For **in the last time,** see on 1 Pet. i. 20 ('in the last of the times'): also Jn. xii. 48 ('on the last day'); Acts ii. 17; 2 Tim. iii. 1 ('in the last days'). All these variant expressions recall the language and ideas of Hebrew prophecy (e.g. Is. ii. 2; Jer. xlix. 39; Hos. iii. 5; Mic. iv. 1), according to which 'the last day' has a twofold aspect, being the day at once of Messianic salvation and of judgment. In the NT these two aspects are held together where the sense of 'realized eschatology' is strongly present (e.g. Acts ii. 17; Heb. i. 2; 1 Pet. i. 20); but in the later writings of the NT, with the growing consciousness that the Messianic time is now past history, there is a tendency to visualize 'the last day' as the day of judgment (e.g. Jn. xii. 48). As 'Jude' sees it, **the last time** is in process of actualization, and he finds proof positive of this, as did others (e.g. 2 Tim. iii. 1; 1 Jn. ii. 18), in the shameless coming forward of blasphemers of God and **scoffers, following their own ungodly desires.**

Literally rendered, the participial clause reads: 'walking according to their own desires of ungodlinesses'; and the participle 'walking' is interpolated between the two nouns. This is clumsily expressed, but not so clumsily as to warrant us in inferring, as some do, that the second noun is an intrusion resulting from a gloss. The textual tradition is strongly against this, and it is possible that the noun is a further reminiscence of the 1 Enoch passage cited in 14 f., in which it occurs. The construction, however, is not clear, If 'of godlinesses' is a subjective genitive, the meaning is 'desires which take their rise in ungodliness'; if an objective genitive, 'desires for ungodly conduct'. In view of the plural, which suggests concrete acts of ungodliness, the latter is more plausible: cf. 'deeds of ungodliness' in 15. In any case what he has in mind (conventional invective apart) is probably the errorists' looseness and immorality (cf. 4; 8; etc.) which, he claims, the apostles accurately anticipated. More difficult to determine is what precisely he intends by **scoffers** (*empaiktai*: only here and 2 Pet. iii. 3 in NT). Relying on the parallel passage in 2 Pet. iii. 3 f., some narrow it down to denoting people who deride the Church's eschatological teaching because of the delay of the Parousia. This is not, however, a subject of controversy in Jude so far as we can see, and the meaning must therefore lie elsewhere. In the OT (e.g. Ps. xxxv. 16; Prov. xiv. 6; xix. 25; 29; LXX Is. iii. 4) the mocker is the man who despises morality and religion, the arrogant and godless libertine. He stands in sharp contrast with the sincerely religious, God-fearing man, and that contrast (which is of a piece with the writer's earlier portrait of the heretics) seems to be clearly intended here.

He adds one further pointed, and for us illuminating, criticism: **These are the people who set up divisions, 19 worldly-minded, lacking the Spirit.** For the withering **These are . . .,** cf. 12; 16: also note on 10a. The verb rendered **set up divisions** (*apodiorizein*) is extremely rare, almost the only example apart from the present verse occurring in Aristotle, *Pol.* iv. 3. 9, where it is used with the sense of defining with a view to classifying (cf. the more frequent *diorizein*, meaning either 'delimit', 'separate', or 'define'). According to many, it is intended to convey here that the false teachers have a divisive effect on the community, splitting it into rival cliques or factions. So far as it goes, this is an acceptable exegesis; it prepares the way for the next verse, where the faithful are urged to 'build themselves up', i.e. consolidate rather than disrupt their corporate unity. It also fits in with evidence from other sources (e.g. 1 Cor. i. 10 ff.; Gal. v. 20; 1 Tim. iv. 1 ff.) of the prevalence of sectarian quarrels and schisms even in the 1st cent. We may doubt, however, whether such a general statement explains the choice of such an unusual verb or does full justice to the idea of definition or classification inherent in it. This difficulty is amply met if we recognize that the words which follow almost certainly throw light on the very special nature of the **divisions** the errorists **set up.** They create schism in the community by classifying its ordinary members, i.e. the faithful to whom 'Jude' writes, as **worldly-minded** (*psuchikoi*), and themselves as 'spiritual' (*pneumatikoi*). His immediate retort is that this is just the reverse of the truth: it is the errorists themselves who are **worldly-minded** and who, so far from being 'spiritual', are in fact 'devoid of' (RSV) **the Spirit.**

This is the only interpretation which succeeds in bringing out the proper force of *apodiorizein*. It is also to be preferred because a mere reference to schism-making of the ordinary kind does nothing to explain the sudden, very pointed, interjection of **worldly-minded** and **lacking the Spirit.** The distinction between the *psuchikos* ('natural') man and the *pneumatikos* ('spiritual') man was familiar to Paul (e.g. 1 Cor. ii. 13-15), the former being the **worldly-minded** person who lives on the natural level and is incapable of grasping the things of God, while the latter is instructed by the Holy Spirit and is capable of judging all things. We know that some 2nd cent. Gnostics (e.g. the Valentinians: cf. Irenaeus, *Haer.* i. 6. 1 ff.; Epiphanius, *Pan. haer.* xxxi. 7) pressed a superficially similar distinction, claiming that in contrast to ordinary Christians the enlightened Gnostic who had become aware of the higher element in him was alone 'spiritual'. Although his language is highly compressed, 'Jude' seems to be countering some such claim here, and affirming by implication that, if there is an élite of 'spiritual persons', it does not consist of men who have acquired some esoteric 'knowledge', but of those who have received the Holy Spirit (that **Spirit** denotes the Holy Spirit, as, e.g., in Jn. iii. 5; Gal. v. 16 ff., seems evident from 20). If correct, this interpretation places it beyond reasonable doubt that the false teachers had Gnostic leanings.

After this parting shot at the trouble-makers, the writer addresses himself directly to his correspondents; his tone becomes positive and constructive as he rapidly summarizes his programme for the way Christians should live in such a situation. Its focal points are faith, prayer, love and hope, a tetrad which reads like an elaboration of the well-known triad faith, hope and love (1 Cor. xiii. 13; Col. i. 4 f.; 1 Thess. i. 3). The triadic pattern Spirit-God-Jesus Christ discernible in 20 f. also deserves attention as indicative of the Church's gradually developing Trinitarian formula (cf. 1 Pet. i. 2 for another archaic example).

As in 17, he starts off with **But you, dear friends** to mark 20 the antithesis between them and the errorists. His first advice is that they should build themselves **up on** (*epoikodomountes*: the present participle) their **most holy faith.** As elsewhere in the NT (cf. 1 Pet. ii. 5 and note), the body of Christian believers is pictured as a building or temple; it is, or should be, a solid, integrated structure which needs to be 'built up on' a firm foundation in order to withstand the onslaughts of heresy. In 1 Cor. iii. 9-17 Jesus Christ is the foundation on which the Christian temple is constructed; in Eph. ii. 20-22 it is the apostles and prophets, while Christ is the corner-stone. Here, in face of the threat of heretical teaching, the foundation which will sustain the building and keep it safe is declared, appropriately enough, to be **your most holy faith.** As in 3, **faith** has the objective sense, connoting the ensemble of apostolic teaching; it is **your faith** as opposed to the innovators' heterodoxy; and it is **most holy** because it has been revealed by the holy God and sanctifies those who hold it. This exegesis of the phrase exposes the main weakness of the alternative rendering sometimes proposed for the clause, viz. 'building yourselves up by means of your most holy faith'. The instrumental dative which it posits is of course possible, but not only does it render the *epi* of *epoikodomountes* otiose, but it also (a) involves our taking **faith** in the subjective sense, i.e. as meaning trust in Christ and adhesion to His doctrine (which conflicts with the sense it bears in 3), and (b) makes **most holy** distinctly awkward.

Secondly, they should continue **praying in the Holy Spirit**. The injunction recalls Paul's in Eph. vi. 18: 'Pray at all times in the Spirit'. Prayer in or by the Spirit is one of the Apostle's great themes (Rom. viii. 26 f.; 1 Cor. xii. 3; Gal. iv. 6), and we may perhaps detect the influence of his theology here. Again a contrast with the errorists is deliberately drawn: they, alas, do not possess the Spirit (19), and so have no true prayer. The faithful, however, building themselves up on the apostolic teaching, enjoy the presence of the Spirit, and the visible fruit of this is prayer.

21   Thirdly, they are to **keep** themselves **in the love of God**. Many prefer the rendering 'in your love for God', arguing that both the preceding admonitions underline positive activity on the part of the correspondents, and that we should therefore expect here an encouragement to them to be firm and steadfast in their love for God. Clearly this interpretation yields an excellent sense: for 'love of God' used objectively in this way, cf. Lk. xi. 42; Jn. v. 42 (probably); 2 Thess. iii. 5; 1 Jn. ii. 5; 15 (probably). On the other hand, (a) the expression seems balanced by **mercy of ... Christ** in the following clause, where the genitive is undoubtedly subjective; (b) the writer has already stressed (1) that Christians are 'beloved in God the Father'; and (c) the full meaning of the verb **keep** (*tērein*: evidently a favourite with 'Jude', since he uses it at 1; twice at 6; 13) is 'keep yourselves safe and unharmed'. These considerations favour the view that it is God's love (cf. Jn. xv. 9; Rom. v. 5; viii. 39; etc.) which is being spoken of. The writer's implied point is that as Christians his readers are the objects of God's love, but through backsliding or infidelity they can lose their awareness of it or erect barriers between themselves and it. They can only 'abide in His love' (Jn. xv. 9 f.) if they keep His commandments. At bottom, however, these subtle distinctions

may not have been present in the author's thoughts; the love which men have for God is itself the flowering of the love which He bestows on them, and the genitive may be what C. Spicq (*Agapè* II, 351-53) has aptly called a 'comprehensive' one, including both.

Fourthly, the writer turns his correspondents' thoughts to the future: they are to look **forward to the mercy of our Lord Jesus Christ** which leads **unto eternal life.** The verb used (*prosdechesthai*: also in a similar setting at Lk. ii. 25; xii. 36; Tit. ii. 13: cf. Heb. ix. 28) well portrays the confident expectation with which the Christian awaits the last day (cf. 1 Pet. iv. 7), a confidence which springs (as 'Jude' has hinted) from loyalty to the faith and from abiding in the Holy Spirit and the love of God. He is confident because Christ Himself will be the judge (for this conviction of the apostolic Church, cf. Mt. xxv. 31-46; xxvi. 64; 2 Cor. v. 10), and while He will condemn the impious (cf. 14 f. above), He will show **mercy** to true believers. There may be an echo here of 1 En. xxvii. 3 f., which eloquently describes how the righteous will bless the Lord at the judgment for the mercy He has shown them. No man can live without sin (1 Jn. i. 8), and therefore even the faithful Christian stands in need of the divine **mercy.** But as a result of that **mercy** he knows that he will enter **eternal life,** i.e. the blessed life in God's kingdom which is in store for the righteous at the resurrection (a conception dear to later Judaism: e.g. Ps. Sol. iii. 16; 1 En. xl. 9; lviii. 3; 2 Macc. vii. 9; 4 Macc. xv. 3: for the NT, cf. Mk. x. 17; 30). In this exegesis **eternal life** is taken closely with **the mercy of our Lord J.C.,** i.e. as expressing the result in which Christ's **mercy** issues. Some commentators prefer to connect the phrase with **keep yourselves** above; but while this gives an admirable sense (by keeping oneself in the love of God one obtains eternal life) and a good grammatical construction, the intervening participial clause makes too big a gap, and in the eschatological context the linking of **eternal life** with **the mercy** of Christ seems entirely natural.

Without any warning of transition, the writer then appends to his brief but splendid analysis of Christian living some counsel about how his correspondents should behave towards fellow-members of the community who have fallen, in greater or less degrees, under the trouble-makers' spell. Difficult in itself, the section is made even more perplexing by the uncertainty of the text, which has come down to us in a peculiarly confused state. From the mass of variants, however, two rival texts by and large emerge. The shorter one, represented by B and also by Clement of Alexandria, is the one translated above, and distinguishes two groups of backsliders. Over against it stands a longer text supported by Codex Sin., A and others; it distinguishes three groups, and in its most plausible form (there are several variants within it) has been rendered (RSV) as follows: 'And convince some, who doubt; save some, by snatching them out of the fire; on some have mercy with fear, hating even the garment spotted by the flesh'. The sense it yields is excellent and calls for little or no comment beyond what is given below. Editors are divided in their evaluation of these texts, and dogmatism is clearly out of the question. The considerations inclining one in favour of the shorter version are (a) its stylistic roughness and sheer difficulty as compared with the smoothness and correctness of the longer one, and (b) the fact that the latter and its variants can be intelligibly explained as attempts to make sense of the abrupt shorter text.

22   If this is accepted, the first of the two groups consists of **the ones who are hesitating.** The verb used in the present participle (*diakrinesthai*) has already appeared at 9 with the meaning 'be at odds with', 'dispute'; and the assumption that this must therefore be its sense here may have caused some MSS to insert *elegchete* ('convince' or 'refute') in place of 'pity' (*eleeite* or *eleate*): cf. NEBm's 'There are some who raise disputes; these you should refute'. In the middle or passive, however, the verb quite frequently (e.g. Mt. xxi. 21; Acts x. 20; Rom. iv. 20; Jas. i. 6) signifies 'be doubtful', 'waver'. This would seem to be its meaning here: the people envisaged have been dangerously attracted by the false teachers, but fortunately still have reservations and so have not taken the fatal step. Hence the faithful are encouraged to **have pity on** them, indeed to
23 make energetic efforts **to save them by snatching them from the fire.** For the image of a 'brand plucked out of the burning', cf. Am. iv. 11; Zech. iii. 2. Here **the fire** into which the unhappy dupes of the errorists are already slipping is the fire reserved for

the punishment of the wicked on the last day (Mt. xiii. 42; 50; xxv. 41).

The second group, on this reading of the text, are in a much worse plight: so far from having doubts, they have been completely carried away by the dangerous propaganda. Even so the church is exhorted to **have pity on** them too (the writer's fine Christian compassion, so different from his polemical fierceness elsewhere, is very evident here), but **with fear.** This **fear** is not so much apprehension of being infected themselves (that is covered by the next clause) as the specifically religious dread, or awe of God, which features so largely in the OT and is so much insisted on in 1 Peter (i. 17—see note; ii. 17; 18; iii. 2; 16). This godly reverence will be shown by their **hating the very clothing which has been contaminated by the flesh.** What this crudely vivid expression is intended to convey is that any kind of contact with these wretched people is to be shunned, even such slight and casual relations as brushing against them in the street. Their **very clothing** (*chitōn*: the inner garment immediately next to the body) has become **contaminated** or polluted by its proximity to their **flesh.** Again the writer is hitting at the immoralities of the false teachers and the corrupting influence they are in consequence likely to have on their associates. The contamination of which he speaks may be understood literally, their dress having been soiled as a result of their dissolute excesses (cf. Rev. iii. 4), or (more probably) the phrase may reflect the primitive belief that spiritual or demonic power can be communicated to, and reside in, a man's very clothes (e.g. Mk. v. 27-30; Acts xix. 11 f.). But there is also present the idea which is so evident in Paul (e.g. Rom. vii. 18; viii. 3: see on 1 Pet. ii. 11) that **the flesh** as such is evil, the seat of sin. In general the advice resembles that given at 1 Cor. v. 9-11; 2 Thess. iii. 14 f. Evil-doers are best left to the judgment of God, but the community should not be lacking in compassion to them. Even if normal social relations should be avoided, it remains possible to 'admonish them as brothers' (2 Thess. iii. 15), and also perhaps to offer intercessory prayer for them, as is recommended in such cases in Ignatius, *Smyrn.* iv. 1; *Did.* ii. 7.

7. CLOSING DOXOLOGY

24-25

(24) To him who is able to keep you safe without falling and to present you faultless, with exultation, before the presence of his glory, (25) the only God our Saviour, through Jesus Christ our Lord, belong glory, majesty, dominion and authority before all time, now, and for all ages. Amen.

The letter concludes without any of the messages to individuals or personal greetings which are customary in NT correspondence. Instead we have an eloquent, liturgical-sounding doxology which at the same time enshrines an aptly phrased prayer for the ultimate welfare of the recipients. In structure and ideas it bears some resemblance to the famous doxology of Rom. xvi. 25-27 (cf. also Eph. iii. 20 f.; 1 Thess. v. 23; 1 Tim. i. 17). It would be rash, however, to conclude that Jude is necessarily dependent on Romans; the un-Pauline character of Rom. xvi. 25-27 is widely acknowledged, and there is much to be said for the view that it is an early 2nd cent. insertion. It is therefore likely that both Romans and Jude are drawing independently on existing liturgical material; a very similar doxology, we should note, appears in *Mart. Polyc.* xx. 2.

In customary fashion the doxology opens with a reference to 24 God's might: **To him who is able.** For the wording (*tōi dunamenōi*), cf. Rom. xvi. 25; Eph. iii. 20; *Mart. Polyc.* xx. 2. The writer is acutely conscious of the perils to which his readers are exposed and which may well bring them to disaster on the last day. Thus he deliberately frames his ascription so as to emphasize that God, and God alone, **is able to keep** them **safe without falling and to present** them **faultless, with exultation, before the presence of his glory.** Left to themselves, they might all too easily lapse and lose their promised inheritance. For the thought, cf. esp. 1 Cor. i. 8 ('who will sustain you to the end, guiltless in the day of our Lord Jesus Christ'), and 1 Thess. v. 23 ('may your spirit, soul and body be kept sound and blameless at the coming of our Lord Jesus Christ'). The

rare adjective **without falling** (*aptaistos*) is found in 3 Macc. vi.
39, which speaks of the Ruler of all delivering the Jews 'without
hurt'. Literally it means 'not stumbling' (cf. Xenophon, *De
re eq*. i. 6, of horses), and metaphorically 'unfaltering' (Marcus
Aurelius, *Med*. v. 9) or 'not giving offence in one's life'
(Epictetus, Fr. 52). Some would paraphrase it here as 'without
sin', pointing to the use of the cognate verb *ptaiein* in the sense
of 'sin' in Jas. ii. 10; iii. 2, but this idea is covered by the next
clause. Here the thought which is foremost, as the verb **keep
safe** suggests, is their preservation from ruin at the judgment.

The second adjective **faultless** (*amōmos*: see on 1 Pet. i. 19)
originally has cultic associations, denoting the sacrificial victim
free from blemish which God requires (Ex. xxix. 1; Lev. i. 3;
10; etc.), but comes to signify the integrity and moral purity
which is what He really demands from His worshippers (Ps.
xv. 2; Prov. xi. 5; Eph. i. 4; v. 27; Heb. ix. 14; Rev. xiv. 15). The
noun **exultation** (*agalliasis*) and the related verb 'exult'
(*agalliasthai*) have special eschatological overtones (see on 1 Pet.
i. 6), denoting the jubilation of God's chosen people at His
manifestation at the End. Here it is parallel to **faultless** and
hints that the readers, as a result of their steadfastness, will
share in the joy of those who are acquitted by the Judge. In
before the presence of his glory we have a conventional
Hebrew periphrasis of reverence for 'in His presence'; God's
glory (see on 1 Pet. i. 7 f.) stands for His radiance and majesty,
which will be specially manifested at the End (Is. xl. 5).

Two further characterizations of God are added to this
elaborate ascription: He is **the only God,** and He is **our**
Saviour. In Rom. xvi. 27 we read 'only wise God', and
should note that many MSS insert 'wise' here, doubtless influenced by this model. Is **only** no more than a stock epithet, a
reiteration of the traditional Judaeo-Christian affirmation of the
uniqueness of God against all forms of polytheism? This is the
view of many scholars; but (a) the adjective is very rarely
applied to God in the NT, no doubt because the truth it contains was taken for granted in most circles; (b) while its use
might be natural in discussion with Gentile Christians with a
polytheist upbringing, its emphatic occurrence here is somewhat strange since 'Jude's' correspondents, though probably

Gentiles, were clearly steeped in the ideas of later Judaism; (c) we cannot fail to recall that the errorists have already been charged (cf. 4) with 'denying the only Master'. It is therefore more than likely that the stress on **only God** here is a further reference to this basic fault in their teaching, and so to their Gnostic leanings. At the same time the hint it conveys is much too slight and vague to justify our attributing to them, as has often been done, the developed ideas of 2nd cent. Gnosticism about the distinction between an inferior creator-God and an unknowable supreme God, and we are left in the dark as to the exact way in which their teachings infringed strict monotheism.

In NT language the title **Saviour** (*sōtēr*) is relatively rare, but in the majority of cases belongs to Jesus Christ; its application to God is confined, apart from Lk. i. 47 (an echo of 1 Sam. ii. 1), to the Pastorals (1 Tim. i. 1; ii. 3; iv. 10; Tit. i. 3; ii. 10; iii. 4—but cf. Tit. ii. 13; iii. 6). The usage derives from Judaism (e.g. Philo, *De confus. ling.* 93) and more particularly from the LXX; but whereas in the latter God is designated Saviour either because He delivers Israel (e.g. Dt. xxxii. 15; Is. xvii. 10; xlv. 15; Ps. lxxix. 9) or because He rescues the believer from some temporal trouble (e.g. Ps. xxv. 5; xxvii. 1; 9), the expression has a strongly eschatological sense in the NT: God is Saviour of all who believe, delivering them from destruction on the last day and bestowing eternal salvation on them.

Opinion is divided as to whether **through Jesus Christ our Lord** (omitted in many late MSS) should be taken with **our Saviour** or with **belong glory** etc. as the punctuation printed above suggests. According to the former interpretation, God effects His saving work through His Son whom He has sent. This yields an unobjectionable sense, for it is NT doctrine that God's activity, whether in creation or redemption (cf. esp. Jn. i. 3; 17; iii. 17; Acts x. 36; 2 Cor. v. 18; Col. i. 20; 1 Tim. ii. 5), is mediated through Christ. On the other hand, this close attachment of the preposition **through** (*dia*) to the noun **Saviour** is difficult and almost unexampled. Further, the alternative interpretation is exactly in line with Rom. vii. 25; xvi. 27; 2 Cor. i. 20; Col. iii. 17; 1 Pet. iv. 11. All these passages illustrate the conviction of 1st cent. Christians that when they ascribe glory to God, they do so **through J.C. our Lord.** The only *prima*

facie serious objection to following this here is the incongruity of
saying that glory belongs to God **through J.C. our Lord,** i.e.
the incarnate Son, **before all time.** Strict precision of language
(no reference to His pre-existence is in any case intended), however, is not to be expected in a sentence built up as this one
is of stereotyped, grandiose-sounding formulae. The omission
of **before all time** in a number of late MSS is probably
prompted by the desire to eliminate this superficial awkwardness, and so supports the view that this was how the words were
commonly construed.

Four attributes are said to **belong** to God. No verb is
expressed in the Greek, and most translations imply that an
optative should be understood; but (a) while one can pray or
wish something for the present or future, one cannot do so for
the past, and (b) consistent NT usage (see note on 1 Pet. iv. 11)
endorses the use of the indicative rather than the optative in
doxologies. In any case the point of a doxology is not to offer
God anything which He does not already possess, but to
acknowledge adoringly the blessedness which is His by right.
The first attribute, **glory,** is almost universally predicated of
God in NT doxologies, and denotes (see on 1 Pet. i. 7) the
effulgent radiance which, according to conceptions going far
back in OT theology, belong to God's very being. Similarly
majesty (*megalōsunē*), a word used only of God in the Bible,
describes His awful transcendence; it is found in a doxology in
1 Chron. xxix. 11 and in equivalent formulae in Dt. xxxii. 3;
Ecclus. xxxix. 15: also in early Christian doxologies independent
of Jude (*1 Clem.* xx. 12; lxi. 3; lxiv; lxv. 2; *Mart. Polyc.* xx. 2;
xxi).

The remaining two attributes, **dominion** (*kratos*) and
authority (*exousia*), are almost synonymous, except that while
dominion denotes that absolute power of God which ensures
Him ultimate victory, **authority** suggests the sovereign freedom of action He enjoys as Creator. In the NT, with the sole
exception of Heb. ii. 14 (where the reference is to a particular
sphere of power), **dominion** is ascribed exclusively to God;
the term is regular in doxologies (1 Tim. vi. 16; 1 Pet. iv. 11;
v. 11; Rev. i. 6; v. 13). **Authority** occurs frequently in the NT,
and with a variety of senses: e.g. Mk. i. 22 (with reference to

Christ's manner of teaching); xi. 28 (of the 'authority' by which He acts); vi. 7 (of power over evil spirits); Mt. xxviii. 18 (of the universal authority given Him by His Father); Eph. iii. 10; vi. 12 (of angelic powers). In the LXX (e.g. Dan. iv. 17) and late Jewish usage it is mentioned as an attribute of God, but is nowhere else found in a doxology.

In a solemn-sounding phrase God is declared to possess these attributes from all eternity: **before all time, now, and for all ages.** Variants of these formulae occur elsewhere in the NT: cf. 'before the ages' in 1 Cor. ii. 7; 'before the foundation of the world' in Jn. xvii. 24; Eph. i. 4; 1 Pet. i. 20; 'for ages' in Rom. i. 25; ix. 5; etc.; 'for the ages of the ages' in Gal. i. 5; Phil. iv. 20; 1 Pet. iv. 11; v. 11. All these expressions and their variants belong to the vocabulary of the LXX and of Hellenistic Judaism. Similarly **Amen** (see on 1 Pet. iv. 11) is the Hebrew affirmation, meaning 'So be it', which regularly concludes prayers and doxologies.

THE SECOND EPISTLE OF PETER

1. GREETINGS AND REMINDER
i. 1-4

(1) Symeon Peter, a servant and apostle of Jesus Christ, to those who have been granted a faith of equal privilege with ours through the justice of our God and Saviour Jesus Christ: (2) May grace and peace be multiplied to you through the knowledge of God and of Jesus our Lord, (3) seeing that his divine power has bestowed on us everything that makes for life and godliness, through the knowledge of him who has called us by his own glory and excellence, (4) by means of which he has bestowed on us his precious and magnificent promises, so that through them you may become sharers of the divine nature, having escaped from the corruption which is in the world as a result of desire.

This exordium combines a salutation of the customary NT type (see on 1 Pet. i. 1; Jud. 1) with a development in which some of the epistle's main themes are foreshadowed. The former is carefully framed so as to convey to the recipients the impression that they are being addressed on terms of complete equality by the chief of the apostles, whose weighty authority thus lies behind the counsel and warnings which follow. The latter introduces us at once to the writer's baroquely opulent diction and partiality for Hellenistic religious concepts and terminology.

Thus he represents himself (for the pseudonymity of the epistle, see Introduction, pp. 235 f.) as **Symeon Peter,** where 1 **Symeon** reproduces the Hebrew *Shim'ōn*. The form is frequent in the LXX and occurs occasionally in the NT (Lk. ii. 25; 34; iii. 30; Acts xiii. 1; xv. 14; Rev. vii. 7), but its choice here is curious. Except in Acts xv. 14, where the Jewish-Christian setting makes 'Symeon' specially suitable, it is the similar-sounding, genuinely Greek 'Simon' which is invariably applied to the Apostle elsewhere in the NT. Possibly the writer considered that this old-fashioned, Semitic touch would add verisimilitude to the letter's claim to come from Peter himself. This claim is quietly reinforced by the reminder that he is **a servant** (see on Jud. 1) **and apostle of Jesus Christ** (see on 1 Pet. i. 1). For the juxtaposition of these two descriptive titles, the one drawing attention to his ministerial role and the other underlining his authoritative commission, cf. Rom. i. 1; Tit. i. 1.

We are given no clue to the identity of the addressees until iii. 1, where he suggests (on the most likely interpretation) that they are the Gentile Christians in Asia Minor to whom 1 Peter was sent. Who in fact they were, on the assumption that the epistle is a piece of genuine correspondence, is a problem which is briefly touched on in the Introduction (p. 237). He describes them as having **been granted a faith of equal privilege** (*isotimon*: 'equally precious') **with ours.** Here **faith** is not used in the Pauline sense of the trust by which a man responds to God's grace, for this does not admit of degrees of worth; as in Jud. 3, it stands for Christian belief as a body of teaching handed down from the apostles (cf. iii. 2). The participle translated **have been granted** belongs to a verb (*lagchanein*) which properly means 'obtain by lot'. Thus it contains a reminder that the saving belief which Christians hold is a gift to them of God's free grace.

Evidently 'Peter' wants to still any anxious fears his readers may have of being under-privileged or second-class Christians. On the contrary, he insists, their **faith** is **of equal privilege with ours** (lit. 'with us'), i.e. it is exactly the same doctrine, and just as precious in the blessings it imparts to its holders, as the faith which he and the group to which he belongs possess. The language is slightly reminiscent of Acts xi. 17, where the real Peter speaks of God bestowing 'the same gift (*isēn dōrean*) upon them [the Gentiles] as upon us', i.e. Jews who have become Christians; and some have deduced that the writer may be here reassuring Gentile readers that they do not rank as in any respect inferior to Jewish converts. But there is not the least vestige in the letter of tension between Christians of Jewish and pagan backgrounds. The contrast which is almost certainly in mind is that between the apostles, who had been the eye-witnesses of the original revelation (cf. i. 16), and the Christians of the second, or even third, generation, for whom the epistle was intended. These might well feel at a disadvantage; and so the writer, speaking in the person of Peter, tactfully assures them that their **faith** admits them to precisely the same privileges as the apostles themselves enjoy. The motive is much the same as the one that moved the Fourth Evangelist to record the Lord's own statement that those who have not seen and have neverthe-less believed can reckon themselves blessed (Jn. xx. 29: cf. also 1 Pet. i. 8 and note).

The reason for this complete equality between the apostles and succeeding generations of Christians is, he explains, **the justice,** i.e. the absolute fairness and lack of favouritism, **of our God and Saviour Jesus Christ.** The Greek noun for **justice** is *dikaiosunē*, the key-word ('righteousness') in the Pauline theology of justification. Some strive to give it a Pauline or near-Pauline sense here, translating 'faith standing in the righteous-ness of . . .'; but in Paul's teaching faith precedes righteousness. Some ancient interpreters, perceiving this, altered the text (changing *en*, which literally means 'in' and is rendered **through,** to *eis*, i.e. 'into', and putting *dikaiosunē* into the accusative in place of the dative) so as to read 'faith issuing in a righteousness . . .'; but such expedients raise other difficulties, and in any case are not called for. In the letter (ii. 5; 21; iii. 13), as in 1 Pet. ii. 24; iii. 14, *dikaiosunē* regularly connotes justice or fair dealing, and that provides an excellent sense here.

As the translation suggests and most modern scholars agree, it is probable that in the phrase which follows **our God** as well as **Saviour** goes closely with **Jesus Christ.** This exegesis gains support from the single definite article in the Greek before **our God,** which seems to govern both nouns. Against this it is pointed out that the absence of an article before **Saviour** is not decisive in Greek of this period (e.g. 1. Tim i. 1); that it would be odd to have Christ called **God** here, with God and Christ distinguished in the very next verse; and that the description of

Christ as **our God** is unacceptably bold. On the other hand, (a) if we are to distinguish two persons here, **our** must be taken exclusively with **God,** and **Saviour Jesus Christ** is an awkward expression when left standing thus on its own. (b) Where **Saviour** occurs elsewhere in the letter (i. 11; ii. 20; iii. 2; 18), it is always in a very similar combination ('our Lord and Saviour J.C.'). (c) There is nothing in the least surprising in Christ's being designated 'God' if a relatively late date is posited for 2 Peter. Rom. ix. 5 possibly provides an early example, but definite instances accumulate as the 1st cent. advances (Jn. xx. 28; Tit. ii. 13; Heb. i. 8), and they become more outspoken in the early decades of the 2nd cent. (e.g. Ignatius, *Eph.* inscr.: 'Jesus Christ our God'; i. 1: 'the blood of God').

Surprising as it may at first seem, the title **Saviour** (*sōtēr*: see on Jud. 25) is applied rather rarely to Christ in the NT generally: only 4 times, in fact, in the acknowledged Paulines (Eph. v. 23; Phil. iii. 20) and the Johannine writings (Jn. iv. 42; 1 Jn. iv. 14). The Pastorals and 2 Peter are striking exceptions, the former employing it 10 times (6 times of God, 4 of Christ) and the latter 5 times (i. 1; 11; ii. 20; iii. 2; 18: always of Christ). In the Hellenistic world rulers were honoured as 'saviours', as were Roman emperors when Caesar-worship came into vogue; and this may in part lie behind the great reserve of the rest of the NT in using the title of Christ. Its prominence in the Pastorals (2 Tim. i. 10; Tit. i. 4; ii. 13; iii. 6) is often explained as reaction to the imperial cult, but this is an overworked theory to which the texts give little, if any, support. In the 2 Peter passages it is formalized, appearing always in solemn-sounding, stereotyped phrases, so that it is useless to attempt to pinpoint its exact theological content. See TWNT VII, 1015-22.

2   The formula **May grace and peace be multiplied** resembles, and is in fact copied from, 1 Pet. i. 2 (see note). These blessings, it is stated, are mediated **through the knowledge of God and of Jesus our Lord,** an expression in which the writer's concern for the soundness of his correspondents' Christian faith shines out. He habitually envisages this as **knowledge** (*epignōsis*), using this characteristic key-term in three further passages (i. 3; 8; ii. 20: cf. *gnōsis* in iii. 18). In all these Christ is the object,

and the composite phrase defines what he regards as essential Christianity. So in 1 Tim. ii. 4; 2 Tim. ii. 25; iii. 7; Tit. i. 1; Heb. x. 26 *epignōsis alētheias*, i.e. 'knowledge of the truth', has become a cliché, and throughout 2 Peter (i. 5; 12; 16; 20; iii. 3; 17) there is a noteworthy stress on 'knowing'. Gnosticism, with its pretensions to have access to an esoteric 'knowledge' (*gnōsis*), was the current danger, and 'Peter' is deliberately setting in opposition to it that authentic **knowledge** which baptized Christians have, which is centred on the God of the Bible and on Christ, and which (as the sequel will show) is expected to issue in a disciplined moral life. For parallel pleas that the instructed Christian is the possessor of the true, saving knowledge, cf. Jud. 5 (see note) and 1 Jn. ii. 20 f.

The Greek text represented by the translation is that given by the majority of MSS, including the most ancient (some important witnesses add 'Christ' after **Jesus,** while Pap. 72 omits *kai*, i.e. **and of**). Side by side with this there is evidence (cf. the Vulgate and Syriac traditions; some rather late MSS) for a shorter text, 'through the knowledge of our Lord'. Several editors prefer this, but it is probably to be explained as a correction intended to harmonize the formula (a) with the references to a single person in 1b and 3a, and (b) with the writer's normal practice (i. 8; ii. 20; iii. 18) of making Christ alone the object of Christian *epignōsis*. But these very points make it difficult to understand how, if the shorter text were original, it ever came to be expanded into the longer one.

The next two verses raise a problem of connection, for in the original the main verb in 3 is a genitive absolute; they may therefore be regarded either as syntactically linked with 2b or as introducing a new paragraph and preparing the ground for the exhortation in 5-7. Either construction makes reasonable sense, but the former seems preferable (a) because the clause reads like an elaboration of the thought of 2b (cf. the repetition of **knowledge**); (b) because the latter requires us to treat 3 f. as an extremely clumsy anacoluthon, with the writer starting a fresh sentence at 5a (see note). While rare, such an expansion of the formal address is not unexampled: cf. Ignatius, *Philad.* inscr.

As the ground therefore of his confidence, the writer recalls that Christians (here **us** does not refer specifically, as in 1, to 3

Peter and his fellow-apostles, but to Christians generally) owe their possession of **everything that makes for life and god-liness,** i.e. eternal life in contrast to corruption and death (cf. 4b) and sound as opposed to erroneous religion, not to any achievement of their own, but to **his divine power.** By **his** he probably means 'God's', in spite of the proximity of **Jesus our Lord;** as Paul remarks in Rom. viii. 32, God has not only given us His Son, but with Him will 'lavish upon us all He has to give' (NEB). This cannot, however, be regarded as certain; some editors are satisfied, because of the position of the words, that the reference must be to Christ's **divine power,** and one is tempted to think that the author had not sorted the matter out clearly in his own mind.

More precisely, Christians have their enjoyment of all these things mediated to them **through the knowledge of him who has called us by his glory and excellence.** There seem to be verbal reminiscences of 1 Peter (e.g. i. 15; ii. 9; v. 10) in the writer's choice of 'call', 'glory' and 'excellence', though it would be rash to assume that he gives these words exactly the same sense as they bear in his model. Again we are faced with a difficult ambiguity, and there has been much debate whether we should take **him who** as denoting God or Christ. A strong argument in favour of the former is that in NT parlance it is almost always God who calls, and this indeed is how 1 Peter understands our calling (e.g. i. 15; ii. 9). If this exegesis is accepted, **us** again stands for Christians generally, not for 'us apostles'. On the other hand, (a) if our exegesis of **his divine power** is correct, we should expect a different subject for **has called,** for 'God has bestowed everything on us through our knowledge of God' is an unnatural way of putting things. (b) When 'Peter' speaks of Christian faith in terms of 'knowledge', it is always, 2b excepted, knowledge of Jesus Christ. (c) His mention of **glory** inevitably makes us think of the glory Christ received from His Father and disclosed to the apostles at the Transfiguration (cf. i. 17). (d) While **excellence** (*aretē*) may well be an echo of 1 Pet. ii. 9, where it denotes God's mighty acts (see note), it is found there (as that meaning requires) in the plural, whereas he uses it here and a few lines below (5) in the singular, in the latter case without any doubt to designate some kind of ethical virtue. For these reasons it seems better to interpret **him who** as referring to Christ, and the call in question as the calling, not of Christians in general, but of the apostles, among whom 'Peter' numbered himself, by the historical Jesus. We might paraphrase: 'God has bestowed all these blessings on us Christians, mediating them to us through our knowledge of the Christ who called us, His apostles, by that divine glory and transcendent virtue which we were privileged to observe in Him'. 'Glory' and 'excellence', we should observe, are coupled in LXX Is. xlii. 8, but even more significant is the fact that they are a stock combination in Hellenistic writers, especially Plutarch. Further, a remark of Plutarch's (*Arist.* vi. 3) is perhaps relevant in this context: 'Divinity, to which men are eager to adapt and conform themselves, seems to have three elements of superiority—incorruption, power, and virtue (*aretē*); and the most impressive, the divinest of these is virtue'.

By means of His **glory and excellence,** or more generally His saving intervention in the incarnation, Christ **has be- 4 stowed on us his precious and magnificent promises.** The idea of God's **promises** was deeply entrenched in OT religion, and a feature of primitive Christian preaching was the announcement (e.g. Acts xiii. 32 f.) that what He had promised to the fathers He had now fulfilled in Christ; here, as befits a very late writing, the **promises** have become Christ's. The perfect tense used here, like the perfect participle in 3a, brings out the finality and permanence of the gift. Specifically the writer is thinking, we may be sure, of the promises of Christ's Second Coming (i. 16; iii. 4; 9 f.; 12), of the establishment of a new heaven and earth (iii. 13: cf. 'his promise'), and of entrance into Christ's kingdom (i. 11). In view of the errorists' scepticism (i. 16; iii. 3 f.) he is anxious to emphasize (this will be his object throughout the letter) that these are firmly guaranteed. And their fulfilment (**through them** is much better construed with **promises** than with **glory and excellence**) will result in believers becoming **sharers of the divine nature** (probably another echo of I Peter, this time of 'a sharer in the glory which is going to be revealed' in v. 1). In other words, they will enter into true union with God, participating in His glory, immortality and blessedness. The thought is similar to that of 1 Jn. i. 3, although there 'our fellowship with the Father and with His Son Jesus Christ' is conceived of as a present experience. This is their certain hope, and it can be theirs because as Christians they have **escaped from the corruption which is in the world as a result of desire.** The aorist participle points to a definitive act, and so there is probably an allusion to their baptism and their renunciation of sin (see on 1 Pet. ii. 1). As in 1 Pet. i. 14 (see note), but even more forcibly, **desire** (*epithumia*) is treated as intrinsically evil; and **the world** (cf. 1 Jn. ii. 17) is branded as subject to **corruption** (*phthora*), i.e. the disintegrating power of evil by which the whole created order, according to Paul (Rom. viii. 21), is enslaved in the present age. In Greek philosophical thinking, too, it was widely accepted as axiomatic that everything contingent, belonging to the world of coming-to-be as opposed to the world of true being, is exposed to *phthora* or decay (e.g. Plato, *Resp.* viii. 546a; Aristotle, *De cael.* i. 279b; 282b).

Though partially veiled in translation, the writer's Hellenized vocabulary and thought-forms are well illustrated in this passage. They are all the more interesting since they are employed to expound a futurist eschatology and have the archaic-sounding 'promises' embedded in them. An obvious example is the repeated **divine** (*theios*), an adjective which in the NT appears only here and in Acts xvii. 29 (significantly, Paul's Areopagus speech), was generally avoided in the LXX (perhaps because of its suggestion of impersonal deity), but was popular in classical and Hellenistic Greek and in Jewish writings influenced by Hellenism (e.g. 4 Macc.—26 times; Philo; Josephus). In particular, **divine power** (*theia dunamis*) and **divine nature** (*theia phusis*) deserve attention: both had been Greek philosophico-religious clichés as early as Plato and Aristotle, were in popular use in the early empire (witness, e.g., the famous inscription of Stratonicea, in Caria, which speaks of 'images testifying to the virtues of the divine power': CIG II, no. 2715), and were current coin in Hellenized Jewish circles in the 1st cent. A.D. Again, **godliness** (*eusebeia*), meaning 'true religion' (NEB) and in the NT found only in Acts, the Pastorals (cf. esp. 1 Tim. iii. 16: 'the mystery of godliness') and 2 Peter (i. 3; 6 f.;

iii. 11), was a specifically Greek and Hellenistic expression, abundantly used in honorific inscriptions lauding the virtues of the deceased and much favoured by 4 Maccabees (47 times), *Ep. Arist.*, Philo and Josephus. Its connotation was wide-ranging: primarily it stands for pious behaviour towards the gods, with particular reference to the punctilious performance of cultic duties, but it also covers religiously motivated moral demeanour (towards parents, the dead, one's country, etc.). If in 6 f. the latter aspect is to the fore, here the accent seems to be on the former.

Most striking of all is **sharers of the divine nature,** associated as it is with **escaping** from the corrupt world. The affinity of these notions with Greek mystical philosophy, with its dualist presuppositions, cannot be disguised. From Plato it had been a commonplace that (*Theaet.* 176ab) 'we ought to try to escape from here to there as quickly as possible; and to escape is to become like God so far as is possible'. Hellenized Jews like Philo reproduce it, urging man (*Migr. Abr.* 9) to get away from his earthy surroundings, escaping from the filthy prison which the body and its lustful pleasures form. In Plato assimilation to God had been the goal, but here it is actual participation in His nature. It may be doubted whether the parallels often cited from Stoicism (e.g. Seneca's 'Man is part of God': *Ep.* xcii. 30) are strictly relevant, given the pantheistic premises of the system. In the 1st and 2nd cents., however, union with the divine was a widely entertained aspiration, being held out as a prize in the mystery cults and in the religion both of ordinary people and of the intelligentsia: cf., e.g., the glowing description of man's deification in Hermetic Tractate XIII. Alexandrian Judaism seems to have been deeply affected by this mystical trend, and so far as language is concerned expressions analogous to 'sharing the divine nature' are abundant in Philo and Josephus (e.g. *Dec.* 104; *C. Ap.* i. 232). We should note, however, that as good Jews they were careful to emphasize (e.g. Philo, *Leg. alleg.* i. 38) that union with God's being was not a natural possession of man but the effect of God's drawing him to Himself.

There is nothing novel in the thesis that Christians enjoy fellowship with God. For Paul they have been made sons of God by the outpouring of the Spirit which He has given them (Rom.

v. 5; viii. 14-17; Gal. iv. 6); they are united with one another
and Him in the body of Christ. For 1 John, too, they are
children of God (ii. 29-iii. 1) and have fellowship with the
Father and His Son Jesus Christ (i. 3); while according to Heb.
iii. 14 they are 'sharers of Christ'. What is interesting about the
present passage is the substitution of a metaphysical terminology for the earlier language of sonship and fellowship, and the
postponement of the realization of the promised grace to the
consummation; it is also to the individual, rather than to Christians as a body, that the grace is promised. We can only guess at
the writer's motive for introducing these changes, but in part at
any rate it is probably his desire, having regard to the situation
in which his readers are placed, to restate the Christian hope in
terms which they will find congenial, and which will also convince them that orthodox Christianity is fully in tune with, and
is uniquely qualified to satisfy, the religious aspirations of the
age. Like the author of 1 John, he 'is naturalizing within
Christian theology a widely diffused mystical tradition' (C. H.
Dodd, on 1 Jn. iii. 2), although he is in no way insinuating, as
that tradition tended to do, either that there is a natural kinship
between the higher part of man and God, or that the **corruption** of the world is in fact its materiality (that, he makes clear, is
the result of sin). His tentative ideas, however, were destined
to provide a firm scriptural foundation for the vast theology of
redemption by the divinization of human nature which, beginning with Clement of Alexandria, was to dominate the patristic
centuries and remains immensely influential in large sections of
the Church down to the present day.

2. THE NEED FOR PERSONAL EFFORT

i. 5-11

**(5) For this very reason, then, apply every effort to sup-
plement your faith with virtue, your virtue with knowledge, (6) your knowledge with self-control, your self-
control with steadfastness, your steadfastness with
godliness, (7) your godliness with brotherly affection, and**

your brotherly affection with love. (8) For if these qualities are yours in abundance, they prevent you from being
ineffective and unfruitful in the knowledge of our Lord
Jesus Christ. (9) For anyone who lacks these is blind and
short-sighted, and has forgotten the cleansing of his
former sins. (10) Because of this, my brothers, make all
the more effort to confirm your calling and election, for if
you do these things you will never come to grief. (11) For
thus you will have an entrance richly provided for you
into the eternal kingdom of our Lord and Saviour Jesus
Christ.

Having briefly sketched the glorious destiny promised them,
'Peter' challengingly reminds his readers that they have a very
necessary part to play in making it secure: **For this very reason, 5
then, apply every effort.** Their dissatisfaction with orthodox
Christianity, he is suggesting, as a result of which some of them
are being attracted by the errorists' distorted presentation of it,
springs in fact from their failure hitherto to make their own
proper contribution: little wonder they are finding their faith
ineffective. To counter this he sets before them a programme of
eight virtues which they must cultivate, starting with **faith** and
ending with **love** (cf. Ignatius, *Eph.* xiv. 1: 'Faith is the beginning, love the culmination'). The number has a mystic significance, for in the ancient world, pagan and Jewish as well as
Christian, eight symbolized perfection. They are arranged in
pairs with rhetorical art, the second in each pair being repeated
as the first in the next (for the same device, cf. Wis. vi. 17-19;
Rom. v. 3-5; viii. 30; x. 14; Jas. i. 2 f.: also Hermas, *Mand.*
v. 2. 4). Catalogues of this kind are frequent in the NT: e.g.
2 Cor. vi. 6; Gal. v. 22; Col. iii. 12-14; 1 Tim. iv. 12; vi. 11;
2 Tim. ii. 22; iii. 10; also outside the NT, *1 Clem.* lxii. 2. All
these include **love** and the last five **faith,** but the vocabulary of
the present list has a much more Hellenistic flavour and, unlike
the others, it reveals little or no affinity with the Qumran community rules. The cultivated Hellenistic atmosphere is further
heightened by the two verbs. As regards the former, while
every effort recalls the identical wording in Jud. 3, 'apply
effort' (*spoudēn pareispherein*, usually *eispherein*) is a very

common late Greek idiom (Polybius, *Hist.* xxi. 29.12; Diodorus
Sic., *Bibl.* i. 83.8; Josephus, *Ant.* xx. 204; the decree of Stratonicea cited on p. 302 above; numerous inscriptions). The second,
epichorēgein (lit. 'supply in addition'), originally signifies the
provision of a choir for a festival with something added, and
in Hellenistic Greek (e.g. Dionysius of Halicarnassus, *Ant. Rom.*
i. 42. 4; Diogenes Laertius, *Vit.* v. 67; Pap. Oxy. 905, 10—of a
husband providing for a wife) comes to mean 'give lavishly, with
generosity'.

The particles (*kai . . . de*) and adverbial phrase (*auto touto*: for
the idiom, cf. Xenophon, *An.* i. 9. 21; Plato, *Prot.* 310e), together rendered **For this very reason, then,** mark a progres-
sion of thought, and thus make it difficult to treat the preceding
two verses as the protasis of the present sentence. We might
paraphrase: 'Since then you have escaped corruption and have
been promised participation in the divine nature'. The readers
are presumed already to have **faith,** here to be understood
subjectively of loyal adhesion to Christian teaching rather than,
as in 1, of that teaching itself. This is to be the foundation of all
their Christian living and of the realization of the hope to which
they look forward. They must **supplement** it, however, with
virtue (*aretē*), a classic term from Greek ethics which, apart
from this verse and 3b (of the moral excellence of the incarnate
Christ), is only so used in the NT at Phil. iv. 8, a passage in
which (we should note) Paul seems to be appropriating the language of current pagan textbook morality. Here it clearly denotes a specific quality, probably moral courage or moral energy.
To this must be added **knowledge** (*gnōsis*), which here stands
not so much for that knowledge of Christ in terms of which the
writer understands Christian faith (see on i. 2), as for discernment of God's will and purpose (cf. Eph. v. 17; Phil. i. 9; Heb.
v. 14); the word contains a critical side-glance at the speculative
gnōsis of the errorists who will soon be coming under attack.

6 Further, **self-control** (*egkrateia*), **steadfastness** (*hupomonē*),
and **godliness** (*eusebeia*) are called for. A key-term in Greek
ethics since Plato and Aristotle to denote self-discipline in all
matters affecting the senses, the first ranks as a fruit of the
Spirit in Gal. v. 23; in choosing it here, 'Peter' is making a
tacit thrust at the heretics' licentiousness (ii. 2; iii. 3). The

second was also much approved in pagan, especially Stoic, morality; as elsewhere in the NT (Rom. v. 4 f.; viii. 25; 1 Tim. vi. 11; Heb. xii. 1 f.; Jas. i. 3 f.; etc.), it underlines the perseverance Christians should show in face of trials and discouragement, but here is given special pointedness by the impatience which the delay of the Parousia is apparently exciting among some of the correspondents (iii. 3 f.). For **godliness**, see on i. 4; again there is a dig at the trouble-makers, who are to be characterized (iii. 7: cf. ii. 6) as 'ungodly' (*asebeis*). Finally come **brotherly affection** (*philadelphia*) and **love** (*agapē*). For the 7 former, see on 1 Pet. i. 22: a further instance of his acquaintance with that epistle. Since it designates the loving spirit which should mark the relations of Christians with one another, the mention of the latter seems to betray a sense that this is not enough. *Agapē* has a universal scope (cf. 1 Thess. iii. 12), for the gospel demands love of our neighbour, whoever he may be (Mt. v. 43-48; Lk. x. 25-37).

The next two verses explain, the first positively and the second negatively, how impoverished and useless the life of a Christian is without these qualities. If he has them, and has them **in abundance, they prevent** him **from being ineffec-** 8 **tive and unfruitful in the knowledge of our Lord Jesus Christ.** The Greek verb *huparchein*, rendered **are yours,** denotes (cf. esp. the papyri) property which one really possesses and which is therefore fully at one's disposal; while *argos*, rendered **ineffective,** basically means 'out of work', and then 'idle', 'slothful', but here, as in Jas. ii. 20 (cf. Wis. xiv. 5; xv. 15; Philo, *Spec. leg.* ii. 86; 88; etc.) expresses the sterility or ineffectiveness in which not being put to work, or sloth, results. The preposition **in** before **the knowledge** (accusative) is *eis*, lit. 'into' or 'to', and most commentators give it the force of 'for', 'with a view to'. According to them, the writer is urging, like Paul in Col. i. 10, that progress in knowledge of Christ is the fruit of moral endeavour. In fact, however, his aim in the whole paragraph is the rather different one of warning his readers against 'receiving the grace of God in vain' (2 Cor. vi. 1). He assumes (i. 2; ii. 20 f.) that they already enjoy knowledge of Christ, but is pointing out that without their active cooperation it will stagnate and become useless. It is therefore more natural to paraphrase *eis* by 'in respect of your knowledge . . .'.

9   The terrible truth is that the Christian who **lacks** the qualities described inevitably becomes **blind and short-sighted,**
i.e. loses his capacity to see and appreciate the truths of revelation originally imparted to him. The image of spiritual blindness
is routine in NT paraenetic teaching (e.g. Mt. xv. 14; xxiii. 16;
Jn. ix. 40 f.; Rev. iii. 17), but the collocation of the adjective and
the participle (lit. 'is blind, being short-sighted') is curious,
especially as the former is a stronger term than the latter. Some
conjecture that **blind** (*tuphlos*: the everyday word) has crept in
as a gloss on the strange, otherwise almost unattested *muōpazōn*
('being short-sighted'). Others give the latter a causal force:
'being short-sighted, he becomes in effect blind'. The correct
solution (C. Spicq) may perhaps lie in the etymology of the verb,
which comes from the adjective *muōps*, i.e. 'closing, or contract-
ing, the eyes', as short-sighted persons tend to do. The meaning
may therefore in fact be 'shutting his eyes to the truth', the
intention being to emphasize the responsibility of the believer.
The unhappy man's plight is more precisely defined in a further
image as having **forgotten the cleansing of his former sins,**
i.e. the forgiveness which he received in baptism (Acts xxii. 16;
1 Cor. vi. 11; Eph. v. 26; Tit. iii. 5; 1 Pet. i. 22) for the sins
committed prior to his conversion (cf. 'passions which in your
ignorance formerly dominated you' in 1 Pet. i. 14). The mention of forgetting one's baptism (there is a distant allusion to it
in 4b) comes in very appropriately after that of spiritual blindness in view of the early Christian understanding of the instruction preceding baptism as an 'enlightenment' (Heb. vi. 4; x. 32).
The Greek periphrasis *lēthēn labōn*, translated **has forgotten**
but literally meaning 'having received forgetfulness', is another
characteristic Hellenistic turn (e.g. Josephus, *Ant.* ii. 163; iv.
304; Aelian, *Var. hist.* iii. 18).

10   'Peter' now reiterates his appeal: **Because of this,** i.e. in the
light of the encouragement and warning given in 8 f., **make all
the more effort** (observe how the verb *spoudasate* echoes the
noun *spoudē* in 5) **to confirm** (lit. 'make secure') **your calling
and election.** The former noun (*klēsis*) harks back to 'him who
called' in 3b; for **election** (*eklogē*), see on 1 Pet. i. 1: this pair of
nouns or their cognates are combined elsewhere in the NT

(e.g. Mt. xxii. 14; Rom. viii. 28-30; 1 Cor. i. 26 f.; 1 Pet. ii. 9; Rev. xvii. 14). It is God who calls and chooses, but a man is expected to make the appropriate moral response if his salvation is to be assured; he should 'walk in a manner worthy of his calling' (Eph. iv. 1). Even allowing for the hortatory setting and the implied critique of the errorists' claim to be above ordinary morality (ii. 19), it is difficult not to conclude from his tone that the writer assigns a greater role to good works than, say, 2 Tim. i. 9. Phil. ii. 12 f. is sometimes cited as a parallel treatment of the paradox of grace and works, but Paul's insistence there that God is at work in us both in our willing and in our acting has no counterpart here. This impression is borne out by the sequel: **if you do these things** (as in 8 and 9, *tauta*, i.e. 'these', refers back to the virtues listed in 5-7), **you will never come to grief.** By **come to grief** (*ptaiein*: a reminiscence of its cognate *aptaistos* in Jud. 24) is meant the disaster which befalls the man who fails to make sure his election. Literally the verb means 'stumble', 'trip', and so comes to mean 'sin' (so Jas. ii. 10; iii. 2). Many prefer this sense here, rendering the sentence (RSV), 'if you do this (i.e. make your calling etc. sure), you will never fall (i.e. sin)', and quoting passages like Ecclus. vii. 36 ('remember the end of your life, and you will never sin'). But (a) *ptaiein* can also have the metaphorical sense 'come to ruin', 'be lost' (e.g. Philo, *De Jos.* 144; Josephus, *Ant.* vii. 75; xiv. 434); (b) *aptaistos* in Jud. 24 seems to denote (see note) not so much freedom from sin as exemption from the disaster on the last day which sin brings down on a man; (c) **these things** is much more naturally referred, like the identical word in 8 and 9, to the virtues mentioned above than to **confirm your calling** etc., but if it is the proposed rendering 'you will never sin' is surely banal in the extreme. The two meanings, of course, overlap, for one 'comes to grief' as the penalty of sinning.

The paragraph is rounded off with an eloquently phrased assurance: **thus you will have an entrance richly provided 11 for you into the eternal kingdom of our Lord and Saviour Jesus Christ.** Once again **thus** (*houtōs*: lit. 'in this way') looks back to the pattern of moral behaviour outlined as the indispensable precondition of salvation. But the divine generosity, and with it the idea of God's grace, are highlighted both in the adverb **richly** (*plousiōs*: cf. Rom. x. 12; xi. 33; Eph. i. 7; ii. 4; 1 Tim. vi. 17) and in the verb *epichorēgein* (cf. Gal. iii. 5: of God's supplying the Spirit), which (as we saw at 5 above) conveys the notion of providing lavishly without cost to the beneficiary. Entering the kingdom is a frequent image in the synoptic gospels (e.g. Mt. vii. 21; xviii. 3; Mk. x. 15), and our Lord is also represented in them as laying down certain conditions for entry (Mt. vii. 21; xviii. 8 f.; xix. 17; Mk. x. 15). Both 'Peter's' manner of describing it, however, and his emphases are different. Whereas they speak of 'the kingdom (or reign) of God', or 'the kingdom of heaven', here we have **the eternal kingdom of our Lord and Saviour Jesus Christ.** Very occasionally in the NT the kingdom is designated as Christ's (e.g. Lk. xxii. 30; Jn. xviii. 36; Eph. v. 5; Col. i. 13; 2 Tim. iv. 1), but in Paul at any rate the 'kingdom of Christ' is the Messianic kingdom which exists between the resurrection and the Parousia, and which He will then hand over to God the Father (1 Cor. xv. 24). Luke indeed, in a text (i. 33) which the Church of the 4th cent. was to exploit effectively against Marcellus of Ancyra, declares that His kingdom will have no end; but only here in the NT (cf. Dan. iv. 3; vii. 27) is the adjective **eternal** (*aiōnios*) applied to it. Thus the eschatological perspective has altered. The kingdom is no longer thought of as coming to men, still less as already present so that they can enter it or as a Messianic kingdom which will last till the End; it lies in the future and is equated with the endless blessedness upon which believers who hold fast will enter at the Parousia. 1 Peter i. 3–9 reaches a similar climax, and there is much in the suggestion (G. H. Boobyer) that our writer is restating, in his own very different forms of expression and with his own characteristic emphases, some of the themes of that passage in this paragraph. The formula **our Lord and Saviour Jesus Christ** also deserves note. Though so familiar to Christians in their ordinary speech since early times, it only appears in the NT in 2 Peter, here and at ii. 20; iii. 2; 18. For **Saviour,** see on i. 1.

3. THE AUTHOR'S MOTIVE FOR WRITING

i. 12-15

(12) For this reason I intend always to remind you of these things, although you are aware of them and are firmly settled in the truth which lies before you. (13) I think it right, however, so long as I am in this tent, to stir you up by way of reminder, (14) knowing as I do that my tent will soon have to be discarded, as indeed our Lord Jesus Christ has revealed to me. (15) So I shall make the effort to see that, even after my departure, you may be able on all occasions to recall these things.

The real aim of the epistle is now unfolded. The author, writing with all the weight of Peter himself, wishes to leave with his readers an authoritative statement, to which they can constantly refer, of the Christian eschatological hope as he has been expounding it (cf. esp. 4 and 11 above) and as he will be further elaborating it later. He makes it all the more impressive and solemn by casting it in the form of a valedictory message, or last testament, penned by the Apostle himself in full consciousness of his imminent martyr-death. In the centuries immediately before and after Christ this was a recognized literary genre, with its own characteristic subject-matter, dramatic setting and even vocabulary. In the NT both Acts xx. 17-38 (Paul's farewell to the Milesian elders) and 2 Tim. iii. i-iv. 8 (his last charge, before his death, to Timothy) can be regarded as belonging to it. The most famous example that has come down to us, *The Testaments of the XII Patriarchs* (mostly 2nd cent. B.C.), has many points of contact with 2 Peter (e.g. its diatribe against immoral priests, its use of visions as a source of revelation, its dark foreboding of the corruption of the last days, its prophecy of cosmic catastrophes).

So 'Peter' begins: **For this reason I intend always to 12 remind you of these things.** By **these things** he means the hope of eternal life, and participation in the divine nature, but also (as in 8, 9 and 10, where the identical word 'these' is employed) the exalted moral qualities and strenuous moral

effort which are necessary to their attainment and on which he
has been dwelling in the previous section. His **reason** is that,
while the prospect is magnificent, its realization, as he has
explained, depends on the degree of cooperation they are
prepared to show. While giving what must be broadly the
correct sense, **I intend** may not be quite right. It represents
mellēsō, 1st person future indicative of *mellein* ('be about to',
'intend'), and though given by the best MSS the tense is
difficult (Mt. xxiv. 6 is not an exact parallel). It has therefore
been corrected in some MSS to *ouk amelēsō*, i.e. 'I shall not
neglect', but this is clearly an expedient to make a smoother
construction. No really satisfactory solution has been advanced.
For the courteous suggestion that the readers **are** already
aware, see on Jud. 5 (a verse from which **remind** as well as
aware seems to have been borrowed). But there is probably
more than conventional politeness in the remark: the writer
presumes that they 'know these things' because, according to
his fiction, they have studied them in 1 Peter and have read
there of the incorruptible inheritance reserved in heaven which
the faithful, if they remain steadfast, will receive at the Parousia
(1 Pet. i. 3-9) as well as of the possibility of sharing in the
divine glory (1 Pet. i. 8; v. 1).

For **firmly settled** (*estērigmenous*), cf. Ecclus. v. 10 ('Be
firmly settled in your understanding'); Lk. xxii. 32 ('settle your
brethren firmly'). The expression **the truth which lies before
you** (*parousēi*: lit. 'is present') recalls Col. i. 5 f.: 'the truth of
the gospel which has come (*parontos*: lit. 'is present') to you'.
But here the import is more far-reaching. Taken in conjunction
with the references to 'reminding' (i. 12 f.; iii. 1: see on Jud. 5)
and passages like ii. 21; iii. 2, it shows that the idea of Christian
teaching as a clearly defined and authoritative corpus of truth is
rapidly taking shape (see on Jud. 3). It is a revelation of which
the apostles are witnesses, which **lies before** the readers,
and to which they are expected to give loyal adherence. The
writer's expression of satisfaction that they are **firmly settled
in** it is a sound psychological touch, for he is in fact only too
conscious that they are in danger of being unsettled by the
deviationists.

While it is his general intention to be **always** (a further hint that this is not his first communication) hammering his message home, he explains that the certain approach of death makes this duty particularly urgent now: **I think it right . . . so long as I** 13 **am in this tent** (i.e. alive in the body), **to stir you up by way of reminder.** The opening words **I think it right,** and the manner and wording, as well as some of the particular admonitions etc., are strikingly reminiscent of the farewell address attributed by Josephus (*Ant.* iv. 177-193: it too begins with 'I have thought it right') to Moses: this letter is to be Peter's testament. Again we have the stress on **reminder** (*hupomnēsis*), a fundamental and constant feature of the early Christian paraenetic style (see on Jud. 5a). The comparison of the body to a **tent** (*skēnōma*) is found in Hermetic texts; *Ep. ad Diogn.* vi. 8; Eusebius, *Hist. eccl.* iii. 31. 1 f. It recalls Paul's 'the earthly tent (*skēnos*) we live in' (2 Cor. v. 1): also Wis. ix. 15; Philo, *Quaest. in Gen.* iv. 11; a host of pagan texts. The imagery is probably drawn from the life of nomads, who can quickly fold up their tents before moving on to fresh pastures; hence Isaiah (xxxviii. 12) can liken the suddenness of death to his dwelling being plucked up and removed 'like a shepherd's tent'.

The writer then explains his sense of urgency: **knowing as I** 14 **do that my tent will soon have to be discarded,** i.e. he will shortly die. The imagery has changed: a **tent** is folded, but the figure has switched to that of doffing a garment. For a similar mixing of metaphors, cf. 2 Cor. v. 1-4. The adjective translated **soon** (*tachinos*) can convey the idea of suddenness (cf. ii. 1, where it is applied to the destruction coming to the errorists) as well as soonness or swiftness (Ecclus. xviii. 26; Wis. xiii. 2; esp. Hermas, *Sim.* viii. 9. 4), and so might suggest a violent death; but this does not seem to suit the context so well. In any case he is absolutely sure that he is going to die because **our Lord Jesus Christ has revealed** it to him. The verb used (*dēloun*) can mean 'inform', 'make clear' (e.g. 1 Cor. i. 11; Col. i. 8), but it is also used of special revelations (e.g. 1 Cor. iii. 13; 1 Pet. i. 11; often in the LXX: see TWNT II, 61). Commentators have speculated what communication he has in mind, many identifying it with the Lord's prophecy to Peter recounted in Jn. xxi. 18 f., and some even with the Quo Vadis legend which we read in *Acts of Peter* xxxv (late 2nd cent.). It should be unnecessary to point out that the logion in Jn. xxi. 18 f. discloses the manner, not the timing, of the Apostle's death, and in any case was uttered soon after the Lord's resurrection, i.e. many years before Peter's actual martyrdom. The discussion is unrealistic, for on the assumption that the epistle is pseudonymous Peter was revered as a glorious martyr at the time it was written (cf. the tribute paid to him in *1 Clem.* v. 1-4: *c.* 95). It came naturally to Christians to believe that the heroes of the faith received premonitions of their approaching martyrdom (e.g. Acts xx. 25 and xxi. 11, of Paul; *Mart. Polyc.* v. 2; *Pass. Perp. et Fel.* iv. 3-10; *Vita Cypr.* xii). The same motive was probably at work here, and it is fruitless to hunt around for any particular incident, historical or legendary; a similar warning to Peter is narrated in the early 3rd cent. Ps. Clementine *Ep. ad Iac.* ii. 2, and the edifying Quo Vadis story fits into the same scheme of things.

15   'Peter's' concern, however, extends far beyond the brief span of life still left to him: he will **make the effort** (again his favourite verb *spoudazein*, as at 10a: cf. also 5a) **to see that, even after** his **departure,** his correspondents (here he seems to be envisaging the Church generally as well) **may be able on all occasions to recall these things.** In other words, he plans to leave behind him a permanent testimony to which they can refer; there is perhaps a hint that apostolic writings were not only treasured but read at services. For **departure** (*exodos*) as a dignified euphemism for death, cf. Lk. ix. 31 (Jesus's death, foreshadowed at the Transfiguration); Wis. iii. 2; vii. 6; Irenaeus, *Haer.* iii. 1. 1 (of the deaths of Peter and Paul). At first sight the cast of the sentence, with its future tense, seems to imply that he is promising a further work, and on the theory of Petrine authorship commentators have often identified this either as some document now lost or as Mark's Gospel, which the ancient Church (e.g. Irenaeus, *Haer.* iii. 1. 1; Eusebius, *Hist. eccl.* ii. 15; iii. 39. 15) regarded as enshrining the Apostle's teaching. Neither conjecture has any plausibility if we are satisfied that 2 Peter is pseudonymous. A serious objection in any case to the latter is that the language used here leads us to expect a work (a) composed by Peter himself, not a disciple, and (b) consisting of exhortation and doctrine (cf. **recall these**

things), not gospel narrative; while the former overlooks the fact that the imagined setting is Peter's fast approaching death. Almost certainly the reference is to the epistle itself. The tense is admittedly difficult, but the whole pericope 12-15 is clumsily and pretentiously composed, and in employing the future the writer is either looking forward to the sections he is about to draft or (more probably) placing himself in the position of his readers when they receive and study his tract. His remark is revealing in other respects, for it savours of an epoch when the living witness of the apostles is no longer operative and the Church feels the need of written texts stamped with their authority.

4. THE VERACITY OF THE APOSTOLIC TESTIMONY
i. 16-21

(16) For we were not following cleverly contrived fables when we made known to you the power of our Lord Jesus Christ and his Coming, but we had been eye-witnesses of his majesty. (17) For having received honour and glory from God the Father, when a voice was borne to him from the Majestic Glory in these terms, 'This is my Son, my beloved, on whom my favour rests'—(18) this very voice we heard borne from heaven when we were with him on the sacred hill. (19) Thus we have confirmation of the prophetic message, to which you would do well to pay attention as to a lamp shining in a darksome place, until the day breaks and the morning star rises in your hearts, (20) understanding this first, that no prophecy in scripture is a matter of one's own interpretation, (21) because no prophecy was ever brought by the volition of man, but men spoke from God under the influence of the Holy Spirit.

The writer now comes to closer grips with his main theme, claiming that the apostolic teaching is firmly founded on a historical revelation which itself only confirms what earlier

16 prophecy foretold. As he puts it, **we were not following cleverly devised fables when we made known to you the power of our Lord Jesus Christ and his Coming, but we had been eye-witnesses of his majesty.** He has quietly slipped, we notice, from the personal 'I' of 12-15 to **we,** thereby associating himself again with the apostles who were privileged to receive the revelation and insinuating that he shares their authority: for this manner of speaking, cf. Jn. i. 14; xix. 35; Acts i. 21 f.; x. 39-41; 1 Jn. i. 1 f.; iv. 14. The exact bearing of **cleverly devised fables** is a little uncertain. The word **fables** (*muthoi*) carried a disparaging flavour in the religious language of the time; it stood for mythical stories about gods, the creation of the world, miraculous happenings, etc., and writers regularly (e.g. Plato, *Tim.* 26e; Philo, *De opif.* 1; *Exsecr.* 162; Josephus, *Ant.* i. 22; *C. Ap.* ii. 256; Plutarch, *De Is. et Os.* 20) draw unfavourable comparisons between 'fictional myths' and authentic accounts. In 1 Tim. i. 4; iv. 7; 2 Tim. iv. 4; Tit. i. 14 the term is applied to the theosophical speculations of the Gnostic-minded teachers there criticized. This obvious parallel has led most commentators to conclude that 'Peter' is attacking the fanciful theorizings of the errorists, contrasting the apostolic version of Christianity, with its secure basis in history, with their allegorization of 'spiritualization' of it; and this interpretation is almost certainly correct. An alternative possibility, however, which is supported by the balance of the sentence, is that he is in fact rebutting an imputation made against his own and the Church's teaching. In effect he may be saying, 'When we preached Christ's Coming to you, we were not, as our opponents allege, foisting an ingenious mythology on you, but were reporting truths of which we had empirical evidence'. In the sequel we do not hear of **fables** put out by the deviationists, but they are represented as questioning the apostolic eschatology; and this may well have taken the form of caricaturing it as 'myths'. These two exegeses need not, of course, be mutually exclusive; and if the former is accepted as giving at any rate part of the meaning (the participle **cleverly devised** certainly reads like a sneer of the writer's), it lends powerful support to the view that the trouble-makers are some kind of Gnostics.

The verb 'make known' (*gnōrizein*) is almost technical in the

NT for imparting a divine mystery (e.g. Lk. ii. 15; Jn. xv. 15; xvii. 26; Rom. xvi. 26; Eph. vi. 19; Col. i. 27). Both **power . . . and his Coming** and **majesty** are to be understood in the setting of the Transfiguration (17 f.), which is taken as a fore-shadowing of Christ's Second Coming in glory. His **power** refers, not to the miraculous deeds He performed during His incarnate life, but to the godlike might which He possesses as risen Lord, which He disclosed by anticipation for a moment on the mount of Transfiguration, and which He will manifest to all when He comes again on the last day. Here, as in the NT generally (e.g. Mt. xxiv. 3; 1 Cor. xv. 23; 1 Thess. ii. 19; 2 Thess. ii. 8; Jas. v. 7 f.; 1 Jn. ii. 28), that great event is described as His **Coming** (*parousia*: lit. 'presence'), a sacral term in Hellenistic religion and the mystery cults for the epiphany of a god which was taken over by Hellenistic Judaism (e.g. Josephus employs it of God's manifestation of His presence: *Ant.* iii. 80; 202; ix. 55— the identical expression 'power and presence'; xviii. 284: cf. Test. Jud. xxii. 2). It was from the latter that primitive Christianity seems to have borrowed it, and it has already become technical when it appears in the NT (see TWNT V, 856-69).

Some scholars contest this commonly accepted interpretation, claiming that *parousia* must here denote the Lord's first Coming, i.e. His earthly ministry, death and resurrection, mainly on the grounds (a) that the gospel narratives (Mt. xvii. 9; Mk. ix. 9 f.: cf. Lk. ix. 31) treat the Transfiguration as pointing forward to the resurrection, not the Second Coming; and (b) that a reference to an as yet unfulfilled event would invert the writer's whole argument, which is that his teaching concerns matters with which he has had direct contact. Against this, however, the following objections may be urged. (a) While *parousia* refers to Christ's incarnate coming or presence in a few late passages (e.g. Ignatius, *Philad.* ix. 2; Justin, *1 Apol.* lii. 3; *Dial.* xiv. 8), it nowhere does so in the NT. (b) Our writer indisputably uses it of a future coming in iii. 4 and 12, and it would be surprising for him to employ it with a different sense here in the course of quite a short tract. (c) As the rest of the letter shows, it was the Lord's present power and future coming, not anything to do with His earthly life, about which (so far as we can see) the errorists were raising doubts and 'Peter' therefore wished to reassure his readers. (d) The section immediately preceding, with its talk about securing entrance into Christ's eternal kingdom, has been preparing us for the theme of the Second Coming. (e) This theme is prominent in 1 Peter, which is constantly speaking of 'the last time' (e.g. i. 5; iv. 7; v. 6) and 'the revelation of our Lord Jesus Christ' (i. 7; 13; iv. 13), where the latter expression denotes the Parousia; and we have reason to believe that its contents were constantly in 'Peter's' thoughts. (f) There is also some slight evidence (Ethiopic version of the *Apocalypse of Peter*; Origen, *Comm. in Matt.* xii. 31) that in the early Church the Transfiguration was interpreted in certain circles as a forecast of the Second Coming. (g) The second of the arguments mentioned above fails to notice that, while the writer certainly claims that his message has a sure basis in the apostles' experience, this in no way implies that this experience may not have been the revelation of a supernatural event to be fully accomplished in the future.

In fact, he claims, he and his companions had been **eye-witnesses of his majesty.** The former noun (*epoptēs*: only here in the NT, but cf. 1 Pet. ii. 12) designated in the mystery religions higher-grade initiates who had been admitted to the spectacle of the *hiera*, or sacred cult objects (e.g. Plutarch, *Alcib.* xxii. 4: also Dittenberger, *Sylloge inscr. Graec.* III, 1052; 1053— the mysteries of Samothrace, 1st cent. B.C.). The word can also bear the more general sense of 'spectator', 'observer' (e.g. Aeschylus, *Prom.* 298 f.; Josephus, *C. Ap.* ii. 187), and this is the meaning which is to the fore here. Nevertheless its choice, inspired probably in the first instance by the use of the cognate verb (*epopteuein*) at 1 Pet. ii. 12; iii. 2, is a further instance of the writer's predilection for Hellenistic religious terminology. He is probably aware that it suggests privileged admission to a divine revelation. The second noun (*megaleiotēs*) describes the content of this vision, viz. **his majesty,** i.e. the supernatural quality of Jesus, unveiled at the Transfiguration, which is seen as a trustworthy anticipation of His Second Coming in might and glory. In Lk. ix. 43 too it connotes the disclosure or revelation of divine power; while Josephus frequently uses it (e.g. *Ant.* i. 24; viii. 111; *C. Ap.* ii. 168) of God's grandeur and sublimity.

'Peter' now indicates more precisely the occasion when he

and his companions had this unique experience: it was when
Jesus **received honour and glory from God the Father** (in 17
the original the verb is a nominative participle, and the sentence
tails off as an anacoluthon, with a fresh construction starting at
18), and **a voice was borne to him from the Majestic Glory.**
As the details, especially the mention of the divine utterance and
the holy mount, clearly indicate, he is recalling the scene of the
Transfiguration. For the stock phrase **honour and glory,** cf. Ps.
viii. 5 (cited in Heb. ii. 7; 9); Rom. ii. 7; 10; 1 Tim. i. 17; 1 Pet.
i. 7; Rev. iv. 9; etc. Here **honour** denotes the exalted status
which the proclamation of Sonship implies, while **glory** (*doxa*)
points to the ethereal radiance of the transfigured Jesus (Mk.
ix. 2 f. and parr.), a radiance which, it is suggested, is a participation in that splendour of light which, according to OT
conceptions (see on 1 Pet. i. 7 f.; Jud. 25), belonged to God's
very being. So in the next clause God is described, with a
characteristically Hebrew avoidance of the divine name, as **the
Majestic Glory:** cf. Test. Lev. iii. 4; 1 En. xiv. 20; Asc. Is. xi.
32, where He is called 'the Great Glory'. The synoptists, we
may note, make no mention of God and represent the voice as
coming 'from the cloud'.

For the statement uttered by the voice, cf. Mt. xvii. 5; Mk.
ix. 7; Lk. ix. 35. The true Greek text here (the MSS have
assimilating variants) comes closest to Matthew's version, but
differs from it (a) in placing **This is** at the end of the first clause
instead of the beginning; (b) in reading **my beloved** instead of
'the beloved'; and (c) in reading **on whom** (*eis hon*) instead of
'in whom' (*en hōi*). The discrepancies are of no significance
since the author's source was probably traditional material, and
not any of the written gospels. He now comes to his main point
and, in his eagerness to stress that he relies on the evidence of
his ears as well as his eyes, breaks off his half-completed sentence
and starts another: **this very voice we heard borne from** 18
heaven when we were with him on the sacred hill. The
former **we** (*hēmeis*) is expressed in the Greek and is emphatic
(almost 'we ourselves'); once again the writer is associating
himself with the other apostles, in this case James and John.
The synoptists' indeterminate 'a high hill' has become **the
sacred hill,** i.e. a specific spot hallowed in the religious con-

sciousness of the Church. 'Peter' is perhaps identifying it with Sion, taking a hint from Ps. ii. 6 f., where Sion is 'the holy hill' on which Yahweh sets up His anointed Son (cf. also Philo, *Leg. alleg.* iii. 142).

Evidently he regards the Transfiguration, with its disclosure of Christ's divine nature and the ratifying of this by the heavenly voice, as confirming His power and future Coming, but scholars have wondered why he did not rather select the resurrection itself. In 1 Peter and other NT writings this is normally seen as the prelude of the Second Coming. Some (e.g. E. Käsemann) have taken the interesting line that he may have considered the resurrection less suitable for his purpose since it affected Christ alone, whereas the Transfiguration reminds us that Christ walked on earth as man with His divinity veiled, and thus holds out the hope not only that He will come again but that human beings will be able to share in His glorification; participation by the faithful in the divine nature (i. 4) is integral to his eschatology. The more usual explanation points out that his interest is focussed on the divine voice; it is the declaration made at the Transfiguration that Christ is God's Son and His beloved that makes it doubly impressive as a guarantee of His coming in glory. An alternative solution that has been advanced (A. Loisy, *La Naissance du christianisme*, p. 42; K. G. Goetz, *Petrus als Gründer und Oberhaupt der Kirche*, p. 89; etc.) is that he may have treated the Transfiguration as a post-resurrection appearance, and it is worth noting that this is how the *Apocalypse of Peter* (*c.* 135) understands it. It must be acknowledged that there are fascinating puzzles here which remain unresolved.

The writer now moves to a further point, perhaps taking his cue from the linking of OT prophets with Christian teachers in 1 Pet. i. 10-12: in the apostles' experience of the Transfiguration 19 **we** (the pronoun covers the faithful generally, not just the chosen disciples as in 18) **have confirmation of the message of prophecy.** AV's 'we have also a more sure word of prophecy' is syntactically acceptable, and is favoured by some on the ground that in the NT prophecy is normally regarded as giving support to gospel events, not the reverse. Against this it may be argued (a) that the event in question here is still in the future; and (b) that it seems paradoxical to attribute greater trustworthiness and 'more sure' authority to OT prophecy than to the direct testimony of God Himself given at the Transfiguration. The true meaning, which the Greek construction fully supports (for parallels to this use of the comparative 'more sure', cf. Isocrates, *Ad Dem.* 36; Stobaeus, *Anthol.* iv. 25. 31), is that in the light of this revelation **the message of prophecy** has been made 'more sure' in the sense both that God has Himself certified it as true and that it is already in process of fulfilment. **The message of prophecy** (lit. 'the prophetic word': so Philo frequently, e.g. *De plant.* 117; *2 Clem.* xi. 2; Justin, *Dial.* lvi. 6) was a current expression embracing the OT as a whole and not simply the prophets proper. The writer probably has no particular passage in mind, but, like other Christians of the apostolic and sub-apostolic period (cf. Peter's statement in Acts iii. 24 that 'all the prophets . . . proclaimed these days'), assumes that the OT in all its parts confidently looked forward to the glorious coming of the Messiah and His subsequent establishment of His kingdom.

He now inserts a warning note: scripture having been thus confirmed, his readers **would do well to pay attention** to it. He is concerned, apparently, at the neglect and misuse (see below) of it encouraged by the false teachers. So he compares it to **a light shining in a darksome place** (*auchmēros topos*: a very rare expression, but paralleled in *Apoc. Pet.* 21). For similar descriptions of God's word, cf. Ps. cxix. 105 ('a lamp to my feet and a light to my path'); 2 Esd. xii. 42 ('a lamp in a dark place'). In this case the **darksome place** is the world as it at present exists, which in the NT (e.g. Jn. i. 5; Eph. vi. 12; 1 Thess. v. 4 f.; 1 Jn. ii. 8) is regularly characterized as darkness. Prophecy, or scripture generally, gives men illumination and therefore guidance as they pass through it, and they will need it **until the day breaks and the morning star rises in their hearts.**

This beautiful sentence needs careful elucidation, but the opening clause at any rate is tolerably clear. By **the day** the writer means primarily Christ's Parousia (cf. Paul's 'the day is at hand' in Rom. xiii. 12), which will dissipate the darkness of the present age just as the dawning day banishes night. The figure, however, contains a secondary layer of meaning as well, hinting at 'the day of the Lord' (iii. 10; 1 Pet. ii. 12; Jud. 6); thus it is intended to impress on the readers that Christ's Coming has a twofold aspect, being a day both of salvation and of judgment. The clause which follows is much more enigmatic. Is it merely a picturesque embroidery of the image of the dawning day? This has been the general view, but it is intrinsically probable that, while the dawn-imagery is being elaborated, a fresh idea or facet is being introduced. In any case, if embroidery had been the sole point of the clause, we should have expected the rising sun to be mentioned rather than **the morning star** (*phōsphoros*), especially as the ancients were fully aware that the morning star, or 'light-bringer' (such is the literal rendering of the word), i.e. the planet Venus, precedes and does not follow the dawn. Hence some scholars have tried to interpret *phōsphoros* as here denoting the sun, but there is no lexical precedent for this; others have recognized that there is a minor inaccuracy of detail here which must he attributed to carelessness on the author's part. The correct solution, however, probably lies in a different direction. Having mentioned the Parousia, the writer wishes to bring in Christ Himself, and this he does by representing Him as **the morning star.** The imagery lay ready to hand, for the famous prophecy in Num. xxiv. 17, 'There shall come a star out of Jacob', was understood in Judaism as pointing to the Messiah (Test. Lev. xviii. 3; Test. Jud. xxiv. 1-5; 1QM xi. 6 f.). It was natural that it should be taken up by Christians, and the fact that in Lk. i. 78 Christ at His first coming is hailed as 'the dawn from on high', and that in Rev. xxii. 16 the risen Lord is spoken of as 'the bright morning star', confirms that it was.

If **the morning star** symbolically stands for Christ, how are we to understand **rises in your hearts?** On any interpretation this is a difficult phrase, and scholars have sometimes tried to ease it by construing the words either with **pay attention** above or with **understanding this** in the next verse. Neither is really a viable expedient, for (a) the distance of **in your hearts** from **pay attention** is by itself against the former, while (b) both the balance of the sentence and the stereotype expression **understanding this first** (*touto prōton ginōskontes*: cf. iii. 3) are against the latter. When Paul (Rom. xiii. 12) uses the transition

from night to day as a metaphor for the Parousia, he is thinking
of a cosmic event which takes place outside the individual. Here
the 'rising in our hearts' obviously points to something which
happens, in a blessed and saving way, to Christians in their
inner selves. The clause must be a pictorial description of the
way in which, at His Coming, Christ will dissipate the doubt
and uncertainty by which their hearts are meanwhile beclouded
and will fill them with a marvellous illumination. As such the
expression finds parallels in 1st cent. Hellenistic Judaism. Philo,
e.g., describes in remarkably similar terms (*Ebr.* 44) how the
pure rays of 'the divine morning star', i.e. God, 'flash on the
eye of the soul'; in much the same way, too, he considers
(*Decal.* 49) the oracles of God as 'stars which usher in the dawn
(*phōsphorountas*) in the soul'. This verse, however, is highly
instructive for the light it throws on the writer's picture of the
End. As we shall see (iii. 10-13), this is largely coloured by the
primitive features of a cosmic transformation; but here, as in
i. 4, his language betrays the beginnings of an attempt to give
eschatology a personal and even psychological orientation. The
Parousia is conceived of as having a transforming effect in the
hearts of faithful believers.

A futher caution, however, is necessary. While Christians
should study the Bible attentively, they ought to accept and
work by the principle **that no prophecy in scripture is a** 20
matter of one's own interpretation. As normally in the NT
(but see on iii. 16), **scripture** (*graphē*) denotes the OT. *Epilusis*
(rendered **interpretation**) occurs only here in the LXX and
NT, but elsewhere the noun or the cognate verb (*epiluein*)
signifies the exposure of fallacies (Philo, *Agric.* 16; Sextus
Empiricus, *Pyrrh.* ii. 246), or (more characteristically) the
explanation of puzzles or riddles (Athenaeus, *Deipn.* x. 450e;
Josephus, *Ant.* viii. 167), dreams (Gen. xl. 8 Aquil.; Heliodorus,
Aethiop. i. 18), difficult passages of scripture (Philo, *Vit. con.* 75),
or parables (Mk. iv. 34; Hermas, *Sim.* v. 5. 1). *Epilusis* is in the
genitive case, and the verb translated **is a matter of** is *ginetai*,
which with a genitive could mean either 'arises from' or
'belongs to', 'comes under the scope of'. Some commentators
opt for the former, paraphrasing the text as 'no prophecy arises
from the prophet's own interpretation, but is given by God';

and they point to 21a for confirmation. But this entails reducing 21a, which professes to give a reason for the statement in 20, to a repetition of it in a different form. Again, it is distinctly awkward to have to take **one's own** (*idias*) as referring to 'the prophet', since no such person has actually been mentioned. The whole expression 'arises from an interpretation' is also puzzling, for an *epilusis* is an explanation of something, but no object is indicated. The 11th cent. Theophylact, often cited in support of this exegesis, seems to have perceived this, for he adds the gloss (PG cxxv, 1265) that the prophets did not work out an explanation (*epilusin*) of the message they had received; but this is to introduce an idea which is alien to the context. Not surprisingly, those who hold that the writer's point is that prophecy comes from God, not the prophet himself, are obliged to admit that *epilusis* must here be virtually equivalent to 'inspiration' (so M. Green); but this is impossible.

Much the most natural meaning, and the one which suits the context best as well as agreeing with the lexical evidence for *epilusis*, is the one implied by the printed translation (so too RV; RSV; NEB; etc.), viz. that no individual is entitled to interpret prophecy, or scripture generally, according to his personal whim. It is precisely this, as we shall later see (iii. 16), that the trouble-makers are guilty of, and it leads in the writer's view to disaster. But if **one's own interpretation** is excluded, what is the approved alternative with which 'Peter' contrasts it? The next verse makes this clear: it is the interpretation intended by the Holy Spirit, whose inspiration lies behind prophecy. In view of his attitude and date there can be little doubt that he is not thinking of the Spirit-endowed individual or prophet in the community, but rather of apostolic authority as embodied in the recognized ministers and charismatic teachers of the local churches who, as he understands it, bear the Spirit's commission. The notion of the official Church as the appointed custodian of scripture is evidently taking shape.

All this, however, is hinted at rather than stated; the straight and obvious reason why individuals have no right to read their 21 arbitrary interpretation out of scripture is that **no prophecy was ever brought** (or, perhaps, 'was brought of old': so AV; NEB) **by the volition of man, but men spoke from God**

under the influence of the Holy Spirit. The inference that consequently a correct understanding of scripture depends upon the aid of the Spirit is implicit but clear. It is sound OT doctrine that only pseudo-prophets prophesy what their own minds prompt them to say (e.g. Jer. xxiii. 16; Ezek. xiii. 3); the genuine prophet's utterance is not his own but 'the word of the Lord' (cf. esp. Jer. i. 4-10), and so far from its resulting from his own **volition** (*thelēma*: 'will'), he on occasion proclaims it only under compulsion (e.g. Jer. xx. 7-10). The inspiration of prophecy was a commonplace with Josephus (e.g. *Ant*. iv. 118 f. and Philo (e.g. *Vit. Mos.* i. 281; *De mut. nom.* 203), as well as with the Qumran sectaries (e.g. 1QS viii. 16; 6QD ii. 12 f.); and it was the rabbinical tradition that the whole OT was the work of God's Spirit (cf. SB IV, i. 435-51). The NT is in full agreement (e.g. Mk. xii. 36; Acts iii. 21; 2 Tim. iii. 16; Heb. i. 1) that it is God's voice that is heard in it.

So widespread indeed was the consensus that **no prophecy was ever brought by the volition of man** that 'Peter's' energetic insistence on the point is surprising; one is tempted to inquire if there were any contemporary circles in which it was denied. If there were, the discovery would enhance our understanding of the verse and throw light on the false teachers' standpoint. E. Molland has pointed out that in the Pseudo-Clementine Homilies (e.g. ii. 6-12; iii. 52-54) we read of Gnostic-minded Jewish Christians who refused to recognize the inspiration of prophets subsequent to Moses, while Methodius of Olympus (*c.* 300) reports (*Conviv.* viii. 10) the 'obstinate assertion' of Ebionite heretics that the prophets were not inspired by the Spirit but 'spoke by their own prompting' (*ex idias kinēseōs*). Epiphanius (*Pan. haer.* xxx. 18. 5) similarly represents the Ebionites as teaching that the prophets relied on their own intelligence, not on the truth. Methodius and Epiphanius are, of course, much later writers than ours, but the material embodied in the Pseudo-Clementines belongs to a period not much removed from that of 2 Peter; and it may well be that the errorists envisaged in the latter shared the same disparagement to prophecy.

5. WARNING AGAINST FALSE TEACHERS

ii. 1-3

(1) But false prophets too appeared among the people, just as there will be false teachers among you also, who will smuggle in destructive heresies, denying even the Master who bought them—bringing swift destruction on themselves. (2) And many will follow their licentiousnesses, and because of them the way of truth will be reviled. (3) In their cupidity they will exploit you with false words; but from of old their condemnation has not been idle, and their destruction is not asleep.

At this point, postponing till ch. iii his further defence and exposition of the Christian eschatological hope, the writer plunges into a warning against, and vehement denunciation of, false teachers who are undermining the Church's faith and practice. Although it might seem a digression, it is not really one, for his positive exhortation in ch. i is, as we have seen, shot through with veiled criticisms of them, and indeed the whole object of his tract (this has come out particularly in the immediately preceding verses) is to set out the true teaching and safeguard it against distortions. The numerous correspondences between this chapter and Jud. 4-16 prove a close literary relationship between the two texts, and there is little doubt (see Introduction, pp. 225-27) that 2 Peter is the borrower. In Jude the errorists are represented as already at work in the communities, but in 2 Peter the writer starts off by predicting their rise in the future. It is apparent, however, that this is an artificial device which he adopts in furtherance of his claim to be the Apostle. In ii. 10 ff. he abandons it and assails them as a present menace.

1   His remarks about prophecy in i. 20 f. give him his cue: **false prophets too,** he recalls, as well as genuinely inspired ones, **appeared among the people,** i.e. God's people Israel (cf. 1 Pet. ii. 10). A 'false prophet' (*pseudoprophētēs*) is one (Dt. xviii. 20) 'who presumes to speak a word in my name which I have not commanded him to speak', and thus leads people

astray. The phenomenon was a familiar one under the old covenant (e.g. Dt. xiii. 1-5; 1 Kgs. xxii. 5-28; Jer. v. 31; Ezek. xiii; Mic. iii. 5-12); and as this was the type of the new covenant, the Church must be prepared for a similar experience. Just as the old Israel had its prophets, so the Church has teachers occupying an authoritative position (Rom. xii. 6-8; 1 Cor. xii. 28 f.; Eph. iv. 11); like Israel too, it must look for the emergence of **false teachers.** Justin also makes the point (*Dial.* lxxxii. 1), in almost identical words, that the false prophets of the Jews are matched by the Church's false teachers. For the apocalyptic belief, widely accepted in primitive Christianity, that the period preceding the End would see the rise of perverse teaching, blasphemy and immorality leading to apostasy, cf. Mk. xiii. 22; 2 Thess. ii. 3; 11 f.; 1 Tim. iv. 1-3; 2 Tim. iii. 1-5. A similar expectation prevailed at Qumran (e.g. 1QpHab ii. 5).

These dangerous deceivers **will smuggle in destructive heresies** (lit. 'heresies of destruction'), thereby (since so, the writer implies, it has been divinely ordained) **bringing swift destruction on themselves.** The verb rendered **smuggle in** (*pareisagein*: cf. *pareisaktos*, i.e. 'secretly bought in', in Gal. ii. 4) suggests introducing in an underhand way; it recalls 'smuggled themselves in' in Jud. 4. In classical Greek, as in Hellenistic Judaism, 'heresy' (*hairesis*) is a neutral term denoting 'choice', and so 'school of thought', 'sect' (so Acts v. 17; xxvi. 5); but it rapidly acquired the pejorative sense it bears here (cf. 1 Cor. xi. 18 f.; Gal. v. 20). The destruction twice referred to is final perdition, in the latter case of the false teachers and in the former both of them and of the unfortunates they succeed in duping; and it will be **swift** (*tachinos*: the same word as is used for 'soon' in i. 14) both because it will come suddenly and because the judgment is near at hand ('Peter' shares this ancient conviction, in spite of what he has to say at iii. 8-10). Their blasphemy is summarily characterized as **denying even the Master who bought them,** which closely reproduces the charge of Jud. 4. **Master,** however, undoubtedly here denotes Christ (there is no question, as in Jude 4, of denying God as well), and its original connotation of owning slaves is still fresh as a metaphor. By His saving act Christ has **bought** us (for the figure, cf. 1 Cor. vi. 20; vii. 23; Gal. iii. 13), and so the Christian belongs and owes allegiance to Him. Instead the errorists 'deny' Him, but as in Jud. 4 we are given no clue to what form or forms their denial took. Many critics infer from the context that it must have been practical (flouting Christ's lordship by their scandalous conduct), but it may also have included specific doctrinal deviations (e.g. the rejection of the Second Coming, or a defective estimate of Christ's divine sonship).

They will, the writer in the person of the Apostle predicts (in fact, he is describing a situation which already exists), have con-
2 siderable success: **many will follow their licentiousnesses, and because of them** (lit. 'because of whom': the reference is clearly to the **many** backsliders) **the way of truth will be reviled.** They are apparently professed antinomians (see on ii. 19), and he is continually recurring, directly or indirectly, to their sensuality (ii. 7; 10; 12; 14; 18; 19; 22; iii. 3). The term (*aselgeia*) which he uses for it, here and again at ii. 7; 18, echoes Jud. 4 (see note), and is also found at 1 Pet. iv. 3; it normally denotes debauchery in general, but in ii. 7; 18 has sexual licence specifically in view. For **the way of truth,** cf. Ps. cxix. 30 ('the way of faithfulness'): also Philo, *Quaest. in Gen.* iv. 125. One of the earliest names for Christianity, as we know, was 'the Way' (Acts ix. 2; xix. 9; 23; xxii. 4; xxiv. 14; 22); it was also called 'the way of the Lord' or 'the way of salvation' (Acts xviii. 25; xvi. 17). In the late apostolic and sub-apostolic age 'the truth' *tout court* came to mean sound Christian teaching (e.g. 1 Tim. vi. 5; 2 Tim. ii. 18; Tit. i. 14; Ignatius, *Eph.* vi. 2; Polycarp, *Phil.* iii. 2: cf. also Valentinus's 2nd cent. *Gospel of Truth,* where the second noun stands for the true teaching of Christianity, as he understood it, as opposed to erroneous versions). Here the whole expression denotes the Christian message and way of life, which are inevitably brought into discredit when their adherents (as the errorists and their followers must have seemed to shocked outsiders) identify themselves with patently immoral courses. Both thought and expression reflect the influence of LXX Is. lii. 5 ('Because of you God's name is reviled among the Gentiles'). Paul cites the text in Rom. ii. 24, and early Christian writers are acutely conscious (e.g. 1 Thess. iv. 12; 1 Tim. vi. 1; Tit. ii. 5; 1 Pet. ii. 12; 15; iii. 16; Ignatius, *Eph.* x. 1) of the impression, favourable or the reverse, which the

pagan world is bound to form of the Church from the conduct of its members.

A further charge is pressed home in a biting sentence. The errorists' driving force, it is alleged, is sheer **cupidity**, i.e. 3 greed of gain (so too ii. 14): the preposition **in,** in Greek *en*, is used, as frequently, of 'attendant circumstances'. Their counterparts in Jude (cf. 11 and 16) are also accused of this distressing weakness. The early Church was constantly warning its officials against the temptations of money (e.g. 1 Tim. iii. 3; Tit. i. 7; 1 Pet. v. 2—see note; *Did*. xi. 12), and Paul took particular care (Acts xx. 33 f.; 1 Thess. ii. 5) to avoid suspicion on this score. As a result **they will exploit** people. The verb (*emporeuesthai*) originally means 'travel' or 'travel on business', then 'carry on business' (e.g. Jas. iv. 13) or 'trade in', and finally 'trade on', 'cheat'. Clearly it has the last sense here, and coupled with **cupidity** insinuates that they will not only deceive people or take them in, but will feather their own nests in the process (how precisely, we are not told). Their **false words** are of course the specious arguments or fictitious claims they will use to buy over converts.

Nevertheless, 'Peter' assures his readers, they will not get away with it: **from of old their condemnation has not been idle** (Jud. 4 also speaks of wicked men who were 'from of old marked out for condemnation'), **and their destruction is not asleep.** There is a solemn rhythm in the threat, and **condemnation** (*krima*, as in Jud. 4) and **destruction** (*apōleia*: in the eschatological sense, as in ii. 1) are almost personified (for a parallel, cf. *Ep. apost.* 7 (8)). When the wicked are successful and their misdeeds go unrequited, men tend to imagine that God is asleep (e.g. Ps. xliv. 23), but His slumber and apparent inactivity should not be misunderstood (Ps. cxxi. 4; 2 Esd. iv. 37). The verdict has already been pronounced on them, and the doom which will surely overtake them has been set in motion **from of old** (*ekpalai*: cf. *palai* in Jud. 4), as will now be demonstrated.

6. EXAMPLES OF PREVIOUS JUDGMENTS
ii. 4-10a

(4) For if God did not spare the angels when they had sinned, but casting them into hell consigned them to pits of darkness to be kept until the judgment; (5) if he did not spare the ancient world, but kept Noah, a herald of righteousness, safe with seven others when he brought the deluge upon a world of ungodly men; (6) if he reduced the towns of Sodom and Gomorrah to ashes and sentenced them to extinction, making them an example of the fate in store for ungodly people; (7) and if he rescued righteous Lot when he was greatly troubled by the licentious behaviour of unprincipled men (8) (for as a result of what he saw and heard that righteous man, as he resided among them, was day after day tortured in his righteous soul by their lawless deeds): (9) then the Lord knows how to rescue the godly from trial, and how to keep the unrighteous under punishment until the day of judgment (10a)—especially those who indulge the flesh with polluting lust and despise authority.

Like the author of Jude (5-7), 'Peter' bases his certainty of divine retribution on God's consistent action in the past and cites three terrifying examples of it. Two of these (the dissolute angels, and Sodom and Gomorrah) agree with 'Jude's', but for the latter's first (the Israelites who 'murmured' in the desert) he substitutes the Flood. This change probably reflects the influence of 1 Pet. iii. 20, and as he places it second he succeeds, unlike 'Jude', in arranging his catastrophes in the correct chronological order. By itself this adjustment favours the inference that his is the dependent text, and a further pointer in this direction is the slightly awkward way in which he interweaves a motif completely absent from Jud. 5-7, viz. the insistence (5; 7; 9) that, while destroying the wicked, God can be trusted to rescue the righteous. This note of reassurance and promise (cf. i. 4; 11; 19; iii. 9; 11-14) may also betray the impact upon him of themes he has come across in 1 Peter.

He begins his argument: **if God did not spare the angels 4 when they had sinned . . .**; the protasis is dragged out with clumsy elaboration in successive clauses, and we only reach the apodosis in 9. As in Jud. 6 (where see note: also note on 1 Pet. iii. 19 f.), **the angels** are the heavenly beings mentioned in Gen. vi. 1-4 who lusted after earthly women and whose subsequent punishment was enlarged upon in late Jewish speculation. Like the author of Jude, 'Peter' is acquainted with Jewish *haggadah* and with apocryphal literature (see on ii. 5-8; iii. 5-10), but is no longer prepared to treat the latter as inspired; hence he is more sparing in the detail he supplies and abstains from direct quotation. According to him, God cast the angels **into hell** and **consigned them to pits of darkness to be kept until the judgment.** The former verb *tartaroun*, which is almost unexampled elsewhere, comes from the proper noun 'Tartarus', the name in classical mythology for the subterranean abyss in which rebellious gods, nefarious human beings, etc., were punished. There is no need, however (see on Jud. 6b), to detect anything beyond an indirect and indeed remote influence of Greek literature in its use, for the noun and its associations had become fully acclimatized in Hellenistic Judaism (e.g. LXX Job xli. 24; 1 En. xx. 2; Philo, *Exsecr.* 152; Josephus, *C. Ap.* ii. 240—an allusion to the Titans being chained in Tartarus). There is some slight uncertainty about the reading **pits** (*seirois*), for some MSS, including Pap. 72, give *seirais*, i.e. 'chains', instead. This agrees with the picture in Jud. 6; but the former noun, as well as fitting **of darkness** (*zophou*) better, is extremely rare, and this fact, in combination with the wording of Jud. 6, probably prompted its alteration. Neither **pits** nor the verb **casting into hell** entails that the location of their prison was underground (see on Jud. 6); indeed it is more likely to have been conceived of as the second heaven.

His second illustration is the Flood, the narrative of which follows closely in Gen. vi on that of the misdemeanours of 'the sons of God' and indeed dovetails with it. Two features, he contends, stand out in that appalling disaster. First, God **did 5 not spare the ancient world** when He saw its corruption (Gen. vi. 12 f.); on the contrary, He did not hesitate to bring **the deluge upon a world of ungodly men** (*asebeis*: his stock term, as it was 'Jude's', for the errorists—cf. ii. 6; iii. 7). Although it contains one of his two principal points, this latter sentence is clumsily expressed in the Greek by a participial phrase added at the end. It is interesting to note the threefold division of history which he seems to envisage: **the ancient world,** i.e. the antediluvian epoch; the present post-Noachian order; and the new world-order which will be ushered in by 'the day of God' (iii. 12 f.). The noun he uses for **world** is in both cases *kosmos*, and while this could denote mankind, it is probable that in this setting he means it to refer to the universe as a whole and conceives of the Flood as causing a cosmic catastrophe (see on iii. 6). Secondly, however, the catastrophe reveals another and definitely hopeful aspect of God's dealings: **he kept Noah, a herald** (*kērux*: for this noun with the sense of 'preacher', cf. 1 Tim. ii. 7) **of righteousness, safe with seven others**; the encouraging innuendo is not meant to be lost on the readers. The reference to **seven others** is again picked up from 'eight persons' in 1 Pet. iii. 20 (see note); the translation paraphrases the laconic Greek idiom 'eighth'. There is no mention in the OT of Noah's actually preaching **righteousness** (*dikaiosunē*: here, as in i. 1; iii. 13; 1 Pet. ii. 24; iii. 13, and generally in the NT outside Paul, the word denotes just or upright moral behaviour) to his contemporaries, but later Jewish and Christian imagination richly expanded its sparse account (Gen. vi. 9) of him as a 'righteous and blameless man'. Josephus, e.g., represents him (*Ant.* i. 74) as disgusted by their conduct and urging them to amend their ways. For samples of moral exhortation attributed to him, cf. Orac. Sib. i. 128 f.; 150-98; Jub. vii. 20-39. For the Christian tradition of his preaching and call to repentance, cf. *1 Clem.* vii. 6; ix. 4; Theophilus, *Ad Autol.* iii. 19.

6   Thirdly, we have the spectacle of **the towns of Sodom and Gomorrah,** which God **reduced ... to ashes and sentenced ... to extinction,** thereby **making them an example of the fate in store for ungodly people.** Both the mention of the Cities of the Plain and the stress on their annihilation as **an example** (*hupodeigma* here, *deigma* there) are clearly inspired by Jud. 7, but there are differences (sentence structure, reference to the method of destruction, omission of the nature of their

crime) which suggest reliance on memory rather than on a text. In Gen. xix. 24-28 it is not stated that God **reduced** the cities **to ashes**, but that He 'rained brimstone and fire' upon them, with the result that 'the smoke of the land went up like the smoke of a furnace'. 'Peter's' source is late Jewish folklore, according to which (e.g. Philo, *Migr. Abr.* 139; *Ebr.* 222 f.; *Vit. Mos.* ii. 56) only ashes were left of them; Strabo (*Geog.* xvi. 2. 44) describes the Dead Sea region as 'a land of ashes'. Instead of **of the fate in store for ungodly people** (*mellontōn asebesin*, lit. 'of things going to befall ungodly people': so Codex Vat.; Codex P; the Syriac version; Pap. 72), the great majority of MSS and versions give 'of people who should prove ungodly in the future' (*mellontōn asebein*). The intended meaning is the same in both cases, but the latter fails to bring it out accurately. The former is closer to Jud. 7, and also makes a more pointed thrust at the present errorists; it may have been altered because of the unusualness of the construction, the verb *mellein* being normally followed by an infinitive and not, as here, by a noun in the dative.

This instance, too, signally shows up, in contrast to God's stern treatment of the wicked, His concern for people who observe His laws: again an aspect passed over in Jud. 7, but completely in tune with our writer's purpose and attitude. While ruthlessly destroying Sodom and Gomorrah, God **res- 7 cued righteous Lot when he was greatly troubled by the licentious behaviour of unprincipled men.** Gen. xix. 15 ff. records the deliverance of Lot and how the Lord was 'merciful to him', an incident not mentioned in Jude, but once again 'Peter' goes beyond the strict narrative of the OT. This represents Lot as a weak and timorous man who, while undoubtedly **greatly troubled** by the boisterous ribaldry of his fellow-citizens (Gen. xix. 4 ff.), seems to have put up no serious resistance to it. Indeed his own conduct is not portrayed (Gen. xix. 8; 32 ff.) as exactly edifying, and in view of this a number of rabbinical texts (SB III, 769-71) treat him as a notorious sinner. In a very different tradition, however, both Jewish and early Christian (e.g. Wis. x. 6; Pirke R. Eliezer, xxv; *1 Clem.* xi. 1), he was saluted as a model of virtue, a striking proof that when castigating evil God will always save the minority who trust in

Him. This whitewashing is to be attributed to the fact that, since the Messiah was to trace his descent through David from Ruth the Moabitess, the unseemly union of Lot with his daughters which is described in Gen. xix. 30-38 and which had resulted in the birth of Moab was interpreted by some rabbis as having served a providential purpose.

The next verse underlines, again with the similar situation of the orthodox readers in view, the anguish and sense of outrage 8 which **that righteous man** suffered; **as he resided among** the Sodomites, **as a result of what he saw and heard,** Lot **was day after day tortured in his righteous soul** (lit. 'was torturing his righteous soul': the verb is, appropriately, the continuous imperfect) **by their lawless deeds.** For the OT's outspoken condemnation of Sodom and Gomorrah, cf. Gen. xviii. 20-32; their abominable conduct became a byword with the rabbis (SB I, 571-74; III, 785 f.). The Greek phrase here rendered **as a result of what he saw and heard** literally means 'in seeing and hearing' (*blemmati kai akoēi*), and comes at the beginning of the sentence immediately before **that righteous man** (*ho dikaios*). As some MSS omit the definite article *ho* before **righteous,** an alternative translation might be 'for righteous as he was in aspect and report, he . . .', and indeed the Vulgate accepts this as the meaning. It is a possible version so far as 'righteous . . . in report' is concerned, but the attempt to extract 'righteous in aspect' from 'righteous in seeing' is extremely dubious. The collocation of two instrumental datives **(as a result of what he saw and heard** and **by their lawless deeds),** both connected with the single verb **tortured,** is admittedly inelegant and awkward, but is not out of keeping with the author's negligent style; in mitigation it may be argued that **lawless deeds** is added to give precision to the rather vague and general 'seeing and hearing'.

At last, after this lengthy build-up (4-8), we are brought to the twofold moral contained in these exemplary stories of the 9 way in which the divine justice works: **the Lord knows how to rescue the godly from trial, and how to keep the unrighteous under punishment until the day of judgment.** The former perspective is absent from Jude, but 'Peter' is anxious to highlight it in order to stiffen his readers' resolution. **Rescue** (*ruesthai*) picks up the same verb (*errusato*) used of Lot's deliverance from his trials at 7. This confirms that the **trial** (*peirasmos*) from which God rescues **the godly** (*eusebeis*: in pointed contrast to 'the ungodly', or *asebeis*) is probably not, as many suppose (cf. Rev. iii. 10), their final testing on the last day, but the affliction of spirit, disillusionment and temptation to lapse (cf. 'in the hour of trial' in Lk. viii. 13) which decent, God-fearing people experience when surrounded by vicious neighbours. Though the suffering involved has a different origin here, the word has the same general sense as in 1 Pet. i. 6. Many exegetes translate the second half of the sentence by 'hold the unrighteous in reserve for punishment on the day of judgment', arguing that this is the correct inference from the catastrophes described and fits the eschatological tension of the letter, and that any other interpretation presupposes a double judgment. But the rendering adopted above (a) accords better with the Greek, in which **under punishment** is represented by a present participle (*kolazomenous*: 'being punished') to which we cannot easily attribute a future sense; (b) reproduces exactly the moral of the OT illustrations cited, which depict God's immediate vengeance on sinners without excluding (cf. esp. ii. 4, where it is expressly stated) the possibility of further punishment on the last day; and (c) is in agreement with current Jewish accounts (e.g. 1 En. xxii; 2 Esd. vii. 75-101: cf. the description of Dives as 'being in torment' in Lk. xvi. 23 f.) of the wretched existence of the wicked between their death and the final judgment.

From the general the writer moves abruptly to the particular, singling out as **especially** the objects of God's wrath **those who** 10a **indulge the flesh** (lit. 'those who walk after the flesh': for this use of *poreuesthai*, i.e. 'walk', see on Jud. 11) **with polluting lust and despise authority** (or 'flout lordship'). This more circumstantial attack is clearly aimed directly at the trouble-makers, and both here and in the more developed onslaught which follows the pretence of prophecy is dropped and they are treated as insidious influences currently at work in the communities. There are close verbal correspondences, as a comparison of the Greek texts shows, with Jud. 7 (*opisō sarkos*, i.e. 'after the flesh' in both); 8 (*miainousin*, i.e. 'pollute': cf. *miasmos*,

335

i.e. 'pollution', here; 'set authority at nought' there, and **despise authority** here); 16 (in both the noun 'lust', or *epithumia*, and the verb 'walk', or *poreuesthai*). The first charge is sexual looseness; this is constantly mentioned or hinted at in the tract, and we can deduce from ii. 19 that the false teachers interpreted their Christian freedom as placing them above ordinary moral rules. The Greek behind **with polluting lust** (*en epithumiāi miasmou*) literally means 'in desire of pollution': if the genitive is objective, the sense is 'in their hankering after pollution', but if subjective (as is more likely), 'in lust which pollutes'. The second charge seems modelled on 'set authority at nought' in Jud. 8 (see note), but we should not infer that the obscure expression necessarily has exactly the same meaning here as it has there. For the reasons given in the note on that verse, it is unlikely, in spite of 10b, that it refers to the errorists' contemptuous attitude to angelic powers and still less to their disregard of ecclesiastical officials. We should probably connect it with ii. 1, where they are accused of 'denying the Master'; the Greek behind **authority** is *kuriotēs*, i.e. the abstract noun 'lordship' related to *kurios*, i.e. 'Lord'. Thus the indictment here, as at ii. 1, is that, in some way that we can only surmise, they depreciated or disparaged Christ's sovereignty or divine status.

7. THE ERRORISTS' WICKEDNESS DENOUNCED
ii. 10b-16

(10b) Brazen and self-willed, they are not afraid to revile the glorious ones, (11) whereas angels, though superior in might and power, do not advance a reviling judgment against them before the Lord. (12) But these people, like irrational animals which according to their nature are born for capture and destruction, reviling in matters where they have no knowledge, will themselves be destroyed in their destruction, (13) suffering injury as the recompense for the injury they have done. They count revelling in the day-time pleasure, and are blots and blemishes as they carouse with you, revelling in their

deceptions. (14) **They have eyes filled with a loose woman and insatiable for sin; they ensnare unstable souls and have hearts well trained in cupidity—accursed creatures! (15) Abandoning the straight path they have gone astray, following the path of Balaam, son of Bosor, who loved profit from wrong-doing, (16) but received a rebuke for his wickedness: a dumb beast spoke with a man's voice and put a stop to the prophet's madness.**

This indictment, with its sequel in 17-22, is the most violent and colourfully expressed tirade in the NT. As before, the writer exploits Jude, selecting and adapting to suit his needs, but supplementing his source with gusto from his own repertory of abuse.

Brazen (*tolmētēs*: cf. the use of *tolmān*, i.e. 'presume', in 10b Jud. 9) **and self-willed** as they are, the false teachers **are not afraid to revile the glorious ones.** No completely satisfactory interpretation of this enigmatic sentence has so far been proposed. It almost exactly reproduces Jud. 8c, and we can reject at once, as we did there, the notion that slandering the church authorities is the misdemeanour to which exception is being taken. The following verse makes this exegesis particularly unsuitable here, for it scarcely makes sense to speak of good angels as being superior to the hierarchy or of the latter as deserving (in the author's view) censure before the Lord. In Jud. 8c 'the glories' (*doxai*, as here) insulted appear (see note) to be heavenly beings in God's service, in all probability good ones. One's first inclination is to understand the word in that sense here too, and so indeed some commentators do; but verse 11 implies quite clearly that **the glorious ones** in fact merit condemnation, though not from human beings. So the most plausible and widely accepted theory is that, while they are celestial beings, they are guilty ones, probably the fallen angels mentioned in ii. 4. If this is correct (the objection that 'the glories' is scarcely an apt description of trespassing angels does not hold, for angels of any sort belong to a higher order than men), we can only speculate what form the errorists' 'reviling' took. Were they crudely disparaging Satan and his angels, claiming that in view of their spiritual standing they were free and that he had no power over them (Knopf)? As Gnostics did they consider themselves sufficiently familiar with the realm of spirits to be entitled to speak contemptuously of its disgraced inhabitants (Schelkle)?

What remains clear is that their attitude, in the writer's eyes, betokens a blasphemous rebellion against the divinely established order of existence. The 'reviling' in which it finds an outlet is

11 all the more presumptuous since even **angels**, in spite of being **superior in might and power** (**superior**, of course, to the erring 'glories', not to the false teachers; that would be the most banal of truisms), **do not advance a reviling judgment against them** (i.e. against the fallen angels) **before the Lord.** The picture presupposed is that of the heavenly court; and in 1 En. ix. f. we have a vivid account of men piteously complaining of the evils which befall them through the machinations of bad angels, and of the archangels then bringing these complaints before God, though without themselves venturing to pass judgment, and of the Most High Himself eventually intervening and chastising the guilty. Here the reserved attitude of the good angels to 'the glories' corresponds to the notable moderation of the archangel Michael in his altercation with the Devil so graphically described in Jud. 9. 'Peter' is obviously drawing on this verse (cf., e.g., *blasphēmon krisin*, i.e. **reviling judgment,** here and *krisin . . . blasphēmias*, i.e. 'judgment of reviling', there), but deliberately omits all reference to the legend from the Assumption of Moses, contenting himself with a general statement which, to say the least, cries out for an explanatory note which he fails to supply. This is in keeping with his tendency to play down reliance on apocryphal writings (cf. his pruning of Jude's more luxuriant detail in ii. 4 and 6, and his entire omission of the quotation from 1 Enoch in Jud. 14 f.), and betokens a later date and also a more 'Catholic' attitude. See Introduction, pp. 226 f.

12 The diatribe continues: **But these people** (adversative, in contrast to the angels who exercise such restraint), **like irrational animals. . . .** The writer is expanding material taken almost word for word from Jude 10, and rearranging it rather clumsily. For example, the comparison with beasts is introduced in Jud. 10, more logically, in connection with the

errorists' physical propensities, but here to illustrate their
ignorant **reviling** and ultimate fate. In abusing 'the glories' in
the ways darkly hinted at, they evidently preen themselves on
their knowledge (a palpable dig at their pretensions to superior
gnōsis), but in fact these are **matters where they have no
knowledge,** any more than brute beasts have. And so, just as
these **according to their nature are born for capture and
destruction** (*phthoran*: in an ordinary context we should have
expected something more specific, like *sphagēn*, i.e. 'slaughter',
but the general noun suits the comparison better), the false
teachers will share their doom and **will themselves be destroyed in their destruction,** i.e. a destruction similar in its
finality to that which befalls wild beasts. They of course come to
a violent end by the huntsman's knife or spear, or by the fangs
of his hounds, but the evil men who live like them will meet
their equally terrible retribution at the final judgment.

Even so, though they will be **suffering injury,** it will be no 13
more than **the** just **recompense for the injury they have
done.** In the original there is an intentional verbal play between
the participle *adikoumenoi* (**suffering injury**) and *adikias*
(**injury**); **as the recompense** (*misthon*) is an appositional
accusative. The basic meaning of the verb (*adikeisthai*) is 'to
suffer injustice', and so a number of MSS and versions replace
the participle by *komioumenoi* (future participle of *komizeshtai*,
i.e. 'to receive'), which would yield the translation 'and will
receive recompense for their wrong-doing'. The motive for the
correction is obviously to smooth out the construction and, more
particularly, eliminate any suggestion that the false teachers
are the victims of injustice; but it not only destroys the verbal
play but is entirely unnecessary, since *adikeisthai* can also bear
the meaning 'be damaged', 'be harmed', without any implication of unjust treatment (e.g. Wis. xiv. 29; 3 Macc. iii. 8;
Rev. ii. 11).

Nevertheless, while this seems the most satisfactory exegesis
(cf. 'wages of sin' in Rom. vi. 23; 'recompense for wickedness'
—the same noun *misthos*—in *Barn.* iv. 12), certain difficulties
remain, notably the use of *misthos adikias* with the sense of
'punishment for sin' here and 'reward for wrong-doing' in 15.
Hence many prefer the alternative rendering 'being defrauded,

or done out of, the reward for their wrong-doing'. This gives an excellent sense, but is syntactically questionable, and we may doubt whether any reader would have naturally read this meaning out of the expression. Somewhat more attractive is P. W. Skehan's proposal (*Biblica* xli. 69-71) that a colon should be placed after *adikoumenoi* and 'reward for wrong-doing' construed with the following clause ('they count pleasure the reward for wrong-doing . . .'). The present verse is then taken to mean, '. . . in their corruption they will suffer damage (*adikoumenoi*) and will be corrupted'. But a major objection to this interpretation is that it extinguishes the parallelism between the beasts, **born for . . . destruction**, and the false teachers. The word *phthora* ('destruction' or 'corruption') and the cognate verb occur in both halves of the sentence, in reference to both the beasts and the errorists, and are most naturally taken in both cases as meaning 'destruction', 'be destroyed'; further **in their destruction**, followed as it is by *kai* in the Greek, must refer to the destruction of the wild beasts, to which that of the errorists is likened.

The attack returns to the immoral life of the latter. In the Greek the several items are strung together in a series of biting participial clauses (cf. Rom. xii. 9-13, where however the participles have the force of imperatives) in loose apposition to **will be destroyed** (they set out the justification for the destruction), but they are more conveniently expressed in English by short finite sentences. The first is clear enough: **They count revelling in the day-time pleasure.** If debauchery has any place at all, the night is the time for it (cf. Rom. xiii. 12 f.), and to practise it by daylight increases its heinousness; darkness is the standard symbol of evil, and by a rationalization night can be regarded as veiling unseemly behaviour in 'decent obscurity'. For the thought, cf. Eccl. x. 16 ('Woe to you, O land, . . . when your princes feast in the morning'); Is. v. 11 ('Woe to those who rise early in the morning that they may run after strong drink'); Ass. Mos. vii. 4 ('they delight in banquets every hour of the day').

The second item is more obscure, mainly owing to an important textual variant. According to the more widely accepted reading, the heretics **are blots and blemishes as they carouse**

with you, revelling in their deceptions. 'Peter' is now plundering Jud. 12, taking over the rare verb **carouse with** (*suneuōcheisthai*), but altering (sure confirmation that he is the later writer) 'Jude's' difficult 'hidden rocks' (*spilades*: see note) to the much easier **blots** (*spiloi*: cf. Eph. v. 27, where *amōmos*, i.e. 'without blemish', may have instigated him to add *mōmoi*, i.e. **blemishes**). Thus the accusation is one of riotous misbehaviour at banquets, and since the correspondents participate in these they would seem to be some kind of community celebrations.

A complication, however, is introduced by **deceptions** (*apatais*: dative), in place of which several good MSS and some versions read 'love-feasts' (*agapais*: in uncials the words look almost identical), which appears in Jud. 12 (see note). Though favoured by AV, RV and many editors, this latter reading can scarcely be original. Had it stood in the text, the only reason for altering it would presumably be disgust that such misconduct should disfigure the Church's sacred meals; but since those responsible were the errorists, the misconduct could only have enhanced their guilt. The most likely explanation of the reading is that it is the result of assimilation to Jud. 12. 'Peter' himself must have deliberately altered what he read there, but it is not easy to fathom his motive. Perhaps the *agapē*, or love-feast, was already obsolete in his area when he wrote. Perhaps he selected the word *apatē* with conscious, stinging irony in order to brand these disgraceful functions as mockeries af *agapai*, pseudo-love-feasts which were in fact **deceptions.** On the other hand, if the parties he has in mind are social ones, without any religious object or atmosphere, this latter word may properly be given the sense of 'dissipations' (so RSV). The 2nd cent. lexicographer Moeris defines (p. 65) *apatē* as signifying 'leading astray among Attic speakers . . . among Greeks delight (*terpsis*)'. The transition from 'guile' or 'deception' to 'sinful pleasure' was natural and easy, and examples of it with the latter connotation are not lacking in late Greek (e.g. Philo, *Dec.* 55; Hermas, *Sim.* vi. 2. 1; 3. 3; 4. 4; 5. 1; Hegemonius, *Arch.* x—in PG x. 1445).

The catalogue builds up: **They have eyes filled with a 14 loose woman** (*moichalis*: lit. 'an adulteress'; but the connotation is probably more general) **and insatiable for sin.** The two descriptive phrases are connected: the errorists have so lost moral self-control that they cannot look at a woman without imagining or wishing themselves in bed with her (cf. Mt. v. 28). The former expression, concrete and intensely graphic, has been corrected in several MSS, the Old Latin version, etc., to the banal 'full of adultery (*moichalias*)'. In fact it is paralleled by the current tag quoted by Plutarch (*Mor.* 528e) and Longinus (*De sub.* iv. 5) that the shameless man 'has harlots, not maidens [*korai*: a pun, since this word also denotes the pupils of the eyes], in his eyes'.

Little wonder that **they ensnare unstable souls,** presumably largely, though not exclusively, recent converts (cf. ii. 18), and thus bring them under their control and initiate them into their own disorderly ways. Philo also (*De praem.* 25) uses the verb **ensnare** (*deleazein*) of the impostor who takes in the young and inexperienced. For **souls** (*psuchai*) virtually meaning 'people', cf. Acts ii. 41; 1 Pet. iii. 20. Their dupes are **unstable** (*astēriktos*: only here and in iii. 16 in the Bible), i.e. they lack a firm foundation in faith and discipline, and so are liable to be unsettled by scandalous conduct or erroneous teaching: the direct opposite of the author's ideal of being 'firmly settled (*estērigmenos*) in the truth' (i. 12). They themselves, by contrast, **have hearts well trained** (*gegumnasmenos*: of athletic training—the term is chosen in conscious antithesis to **unstable**) **in cupidity.** As in Semitic thought generally, the heart is regarded as the seat and principle of affections, emotions, etc. We have already heard (ii. 3) of their greed and improper interest in money-making, so alien from the generosity which should characterize the true believer, and the repetition of the charge here provokes the exclamation **accursed creatures!** For this typically Hebrew expression (lit. 'children of a curse', i.e. God's curse), cf. Is. lvii. 4 ('children of transgression'); Rom. ix. 8 and Gal. iv. 28 ('children of promise'); 1 Pet. i. 14 ('children of obedience'); etc.

15   The writer returns to Jude: **Abandoning the straight path they have gone astray, following the path of Balaam, son of Bosor.** Though corrected to 'Beor' in B, the Philoxenian Syriac and Sahidic versions, etc., the form *Bosor* has massive MS support and clearly ought to be retained. Balaam's father

was of course Beor (Num. xxii. 5; xxiv. 3; 15; etc.), and no plausible explanation of 'Peter's' mistake has been advanced. In Jud. 11 the downfalls of Cain, Balaam and Korah are all lumped together, but he omits the other two and concentrates on Balaam, **who loved profit from wrong-doing** (lit. 'reward of wrong-doing': alternatively the genitive may be a Semitic one of quality, meaning 'wrongful reward'). His reason for making this selection is that his interest is now focussed on the false teachers' avaricious propensities. For the blackening of Balaam's reputation in later Jewish tradition and the portrayal of him as induced by bribes to act wickedly, see on Jud. 11. The comparison of conduct to a 'way' (cf. ii. 2) is found everywhere in the Bible, and upright conduct is pictured as a **straight path** in, e.g., 1 Sam. xii. 23; Hos. xiv. 9; Ps. cvii. 7; Acts xiii. 10. In Prov. ii. 15 the paths of the wicked are described as 'crooked', and in *Did.* i-v (cf. *Barn.* xviii-xxi) the distinction is drawn between 'the way of life' and 'the way of death'. Similarly 'lead astray' (*planan*) and 'go astray' (*planasthai*) are stock expressions in the LXX and the NT (the same imagery was in vogue at Qumran: 1QS iii. 21; 1QH ii. 14; iv. 12; etc.) for corrupting and being corrupted either spiritually or morally (see further in TWNT VI, 230-52).

Breaking away from Jud. 11, where 'Balaam's error' is cursorily mentioned, the writer relates with gusto the humiliating outcome of the Biblical episode (as he understands it) so as to point the moral for the errorists: Balaam **received a rebuke** 16 **for his wickedness,** i.e. his readiness to accept a bribe to curse Israel: **a dumb beast** (*hupozugion*: in general a beast of burden, but more specifically an ass: e.g. Mt. xxi. 5, quoting Zech. ix. 9) **spoke with a man's voice and put a stop to the prophet's madness.** The description of an ass as **dumb** (*aphōnos*) strikes us as faintly comic, but in Greek and Latin the adjective was commonly applied to animals because they appeared to lack articulate speech. According to Num. xxii. 21-35, it was not the ass but the angel of the Lord who administered the rebuke. Aware of the angel's presence, the ass refused to budge, and when Balaam struck her voiced a justified complaint in human language. 'Peter' is drawing on Jewish *haggadah* which developed around the tale (see SB III, 771 f·). The phrase **spoke**

with a man's voice finds an almost exact parallel in Josephus's (*Ant.* iv. 109) expression 'uttering a human voice' in reference to the same incident.

8. THEIR DOOM ASSURED
ii. 17-22

(17) These people are waterless springs and mists blown away by a squall, for whom the gloom of darkness has been reserved. (18) For, declaiming bombastic futilities, they ensnare in fleshly passions, in sensualities, men who are only just escaping from those who live in error. (19) They promise them freedom, although they are them-selves slaves of corruption; for a man becomes the slave of him who overpowers him. (20) For if, after escaping from the pollutions of the world through the knowledge of the Lord and Saviour Jesus Christ, they again get en-tangled in and overpowered by them, their final state is worse than the first. (21) For it would have been better for them not to have got to know the way of righteousness than, having got to know it, to turn back from the holy commandment which was delivered to them. (22) What has happened to them is what the true proverb teaches, 'A dog which has returned to his vomit and a sow which has washed in order to wallow in mire'.

'Peter' now derides the utter vacuity and feebleness of the errorists' teaching, and claims that it is bound to entail their
17 own downfall as well as that of those whom they seduce. **These people** (for the biting **These,** see on Jud. 10), he protests, **are waterless springs and mists blown away by a squall,** and they have **the gloom of darkness . . . reserved** for them. He culls his imagery from Jud. 12 f., carefully omitting allusions to apocryphal myths as well as material already used at ii. 13, abbreviating and trying, mostly but not altogether successfully, to improve on his original. He probably objected to 'Jude's' 'waterless clouds' because all clouds carry water, but his revised comparison of the false teachers to 'wells without

water' (cf. Jer. xiv. 3) is particularly happy. There could be no more bitter symbol of disillusionment to the thirsty traveller or anxious farmer in the east. Equally apt is his substitution of **mists** (*homichlai*), for according to Aristotle (*Meteor*. i. 346b) this rare term denotes the haze which is left after the condensation of cloud into rain. It is, as it were, 'unproductive cloud' heralding dry weather, and both that fact and the ease with which such **mists** are dispersed by sharp gusts of wind (for *lailaps*, i.e. **squall**, cf. Lk. viii. 23) underline the insubstantiality and flimsiness of the teaching. On the other hand, the ominous clause about **the gloom of darkness** (cf. ii. 4) fits less naturally here than in Jud. 13, from which the wording (with the omission of 'for ever') has been taken. In both passages the heretics are being threatened with ultimate destruction, but whereas there (see note) the picturesque imagery springs directly from late Jewish ideas about the fate of 'the wandering stars', here it stands without any such background to give it special appropriateness.

In plain language, their propaganda consists of **declaim- 18 ing bombastic futilities** (lit. 'bombastic words of vanity': *huperogka*, i.e. 'inflated', is borrowed from Jud. 16). By means of this **they ensnare in fleshly passions** (lit. 'passions of the flesh': a stock expression, as we see from, e.g., Gal. v. 16; Eph. ii. 3), **in sensualities, men who are only just escaping** (*apopheugontas*: an ingressive present participle) **from those who live in error,** i.e. novices to Christianity who are still in process of breaking contact with pagan associates. As often in the Bible (e.g. Wis. xii. 24; Rom. i. 27; Tit. iii. 3), **error** (*planē*) stands specifically for idolatry or paganism (see TWNT VI, 230-54). The juxtaposition without connection of two datives, **passions** (*epithumiais*) and **sensualities** (*aselgeiais*), is gauche; either it is a case of asyndeton, to which the author seems partial (cf. i. 9; 17; iii. 2; 14), or the second stands in apposition to and is explicative of the first. It is scarcely surprising that some MSS alter the second to the genitive (*aselgeias*), reading 'in carnal desires for sensuality' (cf. RSV), but this must clearly be rejected as a well-intentioned attempt to improve. There is also a textual variant *ontōs* (i.e. 'really', 'in actual fact') for the adverb translated **only just** (*oligōs*, i.e. either 'very recently' or 'in a small degree'), and indeed it has far the stronger MS support. But (a) it misses the point that beginners in Christianity are more liable to succumb to sensual temptations; and (b) its substitution for *oligōs* is probably due to the unfamiliarity of copyists with the latter (it occurs only here in the Greek Bible and very rarely elsewhere), especially as the two words could easily be confused when written in capitals. There is evidence (see *Revue Biblique* lxiv, 399-401) that the text read by Ephraem Syrus (4th cent.) contained *tous logous* (i.e. 'the words') instead of *oligōs* and inserted the adjectival *tous eutheis* (i.e. 'the straight') with *kai* (i.e. 'and') after 'escaping', the resulting sense of the clause being 'they ensnare . . . those who shun the correct teaching and those who live in error'. This has no support whatever in the MS tradition or the versions, and has all the air of an intelligent, if mistaken, gloss; but the whole sentence in the received text is so clumsily constructed (cf., e.g., the accusative 'those who live . . .' depending on the accusative 'those who are just . . .') that one suspects it may betray a fundamental corruption which cannot now be cured.

19   The bait they hold out to these inexperienced converts is the promise of **freedom,** that liberty (presumably) which believers enjoy in Christ but which the errorists, with their antinomian leanings, misrepresent as exemption from the requirements of the moral law. They have to learn that faith is not enough: it needs to be supplemented by virtue (i. 5). As we shall discover (iii. 16), they habitually misinterpret Paul's teaching, and we know that even in his own lifetime many were seizing on the Apostle's dictum that 'we are not under law but under grace' as giving the green light to indulgence (Rom. vi. 15: for his anxiety to make his true position clear, cf. Rom. iii. 8; Gal. v. 13). The same misapprehension is criticized in 1 Pet. ii. 16 (see note) and in Jud. 4b (see note). This talk of **freedom,** however, does not come very convincingly from people who **are themselves slaves to corruption.** This last word (*phthora*) does not, as is commonly supposed, denote simply moral **corruption;** that sense is certainly present in it, but (as its use at i. 4; ii. 12 indicates) it also conveys the idea of the spiritual death, leading to final destruction, which is in store for sinners. So Paul teaches (Rom. vii. 5) that 'our sinful passions . . . work in our members to bear fruit for death', and the NT generally (cf. 1 Cor. xv.

42 f.; 50; Eph. vi. 24; 2 Tim. i. 10) promises 'incorruption' (*aphtharsia*) to the faithful.

The writer rams home his argument with a proverbial maxim: **for a man becomes the slave of him who overpowers him.** In the Greek the gender of the mastering agent is ambiguous, being either masculine or neuter, and some scholars prefer the latter (so RSV: 'whatever overcomes a man, to that . . .'); but the imagery derives directly from the ancient practice of enslaving an enemy defeated in battle and so made prisoner, and the masculine reflects this more graphically. For the aphorism, cf. Ps. Clem. *Recog.* v. 12. 3: 'Everyone becomes the slave of him to whom he yields subjection'. This applies with fatal force to the man who surrenders himself to sensual passion and the spiritual **corruption** and death it brings with it.

Then follows a sharp warning against lapsing, but while it has of course a general bearing, it is not easy to decide whether it is intended in the first instance for the false teachers themselves or the converts from paganism (cf. 18) they are seeking to mislead. Most editors favour the former on such grounds as that (a) **For** 20 seems to refer back to **slaves of corruption** in 19a, the intervening sentence in 19b being in effect a parenthesis; (b) **overpowered** in 20 picks up **overpowers** (exactly the same verb in the Greek) in 19b, which explains how the errorists are **slaves**; (c) while suitable enough for these latter, the reproaches in 20-22 are too harsh for recent converts who have not yet fallen away; and (d) the whole chapter being a sustained polemic against the heretics, it seems natural that this should continue to the end. Against this, however, it can be argued that (a) **For** really looks back to 18, enlarging on the awful consequences of being caught in the false teachers' snare; (b) this is convincingly borne out by **after escaping** (*apophugontes*), which must surely hark back to **are only just escaping** (*apopheugontas*) in 18, the same verb being used in both cases, as well as by the mention of being plunged afresh in **the pollutions of the world,** which seems an echo of the **fleshly passions** etc. of 18; (c) there is nothing decisive either way in the repetition of 'overpower', for while the immediate purpose of the aphorism in 19b is to illustrate the servitude of the errorists, it contains a dire caution for all; (d) the language of 20 f., cast as it is in a hypothetical form, reads exactly like a deterrent to people who are exposed to severe temptation but have not yet succumbed, whereas we know that 'Peter' has already given up the heretics as irretrievably lost; and (e) strong though the language is, it comes as something of an anticlimax after the terrifying prophecies of certain destruction he has made about these in the previous section, and yet is not inordinately harsh if interpreted as a severe warning to recent converts. On balance, therefore, one is inclined to conclude that his chief concern is with the 'unstable souls'.

His warning is direct and to the point: if Christians revert to pagan moral standards, **their final state is worse than the first** (this will be more fully explained in the next verse). In the parable of the Unclean Spirit (Mt. xii. 43-45; Lk. xi. 24-26) Christ is reported to have used an almost identical expression; it was probably a proverbial turn of speech (cf. Mt. xxvii. 64) which Christians found admirably adapted for describing the condition of the apostate as compared with that of the unconverted (e.g. Hermas, *Sim.* ix. 17. 5; *Mart. Polyc.* xi. 1). The reason why the former was considered much more wretched than the latter was not just because, according to prevailing ways of thinking, there was no possibility of repentance for serious sin after baptism (cf., e.g., Heb. vi. 4-8), but because the deliberate and open-eyed spurning of God's gift seemed a peculiarly appalling evidence of a man's doomed state. Characteristically (cf. i. 4), the writer defines conversion as 'escaping from' **the pollutions of the world,** and as being brought about (cf. i. 2; 3; 8) **through the knowledge of the Lord and Saviour Jesus Christ.** Once again in the latter expression he is pointedly underlining the nature of the true saving *gnōsis*. In the former his language again, as in i. 4, has an unmistakable Hellenistic ring, and while it has no suggestion of radical dualism, it leaves a strong impression that **the world** is in his eyes an evil and contaminating order of existence. Nevertheless we have to recognize that **the pollutions** which sully it, and which it is disastrous to **get entangled in and overpowered by** afresh, are not intrinsic to it, but are the lusts and sensualities mentioned in 18 which wilful men themselves introduce into it.

He reiterates the gravity of the offence, bringing out what it
21 involves: **it would have been better for them not to have**
348

got to know the way of righteousness—in other words, to have remained pagans—**than, having got to know it** by being instructed in the Christian faith and receiving baptism, **to turn back from the holy commandment which was delivered to them.** Lapsed Christians are in a more tragic plight than unconverted pagans because they have rejected the light (cf. Lk. xii. 47 f.). The primitive Church had a horror of apostasy which is vividly illustrated by the teaching of Hebrews (vi. 4-6; x. 26) cited above that the baptized Christian who has been guilty of it has no hope of forgiveness. In 1 Jn. v. 16 'the sin unto death', for which there is no advantage in praying, is almost certainly the deliberate abandonment of the faith or, in the author's own idiom (ii. 8-11), the reversion from light to darkness. This attitude persisted throughout the 2nd cent., and even after the evolution of a penitential system by the 3rd cent. apostasy counted as one of those major sins for which lifelong public penance was necessary before restoration could be granted.

His description of Christianity as **the way of righteousness** is carefully chosen: as in ii. 15 ('the straight path'), he is concerned about the loose living, as he conceives it, into which recent converts are being tempted to relapse. The expression is frequent in the later strata of the OT (e.g. Job xxiv. 13; Prov. xxi. 16), and in Mt. xxi. 32 Jesus speaks of John the Baptist coming 'in the way of righteousness'. The writer has already (ii. 2) defined the Christian message as 'the way of truth', and there is no suggestion (any more than in ii. 5 or 1 Pet. ii. 24) that **righteousness** (*dikaiosunē*) has a legalistic connotation; it is the pattern of well-ordered, righteous behaviour which issues from the Christian's knowledge of Christ, in the profound sense that that knowledge has in the epistle. Again, because the opponents he is criticizing have antinomian tendencies, he castigates apostasy as turning one's back on **the holy commandment** (*entolē*, as in iii. 2: often used in the singular of the law of Moses, as in 4 Macc. xiii. 15; xvi. 24; Rom. vii. 8-12; Heb. vii. 18; ix. 19; in the singular or plural of the commandment or commandments of Christ, as in Jn. xiii. 34; xiv. 15; 21; 1 Cor. xiv. 37; *1 Clem.* xiii. 3; *2 Clem.* iii. 4; vi. 7). A similar anti-Gnostic motive inspires the insistence on 'keeping his commandments' which runs through the Johannine epistles (1 Jn. ii. 3; v. 3; 2 Jn. 6), but there is no

349

need (indeed it would bring in an idea strange to the writer's thought) to identify **the holy commandment** with 'the new commandment' of love mentioned in 1 Jn. ii. 7 f.; iii. 23. As in iii. 2 (where much the same expression recurs), he is thinking of Christianity as a whole way of life which Christ Himself has laid down and into which believers enter through knowledge of Him. It is **holy** because He is its source and inspiring force. And, as he emphasizes, it is not the new-fangled programme of the heretics, but the one which has been **delivered to them.** This last is a key-expression (*paradotheisēs*) which he has taken over from Jud. 3 (see note), and which implies for him (cf. iii. 2) that Christian doctrine with all its ethical implications has been authoritatively handed down by the apostles.

22   In **what has happened** (a dramatic perfect which treats what is certain to befall as already accomplished) to those who apostatize the writer finds verified **what the true proverb teaches.** He quotes a proverbial saying about the disgusting habits of dogs and pigs, species of animals which were tradition-ally coupled together as unclean and beneath contempt (e.g. Mt. vii. 6). Among the Hebrews a proverb was frequently com-posed of two coordinate members (e.g. Prov. x. 1-xxii. 16), and the two clauses here (they are aorist participles in the Greek) should perhaps be treated as a single aphorism. The former, **'A dog which has returned to his vomit'** (although the Greek contains *idion*, i.e. 'own', it is a mistake to express it in trans-lation, for the word has lost its original force), is familiar from Prov. xxvi. 11, where the comparison is with 'a fool who repeats his folly', but the text cited does not coincide with that of the LXX. The second, **'a sow which has washed in order to wallow in mire',** has no parallel in scripture, but is well illus-trated from the widely popular *Story of Ahikar* (viii. 18 in the Syriac): 'You were to me, my son, like a swine which had had a bath, and when it saw a slimy pit went down and bathed in it'. For further background, cf. SB III, 773; TWNT III, 1100-03. Their point, of course, is to show up in a shocking way the folly and shame of reverting voluntarily to the moral squalor of paganism once one has got rid of it through accepting the Chris-tian way. Some commentators detect in **which has washed ...** a covert allusion to the recent converts' (or, if these are the

persons rebuked, the false teachers') cleansing by baptism: cf. Paul's 'but you were washed' in 1 Cor. vi. 11; 'having cleansed her by the washing of water with the word' in Eph. v. 26; 'having our bodies washed with pure water' in Heb. x. 22; etc. This, however, is probably over-subtle, especially as baptism has not been explicitly mentioned and there is no corresponding allusion in the first half of the proverb.

9. THE CERTAINTY OF THE DAY OF THE LORD
iii. 1-13

(1) This is now the second letter, dear friends, that I am writing to you, and in both I am stirring up your pure understanding by way of reminder, (2) that you should remember the words which were spoken before by the holy prophets and the commandment of the Lord and Saviour by your apostles, (3) understanding this first, that scoffers will come in the last days with scoffing, behaving according to their own passions (4) and saying, 'Where is the promise of his coming? For ever since the fathers fell asleep, all things continue exactly as they have done from the beginning of creation'. (5) For in maintaining this they fail to notice that heavens existed long ago and an earth formed out of water and by means of water by the word of God, (6) through which the world that then existed was destroyed, deluged with water. (7) But by the same word the heavens and earth that now exist have been stored up for fire, being reserved until the day of judgment and destruction of ungodly men. (8) But do not you fail to notice this one fact, dear friends, that with the Lord a single day is like a thousand years, and a thousand years like a single day. (9) The Lord is not slow about his promise, as some reckon slowness, but is being forbearing with you, not wishing that any should perish but that all should come to repentance. (10) But the day of the Lord will come like a thief, and on it the heavens will pass away with a rushing sound, the celestial bodies will be set ablaze and disintegrate, and the

**earth and the works it contains—will they be found? (11)
Since all these things are disintegrating in this way, what
sort of people ought you to show yourselves in the holiness
and godliness of your lives, (12) looking forward to and
hastening on the coming of the day of God, because of
which the heavens will be set on fire and disintegrate and
the celestial bodies will melt in flames! (13) But according to his promise we look forward to new heavens and a
new earth in which righteousness dwells.**

His long tirade against the errorists and their scandalous behaviour ended, the writer takes up afresh his principal theme,
viz. the expected coming of 'the day of the Lord'. In i. 16-21 he
has already tried to refute attempts to question or play it down
by setting out some of the grounds, in prophecy and the
apostles' privileged experience, for the Church's hope. Now he
seeks to dissipate any scepticism his readers may feel because of
its apparent delay. He begins by stressing, as he has done before,
1 his personal authority: **This is now the second letter, dear
friends, that I am writing to you.** It is natural to infer that in
these words he is referring to 1 Peter in order to emphasize once
more his very special apostolic standing. But he immediately
adds that **in both** his letters he is **stirring up** their **pure under-**
2 **standing by way of reminder,** so that they may **remember the words which were spoken before by the holy
prophets and the commandment of the Lord and Saviour
by** their **apostles.** This has provoked the objection that, apart
from a brief mention of the nearness of the End at 1 Pet. iv. 7,
the two epistles have none of the community of subject-matter
which seems implied, and indeed that 2 Peter makes hardly any
use of 1 Peter. Some have therefore proposed that the earlier
letter referred to must be some further epistle attributed to the
Apostle which has now vanished without trace but which our
author knew and had perhaps himself written; others that it
should be identified with 2 Pet. i-ii, this third chapter being in
fact an independent document which has been conflated with
its predecessor.

Neither of these hypotheses is in the least plausible. It is
surely a desperate expedient, in the absence of absolutely com-

pelling necessity, to conjure into existence yet another addition to the corpus of Petrine apocrypha, and one moreover of which no hint survives in early Christian literature or anywhere else. As regards the second theory, while there is undoubtedly a break after ch. ii, it is no more than we should expect as the author takes breath after his loose paraphrase of Jude and returns from polemic to the constructive exposition of his main subject. A decisive argument against it is the fact that he carries on (though of course more sparsely, since the material has been mostly used up and is in any case no longer so relevant) with his borrowings from Jude (cf. iii. 2; 3; 14; 18), as well as making occasional allusions to matter in the earlier chapters. Nor is it in fact necessary to hunt around for alternative explanations to the normal and obvious one. We have already had evidence (see on i. 2; 3; 11; 14; ii. 5) that 2 Peter owes much more to 1 Peter than was once supposed. On the major issue the writer's assumption that there is a broad similarity in the contents of 1 and 2 Peter is, from the point of view of what interests him, by no means far-fetched. What he has in mind, we may be sure (see G. H. Boobyer), are not so much slabs of identical material as, in more general terms, 1 Peter's pervasive concern with the avoidance of immorality and with living blameless, holy lives, and with the blessed inheritance for the righteous and the condemnation of the wicked which Christ's revelation in glory will bring (all themes close to his heart), as also the appeal the earlier letter makes to Christ as an example (ii. 21), to the OT as inculcating the good life (i. 16; ii. 6; iii. 10-12) and prophesying doom to evil-doers, and (in one significant passage: i. 10-12) to the combined authority of the OT prophets, the Spirit of Christ, and apostolic teachers.

The recognition that iii. 1 refers to 1 Peter should not lead us to conclude that 2 Peter was necessarily addressed to the identical four Anatolian provinces named in 1 Pet. i. 1. The earlier letter must by now have attained a fairly wide currency, and all we need infer is that the author feels entitled to suppose that it is being read in the particular communities he has in mind in the first instance. These may have been situated somewhere in Asia Minor, but quite conceivably they may not; the local reference is only another prop in the apparatus of pseudonymity.

On the other hand, iii. 1 deserves special note as (a) the first witness to 1 Peter, and (b) evidence of the emergence of a NT canon. The address **dear friends** (*agapētoi*), as well as the exhortation to **remember the words which were spoken before** and the reference to the apostolic tradition, is taken direct from Jud. 17. Only the apostles are mentioned there, but here **the holy prophets** are added, probably as a reminiscence of 1 Pet. i. 10 and so as to link the argument with what has already been said in i. 19-21 about the value of prophecy. So **stirring up . . . by way of reminder** picks up the identical phrase in i. 13 (these points provide valuable proof of the unity of i-ii with iii). In **pure understanding** the noun (*dianoia*) does not denote the mind or intelligence in the intellectual sense but, as often in the NT (e.g. Eph. iv. 18; Col. i. 21; 1 Jn. v. 20) and Hellenistic Greek (e.g. *Ep. Arist.* 292; Josephus, *Ant.* vii. 381; Epictetus, *Diss.* iii. 22. 20), its faculty of spiritual discernment. So *eilikrinēs*, here translated **pure** rather than (e.g. RSV) 'sincere', retains its original meaning (e.g. Plato, *Phaed.* 66a— with *dianoia*; *Phil.* 52d; Wis. vii. 25; Josephus, *Bell. Iud.* ii. 345; *Ant.* xix. 321) of 'unmixed' and so 'unsullied', 'morally sound'.

The coupling together of the prophets (in effect the OT, which was regarded as foretelling Christ) and the apostles as joint witnesses to the Christian revelation (cf. Eph. ii. 20) becomes routine in the early 2nd cent. (e.g. Ignatius, *Philad.* v. 1 f.; ix. 1 f.; Polycarp, *Phil.* vi. 3; Hermas, *Sim.* ix. 15. 4). For **the commandment** (*entolē*), see on ii. 21: almost more concretely than there, Christianity is envisaged as a new law, as in writers of the sub-apostolic age (e.g. *1 Clem.* xiii. 3; Ignatius, *Eph.* ix. 2; *2 Clem.* iii. 4; vi. 7; xvii. 1), and Christ as the lawgiver. In the Greek the construction is cumbersome in the extreme, for the genitive **apostles** is not qualified by any preposition corresponding to the **by** inserted in the translation; a more exact rendering might be 'the commandment of your apostles, viz. that of the Lord . . .' (cf. the similar collocation of two datives in ii. 18, and the note there). The expression **your apostles** could not of course have been penned by the historical Peter; it inadvertently betrays that the writer belongs to an age when the apostles have been elevated to a venerated group who mediate Christ's teaching authoritatively to the whole Church.

He then singles out what, in the present critical juncture, seems to him the specially relevant message of prophecy and the apostolic tradition: **understanding this first** (the identical 3 phrase used at i. 20a), **that scoffers will come in the last days with scoffing, behaving according to their own passions.** In other words, so far from disconcerting good Christians, the appearance of such people should actually fortify their faith, since it has already been divinely foretold and is indeed sure proof of the approaching End. The pleonastic **scoffers ... with scoffing** is a Hebraism: cf. iii. 1 f.; 'reminder ... remember' above; Lk. xxii. 15 ('with desire I have desired'). The mockers are unquestionably the false teachers attacked in ch. ii. Several editors have doubted this on the grounds that (a) a fresh onslaught seems to be mounted in this chapter, and (b) the errorists in Jude, to which ch. ii is so largely indebted, do not appear to have been guilty of sceptical views about the Parousia. But (a) the writer is virtually obliged to make a fresh start after more or less completely incorporating Jude in ch. ii; and (b) it is a mistake to regard the heresies in both epistles as in all respects coincident. The wording of the present verse closely reproduces that of Jud. 18 (see note), where derision of the faith is also linked with immorality (for **behaving** etc., lit. 'walking', cf. ii. 10a and note on Jude 11). There the prophecy is attributed to the apostles, but here to the OT prophets as well. The writer has no particular passages of scripture in mind; he is voicing the general Jewish-Christian expectation (see on ii. 1) that the approach of the End will be marked by moral breakdown and the emergence of saboteurs of sound religion.

Specifically, the **scoffers** hold up to mockery the apparent failure of the hoped for eschatological denouement to materialize, asking **'Where is** (i.e. 'what has become of': a traditional 4 formula for expressing scepticism—e.g. Ps. xlii. 10; Jer. xvii. 15; Mal. ii. 17) **the promise of his coming** (*parousia*)?' It must, they seem to be claiming, be a fanciful deception, **'For ever since the fathers fell asleep** (i.e. 'died': for 'fall asleep' as a metaphor for dying, cf. Mt. xxvii. 52; 1 Cor. xv. 6; 18; 20; etc.), **all things continue exactly as they have done since the beginning of creation'.** By **the fathers** they mean, not the OT fathers as in Jn. vi. 31; Rom. ix. 5; Heb. i. 1, but their own and the readers' parents and other relatives. Evidently the first Christian generation at any rate lies well back in the past. The premisses of their argument are (a) the belief that the Parousia would be accompanied by a world catastrophe ushering in an entirely new order; (b) the conviction of 1st cent. Christians, relying on sayings of the Lord (e.g. Mt. x. 23; Mk. ix. 1; xiii. 30), that He would come again in their lifetime; and (c) the manifest fact that the people to whom this assurance was deemed to refer had all passed away, whereas neither the Lord's Advent nor the anticipated transformation of the created order had taken place. As early as Paul's time anxieties on this score had begun to make themselves felt, and we know something (1 Thess. iv. 13-18) of the explanations he provided so as to quieten them; for similar anxieties, cf. 1 Pet. iv. 6 and note. The 1st cent. Church as a whole came to terms with the problem by accepting the tension inherent in the Christian, as distinct from the OT and late Jewish, eschatological hope: in one sense the End, i.e. the decisive act of God which gives history its meaning, has already been realized in the incarnation, death and resurrection of Christ, but in another sense it remains still to be consummated in His coming as judge. Not surprisingly, however, groups of Christians continued to be perplexed. For example, *1 Clem*. xxiii. 3 f. (*c*. 95: cf. *2 Clem*. xi. 2-4) quotes a 'scripture' rebuking sceptics of the Second Coming who complain, 'We have heard of these things in our fathers' lifetime too, and, see, we have grown old and none of them has come about'. These **scoffers,** however, make things worse by concluding that, since the Parousia and Judgment are apparently a delusion, they are free to conduct their lives (cf. 3) **according to their own passions.**

These doubts and denials, 'Peter' elliptically implies (this is
5 the force of the **For** with which the next sentence opens) rather than states in so many words, are absolutely unfounded; and to refute them he advances four arguments. The first (5-7) challenges their appeal to the stability of the natural order, pointing out that **in maintaining this they fail to notice** that the universe was created **by the word of God,** and that so far from allowing it to continue unaltered from the beginning, He has already destroyed it once at the Flood, and will use His selfsame Word to do so again when the appropriate time comes. But while the

drift of the passage is clear enough, it is beset with grammatical, exegetical and syntactical difficulties which make its analysis in detail tantalizing. The first, in itself of negligible importance, concerns the opening clause just quoted (*lanthanei . . . autous touto thelontas*), a literal rendering of which could be either 'it escapes them when they wish this' or 'this escapes their notice because they wish [to remain ignorant]'. The translation adopted (so NEB: cf. TWNT III, 45) is based on the former; it is supported by the position of *touto* (i.e. 'this') immediately before *thelontas* (i.e. 'wishing') and at a far remove from *lanthanei* (i.e. 'it escapes notice'), and entails giving the verb *thelein* (i.e. 'wish') the unusual, but by no means unexampled (e.g. Epictetus, *Diss.* i. 19. 12; Pausanias, *Descr. Graec.* i. 4. 6; Herodian, *Ab exc. d. Marci* v. 3. 5) sense of 'maintain contrary to the truth of the matter'. Most editors prefer the latter (cf. RSV: 'They deliberately ignore'), but the position of 'this' is a grave obstacle to construing it as subject of *lanthanei*. It would, however, be rash to dogmatize.

The fact the heretics **fail to notice** (or 'wilfully ignore') is **that heavens existed long ago and an earth formed out of water and by means of water by the word of God, through** 6 **which the world that then existed was destroyed, deluged by water.** As the sentence is clumsily constructed in Greek, the translation has been kept as literal and close to the order of the original as possible. One point which seems reasonably clear is that **existed long ago** (*ekpalai*: the same adverb as at ii. 3, but with a slightly different nuance) has **an earth** as well as **heavens** as its combined subject, and that **by the word of God** qualifies it as well as **formed** in spite of being placed immediately after the latter. This is required by the deliberate antithesis between the heavens and earth established in the beginning by God's creative Word and the present heaven and earth which, according to 7 below, are being kept in readiness for destruction by the same Word. For **the word of God** as His creative agent, cf. Gen. i ('God said . . .' *passim*); Ps. xxxiii. 6; Heb. xi. 3; *1 Clem.* xxvii. 4; Hermas, *Vis.* i. 3.4.

Less easy is the exact interpretation of **formed out of water** etc. (a) Does **formed** refer to **an earth** only (so AV; RV; RSV), or to **heavens** as well (so NEB)? The participle (*sunestōsa*) is feminine singular, and so in strict syntax should qualify the former only; but the singular could be the result of attraction to the number and gender of the nearer noun. Of the alternatives the second seems much the more likely since the passage is concerned to emphasize that the entire universe, comprising both heaven and earth, was destroyed by the very element out of which it had been formed; and this is confirmed by Cod. Sinaiticus, which reads (a palpable correction, but one which indicates how the scribe took the meaning) the neuter plural *sunestōta*. The starting-point of the writer's cosmology is Gen. i. 2; 6-8, according to which water was the sole original existent before God created the heavens and the earth. In stating that water was the material out of which He created them he is, of course, reading more into the Genesis narrative than it contains, and the parallels commonly cited (Ps. xxiv. 2; 2 En. xlvii. 4; Hermas, *Vis.* i. 3. 4) do not fit exactly since they affirm merely that God 'established the universe on the waters'. More to the point is Ps. Clem. *Hom.* xi. 24, which attributes the origin of all things to water, and the teaching of Thales of Miletus (*c.* 600 B.C.: cf. H. Diels, *Fragmente der Vorsokratiker*, 1956, 67-81) that water is the basic stuff out of which all things are made and into which they will be dissolved. But behind this teaching itself lay the creation myths of Assyria, Babylon, Egypt, etc., which pictured a primeval ocean as the element out of which the universe originated.

(b) If this is accepted (and again dogmatism is out of place), how are we to understand the curious coupling of **out of water** (*ex hudatos*) and **by means of water** (*di' hudatos*, where *dia* literally means 'through')? The former, as we have seen, is an understandable gloss on Gen. i. 2; 6-8 in the light of a certain cosmological tradition. In the view of many (e.g. RV) the latter would be more aptly rendered 'amidst water'; the reference, on this assumption, is to Gen. i. 6-8, according to which God placed the firmament, which He called heaven, 'in the midst of the waters', and thus there are waters above and below the heavens and the earth is encompassed by water. This is attractive, nor is the local use of the preposition *dia* so unexampled as is sometimes alleged (cf. Homer, *Od.* ix. 298: 'stretched out *among* the sheep'; also its regular use with the meaning 'standing out among'). Certainly, however, it is difficult (the LXX of Gen. i. 6 f., we should note, has *ana meson*, which properly means 'in the midst of'), and it is made all the more so by the fact that *dia* has the meaning 'through' or 'by means of' in the very next clause. Hence most (so RSV; NEB) accept the translation adopted here and interpret the phrase as heavily underlining the role of water: it was not only the elemental stuff out of which the universe was formed, but it was the means or instrument of its creation.

(c) The next clause is even more perplexing, although its gist is sufficiently obvious. By **the world** (*kosmos*) **that then existed** the writer means, as by 'the ancient world' at ii. 5, not just mankind or even the earth, but the entire universe; the nub of his refutation of the mockers is that, so far from remaining stable, the originally created world order has already been annihilated once and has been replaced by the present one (cf. 7a below). Again he is harking back to the Flood theme of which 1 Pet. iii. 19 f. had reminded him. Gen. vii contains no hint that the Flood caused cosmic destruction, but Jewish apocalyptic and speculation dependent on it read this frightening development into the story. So in 1 En. lxxxiii. 3-5 the heavens are depicted as crumbling and collapsing onto the earth, and the earth itself as being swallowed up into a vast abyss. Echoes of this can be heard in Philo's description (*Vit. Mos.* ii. 63-65) of the complete rejuvenation of everything in nature after the Deluge, and of Noah and his family as 'leaders of a regenerated order and initiators of a second cycle', as well as in the statement in *1 Clem.* ix. 4 that Noah 'announced re-creation (*paliggenesia*) to the universe'. Pseudo-Clementine *Hom.* ix. 2 also seems to imply that the Flood extended its effects to 'the kosmos' and not just mankind.

The problem is the meaning of **through which** (*di' hōn*), where the relative pronoun *hōn* is genitive plural. As it stands, the antecedent might be the water twice mentioned in 5 above, first as the stuff and then as the means of creation; but (i) the use of the relative in the plural because the singular antecedent is employed twice in two different ways is, to say the least, strange, and (ii) the repetition of **by water** with **deluged** in the same short clause seems pointless. A more plausible suggestion is that the plural **which** refers to both **water** and **the word of God** in 5, these being 'the two agents of creation cooperating in destruction' (C. Bigg). Objection (ii) above has been urged against this, but it does not really apply since after his (on this exegesis) ambiguous **which** the writer may have felt it desirable to indicate that it was the water which actually overwhelmed the world. It is admittedly awkward to have the antecedent combined out of two ideas which stand in different relations and different cases in the preceding sentence, but 'Peter' for all his pretentious flights is a conspicuously careless stylist. This exegesis finds support in the following verse, where the Word and fire collaborate in their different roles in the second catastrophe. It is also, for all its defects, preferable to the desperate proposal to accept the variant reading (given by a very late minuscule and adopted by J. B. Mayor) *di' hon*, i.e. 'because of which', viz. the Word of God, which certainly provides an admirable sense, but is a transparent attempt to evade the difficulty.

That earlier cosmic disaster, 'Peter' is arguing, gives ground
7 for believing, against the errorists' sneering scepticism, that **by the same word the heavens and earth that now exist have been stored up for fire, being reserved until the day of judgment and destruction of ungodly men.** What has happened in the past, he assumes and wishes his readers to believe, serves as a sign of what will happen in the future, and **ungodly men** (a pointed thrust at the libertinists) should not let the apparent stability of things lull them into a delusive sense of security. In **reserved ... judgment** he is again taking his cue from Jud. 6. His theory that God's earlier judgment on the world by water will be paralleled by another by fire has reflections in late Jewish thought: cf. Josephus, *Ant.* i. 70 and the late 1st cent. *Vit. Ad. et Ev.* xlix. 3, where in the first case Adam and in the second Eve is represented as prophesying this sequence of catastrophes. The idea that the world will be finally annihilated by fire appears only in 2 Peter in the NT, and is indeed in its fully developed form not Biblical at all: in the OT passages sometimes cited to prove the contrary (e.g. Is. xxx. 30; lxvi. 15 f.; Nah. i. 6; Zeph. i. 18; iii. 8) fire is rather the instrument of God's wrath to destroy His enemies (e.g. Ps. xcvii. 3). We can

observe it taking shape, however, in Jewish apocalyptic, particularly in the Sibylline Oracles (ii. 187-213; iii. 83-92; iv. 171-182;
v. 155-161: cf. 1 En. i. 6-9; lii. 6; 2 Esd. xiii. 10 f.), and the
Qumran sectaries seem to have accepted it (e.g. 1QH iii. 29-36).
Outside the NT it is occasionally found in Christian literature
(e.g. Eth. *Apoc. Pet.* v; Hermas, *Vis.* iv. 3. 3), although towards
the middle of the 3rd cent. Origen (*C. Cels.* iv. 11-13) thought it
worth while debating the advantages of the Christian version of
the final conflagration with the pagan intellectual Celsus. There
are obvious similarities, but equally marked differences (cf. esp.
the alternate destructions and renewals of the world presupposed
by the latter), between this teaching and the Stoic doctrine of
ekpurōsis (e.g. Justin, *1 Apol.* xx; Seneca, *Quaest. nat.* iii. 29;
Diogenes Laertius, *Vit. phil.* vii. 134; Plutarch, *Mor.* 1067a),
i.e. that the universe is periodically consumed by fire, and both
were deeply influenced far back by Iranian eschatological conceptions and imagery. See TWNT VI, 927-48.

So much for the first counter-argument, which is aimed
exclusively at the false teachers. But the author appreciates that
the faithful themselves may be disquieted by the delay of the
Parousia, and so in his further arguments he is at least as much
concerned with reassuring them as with refuting error. Secondly,
therefore, he turns to them directly, addressing them as **dear 8
friends** (*agapētoi*, as in iii. 1), and insists that there is **one fact**
which they for their part must **not fail to notice** (he uses the
same expression as at 5 above, emphasizing **you** here in deliberate contrast to **they** there). This is **that with the Lord a single
day is like a thousand years, and a thousand years like a
single day.** In other words, merely human standards of calculation are inappropriate when estimating the slowness or
speed with which God fulfils His promises; what we can and
must be sure about is that He will fulfil them. The sentence is a
remodelling and expansion of Ps. xc. 4, which in the LXX
reads, 'A thousand years are in your eyes like the day of yester-
day which has gone'. By introducing the opening clause **a
single day** etc. the writer at once makes his point more effectively and underlines the utter irrelevance of temporality to God's
eternal counsel. At Qumran the sectaries were similarly exercised by the problem, and found consolation (1QpHab vii. 13 f.)

in the reflection, suggested by Hab. ii. 3, that 'all the ages of God reach their appointed end as He determines for them in the mysteries of His wisdom'. 2 Peter stands alone in using Ps. xc. 4 to explain why we cannot predict accurately the time of the End, but the text was greatly exploited in apocalyptic and rabbinical circles as possibly giving a clue to the meaning of 'day' in the creation story, the messianic age, the duration of the world, etc. (cf. Jub. iv. 30; 2 En. xxxii. ff.: also SB III, 773 f.). Among Christians an excessively literal interpretation of it was to produce the chiliastic theory that the world would last 6000 years, i.e. as many 'days' as God had needed to create it, and then would come a sabbath of 1000 years for His saints (*Barn.* xv. 4-7; Justin, *Dial.* lxxxi. 3 f.; Irenaeus, *Haer.* v. 28. 3).

The third counter-argument, also primarily addressed to ordinary community members, brings us closer to the heart of 9 the matter. It is a grievous error to suppose that **The Lord** (again this refers to God, as in 8) **is . . . slow** (*bradunei*: it carries the pejorative nuance of 'slack') **about his promise** (*epaggelias*: a reference back to the same word in 4 above), **as some reckon slowness**—imagining, e.g., that His apparent inaction is due to impotence or negligence. The contemptuously vague **some** (*tines*: cf. Jud. 4a for the same usage) may include the scoffers, but refers in the main to Christians who have been infected by their scepticism. The true explanation, 'Peter' claims, is to be found in His long-suffering generosity: He **is being forbearing with you, not wishing that any should perish but that all should come to repentance.** This mention of God's 'forbearance' (*makrothumia*) is probably a further reminiscence of 1 Peter (iii. 20). The underlying problem, in their very different context of belief, was no less puzzling to thoughtful pagans, and was sometimes given an analogous solution: cf. the fascinating discussion in Plutarch's *On the Delays of Divine Vengeance*, which points out (*Mor.* 549b) that 'God's slowness (*bradutēs*: the very same noun as here) undermines our belief in providence', but argues (550a) that He knows best the proper moment to intervene, and further (551c) that His delay shows up 'His gentleness and magnanimity', since it enables many to take warning and escape punishment. The Biblical revelation dwells constantly on His mercifulness, slowness to anger, and forbearance (e.g. Ex. xxxiv. 6; Num. xiv. 18; Ps. lxxxvi. 15; Jon. iv. 2; Ecclus. ii. 11; Rom. ii. 4; ix. 22; 1 Pet. iii. 20), and these ideas are expressed in their depth and richness in our Lord's teaching and attitude

The truth that God desires the **repentance** and conversion of all men was perceived by the post-exilic prophets and later Judaism (e.g. Ezek. xviii. 23; xxxiii. 11: for rabbinical material, see SB III, 774 f.), being sometimes related in the latter to His omnipotence (Wis. xi. 23-26; *Ep. Arist.* 194; Philo, *Leg. alleg.* iii. 106); in the NT it is set out or implied in Jn. iii. 16 f.; Rom. xi. 32; 1 Tim. ii. 4 (cf. 1 *Clem.* viii. 5: 'Since then He wishes all His beloved to partake of repentance, He has established it by His almighty will'). Our writer's application of the idea to the particular problem of the delay of the Parousia seems an in- spired insight of his own, but it is one which (though any such notion must have been remote from his thinking) enables the Church to understand its mission as being, in this span between the resurrection and the Second Coming, to proclaim the divine love and lead men to repentance and faith.

His fourth and final argument seems to contradict the sophis- ticated theologizing of his second and third and returns to primitive tradition: **the day of the Lord will come** (the verb 10 is placed for strong emphasis at the beginning of the sentence), but its coming will be **like a thief**, i.e. unexpected and without warning, so that Christians should be on the alert, prepared for it at any moment. Since **the Lord** denotes God in 8 and 9, it is natural to take it so here; thus **the day of the Lord** has the OT sense (Is. xiii. 9; Jer. xlvi. 10; Joel i. 15; etc.) of 'the day of Yahweh' (cf. 'the day of God' in 12 below). So Paul uses the ancient 'day of the Lord', though understanding by 'Lord' the Messiah, in 1 Thess. v. 2; 2 Thess. ii. 2, in contrast to his later preference for 'the day of the Lord Jesus' or the like (1 Cor. i. 8; v. 5; 2 Cor. i. 14). According to the synoptists (Mt. xxiv. 43; Lk. xii. 39), Christ had Himself likened the coming of the Son of Man to the surprise break-in of a thief, and the vigorous image soon fixed itself in the primitive catechesis (1 Thess. v. 2; Rev. iii. 3; xvi. 15).

Moreover, when the day comes, it will be accompanied by a cosmic catastrophe which, the readers are expected to infer, will engulf evil-doers like the false teachers: **the heavens will pass away with a rushing sound, the celestial bodies will be set ablaze and disintegrate,** etc. The sketch of the dissolution of the universe by fire set out at 7 above (where see note) is filled out with colourful details of chaos and destruction in the heavens which find parallels in OT prophecy (Is. xxxiv. 4; Joel iii. 15) and primitive Christian apocalyptic (Mk. xiii. 24-31; Rev. vi. 12-17). The onomatopoeic adverb (*rhoizēdon*) rendered **with a rushing sound** is connected with *rhoizos*, i.e. a whizzing or whistling sound (e.g. of an arrow), and (so Ps. Oecumenius in PG cxix, 616) could connote the crackling noise of objects being consumed by flames. The noun (*stoicheia*) rendered **celestial bodies** can denote (a) the basic elements of which all natural things are composed (e.g. Diogense Laertius, *Vit. phil.* vii. 136; Hermas, *Vis.* iii. 13. 3: 'the earth is maintained by four *stoicheia*'); (b) the sun, moon and principal heavenly bodies (e.g. Diogenes Laertius, *Vit. phil.* vi. 102—of the signs of the zodiac; Justin, *2 Apol.* v. 2; Theophilus of Antioch, *Autol.* ii. 35); or (c) the cosmic spirits supposed to be connected with the elements and the stars and to dominate human destiny (e.g. Gal. iv. 3; Col. ii. 8). Its basic meaning, of course, was 'one of a row, or series', and so it could stand for the elementary sounds represented by the letters of the alphabet, the elements of knowledge or the sciences, etc., but these significations are irrelevant here. Although some editors prefer it, (a) is inappropriate in view of the comprehensive mention of **the heavens** and **the earth**; a more specific reference to their constituent elements is superfluous. The position of *stoicheia* between these two suggests that it signifies a third kind of cosmic entity, viz. **the celestial bodies,** and this seems an entirely suitable exegesis since these are locally situated between heaven and earth and their extinction or collapse was a stock feature of eschatological speculation (Is. xiii. 10; xxxiv. 4; Ezek. xxxii. 7 f.; Joel ii. 10; Mt. xxiv. 29; Mk. xiii. 24 f.; Rev. vi. 13).

It is impossible to decide with any confidence what to make of the next clause, here rendered: **and the earth and the works it contains—will they be found?** By **the earth** is meant, of course, our planet and not, as some advocate, its inhabitants; while **the works** which fill it are not human actions (these are inaptly described as 'the works in it', and in any case they follow their authors to eternity—Rev. xiv. 13), but all the products of nature and, above all, of human culture, civilization, art and technology. The translation printed assumes that the verb is *heurethēsetai*, i.e. 'will be found'; this has much the best MS support (Codex Sin.; B; K; P; Pap. 72; etc.; also the Syrian and Armenian versions; etc.), and is also decidedly the most difficult reading. Those who accept it usually treat the clause as a direct statement (e.g. NEB: 'will be laid bare'), taking the meaning to be that the earth and men's achievements will be discovered and exposed to the divine judgment. They cite, e.g., 1 Cor. iii. 13-15 ('each man's work will become manifest; for the day will disclose it . . .') and *2 Clem.* xvi. 3 ('the day of judgment comes even now . . . and then shall appear the secret and open works of men'); but in both these passages the subject is the revelation of the true character of men's deeds by the refining fires of the last judgment. Here, apart from the great difficulty of giving 'will be found' the sense proposed, the idea which looms in the foreground is rather the annihilation of **the earth** and all it contains; this is demanded both by the preceding two verses and by the opening words of verse 11. The translation adopted follows B. Weiss's suggestion that the clause is in fact a rhetorical question. In the Bible 'find' or 'be found' frequently approximates to 'be' or 'exist', and when used in the negative or cast in the form of a question can convey the sense of non-existence: e.g. LXX Gen. v. 24 ('Enoch . . . was not found'); Ex. xii. 19 ('no leaven shall be found . . .'); Dt. xviii. 10 ('There shall not be found among you anyone who . . .'); LXX Ps. xxxvi. 10 ('You shall look for his place and shall not find it'); Prov. xx. 6 ('but a faithful man who can find?'); xxxi. 10 ('a faithful wife who can find?'); Is. xxxv. 9 ('no ravenous beast shall go up to it or be found there'); Ecclus. xliv. 19 ('no one has been found like him in glory'); Rev. xvi. 20 ('every island fled away, and no mountains were to be found'). There is a closely analogous use of *phainesthai*, i.e. 'appear', which in negative or quasi-negative forms of expression can in effect mean, not simply 'not appear', but 'disappear' or even 'cease to exist'. Cf. Prov. xxiii. 5 ('if you set your eyes on it [wealth], it will not appear'); Tob. vi. 17 (S text) ('the demon will flee and will nowhere appear'); and above all 1 Pet. iv. 18, quoting Prov. xi. 31 ('where will the impious and sinful man appear?').

Admittedly there are difficulties about this exegesis, notably the abrupt switch to an interrogation, but it has the virtues of making sense of what has every claim to be the correct text, and of logically setting the cataclysmic disappearance of the earth and its contents alongside the passing away of the heavens and stars. There are alternative readings, such as *katakaēsetai* ('will be burned up': preferred by AV; RV; RSV) and *aphanisthēsontai* ('will be eliminated'), but these have all the appearance of being makeshifts, and it is hard to imagine why they should ever have been altered if they had been original. The Sahidic implies *ouch* before *heurethēsetai* (i.e. 'will not be found'); this may conceivably point to the omission of the original negative by a scribe through carelessness, but more probably represents an attempt to get rid of the harshness of the sudden question with the minimum of change; in any case it supports the general sense accepted above. An interesting variant is one offered by Pap. 72 alone, viz. *heurethēsetai luomena*, i.e. 'will be found disintegrating'. The insertion of the participle may, of course, have been prompted by the wish to ease a difficult text, but it is just possible that *luomena* is what 'Peter' actually wrote and that it dropped out through haplography owing to the proximity of *luomenōn* in verse 11 and *luthēsontai* in verse 12.

Like other NT writers (e.g. 1 Thess. v. 6 ff.; Heb. x. 25; 1 Pet. iv. 7 ff.), 'Peter' uses the awesome picture of the approaching End, not to strike terror into the hearts of loyal Christians,

11 but as an urgent moral and spiritual challenge: **Since all these things** (i.e. the universe as he has described it) **are disintegrating in this way, what sort of people ought you to show yourselves in the holiness and godliness of your lives.** The participle rendered **are disintegrating** (*luomenōn*) is present in tense; either it has a future force suggested by the context, or (more probably) the writer deliberately chooses it so as to highlight, by its suggestion that the process of dissolution has already started, the immediacy of his summons. The late Greek *potapos* (**what sort of**) has a much more positive flavour (cf. its use in Mt. viii. 27; 1 Jn. iii. 1) than the English conveys; in the context it hints that great things are expected of the

366

readers ('how outstandingly excellent' would be a fair para-phrase). And the reason is not far to seek. Not only are they **looking forward to . . . the coming of the day of God** (it is 12 quietly taken for granted that they have repudiated, or will be repudiating, the errorists' scepticism), but through their faithful conduct they can be actually **hastening** it **on.**

Many versions (e.g. AV; RV) render the second participle (*speudontas*) by 'earnestly desiring' or something equivalent. This is linguistically quite possible (Is. xvi. 5—'earnestly desir-ing justice': cf. Herodotus, *Hist.* i. 38; Thucydides, *Hist.* v. 16. 1), and yields an acceptable sense. But the more usual mean-ing of *speudein* with the accusative is 'set going', 'urge on', 'hasten on', and this fits the context admirably. It ties up with the conviction expressed in iii. 8 that the Coming is held up by the Lord's desire for as many as possible to repent, which pre-sumably has as its corollary that it may be hastened by the faith and good works of believers. That this idea was familiar to later Judaism is shown by the well-known saying in the Talmud (see SB I, 163 f. for it and others like it) that if only the Israelites could really repent for a single day, the Messiah would appear; also by 2 Esd. iv. 38 f., according to which the judgment is kept back because of the sins of mankind. A relevant early Christian parallel is Acts iii. 19 f., which takes it for granted that repent-ance and conversion speed on Christ's advent.

The details of the final catastrophe given here correspond closely with those given at 10 above, with the graphic touch added that **the celestial bodies** (*stoicheia*, as in 10b) **will melt** with the heat: for the image, cf. Is. xxxiv. 4; lxiii. 19; Test. Lev. iv. 1; 2 *Clem.* xvi. 3. We should note, however, (a) the use here, alone in the NT and in contrast to iii. 4a, of *parousia*, i.e. **coming,** with reference to **the day** rather than the person, God or Christ, whose Coming is anticipated (evidently it has become a technical term); (b) the very unusual expression **the day of God,** which suggests the cosmic finale rather than Christ's per-sonal advent, instead of the normal NT 'day of the Lord' or the like (only Rev. xvi. 14 is strictly comparable); (c) the implication in **because of** that the universal disintegration will not be the result of any natural cyclic process, like the periodical con-flagration of the universe envisaged in Stoic thought, but the direct effect of God's all-sovereign will.

Christians, however, the writer proceeds, are aware that these terrifyingly catastrophic events are the prelude to the creation 13 of a fresh and perfectly ordered world. Thus, relying on **his** (i.e. God's: cf. **day of God** in 12) **promise we look forward to new heavens and a new earth in which righteousness dwells.** For God's magnificent promises, cf. i. 4a. Christ Himself had spoken (Mt. xix. 28) of 'the new age when the Son of Man shall sit on his glorious throne', and which would be the setting of the Messianic banquet (Mk. xiv. 25), and in Paul's view (Rom. viii. 19-22) the present creation is in travail with the birth of a more glorious one. These eager eschatological expectations of early Christianity found their most colourful expression in Revelation, with its affirmation (xxi. 5) that the risen Christ 'makes all things new' and its vision (xxi. 1 f.; 10-27) of a new heaven and earth and a new Jerusalem. All this imagery is a Christian development and adaptation of older Jewish hopes and yearnings, especially as set out in Is. lxv. 17 and lxvi. 22, which specifically forecast the creation of **new heavens and a new earth**; these passages presumably contain the divine **promise** alluded to here (cf. 1 En. lxxii. 1, which also predicts a new creation), and are in our writer's mind. Unlike the author of Rev. xxi f., however, he makes no attempt to describe the re-created world by symbols, however splendid, borrowed from the present material and transient order. In the more spiritual strata of the OT (e.g. Jer. xxiii. 5 f.; Zech. ix. 9; Wis. ii. 18) and of later Judaism (e.g. Ps. Sol. xvii. 35) the Messiah is represented as the righteous One, and **righteousness** or justice is depicted as a characteristic of the Messianic age (e.g. Is. xxxii. 16-18; lxi. 3; Ps. Sol. xvii. 36; 1 En. xlv. 4-6; xlviii. 1-4; li. 4 f.; esp. 2 En. lxv. 8—'the great age of the righteous'). In the NT too the Christian is encouraged (Mt. v. 6) to 'hunger and thirst after righteousness', and the risen Lord is portrayed (Acts xvii. 31; Rev. xix. 11) as judging the world 'in righteousness'. So it is natural that he should delineate the coming new order to his readers simply as one **in which righteousness dwells.** It will be the precise opposite of the present order, dominated as it is by desire and corruption (i. 4).

10. CLOSING ADMONITIONS
iii. 14-18

(14) Since therefore, dear friends, you have these things to look forward to, make the effort to be found without spot or blemish in his sight, at peace, (15) and reckon the forbearance of our Lord as salvation, just as our dear brother Paul also has written to you in virtue of the wisdom granted to him, (16) as indeed in all his letters when speaking of these things; but in them there are passages hard to understand, which ignorant and unstable people twist (as they do the other scriptures too) to their own destruction. (17) You therefore, dear friends, since you know in advance, be on your guard so as not to be carried away by the error of unprincipled men and dislodged from your firm stance. (18) But grow in grace and the knowledge of our Lord and Saviour Jesus Christ. To him belongs glory both now and to the day of eternity.

In this brief concluding section (the particle *Dio*, i.e. **there-** **fore,** and the resumed **dear friends** mark the transition to a new paragraph) the writer reiterates the need, in view of the approaching End and the blessed transformation it is going to bring about, for exalted moral standards and unflinching fidelity, throwing in an unexpected appeal to the authority of the apostle Paul. **Since** his readers **have these things,** i.e. a freshly created heaven and earth where God's will is paramount, **to look forward to** (*prosdokān*: the verb of 13 above repeated), they should **make the effort to be found without spot or blemish in his sight, at peace.** The verb **make the effort** (*spoudazein*) is characteristic with him: cf. i. 10; 15. The exhortation to be **without spot or blemish** contains a barely concealed thrust at the trouble-makers, whom he has branded at ii. 13 as 'spots and blemishes'. The phrase itself (*aspiloi kai amōmētoi*) reflects the impact of 1 Pet. i. 19 (*amōmos kai aspilos*: of Christ), and probably also of Jud. 24 (*amōmous*: in an eschatological context there too). Being **at peace** does not denote either the untroubled

369

conscience of the good Christian or the brotherly relations of
the members of the communities with one another; rather it describes the state of reconciliation with God which the restored
sinner enjoys (see on 1 Pet. i. 2; Jud. 2). The addition of this
second predicate without a connecting particle is a little awkward
stylistically, but is another example of the writer's penchant for
asyndeton (see on ii. 18). By **be found** he means 'by the Lord
when He comes', while **in his sight** (lit. 'to him': the dative in
the Greek) is a clear reference to the judgment.

15   Furthermore, the readers should **reckon the forbearance
of our Lord as salvation.** This recapitulates the explanation of
the delay of the Parousia given at iii. 9, setting **reckon as salvation** (*sōtērian hēgeisthe*) in pointed antithesis to 'reckon slowness' (*bradutēta hēgountai*) there; the delay in fact reveals God's
patient desire to give us all an opportunity to repent, accept
Christ and be saved. It seems probable that **our Lord** here denotes God; this sense of the expression is extremely rare (cf.
Rev. xi. 15), but is practically demanded by the use of 'Lord' in
iii. 8; 9; 10 and of 'day of God' in iii. 12. And this teaching he is
giving, the writer interjects, corresponds with that which **our
dear brother Paul also** has given **you in virtue of the wis-
16 dom granted to him**, and which he has repeated **in all his
letters when speaking of these things.**

Here again he is seeking to bolster his own authority by
identifying himself with the historical Peter and claiming Paul as
his **dear brother,** i.e. not simply as a fellow-Christian, but as a
fellow-apostle (for 'brother' in this specialized sense, cf. Eph.
vi. 21; Col. iv. 7; 1 Thess. iii. 2). But his manner of doing this
betrays, almost more than any other passage in the letter, that
the apostolic age, with its tensions between Peter and Paul (e.g.
Gal. ii. 11-16) on the one hand and Paul and the original apostolic
group on the other, lies in the misty past. Peter and Paul are now
venerated together as the joint leaders and heroes of the apostolic Church, as in Acts; *1 Clem.* v. 3-7 ('Let us set before our
eyes the good apostles, Peter . . . Paul'); Ignatius, *Rom.* iv. 3 ('I
do not give you orders, as Peter and Paul did'); *Ep. apost.* xxxi
ff.; etc. His reference to Paul's correspondence (cf. **in all his
letters**) points in the same direction. Evidently he is living at a
time when the Apostle's letters, originally despatched separately

to distinct churches or individuals, have begun to be collected
together: cf. Ignatius, *Eph.* xii. 2 ('Paul . . . who in every letter
. . .'). It would appear that a Pauline canon is in process of being
assembled and given official recognition, although we have no
clue whether at this stage it comprised all, or only a selection of,
the letters included in the NT.

The expression **in virtue of the wisdom granted to him**
also deserves notice. Paul himself was conscious of being the
conveyor of 'God's secret and hidden wisdom' (1 Cor. ii. 6 f.: cf.
Col. i. 28), and of imparting God's gifts under the influence of
the Spirit (1 Cor. ii. 12 f.); he even recalls (Gal. ii. 9), in words
of which these seem an echo, that the apostles 'perceived the
grace granted to me'—the same participle *dotheisan* as here.
The author of *1 Clem.* xlvii. 3 acknowledges that Paul wrote 1
Corinthians 'under the influence of the Spirit', while Polycarp
(*Phil.* iii. 2) speaks of 'the wisdom of the blessed and glorious
Paul'. Here we have a pointer to the official endorsement of his
writings as inspired, and 16b confirms that they now count as
'scripture'.

Two connected questions which have caused scholars in-
ordinate trouble are (a) what particular items in his own teaching
the writer professes to find supported by Paul; and (b) which of
the Apostle's letters he is alluding to in the phrase **has written
to you.** The answer to (a) can only be: the exhortation beginning
in 14 to lead blameless lives in view of the approach of the
Parousia and the need to use the intervening time as an opportunity for making one's salvation sure. It is quite unjustified to
ransack the rest of the epistle for doctrinal overlaps with Paul,
for **just as** (*kathōs*) firmly ties the following clause to the immediately preceding context. Within this context it is equally
unjustifiable to regard 14b and 15a as mutually exclusive alternatives; both are indissoluble elements in the one paraenesis.
That the End is approaching, and that Christians should adopt
the standards and moral attitudes appropriate to it, are such
common themes in Paul that the listing of parallels is scarcely
called for; 'Peter's' reference is (as we shall see) general. More
specifically, however, the Apostle dwells on God's forbearance
in Rom. ii. 4; iii. 25 f.; ix. 22 f.; xi. 22 f.; and on the need to be
morally prepared for the Coming in Rom. xiii. 11-14; 1 Cor. i. 7;

vii. 29-35; 2 Cor. v. 6-10; Eph. iv. 30-32; Phil. ii. 15 f.; Col. iii. 4-17; 1 Thess. v. 4-11.

The problem of (b) arises from the fact that, while in iii. 1 the writer alleges he is writing to the recipients of 1 Peter, we know of no single letter of Paul's addressed to that particular group of congregations in Asia Minor. Some have argued that Galatians and Colossians, or more plausibly (in view of the theory that it is a circular letter) Ephesians, might meet the requirements. None of these exactly fits, although one or more of them might at a pinch be acceptable if we felt compelled to detect a reference to a particular letter or letters in **has written to you.** We should certainly discard the conjecture that some letter of the Apostle's which is now lost is intended; while his correspondence must have been extensive, it is intrinsically improbable that any more of his letters survived in the age when 'Peter' wrote than we have at our disposal today. J. B. Mayor takes a very different line, claiming that the writer is seeking Pauline support only for his teaching about the Lord's forbearance in 15a, and that therefore the reference is probably specifically to Romans (esp. Rom. ii. 4; iii. 25 f.; etc.); but it seems arbitrary to exclude 14 from the scope of his appeal to the Apostle. All such speculations, however, like the premisses on which they are based, are almost certainly wide of the mark. For the writer, as we have seen, the Pauline letters had a quasi-canonical status, and as such he probably regarded them as the common property of Christians everywhere. As the Muratorian Canon (Roman: late 2nd cent.) was later to argue, though sent in the first instance to seven distinct communities, they were in effect addressed to the world-wide Church. He tacitly reveals that this is his attitude to 1 Peter too, for in spite of iii. 1 his introductory words at i. 1 convey the impression that he is aiming his own letter at a more general destination. So when he speaks of Paul writing **to you,** it is unnecessary to press his language too strictly and infer that he has any particular locality or epistle in mind; **you** covers any community his letter may reach, for he knows that every Christian congregation must have in its possession some letter of the Apostle's where **these things** are treated. Nor should we assume that in 15b and 16a he is distinguishing between one particular letter of Paul's and the rest of his correspondence; in 16b he is merely elaborating the point he has just made by emphasizing the consistency of the Apostle's teaching on these subjects.

But must he not have some special motive for suddenly dragging Paul in? We are given a clue in the statement that his letters contain **passages hard to understand, which ignorant and unstable people twist (as they do the other scriptures too) to their own destruction.** The former clause gives interesting testimony to the perplexities early aroused by the Pauline theology; the adjective *dusnoētos*, rendered **hard to understand,** which is extremely rare, is used by Lucian (*Alex.* 54) of oracles which are incomprehensible, but in Diogenes Laertius (*Vit. phil.* ix. 13) is applied, along with *dusexēgētos*, to a treatise by Heracleitus, which is thus 'difficult to understand and interpret' —exactly the sense the word has here. The latter clause, with its unflattering epithets, is clearly aimed at the errorists: being **ignorant,** i.e. uninstructed in and unwilling to learn the traditional teaching, and **unstable** (cf. ii. 14) in character as well, they are not qualified to expound such recondite documents. It was they, apparently, who had brought the Apostle into the debate, seeking to buttress their own opinions with the immense authority of his name, and 'Peter' deems it necessary to warn both them and his readers how easy it is to misrepresent his authentic message. He has already (i. 20) rebuked them for their arbitrary misuse of prophecy, and now adds the complaint that their handling of scripture generally (cf. **the other scriptures,** i.e. the OT and the embryonic NT canon now in process of formation) is partisan and mischievous, deviating from the accepted exegesis. He has himself propounded the principle (see on i. 21 f.) that the Church, and no individual or group, is the proper interpreter of scripture; and this must apply with redoubled force to writings so difficult as Paul's.

His implied charge must be that they are 'twisting' (*strebloun*: originally of tightening a cable with a windlass, and then of perverting the meaning of words) Pauline texts in the interest of their own ethical libertinism (cf. ii. 19 and note) and defective eschatology, since these are the errors he is chiefly concerned to protest against. While he furnishes no details, we know from Irenaeus and Tertullian that similar-minded, though more

advanced and sophisticated, Gnostics of the second half of the
2nd cent. constantly appealed to such passages as Rom. viii. 21;
2 Cor. iii. 17; Gal. v. 13 as supporting antinomianism. We can
only speculate what texts the trouble-makers interpreted as
favouring their scepticism about the Parousia (the Apostle himself complains in 2 Thess. ii. 2 that he has been misrepresented
as teaching that it has already taken place), but later Gnostics
made considerable capital out of passages like 1 Cor. xv. 50; 53,
or again Rom. vi. 3 ff., arguing that they contained a more
'spiritual' doctrine of resurrection than the 'materialist' one of
the orthodox. For fuller particulars of the Gnostic use, or misuse, of the Pauline letters, see W. Bauer, *Rechtgläubigkeit und
Ketzerei im ältesten Christentum* (1934), 227; E. Aleith, *Paulusver-
ständnis in der alten Kirche* (Beiheft 18 to ZNTW, 1937). In any
case the writer is satisfied that such distorted exegeses can only
lead **to their own destruction** (*apōleia*: again, as at ii. 1; 3;
iii. 7, with reference to the judgment on the last day).

He concludes his letter with a double exhortation which
succinctly gathers the themes treated in chaps. ii and i respec-
17 tively. Negatively he urges his **dear friends** to **be on** their
**guard so as not to be carried away by the error of un-
principled men and dislodged from** their **firm stance.** The
noun represented by these last two words is the rare *stērigmos*;
it connotes fixity as opposed to movement, and is used in conscious contrast to **unstable** (*astēriktos*) above, the characteristic
of the heretics and their dupes (ii. 14). Stability, or being firmly
established in the faith (cf. i. 12), is clearly a quality which he
greatly esteems. It is the best defence against the fatal fascination
of the false teachers' antinomianism which he finds so worrying.
As in Jud. 11 (see note), **error** (*planē*) may have the passive sense
of mistaken teaching (so the translation), or may actively connote 'leading astray'. His readers, however, should be well
equipped to resist temptation since, unlike the **unprincipled**
(*athesmoi*, as at ii. 7) men who try to seduce them, they **know in
advance,** i.e. have been forewarned in this letter in which the
'apostle' has been at pains to set out these very dangers (cf.
i. 12-15; iii. 1-3). The phrase recalls Jud. 5 ('you who have been
informed of all things once for all').

Positively, in recapitulation of his advice in i. 3-11, he bids them **grow in grace and the knowledge of our Lord and** 18 **Saviour Jesus Christ.** Instead of **grow in** some (e.g. NEBm) prefer to translate 'grow with the help of'; but cf. Col. i. 10 ('growing in the knowledge of God'). By **grace** is meant, as at i. 2, favour with God; for the writer's conception of Christianity as consisting in **the knowledge of . . . Jesus Christ,** see on i. 2. The translation adopted seems preferable to the more common one, viz. 'in the grace and knowledge of . . . Jesus Christ', since the latter requires us to treat the genitive **of . . . Jesus Christ** as simultaneously subjective (in relation to **grace**) and objective (in relation to **knowledge**), which while not impossible makes a very harsh construction. For the formula **our Lord and Saviour Jesus Christ,** cf. i. 11; ii. 20; iii. 2.

The doxology, **To him belongs glory both now and to the day of eternity,** and the corresponding one at 2 Tim. iv. 18 are the only ones in the NT in which Christ alone is unmistakably the object; those at Heb. xiii. 21 and 1 Pet. iv. 11 (see note) probably have God in view. Several exhibit an intermediate stage, either ascribing **glory** (for its meaning, see on 1 Pet. i. 7; Jud. 25) to God 'through Jesus Christ' (Rom. vii. 25; xvi. 27; Jud. 25) or working in Christ's name in some other way (1 Cor. xv. 57; Eph. iii. 21). As is usual, no verb is expressed in the original; for the insertion of **belongs** rather than 'be', see on 1 Pet. iv. 11; Jud. 25. The phrase **the day of eternity** (lit. 'the day of the age') is unique in the NT, but is paralleled in Ecclus. xviii. 10 ('Like a drop of water . . ., so are a few years in the day of eternity'). The customary expression in doxologies (e.g. Rom. xvi. 27) is 'for all eternity' (lit. 'unto the ages of the ages'), and that may be the meaning here. Alternatively the writer, thinking of the approaching day of the Lord (iii. 10; 12), may have chosen this unusual and striking wording so as to indicate the day on which the eternal and blessed age inaugurated by Christ's Coming will begin.

INDEX

INDEX

Cybele, 49, 85, 210
Cyprian, 122, 129, 158, 188
Cyril of Alexandria, 42, 150, 163, 173
Cyril of Jerusalem 84, 87, 153, 211
Cyrus, 114

Dalton, W. J., 21, 151, 161, 174
Dathan, 268
David, 241, 334
Day of the Lord, 55, 59, 236, 290, 321, 352, 363, 367, 375; of God, 332, 363, 367 f.
Dead Sea, 259, 333
'Defence' (*apologia*), 6 f., 142 f.
Demetrius, 216
Demiurge, 231, 253, 264, 267, 292
Descent to Hell, 153, 172 f.
De sectis, 227
Devil (Satan), 9, 25, 26, 54, 74, 207, 209 f., 263, 264 f., 266, 337, 338
Dibelius, M., 13
Didache, 67, 107, 115, 126, 135, 178, 179, 190, 201, 252, 262, 268, 269, 282, 289, 329, 343
Didascalia apostolorum, 178
Didymus of Alexandria, 224, 265
Diels, H., 358
Dietrich, A., 49
Dikaiosunē ('upright conduct', etc.), 123, 140 f., 297, 332, 349, 368
Diodorus Siculus, 168, 263, 306
Diogenes Laertius, 168, 306, 361, 364, 373
Diognetus, Epistle to, 41, 313
Dionysius of Corinth, 215
Dionysius of Halicarnassus, 306
Dispersion, diaspora, 4, 40 f., 81, 197, 219
Dittenberger, W., 85, 136, 318
Divine nature, 224, 301-304, 306, 311
Divine plan, 61, 64
Dodd, C. H. 304
Domitian, 27, 28, 232
Doom of the wicked, unbelievers, 1, 20, 23, 24, 59, 93 f., 95, 138, 157, 193 f., 225, 249-251, 254 ff., 268 f., 272-275, 276 f., 327, 329, 330 ff., 339 f., 344 ff., 353
Doxology, 15, 18, 20, 21, 181 f., 183, 213, 290-294, 375
Dreamers, 260 f.

Easter, 18 f., 159
Ebionites, 325
Egypt, 68, 72, 73, 75, 88, 109, 208, 218, 237, 254-256, 358
Eight, symbolism of, 159, 305
Eighteen Benedictions, 47
Elder, elders, 3, 5, 24, 30, 196-198, 199-203, 204 f.
Eleazer, Rabbi, 143
Election, elect, 40, 42-44, 82, 95 f., 98, 99, 101, 194, 212, 216, 217 f., 276, 308
Elliott, J. H., 97, 98
Emperor, 6, 29, 109, 110, 112, 113, 114, 219, 298
End, the, 1, 8, 10, 26, 52, 56, 57, 60, 64, 115, 139, 164, 169, 171, 176 f., 179, 185, 188, 193, 199, 208, 209, 229, 257, 287, 291, 304, 310, 323, 327, 352, 355, 356, 362, 366, 369, 371
Enoch, 152, 154, 155, 156, 227, 257, 274, 275-279, 365
1 Enoch, 50, 52, 62, 63, 76, 154 f., 167, 224, 227, 250, 252, 257 f., 262, 264, 265, 266, 269, 274, 276, 277, 278, 279, 283, 287, 319, 331, 335, 338, 359, 361, 368; considered inspired, 154, 227, 278
2 Enoch, 63, 137, 155, 257, 262, 265, 358, 368
Ephesians, Epistle to the, 11, 13, 14, 32, 372
Ephesus, 3, 41 f., 143, 192, 197
Ephraem Syrus, 346
Ephraim, 94
Epictetus, 85, 108, 129, 291, 354, 357
Epiphanius, 150, 189, 224, 261, 267, 284, 325
Epistula apostolorum, 269, 329, 370
Erasmus, 4, 223
Esau, 267
Eschatology, 1, 8, 10, 15, 16, 20, 22, 26, 30, 45, 52, 66, 72, 100, 102, 106, 114, 175, 177, 178, 181, 184, 192 f., 194, 203, 208, 223, 229, 244, 246, 273, 282 f., 287, 291, 292, 302, 310, 311, 316, 323, 329, 335, 355, 356, 364, 368, 369, 373 f.
Essenes, 205

379

INDEX